W9-CZT-964

DISCARDED

Gleanings in Europe: Switzerland

The Writings of
James Fenimore Cooper

JAMES FRANKLIN BEARD, Editor-in-Chief

JAMES P. ELLIOTT, Textual Editor

Sponsors

Series Sponsors

CLARK UNIVERSITY

AMERICAN ANTIQUARIAN SOCIETY

Volume Sponsor

TRINITY UNIVERSITY

Editorial Board

JAMES FRANKLIN BEARD, Chairman

JAMES P. ELLIOTT

KAY SEYMOUR HOUSE

THOMAS L. PHILBRICK

DONALD A. RINGE

WARREN S. WALKER

Advisory Committee

ROBERT E. SPILLER, Chairman

HARRY C. ALLEN, JR.

CLIFTON WALLER BARRETT

HENRY S. F. COOPER, JR.

WILLIAM EASTMAN

MARCUS MC CORISON

Gleanings in Europe

Switzerland

James Fenimore Cooper

Historical Introduction and
Explanatory Notes by Robert E. Spiller
and James F. Beard
Text Established by Kenneth W. Staggs
and James P. Elliott

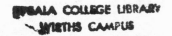
UPSALA COLLEGE LIBRARY
WIRTHS CAMPUS

State University of New York Press   Albany,

DQ
23
.C6
1980

The preparation of this volume was made possible (in part) by a grant from the Program for Editions of the National Endowment for the Humanities, an independent Federal agency.

CENTER FOR EDITIONS OF
AMERICAN AUTHORS

AN APPROVED TEXT

MODERN LANGUAGE
ASSOCIATION OF AMERICA

®

The Center emblem means that one of a panel of textual experts serving the Center has reviewed the text and textual apparatus of the printer's copy by thorough and scrupulous sampling, and has approved them for sound and consistent editorial principles employed and maximum accuracy attained. The accuracy of the text has been guarded by careful and repeated proofreading according to standards set by the Center.

Published by
State University of New York Press, Albany

©1980 State University of New York

All rights reserved

Printed in the United States of America

No part of this book may be used or reproduced in any manner whatsoever without written permission except for brief quotations embodied in critical articles and reviews.

For information, address State University of New York Press, State University Plaza, Albany, N.Y., 12246

Library of Congress Cataloging in Publication Data
Cooper, James Fenimore, 1789–1851.
   Gleanings in Europe, Switzerland.

   (The writings of James Fenimore Cooper)
   Originally published under title: Sketches of Switzerland.
   Includes index.
   1. Switzerland—Description and travel.   2. Cooper, James Fenimore,
1789–1851—Journeys—Switzerland.   I. Title.   II. Series: Cooper, James
Fenimore, 1789–1851.   Works.   1979.
DQ23.C6 1979   914.94'04'6   79-13133
ISBN 0-87395-364-9

Contents

Acknowledgements   ix

Illustrations   xiii

Historical Introduction   xvii

Preface   1

Gleanings in Europe: Switzerland   5

Explanatory Notes   301

Appendix A   Bentley's analytical Table of Contents   317

Appendix B   Guide to parallel passages in 1828 Swiss Journal and expanded 1836 Text   323

Textual Commentary   327

Textual Notes   341

Emendations   345

Word-Division   351

Index   359

015081

Maps

The routes followed by Cooper and his family in their Swiss travels during the summer of 1828 have been traced for this volume on appropriate sections of a large folding map presumably identical to the map Cooper used. The reproductions were prepared by courtesy of the Free Library of Philadelphia from its copy of

CARTE ITINERAIRE DE LA SUISSE
Revue et Corrigée d'après le Manuel du Voyageur dans ce Pays
par Ebel
A Paris
chez Haycinthe Langlois, Géographe
Rue de Bussy, No. 16 F.ᵈ S.ᵗ G.ᵐ

1827

Between pages 180 and 181
Map 1. Arrival at La Lorraine, Bern (mid-July), and first excursion to the Bernese Oberland (4–10 August).
Map 2. Second excursion. To Constance via Schaffhausen and return via Zurich and Lucerne (25 August–2 September).
Map 3. Eastern part of second excursion.
Map 4. Third excursion. To the shrine of Einsiedeln and Wallenstadt via Lake of Lucerne; then to the source of the Rhine following the river south and southwest; then to Meyringen by the St. Gothard Pass and back to Bern (8–19 September).
Map 5. Eastern part of third excursion.
Map 6. Fourth excursion. To Geneva and back to Bern (24 September–1 October).
Map 7. Departure for Italy via Martigny and the Rhone valley to Brig; then over the Simplon pass to Milan (8–14 October). *See also* Map 6.
Map 8. Plan of La Lorraine manorial estate, circa 1800, showing the house occupied by the Cooper family. Courtesy Paul Haupt Berne Publishers.

Acknowledgments

The present edition of the *Writings of James Fenimore Cooper* was initiated in the late 1960s at a series of conferences of American Literature scholars arranged through the courtesy of Professor William M. Gibson, then Director of the Center for Editions of American Authors, at annual meetings of the Modern Language Association. At that time, four-fifths of Cooper's published works were out of print and no book of his had ever been edited according to the standards of modern textual bibliography. Preliminary study of his literary manuscripts and printed texts had resulted in surprising discoveries; and the need for a new edition of his *Writings*, as complete as it was possible to make it, seemed obvious. Dr. Henry S. Fenimore Cooper and the late Paul Fenimore Cooper, great-grandsons of the novelist, responded to the proposal with generous encouragement and cooperation as did other members of the Cooper family, especially Dr. Paul Fenimore Cooper, Jr., and Henry S. Fenimore Cooper, the author's great-great-grandsons.

For institutional support, the editors wish to thank the late President James N. Laurie of Trinity University; Presidents Frederick H. Jackson, Glenn W. Ferguson, and Mortimer H. Appley of Clark University; and Marcus McCorison, Director and Librarian of the American Antiquarian Society, together with the Faculty Research and Development Committee of Trinity University and the Research Committee of Clark University. At a crucial stage of the work, presidents of three of the Worcester Consortium institutions—the Reverend John E. Brooks, S.J., President of the College of the Holy Cross; President George H. Hazzard of the Worcester Polytechnic Institute, and President Mortimer H. Appley of Clark University—generously shared with the Cooper Edition part of a Mellon Foundation Grant to the institutions. Timely assistance from the National Endowment for the Humanities ensured the completion of this and other volumes.

Among the many librarians and curators who helped in the preparation of this book, the editors wish especially to mention Frederick E. Bauer, Jr., Mary E. Brown, Marion R. Snow, Carolyn A. Allen, and Dorothy M. Gleason of the American Antiquarian Society; Tilton M. Barron, Marion Henderson, and Irene Walch of the Goddard Library of Clark University; Donald C. Gallup of the Beinecke Library of Yale University; Kathleen Blow and June Moll of the University of Texas at Austin; Charles R. Andrews of Case Western Reserve University; David Estes of Emory University; Arthur T. Hamilton of the University of Cincinnati; Ruth M. Kirk of the University of Washington; L. Quincy Mumford of the Library of Congress; M. A. Pegg of the National Library of Scotland; J. Richard Phillips of the Robert Frost Library of Amherst College; Felix Pollack of the University of Wisconsin Library at Madison; Nathaniel H. Puffer of the University of Delaware; the late David A. Randall of the Lilly Library of Indiana University; Lawrence E. Wikander of Williams College; and J. B. Post, Map Librarian of the Free Library of Philadelphia.

Mr. Spiller wishes to express his indebtedness to the John Simon Guggenheim Memorial Foundation, and the late Henry Allen Moe, its then Executive Secretary, for a fellowship in 1928–29 to enable him to follow Cooper's routes and to identify his residences in Europe for an edition of the then largely-forgotten five volumes of travels. Two volumes only were published in a semi-modernized text, *France* (1928), and *England* (1930) when it became apparent that a definitive edition was needed. He then postponed the project and put his findings into a single volume, *Fenimore Cooper, Critic of His Times* (1931). He is also indebted to the late James Fenimore Cooper, Esq. of Albany, grandson of the novelist; to Donald Heath, then American Consul at Berne; to Hans Bloesch, then Director of the Stadtbibliothek; to Charles Wirz, Curator of the Institut et Musée Voltaire, Geneva, and to many others.

Mr. Staggs wishes to acknowledge a Young Humanist Grant from the National Endowment for the Humanities that enabled him to visit England and Switzerland in the summer of 1971.

He recalls with appreciation students who volunteered their time, especially Thomas Barth, Kelley Casey, Susan Cruz, Steven Curtis, Brenda De Leon, Wendy Glass, Susan Greenhill, Joseph Harmes, Ricki Harner, Virginia Martinez, Mollie Nethery, Sherry Thomas and Anne Wappler.

Mr. Beard and Mr. Elliott wish to thank their colleagues Professors Karl J. R. Arndt, John Conron, Maurice Geracht, J. E. Parsons, and Donald A. Ringe, their research assistant Betty Murdock, student assistants Francine Greenberg, Kimball Beck, Carl Weinstein, Karen Markin, Lori Van Dusen, Corinne Howard, and Brad Wong, and Mrs. Ella Conger for her expert secretarial assistance.

For permissions to use manuscripts, the editors express their appreciation to the Fenimore Cooper family, to the Trustees of the Richard Bentley Estate, to Lea and Febiger of Philadelphia— successors of Carey, Lea and Blanchard, to the Beinecke Rare Book and Manuscript Library of Yale University, to the British Museum, and to the Miriam Lutcher Stark Library of the University of Texas at Austin. For permission to reproduce the page showing the plan and buildings of La Lorraine from Adolf Hebeisen's *Die Lorraine in Bern*, the editors wish to thank Wilhelm Jost of PAUL HAUPT BERNE PUBLISHERS.

For invaluable assistance and advice of various kinds, the editors wish to thank Leonard Berry, Dean Carey Brush, Alan Degutis, Richard Hendel, Louis C. Jones, Norman Mangouni, Richard Mirick, and David Nordloh.

And, finally, to all who have helped, unmentioned as well as mentioned, the editors extend deepest gratitude, not forgetting Hans-Werner Grüninger, teacher and citizen of Bern, Switzerland, who most generously furnished the editors with a copy of his doctoral thesis at the Sorbonne (1963): *James Fenimore Cooper: Voyageur en Suisse*.

The Index has been prepared by Betty Murdock, the illustrations by Herbert Walden.

Illustrations

The engravings selected for the present edition of Cooper's *Switzerland* are reproduced from a copiously illustrated, two-volume work entitled *Switzerland by William Beattie, M.D., Illustrated in a Series of Views Taken on the Spot and Expressly for This Work, by W. H. Bartlett, Esq.* and published in London in 1836, the same year as Cooper's *Switzerland*. Since Cooper visited and described numerous scenes chosen also by Beattie and Bartlett, many of Bartlett's illustrations are as appropriate for Cooper's text as for Beattie's, and Bartlett's stylized visual record may suggest to the modern reader how Cooper's verbal record derives from the picturesque conventions Cooper and Bartlett shared.

Though not a great or perhaps even superior artist, William Henry Bartlett (1809–1854) was one of England's most fashionable and prolific topographic illustrators. He travelled incessantly, producing hundreds of drawings from the Middle East and remote scenic spots in Europe and his own country, enough to illustrate more than three dozen volumes, and writing the letterpress for some of them. In 1836 and 1837, just after the publication of Cooper's *Switzerland*, Nathaniel P. Willis began energetically to promote the picturesque in the United States, accompanying Bartlett on a grand tour of North America to write the letterpress for their collaborative *American Scenery* (1840) and *Canadian Scenery* (1842). "There is a field for the artist in this country (of which this publication reaps almost the first fruits)," proclaimed Willis in his Introduction to *American Scenery*, "which surpasses every other in richness of picturesque." And he hinted that a comparison of "the sublime of the Western Continent and the sublime of Switzerland" (Bartlett's drawings of Switzerland and the United States were obviously to be the basis for comparison) would not disappoint the American Reader.

Following page 32

Plate I.   Bern, with the Alps of   Cooper's text, *Switzer-*
              the Oberland   *land*, 32–33
              Bartlett, II, facing p. 78

Plate II.   The Valley of   *Switzerland,*
              Lauterbrunnen   48–50
              Bartlett, II, facing p. 94

Plate III.   Thun, with the   *Switzerland,*
              Bernese Alps   43–44, 130–
              Bartlett, II, facing p. 83   31

Plate IV.   The Jungfrau   *Switzerland,*
              Bartlett, II, facing p. 96   50, 65

Following page 150

Plate V.   The Upper Cascade of   *Switzerland*, 63
              the Reichenbach
              Bartlett, II, facing p. 100

Plate VI.   The Valley of   *Switzerland,*
              Grindelwald   55–59
              Bartlett, II, facing p. 97

Plate VII.   Castle of Spietz, Lake *Switzerland,*
              of Thun   45–47
              Bartlett, II, facing p. 87

Plate VIII.   Statue of Arnold von   *Switzerland,*
              Winkelreid, at Stantz   150
              Bartlett, II, facing p. 121

Following page 212

Plate IX.   The Devil's Bridge   *Switzerland,*
              Bartlett, I, facing p. 133   212–14

Plate X.   Unterseen   *Switzerland,*
               Bartlett, II, facing p. 89   48, 223–24

Plate XI.   The Castle of Chillon,   *Switzerland,*
               by Moonlight   267
               Bartlett, II, facing p. 149

Plate XII.   The Abbey of Einsiedeln   *Switzerland,*
               Bartlett, I, facing p. 163   165–66

Following page 278

Plate XIII.   The Gorge of the   *Switzerland,*
               Tamina   185–87
               Bartlett, I, facing p. 180

Plate XIV.   Tell's Chapel and the   *Switzerland,*
               Meadow of Grütli   155–57
               Bartlett, I, facing p. 142

Plate XV.   Baths of Pfeffers   *Switzerland,*
               Bartlett, I, facing p. 177   184

Plate XVI.   The Simplon Pass   *Switzerland,*
               (showing the Bernese   278–82
               Alps)
               Bartlett, I, facing p. 57

HISTORICAL INTRODUCTION

Historical Introduction

Gleanings in Europe: Switzerland, published in Philadelphia on 20 May 1836 with the title *Sketches of Switzerland* [Part One], was the first of five epistolary travel narratives completed by James Fenimore Cooper between 1836 and 1838. Though their primary motive was not autobiography, these books furnished a selectively autobiographical and critical account of his experience of France, England, Switzerland, Italy, the Low Countries and the Rhine from his landing at Cowes, Isle of Wight, on 2 July 1826 to his re-embarkation from London on 28 September 1833.

According to its Preface, the present work—and presumably the four travel books that followed it—contain "fragments . . . of a much more extensive work"[1] Cooper originally intended to publish. How much, if any, of this opus already existed in draft is not now clear.[2] Except for the epistolary frame, it would seem not to have taken definitive form in the author's mind. In subject, tone, structure and impact, each of the published books differs markedly from the others; and all available evidence indicates that the individual "letters" were written for the specific places they occupy in the various narratives. Not unnaturally, some letters bear topical resemblances to actual letters Cooper sent to family and friends, but no known evidence suggests that he collected such letters for use or publication. In short, the project of the European travel volumes, as it exists, appears to have evolved open-endedly, each work assuming its distinctive form as the author proceeded. "It was my intention," Cooper informed a young admirer in 1841, "to give another, and far more elaborate book on France, a second on England, and one on Germany, but want of encouragement has induced an abandonment of the design."[3] Although the emphasis of all five travel books was social and political, the special nature of the subject made the *Switzerland* volume primarily a study in the description of nature.

Issued at Philadelphia and London in a sequence that does not correspond to the chronology of the travels, under a confusing array of variant titles, some of which were selected by the English publisher for his own editions, these works are here assigned the composite title *Gleanings in Europe* which Cooper himself chose for the last three, supplemented by the appropriate geographical designation. The chart below shows the chronology of the travels, the relationships among the titles and the order of publication:

Chronology	Title in Cooper Edition	Title in American First Edition	Title in British First Edition
14 July—15 Oct. 1828	Gleanings in Europe: Switzerland	Sketches of Switzerland (1836)	Excursions in Switzerland (1836)
20 Aug. 1830—17 July 1832 passim 18 July—11 Oct. 1832	Gleanings in Europe: the Rhine	Sketches of Switzerland. Part Second (1836)	A Residence in France; with an Excursion up the Rhine, and a Second Visit to Switzerland (1836)
1 June 1826—27 Feb. 1828	Gleanings in Europe: France	Gleanings in Europe (1837)	Recollections of Europe (1837)
28 Feb.—29 May 1828	Gleanings in Europe: England	Gleanings in Europe. England (1837)	England. With Sketches of Society in the Metropolis (1837)
16 Oct. 1828—11 May 1830	Gleanings in Europe: Italy	Gleanings in Europe. Italy (1838)	Excursions in Italy (1838)

II.

On 14 July 1828, almost exactly two years after his arrival in Europe, Cooper set out from Paris with his family for a summer in Switzerland. He was at a turning point in his career. With his children in a private school in Paris during the previous two years, he had had time to complete *The Prairie* and write *The Red Rover;* and he had achieved one of the purposes of his European trip, an arrangement for the profitable publication and translation of his works in England, Germany and France. Now, physically exhausted from writing the greater part of his *Notions of the Americans* and seeing it through the press in a single three-month stint in London, he was not yet prepared to immerse himself in another major novel. A vacation was in order.

The excursion into Switzerland was utterly different from the summer Cooper had planned. Originally, he had projected an ambitious tour of Northern Europe with his friend Gouverneur Wilkins, an exploring expedition to satisfy his curiosity about Europe. "I have many journals in store for you," he wrote Carey, Lea and Carey, his American publishers, on 11 March 1828:

> About the 1st of June I leave the Rhine in company with a friend, leaving my family at Fra[n]cfort on the Maine. We shall pass through the Netherlands, Amsterdam, Hamburgh, Hanover &c. to Keil, Copenhagen, Norway, Sweden, round the gulf of Bothnia to the Arctic Circle, St. Petersburgh, Moscow, Warsaw, Berlin back again. I devote six months to this tour. At my return there will be a book for America. This will be the first of a series written especially for my own Countrymen. I shall be stationary in the winter at Paris, and finish a tale, which is already on the Anvil—We shall then have a touch at France also Switzerland, and perhaps of Austria, Hungary, &c. &c. in another, and so on till we work our way out at the South of Europe —I have no idea of boring mankind with statistics, and dry essays on Politics, but to give only, rapid sketches of what I shall see, with *American* eyes.[4]

Introducing American readers to Europe through *"American eyes"* was, obviously, an inversion of Cooper's strategy in *Notions of the Americans*. In *Notions*, he had intended to promote international understanding by interpreting the United States to European readers. In the various *Gleanings*, Cooper would assume that whatever attracted his *"American* eyes" in different European countries would be interesting or informative to his countrymen.

When delays with *Notions* and Mrs. Cooper's distress at learning of the death of her father, John Peter De Lancey, in Mamaroneck, New York, induced the novelist to postpone his Northern tour, a new itinerary was devised. To the unconcealed delight of the entire family, it would take them to Switzerland for the summer and to Italy in the fall. The party consisted of Cooper himself, then an energetic thirty-nine, his wife Susan Augusta, their five children, Susan, Caroline Martha, Anne

Charlotte, Maria Frances, and Paul Fenimore (ranging in age from fifteen to four), Cooper's young nephew and secretary, William Cooper, and the household help. Preparation for the trip required a month's delay in Paris. The moment of departure, according to Cooper, was heightened by a "glorious anticipation," for "a common-place converse with men was about to give place to a sublime communion with nature."[5]

The Coopers left Paris in a newly-purchased calèche, or large travelling carriage, complete with postillion and baggage, on the road to Bern, via Fontainebleau, Pontarlier on the border, and Neuchâtel (see Map 1, facing p. 180). Shortly after their arrival in Bern on 22 July, Cooper rented a comfortable villa, on the far bank of the Aar. It was an old stone house, with an excellent outlook, called La Lorraine, the property of Count Louis de Pourtalès. Here the family established headquarters and began immediately to enjoy local excursions and to project longer ones into the mountain and lake regions of central Switzerland.

To a vigorous writer whose interests were equally divided between the grand and strange in nature and the complex varieties of human society, probably no country in the world was more inviting than Switzerland. Roads and trails penetrated to the base of the snow-capped mountains and glaciers, boats plied the long, thin lakes that filled the narrow valleys, and inns and stables made travel relatively easy. And for the study of man's social and political evolution and patterns of behavior, Switzerland, past and present, offered a complete laboratory.

The Coopers had evidently done little to brief themselves specifically for the Swiss adventure, except to address queries to Louis Simond, a resident of Geneva and a family connection of Mrs. Cooper,[6] and to obtain a copy of Simond's *Switzerland, or a Journal of a Tour and Residence in that Country* (Boston, London, Paris, 1822). At Neuchâtel, *en route*, Cooper bought the standard traveller's guide of the period, *Manuel du Voyageur en Suisse*, by M. J. G. Ebel, the seventh French edition of which was published in Paris in 1827 and came, boxed, with a corrected and linen-backed copy of the *Carte Itinéraire de la Suisse*, by Henry Keller, also a German, also dated 1827, also published (by Langlois) in Paris. Cooper's frequent references to Ebel indicate that it was, by far, his principal resource for advance planning of trips, laying out of itineraries, determining modes of travel, and choosing the scenes and places to observe closely and describe in his narrative. As a check to Ebel's notes on history and statistics, the authority he most frequently consulted was *Statistique de la Suisse*, by J. Picot, of Geneva, which had appeared in 1819.

In Bern Cooper could and did rely on the excellent little Stadt-bibliothek on the Kesslergasse, imposing even in 1828 for the richness of its collection on the history of all the cantons, but particularly of Bern. During the reactionary period following the Napoleonic era, the twenty-two cantons, of almost every political coloring from the town-meeting to oligarchic class-rule, had relapsed into the loose affiliation they had enjoyed since the fourteenth century. Napoleon's efforts at federalizing the government under French rule had failed with the Second Treaty of Paris in 1815, and it was not until the liberalizing movements of the 30s throughout Europe that the generally conservative and aristocratic governments of most of the cantons gave way and the more democratic modern Swiss Confederation began to take form. The Switzerland Cooper visited in 1828 was therefore quite different economically and politically from that he was to visit in 1832, and the Switzerland of 1836, when his book was published, was even more changed. The time he spent in the circulating library at Bern "devouring," as he says, "all the works on this country that can be had"[7] was evidently seminal for his later social and political criticism and his use of European history to teach political lessons to post-Federal America. But for the moment, the adventure into nature's greatest wonders was paramount.

III.

For the first two weeks in Bern, the travellers rested, read, and visited novel sites in and around the town that would live in Cooper's memory as "one of the most striking" in Europe. On 4 August, he—together with Mrs. Cooper, Susan and William —set out on the first of four longer trips. Moving by carriage, by boat, by horseback and on foot, as terrain permitted, they went from Bern to Thun and Unterseen, then round the circle by way of Lauterbrunnen, Grindelwald and Interlachen, then back to Thun and Bern on 7 August. This is the grand tour of the Bernese Oberland, known by all travellers in Switzerland to this day, and including a near view of the Jungfrau. (The routes of each of the four trips are here traced on sections of the Keller map of 1827, reproduced in this volume between pages 180–181.)

On the second trip (25 August to 4 September), Cooper, again accompanied by his wife, oldest daughter and William, took the road to the northeast to Schaffhausen, skirting the German border, penetrating the Austrian Tyrol briefly, and returning by way of Zurich and Lucerne. The third trip (8 September to 19 September), made only with a guide, took Cooper again through Unterseen and Meyringen, the lakes of Lucerne and Zurich, then to Glaris and St. Gall, with a stop at the monastery of Einsiedeln, and finally from Coire southwest through rugged country to the source of the Rhine, and north over the Grimsel to Meyringen again and back to Bern. The last (24 September to 1 October), again taken by Cooper alone, was a less strenuous excursion southwest from Bern to Lausanne on Lake Geneva, then by boat to Geneva with a brief visit to Voltaire's home at Ferney, and back by the same route.

Meanwhile, though Cooper had postponed his Northern tour (and would eventually abandon it), he had not forgot the promised travel books. On each of the four Swiss tours, he carried a stiff, serviceable notebook (measuring 16.7 cm. x 21 cm.), sewn but unlined, into which he faithfully entered his movements and impressions.[8] In the fifty-two pages pertaining to Switzerland, detail succeeds detail in a stripped-down, factual sequence that effectually conceals the rich aesthetic experience they registered. Compare, for example, the following Journal entry for 25 September with its expansion on pages 239–44 of the present text:

> Quit Payerne on foot. Heavy fog conceals the view, rises about 10 and [I] find myself in a lovely valley through which the Broye flows. Views of chateaux. Lucens a fine old chateau overhangs the town. Get into a return carriage, in which find a little Swiss woman. Her conversation. Her notions of America, where she thinks there is enough to eat, but not to wear &c. Her account of the dominion of

the Bernois—Moudon. Roman town &c—Jorat. Get a view
of the Dents, and of the mountains of Valais. Appearance
of the Country around Lausanne. Arrival of the Grand
Duchess—[9]

Making no secret of his intended use of this Journal, Cooper
observed with care, revisiting some Swiss landscapes for further
study and, on occasion, erasing and rewriting entries. "I am to
cross the St. Gotthard and recross by the Grimsel, Meyringen,
where we have been already, and take a second look at the
Oberland," he wrote his friend Luther Bradish on 16 August
1828, "as I hope to give the first volume of my intended travels
(including Holland and Switzerland) next season."[10]

Delightful as they were, these excursions had to be interrupted when the light snows of early October warned it was
time to leave La Lorraine. The Cooper family again took the
road toward Lausanne, but cut off at the village of Carrouge
to Vevey on Lake Geneva, continuing around the upper end of
the lake, then up the circuitous route to Brig and finally south
across the Simplon, past Lake Maggiore, and on to Milan and
Florence. Four years later, in the summer of 1832, they made
another excursion into Switzerland, this time up the Rhine to
its source. Again Cooper faithfully recorded his experiences in
a Journal, but the books for which both Journals were preliminary remained in incubation.[11]

IV.

Cooper did not actively revive his project of the travel books
until eighteen months after his return to New York City in November 1833. Even then, seven years after his first visit to Switzerland, he was undecided about the size and format of the series. "In my last," he wrote Richard Bentley, his English publisher, on 5 May 1835, "I mentioned an intention to bring out
a book of travels. This work may extend to two large Octavo
vol. or to three such Vol. as [Richard] Rush's [*Narrative of a
Residence at the Court of London*]. It will include the years 1826
down to 1833. France, England, Switzerland, Holland, Ger-

many, Italy, Belgium. Four visits to London, with views at different times—Five to Paris &c &c. I wish you to state what you think such a work ought to bring in *your market*—."[12] After another three weeks, on 27 May, he proposed further revisions,[13] but by summer when he was actually ready to write, he had decided to proceed with the two Switzerland volumes alone and, it would seem, to postpone or abandon the other volumes.[14]

Cooper's long delay in resuming work on the travel books is attributable, at least in part, to the almost total transformation of his fortunes as a writer. *Notions of the Americans* (1828), his first extended nonfictional venture, had been a failure so complete that he had had difficulty comprehending or assimilating it. Not wishing to jeopardize his popularity as novelist, he proceeded to complete *The Wept of Wish-ton-Wish* (1829), wrote *The Water-Witch* (1830), and avoided public expression of his displeasure. His interest in European literary materials expressed itself, nevertheless, in some aspects of *The Water-Witch* and, comprehensively, in a trilogy of historical novels with European settings designed to comment by analogy or implication on social and political struggles at home. These books drew heavily on his observation and memory of scenes he had visited abroad and on his studies of the politics of the medieval church and state: *The Bravo* (1831) on Venice with its lagoons and its Doges; *The Heidenmauer* (1832) on Durkheim, Rhenish Bavaria, and the monastery at Einsiedeln; and *The Headsman* (1833), on Bern, Geneva, Lake Leman, Vevey and the hospice of the Great St. Bernard. The profoundly democratic, anti-monarchical, anti-aristocratic bias of these works produced a reaction so vicious, particularly in the Whig segments of the American press, that Cooper was made to feel a man without a country.

Stunned by his supposed rejection in the United States, Cooper pronounced a *nunc dimittis* to his career as a novelist in *A Letter to His Countrymen* (1834). His immediate reaction was to turn to projects outside the realm of romance: *The Monikins*, a Swiftian satire on England, France and his own country; the European travel books, and the history of the navy of the United States. By April 1835, Cooper was completing work on *The Monikins*, to be published in New York and London in July, and preparing to turn his attention once more to the long-neglected but not forgotten travel books, at least to the two Switzerland volumes.

Neither Henry C. Carey nor Richard Bentley could have been pleased with this prospect. Bentley undoubtedly voiced Carey's opinion as well as his own in his blunt reply on 14 May to Cooper's overture of 14 April: "In reference to your Travels in Europe, I think it necessary to say that works of that class do not succeed here nearly as well as popular novels."[15] The subsequent failure of *The Monikins* intensified their fears. Yet both publishers were enlightened, indulgent men who thoroughly appreciated Cooper's genius, respected his honesty and courage, and hoped he would retrieve his own fortunes—and augment theirs—by resuming the writing of fiction while they cautiously continued to back him financially. If the agreements for *Switzerland*—or for any of the travel books—seemed satisfactory to him, it was only because, for a variety of reasons, Cooper wanted to write them.[16]

V.

Actual composition began, apparently, during the summer of 1835 while Cooper was supervising the renovation of Otsego Hall, preparatory to the family's move from New York City to Cooperstown. "I have been passing the summer in the country," he wrote Bentley from New York on 18 September, "and have been occupied, first, in repairing an old house, secondly, in arranging my journal through *Switzerland* in 1828, and in 1832, for the press."[17] Susan Cooper described her father's creative process in a head-note to selected passages from the 1828 Journal she published in *Putnam's Magazine* in 1868:

> The diary, when he was in movement, was often brief. A few words would bring back to his memory, long afterwards, a throng of images to fill up the picture, while fresh thoughts and fancies would arise unbidden, and blend with the recollections of the past. The very activity of his mind sometimes made his style brief, laconic . . . . Affluence of thought, and feeling, and memory, always followed, when he returned to fix his attention upon the same fact.[18]

The reader can follow the transformation of specific entries in the Journal text (*Letters and Journals*, Volume I) into the epistolary narrative of this edition by using the "Guide to Parallel Passages" (Appendix B, pages 321–322). The movement is consecutive. In a few instances only does Cooper omit details present in the Journal or disperse matter in one entry through more than one passage in the book. These jottings, cryptic and random as they are, summoned up in Cooper's memory resplendent, long-dormant images for conversion into verbal landscapes, immediate and full in their kinesthetic reality. For historical or geographical facts he consulted his Ebel, Picot, Simond, and Engelmann and Reichard (the last bought at Munich in 1830 and then annotated), but his indispensable resources were his gift of total recall and his virtuosity at creating prose pictures in the then fashionable mode known as picturesque or *pittoresque* by late eighteenth and early nineteenth-century connoisseurs of natural scenery.

Already one of its most prominent practitioners, Cooper was fully habituated to the mode—its poetry, fiction, painting, landscape gardening and architecture; and he drew on its conventions in *Switzerland* more self-consciously than usual, perhaps to suggest to "matter-of-fact, utility-loving, and picturesque-despising America"[19] how to appreciate its own scenery more justly. Early British theorists of the picturesque (William Gilpin, Uvedale Price, and Richard Payne Knight) had apparently not been published in the United States, but they were sufficiently well known that William Combe's delightful burlesque *The Tour of Doctor Syntax, In Search of the Picturesque* ("I'll prose it here, I'll verse it there, / And picturesque it everywhere") was reprinted in Philadelphia in 1813, only a year after its appearance in book form in London.[20] Outliving the early excesses of the cult, the picturesque gradually captivated the sensibility of Western Europe and the United States.[21] Cooper had responded to its influence before going abroad, as his early novels reveal; but he was exposed to the full contagion of the vogue in the London, Paris, and Rome of the 1820s and 1830s, where the picturesque was omnipresent, flourishing in drawings, paintings and engravings, adorning walls, portfolios and travel books, sustaining artists of every degree of ability, and inspiring publications such as *The Yearbook of Landscape* (London, 1830–1839) and *Magasin Pittoresque* (Paris, 1833–1882).[22]

Cooper left no doubt of his intention. *Switzerland* was, he wrote Bentley in 1837, "a *picturesque* book."[23] A reviewer for *Waldie's* (31 May 1836) complained that its "pictures of scenery would have been more effective, had [the author] not taken so much pains to inform us of what does or does not add to the picturesque. Indeed, the use of this word is so frequent, that we should not be astonished to hear the work maliciously nicknamed 'Syntax Redivivus.'"[24] Cooper would justly have resisted the insinuation; but he had used William Gilpin's convention of the "picturesque traveller," who sets out, sketchbook in hand, "*searching after effects*," assured that "the great works of nature, in her simplest and purest stile, open inexhausted springs of amusement," and confident in his "expectation of new scenes continually opening, and arising to his view."[25] These "effects," "scenes," or "picturesque compositions" were Nature's incomparable originals to be admired, studied, copied, and—Gilpin would have it—improved, though the aesthetic values for which the "traveller" searched derived, originally, from the paintings of Claude Lorrain, Salvator Rosa, Nicolas Poussin, and the Dutch genre painters; from the poetry of John Dyer, James Thomson, Thomas Gray, and Edward Young; from the fiction of Ann Radcliffe and Sir Walter Scott; and the "picturesque" travels of—among others—Arthur Young, Thomas Gray, and William Gilpin himself.

Cooper's version of the picturesque as it appears in *Switzerland* must be inferred from his remarks and practices in the broad context of picturesque aesthetics, for his indebtedness was general and he nowhere attempted an exact formulation.[26] Scenes of "a thoroughly Swiss, and, consequently, a truly picturesque character," he repeatedly suggested, were those in which Alpine grandeur furnished "a background of sublimity to a foreground of surpassing loveliness."[27] The implied distinction or discontinuity between "sublimity" and "loveliness" is crucial, for it alludes to the subtle, diffused, and unresolved tension at the heart of the picturesque. According to Uvedale Price, it is "that disposition of objects, which, by a partial and uncertain concealment, excites and nourishes curiosity."[28] In

Switzerland, it is usually a visual interplay in which physical
nature in the background evokes the sublime with its intense,
at times terrifying intimation of the ineffable or inexplicable,
while persons, places or things in the foreground present en-
gaging or expressive reminders of the human or familiar or
proportioned (the *beau*) in the microcosmic design. Transcend-
ing the "lower picturesque" of Gilpin and his followers, this
symbolism explores the moral, religious, and metaphysical
dimensions of the mode, approximating what John Ruskin
called the "higher picturesque" in the paintings of J. M. W.
Turner.[29]

For Cooper, the identity between Swiss scenery and the picturesque was pervasive. Wherever his "picturesque eye" turned,
it found the requisite combinations, contrasts, and tensions.
For the sublime effect, the wild, the abrupt, the ragged, the
rough, the irregular or asymmetrical were present in every conceivable shape and size: mountains, gorges, precipices, glaciers,
waterfalls, avalanches, lakes, landslides, and torrents—all subject to spectacular atmospheric displays, particularly of color
and mist. The mere presence of man against a background so
insistent on "the sublimity of desolation"[30] was, Cooper in-
creasingly felt, a jarring discordancy. Yet man *was* present (and
not coincidentally) in forms approved by picturesque convention: peasants, soldiers, guides, beggars, innkeepers, coachmen, fellow travellers, and even banditti. Among other conventional accessories to the picturesque were ruins, castles, abbeys,
inns, chalets, towers, chapels, animals, graveyards, monuments,
grottoes, roadside crosses, and colorful costumes—most or all
of which came highly recommended in handbooks for the picturesque.

Resolved to avoid "common-place accounts of common-place
things,"[31] Cooper chose subjects for their intrinsic painterly
appeal and employed personal narrative to frame his sketches
and impart momentum and enthusiasm, carefully varying their
lengths, their perspectives, their composition, and their tex-
tures. Especially, he exploited sources of narrative interest.
From the first extended landscape (pages 12–14), culminating
in a momentary, breathtaking glimpse of Mt. Blanc across two
cantons and half of Savoy, to the final prospect view of the
variegated Italian countryside from the roof of the Duomo at

Milan (page 299), he conceived his pictures as moving panoramas (or dioramas), developed climaxes from the interaction
between the sublime and the familiar, and employed tested
storytelling devices: anticipatory preparation, foreshadowing,
suspense, surprise, and anecdotal elaboration.

The cumulative and associative effects of language do not so
much compensate for the absence of the artist's brush as provide an analogous kind of immediacy. No painting could cap-
ture the transitional effect of the sudden and "thrillingly exquisite" play of spectral light on the Oberland Alps as seen
from the terrace of La Lorraine at sunset or the awesome ex-
hilaration of a sight of this massive range, bathed in "powerful
splendour," seemingly cut off from its base and floating in air
(pages 39–41). Letter VI, a good sample of Cooper's kinesthetic flair, lifts the reader to the heights above Lauterbrunnen
where, among other sensations, he shares the author's experience "of riding a mountain" like a horse "of uncommon
power," and watches as a "picturesque avalanche"—at first a
small speck, then a large field of snow—gradually filters down
"to the very verge of the green pastures." But if mountains
like the "Blümlis Alp, radiant, pure, and shining like a glory,"[32]
can invigorate and inspire, they can also make man, "his dwelling, and his estate, sudden sacrifices to the sublime and beautiful."[33] Discovering an eyewitness of the Fall of the Rossberg at
Goldau, Cooper provided a chilling account of the vast mud-
slide that many years before had displaced a lake, destroyed a
village, and in one vale left a mass of rocks "like a battle ground,
where Milton's angels had contended," in ironic juxtaposition
to "the exquisite loveliness of the meadows that closely embrace
its sides."[34]

As Uvedale Price had noted, the picturesque habit of mind,
with its deliberate celebration of the accidental and the incon-
gruous, readily lent itself in prose to "quick, lively, and sudden turns of fancy."[35] Cooper obviously enjoys this spontaneous imaginative play and indulges it, as the ductility of the
mode and the variety of possible topics permits, in a diversified pattern of observations, descriptive asides, and anecdotes.
These passages enrich and complicate the texture of the prose,
reinforcing the effects of the larger canvases by extending the
range of pointed dissociation between the expected and the

actual, the normative and the absurd, and appearance and reality. Characteristically, Cooper selects anomalies broadly applicable to human nature. He retells, for instance, a story of the minister in the Valois (noted for its goitres) who reminds his impolitely curious parishioners that it is not the fault of a visiting stranger "if he had no *goître!*"[36] Or, observing a group of cretins "basking in the sun, with goggling, unmeaning eyes, [and] livid, slavering lips," he reverts to the mordant irony of *The Monikins* and reflects on the thin line "between the material and immaterial" in the human constitution and on the possibility that "nature, weary with fruitless efforts," might, "in the end decree a final divorce."[37] At times, he uses the picturesque to comment on the picturesque, as when he notices "the Corydons and Floras of the vale . . . speculating on the picturesque,"[38] and his description of Samuel Nahl's grave sculpture for the tomb of Mme. Langhans and her child in the church at Hindelbank (pages 35–37) skillfully epitomizes the elements of the picturesque as they obtain in an art other than painting.

So long as he was faithful to his experience in 1828 Cooper had little difficulty with the picturesque idiom; but the mode was not always congenial to him in 1835 and 1836. An outcropping of skepticism in *Switzerland* betrays that he had not adjusted to the shattering of his expectation for the rapid emergence of a new, informed, self-confident civilization in the United States, in harmony with the superiority of its institutions; and he was still sensitive to the hostility shown him by the American press. Given the freedom to improvise which the picturesque offered, or seemed to offer, he used it to voice his current social and political concerns, though they had no source in his manuscript Journal and bore slight relationship to Switzerland or the picturesque. These passages, which are relevant only to the overall concerns of the travel series, occupy no more than five percent of the text; but no ingenuity could reconcile his desire to make a social or political comment with a formal description of nature. At times the mixture of modes resulted in prose that lent itself to misconstruction by unsympathetic readers. More often, it resulted in digressions. For example, in one footnote occupying several pages, Cooper revealed his deeper concerns by anatomizing the workings of the British and American constitutional systems; and, several pages into another digression later on in the book, he caught himself and the reader up sharply with *"Revenons à nos Suisses."*[39]

Despite this division of purpose and a persistent uncertainty about format, Cooper's letters from his publishers (his letters to Carey, if extant, are unlocated) suggest that *Switzerland* was carefully composed and closely proofread. Cooper asserted that it was his only travel book "printed even decently."[40] Having spent the summer of 1835 turning his two Swiss Journals into travel narratives, he wrote Bentley from New York on 18 September that the work would be in the hands of the printers about 1 November.[41] Ten weeks later the matter was still unsettled, and on 3 December Carey queried Cooper seriatim:

> I—How many volumes like your novels will it make? II—How do you propose to publish in Europe? III—If we conclude to divide it into several volumes can you arrange it so as to make each complete in itself—For instance you say that you must include part of Paris—Switzerland— Italy &c—Can you make three parts of it that would do to publish separately & that would not seem like odd volumes?
>
> IV. If we should prefer that mode of publication can you have the same done in England? It would not answer well to do so here unless they were to follow our example— Let me know what you think of all these matters—& when you can go to press—[42]

Cooper's reply was evidently reassuring, for Carey wrote on 9 December: "Let us have the copy as soon as possible."[43]

The printing, begun in Philadelphia in mid-December, would have gone faster if Cooper had not read proof in New York. As the setting began, he was apparently still composing or revising, for his copy arrived in miniscule installments and the printer assigned a small force to the work. Communication was the serious problem, and one shipment was lost in the mails.[44] When the sheets finally began to shuttle regularly overnight from Philadelphia to New York in February, Cooper was apparently still preoccupied with his copy; for the cry from the printers—who could set a gathering or twelve pages a day—was for more manuscript. By 18 February, they were nearing the cutoff point for Volume I[45] and by 12 March it was completed, except for late revisions in the stereotype plates.[46] On 18 February, in an effort to hurry Cooper on, the publisher informed him: the printer "has now on it a large force & can [drive?] it out at once."[47] Still, Volume II seems not to have been finished until about 18 April, when Cooper advised Bentley he would forward a full set of sheets in two days.[48]

VII.

Until proved wrong, Cooper was inclined to be optimistic about the reception of his books, especially in letters to his wife. On 1 July 1836, about five weeks after the publication of *Switzerland*, he wrote confidently to her: "Part 1st I fancy, has done pretty well—at least Bryant says that all but the extreme aristocrats like it. They complain of its democracy."[49] On 10 July, he was still hopeful:

> The Sketches have not sold very well, but stand very fair. About twice as many have sold as of Slidell's book [*Spain Revisited*], but they are puffing away at him, might and main. There is another work on Switzerland [*The Old World and the New*] by a Mr. Orville Dewey, that has just appeared, and he writes of fine scenery like a Yankee meeting his mother after an absence of forty years—"Why! mother—is it you?"[50]

But when Cooper informed his wife on 4 November, "Switzerland, I see, has gone to a second edition" in England,[51] he was misinformed. Bentley had merely reissued the first sheets with a new, tipped-in title page designated "New Edition." Much later, in 1843, Cooper acknowledged the fate of *Switzerland* and of the other *Gleanings* in a set of autobiographical notes sent to Rufus W. Griswold:

> These failed, five books in all, scarce paying for printing. I say failed, meaning in America; though, I am told they have done better abroad; Switzerland in particular having become a sort of guide book.[52]

Even on the last point, Cooper seems to have been oversanguine. *Switzerland* was reprinted in English at Paris and issued in a French and in two German translations (one slightly abridged),[53] but no evidence of its service as a guide book has been discovered.

In a letter written on 27 May 1836, exactly a week after publication, Cooper's friend and confidant Samuel F. B. Morse accurately predicted an ambivalent reception by reviewers:[54] "I am reading your *Switzerland*. I like it very much, but this is doubtless to be set down by the [New-York] American *et omne id genus* as prejudice."[55] The *New-York American* review the following day was unexpectedly favorable, dissenting only from Cooper's politics; but Morse's "*omne id genus*" was at large in the land. The [Boston] *Evening Gazette* (28 May) denounced Cooper's political "monomania" through almost the whole of a jumbled newspaper column. *Waldie's Journal of Belles Lettres* (31 May) twisted Cooper's qualified expression of confidence in popular judgment on "the great principles which ought to predominate in the control of human affairs" into an effort to curry favor with the Trade Unionists; and *The New-York Mirror* (11 June) condemned as "very offensive . . . the careful and elaborate details entered into of the slighting and insulting manner in which Americans are looked upon in Europe."

The American press not only tended to exaggerate and distort the small proportion of *Switzerland* explicitly or implicitly controversial, it also expressed displeasure that "the Leviathan of our literature,"[56] "one of the first American writers of the day,"[57] should have forsaken the romance—a form in which he excelled—for an inferior, less congenial, less satisfying form. That he condescended to implicate himself in politics at all roused suspicions about ulterior motives. And the motives adduced—the supposed flirtation with Trade Unionism, for example—were usually wild fabrications. Edgar Allan Poe was closer to the mark when he noted in the *Southern Literary Messenger* (May) that Cooper seemed in "a degree of splenetic ill humor with both himself and his countrymen, quite different from the usual manner of the novelist, and evincing something akin to resentment for real or imaginary ill usage."[58] So fierce was this post-publication outcry that the *Saturday Evening Post*, which had praised Cooper on 28 May for being "what Rembrandt was amongst Painters, and Crabbe amongst Poets, the 'Sternest, but the best,'" returned to defend him on 4 June, explaining: "we have observed so much illiberal censure heaped upon [*Switzerland*] by the personal enemies of the author, that we are induced to give further expression to our opinions upon it, believing it to be worthy of unqualified encomium." William Cullen Bryant followed with a loyal defense in his *Evening Post* on 25 June, but Cooper's friends were essentially powerless to protect him from what even they saw as a misguided confrontation.

When reviewers, hostile or not, paused to judge *Switzerland* for what it was, a travel book whose intended effects were limited and special, their comments were almost always favorable, though praise was likely to be tucked inconspicuously into afterthoughts. Even the bristling, grossly distorted review in the Boston *Evening Gazette* found *Switzerland* "a very interesting work—the majestic scenery of the Alps is described with feeling and strength"; and the review by the Reverend John G. Palfrey in *The North American Review* (July) exhibited a calculated ambivalence: one paragraph praising the pictures of "noble scenery" and another objecting to the "political mania" that profaned it.[59] *Waldie's*, unable to accommodate to the aesthetic motive at all, complained of Cooper's being "too much on the *qui vive* for the 'picturesque' to waste any time on the useful." A few American journals, less narrowly partisan or journalistic, caught more of Cooper's intention and recognized that *Switzerland* altogether surpassed routine travel books in its kinesthetic evocations of landscape. *The Knickerbocker Magazine* (July) declared Cooper's "conceptions of the sublime country" original and "very perfect," "without so much as a borrowed shade or tint."[60] And a fellow connoisseur of Swiss scenery, in a long essay in the September *American Quarterly Review*, pronounced the book a "lively, and well-written" attempt to communicate what language could probably not express, quoted the set pieces copiously, and ostentatiously compared his own "feelings and impressions with those of the author of the Spy and the Red Rover."[61] For Cooper's politics, he professed disdain.

British journals were more favorable. Reviewers were less sensitive to the hypertensions of American politics and more informed about the picturesque. *The Spectator* (June), in a review reprinted in the United States in *The Museum of Foreign Literature* (July),[62] differentiated *Switzerland* sharply "from the class of sketchy tours" or the kind of book that was "a mere 'tour in search of the picturesque.'" Its superiority, according to the reviewer, lay in its narrative strength and in the peculiar endowments of the author: a highly instructed eye, a skillful pen, a critical discrimination sufficient to hold democracy "sacred" but democrats "fair game," and a disposition to be "a bit of a political philosopher, who whiles away the tedium of a dull road or a wet day by spinning theories, amusing if not instructive." *The Athenaeum* (18 June) agreed that Cooper's "keen sensibility" for "alpine scenery" kept *Switzerland* from being a "superfluity" among the "surplusage" of books "on that country of miracles" and stressed Cooper's rapport with his subject: "as he observes *con amore*, so he describes in all the warm colours and graphic perspicuity of a poetic imagination." "His descriptions have all the minuteness and reality of a Dutch picture," the reviewer continued, "yet are massive and picturesque as the originals from which they are taken." Cooper's extraordinary affinity for Swiss scenery and his alienation from his countrymen might both, the reviewer intimated, derive from "that elevation of character" which drives its "possessors away from the scenes of coarse and vulgar contention." And he remarked prophetically that Cooper was "still more likely to offend his countrymen by the social verities which he thrusts into their rather unwilling ears, than by his political opinions," verities the reviewer regarded as inevitable in the unfinished state of American culture in 1836.[63] A long, generally laudatory essay in *The London and Westminster Review* (October) by an extravagant admirer of Byron accorded *Switzerland* "a commanding superiority." "We have never before," he exclaimed, "perused so vivid, yet accurate, a delineation of the stupendous scenery of the Oberland." His appetite for the Byronic was insatiable, however; and perhaps because Cooper failed to gratify it, he confessed that "to a certain extent" the considerable expectation aroused by "Mr. Cooper's particular genius" had "not been realized."[64]

Switzerland was followed by its titular sequel, *Gleanings in Europe: the Rhine* [*Sketches of Switzerland. Part Second*], only four months after publication, and the former was soon forgotten. Its rapid eclipse may have had several causes: the halting of reviews and the shifting of attention to the later *Gleanings* that followed each other briskly, the glut of books about Switzerland, the preference for Cooper's fiction, the intrusion of political and "social verities," or, simply, the inability of readers to respond to the picturesque. Doubtless Cooper would have favored the last explanation. While he was awaiting the popular verdict on *Switzerland*, he advised his friend Horatio Greenough: "this is no region for poets, so sell them your wares, and shut your ears."[65] Unwilling or unable to follow this course himself, Cooper turned his attention to more basic weaknesses in American civilization. Many would doubt his wisdom, but few would question his courage. Edgar Allan Poe, who a few months earlier had interpreted Cooper's belligerence as an expression of personal pique, wrote in the *Southern Literary Messenger* (October), commenting on the Rhine volume but also on its predecessor: "We are a bull-headed and prejudiced people, and it were well if we had a few more of the stamp of Mr. Cooper who would feel themselves at liberty to tell us so to our teeth."[66]

NOTES

1. *Gleanings in Europe: Switzerland*, p. 1 (hereafter cited as *Switzerland*).
2. At several points in *Switzerland* Cooper refers to "former letters" as if they were already written or published. They had not been published; but they may have existed in draft or, more likely, in Cooper's projections for future travel books. See, for example, the reference to Osage Indians visiting in Europe, p. 10, or the description of the orange tree at Versailles, p. 85.
3. *The Letters and Journals of James Fenimore Cooper*, ed. James Franklin Beard. 6 vols. (Cambridge: Harvard University Press, Belknap Press, 1960–1968), IV, 194 (hereafter cited as *Letters and Journals*).
4. Ibid., I, 258.
5. *Switzerland*, p. [5].
6. In a letter dated Bern, 24 August [1828], Mrs. Cooper thanked Louis Simond "for his kind attention, in answering our inquiries respecting Geneva." The "inquiries" had apparently been sent from Paris when the Coopers "intended being at Geneva very shortly." Bibliothèque Genève, Geneva, Switzerland.

7. *Switzerland*, p. 41.
8. The text is published in *Letters and Journals*, I, 270–384. The holograph is in the Collection of American Literature, Beinecke Rare Book and Manuscript Library, Yale University (hereafter cited as YCAL).
9. *Letters and Journals*, I, 341.
10. Ibid., I, 286.
11. The manuscript Journal including Cooper's entries for his 1832 visit to Belgium, Germany, and Switzerland is published in *Letters and Journals*, II, 275–348.
12. *Letters and Journals*, III, 152. On 14 April 1835, Cooper had written Bentley: "I shall shortly publish an account of the Foreign Policy of the U— States, with an examination of the naval power of the country—also I think two or three vol. of travels. I should like to hear from you on both these subjects— The first would make a moderate-sized royal duodecimo—The last would be in vol—embracing travels in England, France, Germany, Switzerland &c, during seven years—Holland—Belgium &c—" (*Letters and Journals*, III, 149).
13. In a letter to Bentley of 27 May, Cooper proposed bringing out the "Travels. . . . in a single octavo vol. a little larger than Mr. Rush's. Vol. I. will conclude with a first visit to France—Vol— IId. will contain a visit or a winter in London—Vol. III. Switzerland &c. The first vol. will be ready for press in Oct." (*Letters and Journals*, III, 155–56).
14. The Preface to *Switzerland* implies clearly that Cooper intended to restrict his travel books to those recounting his experiences in Switzerland in 1828 and 1832.
15. Richard Bentley to JFC, 14 May 1835; MS: YCAL.
16. Bentley apparently paid £200 for *Switzerland* (about half the sum he had paid for *The Headsman*, Cooper's most recent romance), though the publisher's initial offer was £150 (Bentley to JFC, 27 April 1836; MS: YCAL). Carey paid a mere $1,000 for *Switzerland*, about seventy percent less than for *The Headsman* (Carey to JFC, 29 April 1836; MS: YCAL. JFC to Bentley, 23 April 1836; MS: Miriam Lutcher Stark Library, University of Texas).
17. *Letters and Journals*, III, 171.
18. *Putnam's Magazine*, n.s. 1 (June 1868), 730.
19. *Switzerland*, p. 221.
20. The quotation is from Canto I, lines 129–30.
21. The apotheosis of the picturesque in the United States came somewhat later, perhaps in the compendious, sumptuously

illustrated *Picturesque America* (1872), to which William Cullen
Bryant lent his name. Cooper himself contributed an essay
entitled "American and European Scenery Compared" to G. P.
Putnam's *The Home Book of the Picturesque* (1851).

22. Early celebrated for the prose pictures in his fiction, and recog-
nized as "Constitution" and guiding spirit of the Bread and
Cheese Club in New York City between 1822 and 1826,
Cooper had occupied a position of cultural leadership in the
United States almost from the outset of his career as novelist.
By the 1830s, he had become a close friend and patron of such
artists as William Dunlap, Horatio Greenough, and Samuel F.
B. Morse. In Europe between 1826 and 1833, he was immediately accepted into the highest artistic and cultural circles. He
was an enthusiastic visitor at art museums and exhibits, public
and private, in Paris, London, Florence, and Rome; and he
became something of a collector. He commissioned what was
presumably the first "group" by an American, the "Chanting
Cherubs," by Horatio Greenough, and a Thomas Cole painting
as a personal gift to Samuel Rogers. At the home of Rogers and
other London friends, he met many of the leading British
artists of the day. Since he kept no list of his readings, any effort to reconstruct his readings on the picturesque would be
conjectural, though we know he read omnivorously and was
well informed on the subject. While writing *Switzerland*, he
was remodeling Otsego Hall in the picturesque style according
to a plan said to have suggested by S. F. B. Morse.

23. *Letters and Journals*, III, 261.

24. *Waldie's Journal of Belles Lettres*, No. 22, Part 1 (31 May 1836), n.p.

25. William Gilpin, *Three Essays: On Picturesque Beauty; On Picturesque
Travel; and On Sketching Landscape: to Which is Added a Poem,
On Landscape Painting*, 3d ed. (London, 1808), pp. 41, 44, 47.
The quotations are from the essay "On Picturesque Travel."

26. In *Cooper's Landscapes: An Essay on the Picturesque Vision* (Berkeley
and Los Angeles: University of California Press, 1976), Blake
Nevius traces the development of Cooper's picturesque conventions through his fiction and nonfiction, emphasizing the
effect of his European experience on his mode of scenic representation. This useful monograph minimizes the extent to
which picturesque conventions were available to Cooper before
1826 and the extent to which his version or versions of the
picturesque included the sublime, and hence the metaphysical
and religious dimensions. Donald A. Ringe's *The Pictorial Mode:
Space and Time in the Art of Bryant, Irving and Cooper* (Lexington,

Ky.: University Press of Kentucky, 1971) contains a more comprehensive consideration of the expressive elements in Cooper's scenic art, stressing the symbolic values in Cooper's mode of representation. The approaches are different but not, one suspects, incompatible.

27. *Switzerland*, pp. 48, 32.

28. Sir Thomas D. Lauder, *Sir Uvedale Price on the Picturesque; with an Essay on the Origin of Taste, and Much Original Matter, by Sir Thomas Dick Lauder, Bart.* . . . (London, 1842), p. 69. Coleridge describes the picturesque impression as one in which "the parts by their harmony produce an effect of a whole, but where there is no seen form of a whole producing or explaining the parts of it, where the parts only are seen and distinguished, but the whole is felt" (*Biographia Literaria*, ed. J. Shawcross [London, 1909], II, 309).

29. Ruskin's distinction between the "lower" or "surface" picturesque and the "higher" or "noble" picturesque differentiated between the serious art of J. M. W. Turner, which involved the artist's full moral or metaphysical engagement with his subject, and the merely decorative or illustrative (*Modern Painters*, Chapter I, Book V, Volume IV). Both kinds of picturesque owed much to the tradition begun by William Gilpin, but the aesthetic results were at polar extremes. Gilpin had allowed for this possibility. Writing for "gentlemen-artists" of the leisure class who drew "only for amusement" and could not be expected to excel, he did not expect a high level of accomplishment among his readers, though he recognized the desirability of "*ethical* compositions," works representing achievement of "a *higher character* in landscape." He also recognized that to convey "ideas of this kind is the perfection of the art" (Gilpin, *op. cit.*, pp. 164–65).

30. *Gleanings in Europe. Italy* (Philadelphia, 1838), I, 215–16.

31. *Switzerland*, p. 23.

32. Ibid., p. 131.

33. Ibid., p. 153.

34. Ibid., p. 163.

35. Sir Uvedale Price, *Essays on the Picturesque* (London, 1810), I, 341–42. This passage is quoted, with a longer excerpt, in Martin Price, "The Picturesque Moment," in *From Sensibility to Romanticism: Essays Presented to Frederick A. Pottle* (New York: Oxford University Press, 1965), pp. 259–92. Martin Price's essay is an excellent summary of picturesque aesthetics.

36. *Switzerland*, p. 67.

37. Ibid., pp. 270–71.
38. Ibid., p. 60.
39. Ibid., p. 230.
40. *Letters and Journals*, III, 329.
41. Ibid., p. 171. In the letter to Bentley of 18 September 1835, Cooper indicated that the work on Switzerland (evidently he was referring to both the 1828 and 1832 accounts) would make "two octavo volumes each about as large as the Travels of Mr. Rush." Carey was not satisfied with this format, however; and he suggested on 12 November that the most favorable sale might be assured by publishing "in 3 volumes of moderate size to appear at intervals of a month or six weeks to be followed by the other parts of your travels" (Carey to JFC, 12 November 1835; MS: YCAL).
42. Carey to JFC, 3 December 1835; MS: YCAL.
43. Carey to JFC, 9 December 1835; MS: YCAL. The letter continued: "We shall put the first part in two 12mo volumes, instead of one 8mo as you suggested—The page will be of same size as the novels, but it will be leaded, so as to make the same quantity of matter cover more space. The leads will be as thick as you may direct. You know the quantity of matter, & will be able to say how much should go in a page so as to make the whole extend to about 500 pages—"
44. Carey's letter of 21 December 1835, which covered the first parcel of sheets and which was temporarily lost in the mails, read: "We send 12 pages. They take in 5 pages of Mss including the note—to make 2 vols of about 250 pages each will take 210 pages of your mss like that sent on—Will you have more or less—where [do] you deem it advisable to stop the first part— Can you return the proofs recd. by the mornings mail to the office by 4 o clock in the afternoon of the same day—it will expedite the matter.
   The second parcel of Mss is at hand—" (MS: YCAL).
45. Carey, Lea and Co. to JFC, 18 February 1836; MS: YCAL.
46. Carey, Lea and Co. to JFC, 12 March 1836; MS: YCAL.
47. Carey, Lea and Co. to JFC, 18 February 1836; MS: YCAL.
48. *Letters and Journals*, III, 209.
49. Ibid., p. 223.
50. Ibid., p. 228.
51. Ibid., p. 248.
52. Ibid., IV, 344.
53. *Excursions d'une Famille Américaine en Suisse*. Traduit par A. J. B. Defauconpret. 3 vols. Paris: Gosselin, 1836.

Ausflüge in die Schweiz. Aus dem Englischen von C. F. Nietsch. 6 vols. in 2. Frankfurt-am-Main: J. D. Sauerländer, 1836. *Streifreisen durch die Schweiz*. Nach dem Englischen von Dr. Georg Nicolaus Bärmann. 2 vols. Berlin: Duncker und Humblot, 1836. (Abridged)

54. The following citations locate contemporaneous reviews of *Gleanings in Europe: Switzerland* mentioned or quoted in the Historical Introduction: *The* [London] *Athenæum*, No. 451 (18 June 1836), 429–30; *American Quarterly Review*, 20 (September 1836), 228–44; *The* [Boston] *Evening Gazette*, 28 May 1836; *The Knickerbocker, or New-York Monthly Magazine*, 7 (June 1836), 647, also 8 (July 1836), 102–3; *The Museum of Foreign Literature*, 29 (July 1836), 461–63, an American reprinting of the review from *The* [London] *Spectator* cited below; *New-York American*, 28 May 1836; *The* [New York] *Evening Post*, 25 June 1836; *The New-York Mirror*, 8 (11 June 1836), 399; *The North American Review*, 43 (July 1836), 280; [Philadelphia] *Saturday Evening Post*, 15 (28 May 1836), 3, also 15 (4 June 1836), 3; *Southern Literary Messenger*, 2 (May 1836), 401–3, also 2 (October 1836), 720–21; *The* [London] *Spectator*, No. 416 (18 June 1836), 586–87; *Waldie's Journal of Belles Lettres*, No. 22, Part I (31 May 1836); *The Westminster Review*, 4 (October 1836), 155–74.

55. *The Correspondence of James Fenimore-Cooper*, ed. James Fenimore Cooper [the novelist's grandson], (New Haven, 1922), I, 355–56.

56. *American Quarterly Review*, 20 (September 1836), 240.

57. *The New-York Mirror*, 8 (June 1836), 399.

58. *Southern Literary Messenger*, 2 (May 1836), 401. Poe wrote the notices for the *Messenger* for October, according to Arthur H. Quinn, *Edgar Allan Poe* (New York, 1941), p. 258. The reviewer of *Sketches of Switzerland . . . Part Second* in the October issue, p. 721, identifies himself as author of the review of *Sketches* in the May issue.

59. *The North American Review*, 43 (July 1836), 280.

60. *The Knickerbocker Magazine*, 8 (July 1836), 102.

61. *American Quarterly Review*, 20 (September 1836), 244.

62. *The* [London] *Spectator*, No. 416 (18 June 1836), 586.

63. *The* [London] *Athenæum*, No. 451 (18 June 1836), 429.

64. *The London and Westminster Review*, 4 (October 1836), 161, 174.

65. *Letters and Journals*, III, 220.

66. *Southern Literary Messenger*, 2 (October 1836), 721.

Preface

THE fragments of travels that are here laid before the reader are parts of a much more extensive work, that it was, originally, the intention of the writer to publish. This intention (for reasons on which it is unnecessary to dwell) has been, in a great measure, abandoned; though motives, that may possibly become apparent in the course of the work, more especially in its Second Part, have induced him to make the selection which is now printed.

The narrative form is the best for a book of travels, for, besides possessing the most interest, it enables the reader to understand the circumstances under which one, who appears as a witness, has obtained his facts. This form, therefore, has been adhered to here; though it is hoped that the personal details have nowhere been permitted to trespass on the more material objects of the work.

There is a certain peculiarity which all, who have seen much of different countries, must have observed to exist everywhere, simply because it belongs to human frailty. No nation is probably to be found, in which the mass of the people do not believe themselves to be more highly endowed with the better qualities of our nature, than any of their neighbours. It is one of the fruits of travelling to cure individuals of this weakness; but, in many cases, this cure is succeeded by a state of indiscriminating and generalizing indifference, on which those who are termed "men of the world" are a little too apt to pride themselves, mistaking it for liberality and philosophy; while, in fact, they are nearly as far from the truth as when they were in the state of national complacency from which they have so lately emerged. Although communities are merely aggregations of human beings, they have their peculiar and distinctive traits, as well as individuals; and no account of nations can be of value, beyond descriptions of material things, that has not consulted the circumstances which produce those modifications of character that make up the sum of national differences.

In these volumes, however, little beyond descriptions of natural objects has been attempted; for Switzerland, enjoying probably the sublimest as well as the most diversified beauties of this sort that exist on the globe, would seem to have a claim to be treated *sui generis*. Man appears almost to sink to a secondary rank in such a country; and the writer, in this portion of his travels, has gone little out of the way, to give him a place in the picture.

The vacuum in the narrative, and the abrupt manner in which it is laid before the reader, demand a word of explanation. The year 1828 was commenced in Paris. Thence the writer went early to England; returning, however, to France, in June, by the way of Holland and Belgium. At Paris, after this return, the narrative of Part I. commences; terminating at Milan. The rest of the year 1828, and those of 1829, 1830, and 1831, with part of that of 1832, were passed between Italy, (where the writer remained nearly two years,) Germany, Belgium, and France. The narrative in Part II. recommences at Paris, after which it tells its own tale, up to a time when all the interest of the reader in the subject will most probably cease.

Had the other portions of these letters been published, it is probable that their writer would not have escaped some imputations on his patriotism,—for, in making the comparisons that naturally arose from his subject, he has spoken in favour of American principles much oftener than in favour of American things; always, indeed, except in those instances in which his eyes gave him reason to think that the latter really deserved the preference. Just and simple as this rule would seem to be, it is much too discriminating for a numerous class of native critics, who appear to think that a man must take leave not only of his sense, but of his senses, in order to maintain the character of a faithful son of the soil. The superiority of Switzerland, in its peculiar excellence, however, is so generally admitted, that it is to be hoped one may actually venture to assert that a mountain fifteen thousand feet high is more lofty than one of fifteen hundred, or that Mont Blanc is a more sublime object than Butter Hill!

The writer does not expect much favour for the political opinions that occasionally appear in these letters. He has the misfortune to belong to neither of the two great parties that divide the country, and which, though so bitterly hostile and distrustful of each other, will admit of no neutrality. It is a menacing symptom that there is a disposition to seek for a base motive, whenever a citizen may not choose to plunge into the extremes that characterize the movements of political factions. This besetting vice is accompanied by another feeling, that is so singularly opposed to that which everybody is ready to affirm is the governing principle of the institutions, that it may do no harm slightly to advert to it. Any one who may choose to set up a semi-official organ of public opinion, called a newspaper, however illiterate, base, flagrantly corrupt, and absolutely destitute of the confidence and respect of every man in the community, may daily pour out upon the public his falsehoods, his contradictions, his ignorance, and his corruption, treating the national interests as familiarly as "household terms," and all because he is acting in an admitted vocation; the public servant, commissioned to execute the public will, may even turn upon his masters, and tell them not only in what light they are to view him and his conduct, but in what light they are also to view the conduct of his associates in trust; in short, tell them how to make up their judgments on himself and others; and all because he *is* a public servant, and the public is his master: but the private citizen, who merely forms a part of that public, is denounced for his presumption, should he dare to speak of matters of general concernment, except under such high sanction, or as the organ of party.

It may be well to say at once, that this peculiar feeling has not been permitted to influence the tone of these letters, which have been written, in all respects, as if the republic did not contain one of those privileged persons, honoured as "patriots" and "godlikes," but as if both classes were as actually unknown to the country as they are certainly unknown to the spirit and letter of its institutions.

When the writer first arrived in Europe, he had occasion to remark, almost daily, the number and magnitude of the errors that existed in relation to the state of this country. Allusions are occasionally made to this subject, in the course of these letters, but not always with the same degree of surprise, or with precisely the same conclusions. The apparent discrepancies on this head, as well, perhaps, as on one or two other points of opinion, have arisen as a natural consequence from the difference in the order of time. At the period when Part I. commences, the writer had been in Europe but two years; whereas his visit had already extended to six, before the journey related in Part II. was begun. It has been believed to be the fairest course to leave the impressions as they originally stood in his journal, or rather letters, for many of these letters were actually written at, or near, the period of their dates.

As so much of Part II. relates to other countries besides Switzerland, the writer, lest some one, misled by the title he has selected, may feel disposed to complain, deems it no more than fair to admit the fact in the Preface. Switzerland certainly is the leading point in the whole work, and it has been thought sufficiently so, to authorize the use of its name in the title page.

Letter I.

D<small>E A R</small>————,

It was a moment of glorious anticipation, when the carriage drove through the *porte cochère*, into the *rue de Sèvres*, and we found ourselves fairly on the road to Switzerland! Two seasons in Paris, and one in London, had shown us our fellows, to dull satiety; and, apart from the delights of novelty, a commonplace converse with men was about to give place to a sublime communion with nature. The recent journey through Holland, too, served to increase the satisfaction; for it was like bringing the two extremes of scenery into the same picture, to hurry thus from the most artificial and the tamest of all landscapes that has any pretensions to beauty, into the very presence of all that is grand and magnificent in natural formation. The streets of Paris seemed interminable, nor do I think I breathed without restraint until, leaving the *barrière du Trône* behind us, we began to scour along the highway towards Charenton. We passed the little brick edifice in which the gallant Henri IV. is said to have lodged *la belle Gabrielle*, and, descending the declivity to whose side the village clings, crossed the Marne, and were again in the country.

It had rained a little in the morning, and, as what is called the *gras de Paris* is, in truth, the *gras* of all around Paris, the roads were greasy—I know no better word—and, for horses that are never corked, not entirely without danger. We were travelling *limonière;* or, in other words, in the place of the pole a pair of shafts had been attached to the carriage, and our team was composed of three of the sturdy Norman horses so well known on the French roads; the postilion riding the near horse, with traces so long as to enable him to travel wide of the others, and to control the movement. This beast slipped and fell. Rolling over, he caught the leg of his rider beneath his body. The precious Gorcum coach, of which you have heard, was left in Paris on sale, as worthless, and a French travelling *calèche* had been purchased in its place. The latter had a dicky and a rumble. I was seated on the former when the accident happened. Jumping down, the horses were backed, and the postilion, who lay quite helpless, was enabled to extricate his limb. The poor fellow muttered a few *sacr-r-r-es*, made a wry face or two, and limped back into the saddle. At the next relay he still walked, but with difficulty.

At Melun this accident became the subject of conversation among the postilions and stable-boys, most of whom were men of *la nouvelle France*, or youths who no longer adhere to the prejudices of their fathers, and who admire the new philosophy and the new fashioned boots. There was, however, a solitary relic of the *ancien régime* present, in the person of an old man, who wore a powdered club as thick as a large beet-root, and whose whole air had that *recherché* character, that always distinguishes the Frenchman of 1786 from him whose proper element appears to be revolution. The old man listened to the account of the tumble with great gravity; nor did he utter a syllable until he had satisfactorily ascertained that no bones had been broken. Then, approaching with a politeness that would be deemed *ultra* at Washington, he enquired if *"Monsieur* knew whether the postilion, who had met with the fall, wore the ancient or the modern boot?" When told the former, he turned to his noisy revolutionary comrades, with a grimace replete with sarcasm, and cried, *"Aha! voyez-vous, mes enfans—les anciennes modes ont aussi leur mérite!"*

The old man was right. But for the celebrated boot at which travellers are so apt to laugh, it is probable the limb would have snapped like a pipe-stem. When one sees the manner in which French horses go skating along the slippery roads, he understands, at once, the whole mystery of this extraordinary part of a postilion's equipments.

We intended to look at Fontainebleau, and it was yet early when we drove into the forest, which, by the way, will not compare with that of Compiègne, of which you have already had some account. The town, like nearly every other French country town, is of no great beauty or cleanliness, though, perhaps, a little better than common, as respects the latter property. We ordered dinner, and hastened to the *château*.

This palace was principally built by François I., in the well-known style of his age—a sort of French-Elizabethan architecture. It has not been much frequented since the accession of the Bourbons, though Henry IV., the first of that line,* was accustomed to pass some of his time at it. It is scarcely royal, except in extent, having but few magnificent rooms, and I think none that are in very good taste. At least, none such were shown to us. The principal apartment was a *salle de Diane*, a gallery of some size, but of more tawdriness than taste. Of course, we saw the rooms of Napoleon, the table of abdication, and the leg that was kicked. I was more struck with the imperial wash-basin, than with any thing else. It was of truly regal dimensions. The emperor appears to have been a connoisseur in this piece of furniture, for this was the fourth or fifth of his wash-basins I have seen and coveted, all being of most enviable dimensions; though I have never yet been able to find their pendants in any shop, except in the shape of punch-bowls.

The rooms occupied by Pius VII. are large, airy, and commodious—the best, indeed, in the palace; though far from being either rich or regal.

I did not like the little we saw of the gardens. It is not an easy matter to make trees and water and verdure disagreeable to the

---

* Every one knows that the French crown descends in the male line only. In 1270, Louis IX., commonly called St. Louis, was on the throne. This king left many sons; the eldest, as a matter of course, succeeding. The sixth and youngest, was Robert, Comte de Clermont; who married the heiress of the Baron de Bourbon, one of the great nobles of the kingdom. In 1327, Louis de Clermont, their son, was created Duc de Bourbon, and Peer of France. In the 14th century, Anthony Duc de Bourbon, the head of this branch of the royal family, married the heiress of the little kingdom of Navarre, and assumed, in his own person, the title of king. By the deaths of the three brothers, Francis II., Charles IX., and Henry III., Henry, King of Navarre, became the head of his family, and mounted the throne of France, as Henry IV., in 1589. He was, of course, the first sovereign of the family of Bourbon, though always of the ancient race. He was related, *by the male line*, or by that line which carried title, only in the 21st degree to his predecessor, though there had been many intermarriages. By the female he was closely connected with the three last kings. Three hundred and nineteen years elapsed between the death of St. Louis and the succession of his descendant Henry IV. The Princes of Condé were descended from a Duc de Bourbon, the grandfather of Henry IV., and the Princes of Conti were descended from the Princes of Condé. The Princes of Conti have been extinct for some time, but the last Prince of Condé (the father of the Duc d'Enghein) committed suicide in 1830. He was the *cadet* of the

eye; but it would be quite easy to make their combination more agreeable than it is found to be here. One or two vistas, into the forest, too, were any thing but successful.

There was one gallery filled with busts, that looked more like a travelling exhibition of wax-work, than any thing of the kind I remember to have seen. Washington's head was among them.

We did not see the room that was the scene of the tragedy of Monaldeschi. It was described to us as being beneath the aforesaid *salle de Diane*. What a revolution in opinions, since the days when a queen who had abdicated, dared to cause a follower, and he not a natural born subject, to be executed in the palace of a prince, of whom she was merely a guest!

We left the *château* by its great court, an area of some two of three acres, in which the grass was literally growing; a certain proof that the palace was not in favour; for of all probable events, I take it, grass would be the least likely to grow beneath the feet of courtiers. Courtiers and demagogues, you know, are my especial aversion. They are animals of the same genus, classed in different species by the accidents of position.

The next day we posted on, leisurely, to Auxerre, passing the Yonne at its celebrated bridge. This river, a stream of the size of the Mohawk, murmured before the door of the inn where we lodged.

We were now quite without the influence of Paris, and effec-

house of Bourbon, tracing his descent, *in the male line*, to no king nearer than St. Louis, or through an interval of 560 years. The house of Orleans branched off from Louis XIII. in 1643, or 187 years before its accession. Louis XIV., the grandson of Henry IV., succeeded in placing his second grandson, Philippe d'Anjou, on the Spanish throne. From him are descended (always in the male line, none other counting in this family until the recent accession of Donna Isabella II.) the sovereigns of Spain and Naples, and the Duke of Lucca, who stands next in reversion to the Duchy of Parma. It follows that Louis Philippe I., of France, is the youngest prince of his family, his own children excepted, according to the order of primogeniture; Charles X., the Dauphin, the Duc de Bordeaux, all the Spanish, Neapolitan, and Lucchese princes coming before him. When the other powers of Europe consented to the accession of Philippe of Anjou to the throne of Spain, they conditioned with Louis XIV., his grandfather, that he should renounce, for himself and his successors, all claims to that of France. Louis signed the treaty, but protested, at the time; saying that the rights of primogeniture were a fundamental law of the monarchy, and that no head of the family could bind a successor to their relinquishment.

tually in the provinces. The real rusticity of France, to say the truth, is very rustic! The country was beginning to be vine-growing, and, for a great relief, it became decidedly uneven. Rain—rain—rain. I stuck to the dickey, however, to the last, and was compelled to stop at a place called Avallon, with a slight cold and fever. An hour's rest subdued the latter, but it was determined to pass the third night where we were, or at the distance of only twenty-seven posts from the capital. This was not hurrying on towards the great object of our destination, certainly, but then the landlady gravely assured us, the environs of the place were not only called, but were moreover worthy to be called, *la petite Suisse*.

We wasted an hour in looking at the *fauxbourgs*, which were pretty enough, but which were much farther from Switzerland in character, than in distance. Our salon at the inn was decorated with pictures, emblematical of different countries. One was a belle of fair hair and rosy checks; another, a belle of raven locks and pencilled eyebrows; a third, a belle of brown ringlets and azure orbs. Les Etats Unis were particularized in the person of—to use the southern vernacular—a *wench*, as black as a coal!

If it were possible to take the sense of the people of Europe on the subject, I am persuaded it would be found that nine out of ten believe the Americans are any thing but white. You may remember the account I have given you of our residence on the banks of the Seine, in a small country house, that was once a sort of hunting lodge of Louis XV. One day, while in the grounds, overlooking the gardener, a servant ran to inform me that the carriage of *"son excellence,"* the American minister, had driven into the court. He was told to return, and to say I would join *"son excellence"* in a few minutes. *"Monsieur l'ambassadeur,"* said honest Pierre, the gardener, *"est un grand?"* I told him he stood six feet four inches, English, in his stockings. Pierre had seen him one day, on the boulevards at Paris. Curious to know how the minister could have been recognised, under such circumstances, I delayed paying my respects to *"son excellence,"* another minute, in order to inquire. Pierre had taken an interest in America, on account of our relations, and had learned, in the course of his gossiping, that the minister was *"un grand,"* and meeting a strapping negro on the boulevards, he jumped to his conclusion. These things sound odd to us, and I can remember the time when I used to set them down as traveller's wonders, but, believe me, they are religiously true.

From Avallon, the country became more pleasing, and, occasionally—a rare quality in France—it approached the picturesque. *La belle France* ought to be construed into *la France utile*, for the beautiful in this sense means no more than the beautiful of a husbandman; that is to say, easy to plough, and well ploughed.

One league of the road I well remember, for it was the first really beautiful bit of natural scenery I had then met with in the country. There was a deep and bold valley, a curious geological formation of rock, and a tumbling water-course. All this was greatly aided by a hamlet, half buried in trees, which stood on a sort of promontory, and which terminated in a ruin; woods finely scattered, and the temporary disappearance of vineyards; for the vine, though so high-sounding and oriental in the pages of a book, like the olive, invariably lessens the beauty of a country, except it fringes mountain terraces, where, indeed, both help to make up the sum of the picturesque, though quite as much through association as through the eye.

In the course of the last day, we had more than once seen cows at work in the plough, and, in one instance, we saw a woman added to the team. The country physicians, too, with their saddle-bags and hardy roadsters, had a rural look. If you had travelled through endless lines of nearly leafless trees, over paved roads, and athwart open wastes covered with stubble, unrelieved by even a house, except those which are crowded into dirty, squalid, monotonous villages, for leagues—leagues—leagues, you would know how to prize the appearance of even an apothecary on horseback! Most of these travelling leeches, I observed, had holsters; but whether they contained pistols, or something more dangerous, I could not ascertain.

We reached Dijon, the ancient, storied capital of Burgundy, in good time for dinner. The Osages, of whom I spoke in a former letter, had preceded us, and were making a sensation. I believe, however, I forgot to give you the history of this portion of our red brethren. They had been induced by a Frenchman to come to Europe on a speculation. As this motive was altogether too vulgar to be openly attributed to men who were to pass for warriors and heroes, it was varied according to circumstances. With the pious, they came for the good of their souls; with the refined, to get a few hints on civilization; and with the political, to lay the ground-work of future alliances, against the day when they were to wage war on the Americans! Absurd as the latter may seem, I have been distinctly told it, and believe it to be true. It is not an easy matter to make an American who has never been abroad comprehend the great ignorance of our situation which prevails all over Europe;—I know nothing to which it can be so aptly compared, as it may be to the ignorance of Europe which exists all over America. I was shown, at Paris, a memorial addressed to the French government by the speculator in question, in which he laid great stress on the benefit France might anticipate from a trade with this powerful tribe; a trade that, every one knows, cannot take place so long as this republic holds its present authority over the territory they occupy. Mrs. ——, a countrywoman of ours, who circulated freely in high French society, related to me an amusing *contre tems* that occurred to herself, in connexion with these very Osages. She was making a morning call, and, speaking French fluently, was not recognised by another visiter, who had just come from the levee of these gentlemen. The latter was voluble in their praises, and from extolling their paint, big ears, and tomahawks, she had got as far as the *ulterior political views*, connected with a visit to France, when she was stopped by the mistress of the house, who *did* know Mrs. ——, and thought the other indiscreet. The latter had got so far, before she was stopped, however, as to have expatiated on the warm attachment of the travelling heroes to France, and on their utter detestation of the Americans.*

Dijon has some remains of the middle ages, but of what interest are such things to one who is within forty leagues of Switzerland, and who is actually in sight of the Jura?

* It is now some eight years since these savages awakened the hopes of certain French statesmen, and yet the republic still holds quiet sway over Louisiana, and the Osages; and Charles the Xth—where is he? America has never yet been told the half that is meditated against her on the other side of the Atlantic, for little besides silly and fulsome panegyrics have been repeated at home; little else, it is to be feared, being found acceptable.

As for our red brethren, in the end, I believe, they succeeded in piously *humbugging* the Holy Father himself.

Letter II.

MY DEAR————,
This was the 17th of July, 1828, and on the 18th July, 1826, we first put foot in France. We were about to quit it that day two years. How much is there to admire in that great country; how much to shut the eyes to in disgust!

The first relay, after quitting Dijon, was at an insignificant hamlet, called Genlis. Struck by the name, and by the sight of a herd of cows, and of that of a small *château* near the post-house, by a queer association we were led to inquire if this was the spot where *Mesdames de Silléry et de Genlis* took the baths of milk? The good woman of the house laughed at the question, and protested that there was not milk enough in the whole village to furnish baths for two so great ladies. Though often mistaken for such, this is not *the* Genlis. The latter is further north, at no great distance from Paris.

By the way, this word *château* is greatly abused of late. It properly signifies, I believe, a castellated and moated edifice; but it is now applied, without distinction, to every thing that looks like the residence of a country gentleman. The French usually term the palace of the Tuileries the *château*. The old Louvre *was* a *château;* the name, I presume, has been transferred insensibly to the more modern abode of royalty.

We had before us, now, a plain of great extent, whose eastern boundary was a faint line of blue. This was the beginning of those vast ranges of mountains, which, commencing in nearly perpendicular walls of rocks on the shores of the Mediterranean, are only lost in the remotest provinces of eastern Europe. It is true that those before us were merely a sort of outwork of the Alps, the Jura; but they bear such a relation to this grand geological formation, as the bastion bears to the citadel. We tried to believe that some of the distant ridges were in Neuchâtel, a small territory that, by one of the late political changes, has become a part of the Helvetic Confederation.

About noon we came to the margin of our plain, which is watered by the Saone, on crossing which we entered Auxonne, one of the fortresses of this frontier, and a place that is now celebrated as the spot where Napoleon received his military education. You know that France is girt with triple lines of fortresses on the side of the continent; though these near the mountains are of much less magnitude and strength than those which lie nearer to Belgium and Germany. Diplomacy is made to perform the part of ramparts in this region, Switzerland being as good a fortress, in the hands of friends, as can be desired.

We began to ascend gently on quitting Auxonne, and we were soon beyond the limits of Burgundy, and within those of Franche Comté. This large and important province was one of the acquisitions that Louis XIV. was enabled to keep. On a height, that lay a short distance on our left, was a ruin, which the guide-books say was formerly a castle of Roland. This prince and Cæsar seem to divide the French ruins between them, as the parchments have it, "share and share alike." They are tenants in common of half the round towers one meets with between Calais and Marseilles.

The day was lovely, and I had persuaded [Mrs. Cooper] to share my seat on the carriage box. As we rounded the little height on which the ruin is seated, she exclaimed, "What a beautifully white cloud!" Taking the direction from her finger, I saw an accurately defined mass, that resembled the highest wreath of a cloud whose volume was concealed behind the mountains of the Jura, which, by this time, were so near as to be quite distinct. There was something that was not cloudy, too, in its appearance. Its outline was like that of a chiseled rock, and its whiteness greatly surpassed the brilliancy of vapour. I called to the postilion, and pointed out this extraordinary object. "*Mont Blanc, monsieur.*" We were, according to the maps, at least seventy miles from it, in an air line!

I shall never forget the thrill of that moment. There is a feeling allied to the universal love of the mysterious, that causes us all to look with pleasure at any distant object which insensibly leads the mind to the contemplation of things that are invisible. The imagination steals down the sides of distant peaks into the valleys, which it is apt to people with creatures from its stores of recollections, or, perhaps, by its own creative powers. This glimpse of the glacier, for it was only a glimpse, the shining mass settling behind the Jura as we descended on a gallop towards Dole, transported us all, over a long line of road, into the very heart of the country towards which we were hastening. Mont Blanc, it is true, is not in Switzerland, but it is a part of the same wonderful formation that renders Switzerland so remarkable, and the eye actually swept across two of the cantons, and half of Savoy, to take in this speck of aerial brightness. I never before so ardently longed for wings, though their possession used to be one of the most constant of my youthful aspirations.

After quitting Dole we traversed another wide valley, that is watered by the Doubs and its tributaries, until we reached the foot of the Jura. Here, for the first time in Europe, we saw Indian corn, though of a quality much inferior to the luxuriant growth we have at home. It was a great relief to be fairly rid of the monotony of French husbandry, and of the fatiguing plains, for a nature that in a great degree defied the labours of man. The ascent was rather gradual than severe, but we made an entire relay of two posts, without breaking into a trot. The weariness of the ascent was relieved by glimpses at the country just passed, and at nightfall we drew near a wild gorge, (the first of the hundreds it has been our good fortune since to look upon and dwell amongst,) which had that pleasing mixture of nature and art that is wanting in America, but which abounds over all the more ancient regions of the eastern hemisphere. Precipitous rocks rose to a great height on both sides of the pass (the only one practicable for a road) crowned with the ruins of castles, and fortified by works that are not yet considered useless. In the very pass, which is only a few hundred feet in width, is crowded a town called Salins.This place had, in a great degree, been destroyed by fire, and, although it was rising from the desolation in better buildings than before, I do not remember to have entered a scene of greater confusion and ruin, than was presented, as we slowly dragged our way, in the gloom of twilight, into its narrow and dilapidated streets.

Salins, as the name would indicate, is connected with the manufactory of salt. The town was so filled that we found lodgings with difficulty. We got in, at length, at an inferior tavern, where, as usual, we were made to pay more than common prices, for fare that was worse than common. Take counsel of an old traveller, and never go to a second-rate house, in any town less than a capital, such invariably being the penalty. We had ordered tea, and when we hinted that its colour was not quite as high as would be agreeable, the mistress of the house gravely assured us it must be good, as she had that moment procured it *from the apothecary!* The good woman believed she was administering medicine. The virtues of tea, as a common beverage, had not yet penetrated this part of the Jura.

The *chevaux de renfort*, on the following morning, gave notice that we were to climb; and climb we did, scarcely crawling for the first hour or two. Slow as was our progress, we soon ascended into an entirely new world. The runs of water were no longer turbid and dirty, as was the case, almost without exception, from Calais to Dole; the houses, though still wanting in neatness, became picturesque and rural in their forms, ingredients in a landscape in which most of France is greatly deficient. Their roofs projected, to cast the snows from the doors, and the layers of shingles were bound to the rafters by poles loaded with large flat stones. The panoramas and engravings had already taught us that this usage was Swiss. The whole character of the country too, was changed, for, although we occasionally descended to cross a wide valley, the region, as a whole, was mountainous and savage. In one instance, we went up a long hill-side, and plunged into a dark forest of larches, that, at once, transported us back to America. I do not mean that the larch is common in our woods, for it is not; but the general features of these Jura wilds are sufficiently like those of the pine, to maintain the resemblance.

We reached at last, a point where the road overlooked another broad valley, or plain, through which flowed a stream of some size, and at whose farther side stood a town. The mountain rose like a wall beyond, to an elevation much greater than any thing we had yet seen. The river ran northward, and yet it was the Doubs, a tributary of the Rhone. It makes a circuit here among the hills, inclining to the southward, however, before it arrives at Besançon.

It began to rain, and the clouds settled in dense mist on the black fields of larches. In this state of things, we dashed into

Pontarlier, the last town of France, and the end of the post route. This place, though particularly well washed on the present occasion, had an air of general neatness that is not common in French villages. Its principal street was wide and clean, the houses appearing much more comfortable than usual; but I owe it to this part of France to say, that a want of filth is much more prevalent here than it is farther west.

There are no post routes established by law in Switzerland; but on every road that touches one from any other country, arrangements are made to transport the traveller as far as the nearest town. The post-master at Pontarlier agreed to send us on, forthwith, to Val Travers, or half the distance to Neuchâtel.

It rained when we left the post-house, but not hard enough to drive [Mrs. Cooper] and myself from the carriage box. Enveloped in a good cloth cloak, and protected by an umbrella, we determined to brave the weather, and to enter Switzerland with our eyes open. That dark misty barrier of mountain, which crossed our path like a wall, and which loomed before us through the warm mist, powerfully awakened curiosity, and we were desirous of witnessing the rising of the curtain.

We were soon at the base of the hills, where the road inclined southwardly. At times, the mist descended nearly to our own level, (we were already at a great elevation, though in a valley,) completely shutting out the view of the mountain. Then it rained like a deluge, and we were glad to ensconce ourselves in the cloth. Presently the wind blew in our teeth as if discharged by a pair of gigantic bellows, and the carriage inclined more to the eastward. In the midst of the *mêlée* of wind, mist, and rain, I perceived that we were galloping through a narrow gorge, the road the whole time being excellent, and as level as a floor.

The wind and rain ceased, leaving the atmosphere charged with humidity, the hills loaded with vapour, and the air mild and balmy. Casting aside the cloak, and lowering the umbrella, we looked eagerly around. The gorge that had just been passed it would scarely be exaggerated to term a mountain-gateway, and we were in a strait and deep valley, which soon diverged into two, one leading northward, the other in a north-easterly direction. At the point of separation a high rocky promontory obtruded itself, directly across the line of our route, commanding by its position both passes. It was crowned by long irregular piles of buildings, castellated and fortified, that frowned on the very margin of the precipice. This was the Château de Joux, the last hold of France on this road, and celebrated as the prison in which the ruthless policy of Napoleon caused Toussaint to linger out the close of a life that had commenced within the tropics. The transition from the climate of St. Domingo to that of the Jura, was in itself a cruel, and, in this case, a most unmerited punishment.

When will mankind cease to regard only the gorgeous points in the history of this extraordinary soldier, and to weigh him and his career in the scales of eternal justice? I can answer my own question. This will happen, when men cease to say, "such and such acts are for my interests," substituting, "such is my duty." Our own country is filled with Napoleons on a small scale. How often is the word *"interest"* dinging in our ears, and how seldom are we required to recollect that there is such a thing as principle at all! I perfectly agree with the English traveller who asserts that the freedom with which selfish and improper motives and acts are avowed, in our native land, is quite astounding. I do not believe we are much worse than the best of our neighbours, and I do believe that we are much better than the worst of them; but I know no people who tear away the veil from human infirmities with half the reckless hardihood.

The carriage whirled beneath the beetling battlements of Joux, inclining northward. The vapour began to lift, and there were moments when it rolled upwards until it exposed a thousand feet of gloomy larches, a dark array that left the fancy to fix the limits to their aerial boundary. Half an hour of such varying scenery, during which it was scarcely possible to say which received the most pleasure, the eye or the imagination, was sufficient to persuade us to belong to that class of picturesque hunters, who prefer mists to a bright sun. But I have already given in my adhesion on this point, in the description of Paris, as seen from Montmartre.

Common honesty requires I should add, that we were still in France, a country to whose nature, as you well know, I have been no flatterer. But the greater reputation of the cantons has swallowed up all conflicting claims of this sort, in their own neighbourhood, and few people think, I verily believe, of Mont

Blanc, without passing it, incontinently, to the credit of the Swiss. Thus do we claim Niagara as our own, while both the English and French attribute them to the Canadas; the first because they own those provinces, and the last because they once *did* own them.

We soon stopped at an insignificant hamlet, of unexceptionable neatness, and even of picturesque beauty, and *still* it was France. A *gens d'armes* examined the passport, and we proceeded. The postillion pointed to a sort of vista in the larches, which descended from the clouds to the meadows, and gave us the agreeable information, as we came abreast of it, that it separated the two countries. A house stood near the road, for ever since quitting Salins, isolated farm-houses had, more or less, adorned the fields, and this, we were told, stood in France, while its nearest meadow was in Switzerland.

The republic has no custom-houses, nor any import duties, and we passed the frontier on a brisk trot. To render the *entrée* more agreeable, the sun began to stir the mists, and we had the pleasure of their company without the apprehension of rain.

Although the country had been gradually improving in the picturesque and in neatness for the last eight or ten posts, the change in its appearance now became truly magical. Cottages of admirable forms and of faultless neatness were scattered profusely along the road side, the path itself being narrowed to the width which is exactly suited to good taste. The verdure, in the valley, rivalled the emerald, while the mountains loomed out from behind their curtains of vapour in dark patches of rock and larches. We hear a great deal of the verdure of England; but I have already told you that it is the winter rather than the summer verdure of that country, which occasions surprise. The liveliest verdure of England does not equal the liveliest verdure of even New York, more especially in the forests; but the imagination can scarce conceive of any vegetation of a purer tint or more even texture, than that of the meadows which covered the entire valley through which we were trotting, and this, too, along a road that absolutely was wanting in nothing to render it both good and beautiful. What a change from the wearying *pavés* of the *routes royales*, their everlasting sameness, and the avenues of dusty elms!

The dwellings were uniformly at some little distance from the highway, and, so tenacious are these mountaineers of their soil, not an inch of naked earth was visible, with the exception of here and there a foot-path that went serpenting from cottage to cottage, through the emerald lawns, in a way to give the whole valley the appearance of a vast extent of pleasure-grounds, laid out with the most admirable simplicity.

The effect of this sudden transition on us all, was like that of passing into a new world. We had never before witnessed such a nature, and to me it really seemed that I had never before seen so faultless an exhibition of art. The horses trotted merrily through this little valley, and, as Byron was wont facetiously to imitate some murderer of English, we followed in their train, absolutely overflowing with "*touzy-mouzy*".

We caught glimpses of the people, which bespoke a population entirely different from the field-going, brown, and semi-barbarous peasantry of France. The women were quietly seated at the windows, employed in proper female pursuits, instead of trampling in the mud with wooden shoes, or carrying panniers like beasts of burden; and the men appeared to have little to do in the fields beyond trimming the meadows to their beautiful coats of velvet. Husbandry, in these high and moist regions, is principally confined to the wants of the dairy; and the Neuchâtelois are much addicted to the fabrication of watches. Instead of assembling in towns, the labour is carried on in the cottages, and no doubt a great deal of the ease and neatness which so agreeably surprised us, proceeded from this source.

We left this valley by a pass so narrow that there was barely room for the road, between the beetling rock on one side and a dark ravine on the other. Through the latter brawled the little river that was formed by the contributions of the adjoining hills. The Swiss, at the period of the last great invasion, drew an enormous chain across this road, to intercept the artillery and baggage of their enemies, which the French broke, by running the muzzle of a gun against it, while their own light troops kept the riflemen who defended the pass well occupied. Some of the huge staples still remain imbedded in the stone.

At the point just mentioned, we began to descend, by sharp and steep turns, which carried us down into the celebrated Val

Travers. Here our French postilion took his leave, committing us to the hands of the Swiss, for the next three months.

Although this valley is larger and even more beautiful than that of les Verrières, (the one just passed,) and the habitations are much superior, the neatness and verdure being everywhere the same, I do not think we were as much struck with it as with the latter. We were not taken so completely by surprise, and there had been some abuses committed, in the shape of architectural innovations, with which we could have dispensed. Some, who had visited other lands and returned rich, have dared to introduce colonnades and pediments, among the cottages of larch. A real Swiss cottage is as much adapted to Swiss scenery, as the gothic is suited to the holy and sublime feelings of devotion, and evil be the hour when any inhabitant of these mountains was beset with the ambitious desire of imitating Phidias! We are not guiltless of this pretension ourselves, for there is scarce a shingle village throughout the country, that has not more or less of these classical caricatures, and half the divines seem to think their theology imperfect, unless it can be inculcated beneath a dome that looks like a cracked tea-cup, or from among ill-proportioned pine columns that are rent by the heat of two or three Nott stoves.

The evening was beautiful when we left Val Travers. The mists had joined the clouds, or were already lost in the void, and the sun was tinging the view with a yellow light that harmonized gloriously with the dark forests and verdant meadows. As the carriage began to ascend a mountain, we all got out and walked at least a mile, enjoying the beauties of such a scene, to the "top of our bent." A solitary pedestrian was toiling his way up the mountain; and, leaving the rest of the party, I joined him, and got into discourse. His *"bon soir, monsieur,"* air, accent, and *"tournure,"* though those of an artisan, were all decidedly French. *"Monsieur comes from Paris?"* after a little familiarity was established between us. *"Oui."* *"Apparemment, monsieur est Anglais?"* *"Non; Américain."* *"Ah! Anglo-Américain, n'est-ce pas, monsieur?"* glancing his eye back at the group in the rear, most probably to see if they were black. *"Des Etats Unis, mon ami."* *"C'est un beau pays, là bas?"* *"Ma foi, comme ça; ce n'est pas à comparer avec celui-ci, pourtant."* *"Comment!——monsieur, croit que ceci est beau! moi, je ne le crois pas beau; c'est pittoresque, mais pas beau; à mon idée, un pays comme celui auprès de Dijon est beau; là les champs sont plats, et dignes d'être cultivé.*" At present, you have a Frenchman's distinction between the *beau* and the *pittoresque*. There was nothing to be said against it, and we changed the discourse, I being obliged tacitly to admit that Neuchâtel is picturesque but not beautiful.

The approach of night compelled the whole of us to take refuge in the carriage. It soon became very dark, neither moon nor star shedding its light upon us, and we toiled on for an hour, literally without being able to see each other's faces. Every one was convinced that we were travelling amid scenes that would have delighted us, which made the road still more fatiguing, and, in truth, I learned soon after, that we had passed one of the most extraordinary *coup d'œils* in Europe, in this blind and unsatisfactory manner. I then determined so to measure my *étapes*, as never to go a mile in Switzerland again after dark; a resolution that was faithfully adhered to.

We found we were going down—down—down—until we began to apprehend a return to the lower regions, or to the level from which we had been gradually rising for the last two days, but, in point of fact, we were only descending the last and highest range of the Jura. About nine, the carriage stopped before the principal inn in the town of Neuchâtel.

Letter III.

My DEAR————,

On rising this morning, we found ourselves again in a new world. Neuchâtel lies on the west side of the lake which gives its name to both the canton and the town, and directly at the base of the eastern range of the Jura, which stretches like a wall along the water and the valley, for the distance of a hundred miles. The town itself, though of no great size, is neat and well placed, having its business parts on the very strand, and its better habitations more retired. Many of the latter cling to the hillside, and are buried among vineyards. The place is neat, and apparently thrifty.

But the town was scarcely regarded, among the sublime objects that here met us. W[illiam] was the first afoot, and he had not been out of the house five minutes, before he came panting back to hurry us forth to enjoy the view. We followed as fast as we could, and were, indeed, well rewarded for the pains.

The lake, which is some thirty miles in length, by some five or six in width, was, as a matter of course, the nearest object. Our own shore was the wall of the Jura, sufficiently varied by promontories and ravines to be striking. The opposite was an undulating, but comparatively champaign country, and beyond this rose in grandeur, the entire range of the Oberland distinctly visible for a distance of sixty or eighty miles.

Before this sublime sight, all that we had yet seen, even to the glittering peak of Mont Blanc, sunk into insignificance. It is not easy to convey a sufficiently vivid picture of a view so glorious with the pen, and I hardly know how to set about it; for I am fully aware that however kindly you may be disposed to be satisfied with an imperfect description, it is not easy for one who has actually looked upon it to please himself. You must imagine, therefore, as well as you can, what would be the appearance of frozen snow piled in the heavens to the height of a mile, and stretching twenty leagues across the boundary of an

otherwise beautiful view, having its sides shaded by innumera-
ble ravines, or rather valleys, with, here and there, a patch of
hoary naked rock, and the upper line of all tossed into peaks,
mountain tops, and swelling ridges, like the waves of a colossal
ocean. The very *beau idéal* of whiteness is not purer than the
congealed element, or chiselled marble better defined.

After all, we had seen nothing, knew nothing of Switzerland,
until now! Even what we there beheld was at the distance of
some sixty miles, and again I wished for wings, that I might fly
towards the glittering piles; Neuchâtel, its lake, its beautiful environs, and all the near view, being unable to divert the spirit an
instant from the study of objects so sublime.

Throughout the day, which was beautiful and a Sunday, we
could scarcely keep our eyes from this glorious sight, which
seemed to belong as much to heaven as to earth; and, fatigued
as we had been by the late journey, if it had not been a day
when business could not be done, or my purse had not been
exhausted, which rendered an interview with a banker necessary, I fear we might have hurried on to get nearer to the bases
of these wonderful Alps. As it was, we gazed at them in the
distance, and imagined what would be their appearance when
actually among the frozen piles.

I might here commence a tiresome and grave account of
Neuchâtel; but it is my intention to save you, as far as possible,
from reading common-place accounts of common-place things.
There is one peculiarity in regard to this little territory, however, that it may be well enough to mention. Although, to all
intents and purposes, one of the twenty-two cantons of the
Helvetic Confederation, it is a principality, and the King of
Prussia is its prince. This sovereign, therefore, like the King of
Great Britain, may be made to wage war on himself. Neuchâtel
was formerly an independent state, under the sway of a petty
prince, on the failure of whose line, about a century since, it
passed, either by consanguinity or selection, (I believe the latter,) to the house of Brandenburgh. Like most of the other
small states that surrounded Switzerland, it had long been an
ally of the republic; but, at the peace of 1814, when the country
was again remodelled, it was admitted, with others, to the rank
of a canton. You are probably aware that an ally was connected
by no other tie than a treaty, while the canton formed a part of

the confederation, and had a vote in the national diet. There are no more allies, I believe. Napoleon made Marshal Berthier Duke of Neuchâtel, although he was better known by the title of Prince of Wagram. Some of the coin struck during his ephemeral reign is still to be met with.*

The Neuchâtelois speak French, and the canton, like its sisters of Geneva, Vaud, and Valais, may be included among those of a French character; though it is a character greatly modified by the circumstances of situation, government, religion, and pursuits.

On Monday morning, we provided ourselves with maps, and with a copy of Ebel, a work of great utility, though not without errors, and, what is of more importance, still, in Helvetia, with cash. But what book of travels is free from gross faults of this kind? I do not flatter myself that these letters will form an exception, while it has been, and shall continue to be, my object to render them as little obnoxious to the charge as circumstances, my own ignorance included, will allow.

After breakfast we left Neuchâtel, to plunge deeper into Switzerland, of which I began to think, after all the beauties of Val Travers, we had, as yet, enjoyed but a distant view. The three horses were attached to the *calèche*, unicorn, or *à la mode de l'Allemagne*, and away we trotted, on as fair a day as ever smiled on the creation.

There is a plain of some ten or fifteen leagues in width between the Jura and the Alps, athwart which, in a diagonal line, lay our road. Its surface is broken, though not so much as to render tillage painful, and it is everywhere beautifully sprinkled with wood, and in high order. Through this broad valley flows the Aar, one of the principal rivers of Switzerland. Its course is northward, until it meets the Limmat and the Reuss, when the three pour their waters in a body into the Rhine, at no great distance above Basle.

The roads are as fine as possible, and the scenery quite like our own better sort of country scenery, with here and there a memorial of the middle ages, things that are known to us only

---

* During the convulsive movements of 1831, Neuchâtel formally separated from the Swiss Confederation, and it now makes merely a portion of the Prussian states, though probably in possession, still, of its peculiar immunities. As a canton, it was decidedly aristocratic.

in story. We had a glimpse of the lake of Bienne, and of the island of Rousseau; but the former seemed tame, even compared with its near neighbour of Neuchâtel, which is, by no means, celebrated among the waters of these mountains.

We had a *goûter* at Aarberg, a small town that is surrounded by the Aar; and a league or two beyond it, we passed, or rather passed through, the first Swiss *château* we had yet seen. The road actually runs through the court of this building, which is an inconsiderable pile, like most Swiss edifices, irregular, and of no architectural pretension. It was formerly the abode of a feudal baron, notwithstanding; nobility, like every other mundane quality, being a comparative and not a positive condition of man. The English gentleman, in every important requisite, is more of a nobleman than half the nobles of the continent, and, were it not for the manner in which gentility is diluted by distances in America, the same would be true of our own gentlemen. But my moral will be more evident, by simply saying that a King of the Pottowattomies and a King of France fill very different stations in life.

We came into the canton of Berne, after the first two leagues of road, and in territory, at least, we were now in the real, ancient Switzerland, Berne being the eighth canton admitted into the Confederation; an event which occurred as far back as the year 1353. It has long been the most important of the sisterhood, by its territories, wealth, and population; taking rank as the second in the ancient order of cantonal precedency. It is the empire-canton of the Confederation, as we of New York so modestly term our own vigorous political sprout, which, a wilderness the other day, now contains ten times the wealth, twice the cultivated territory, a greater population, and more resources than the whole of even the Helvetia of our own times.

Throughout the day we saw nothing of the Alps; for the inequalities of the ground along which we were travelling, and the great quantity of wood that is scattered over the valley limited the view. But towards evening, on turning the swell of a ridge, the whole range, or rather the whole of its finest parts, stood suddenly before us. We had sensibly lessened the distance between us and the peaks, since quitting Neuchâtel; and, as the sun threw its light from behind us, it was not difficult to distinguish even the icy ravines that furrow their sides. The meeting was quite unexpected, and it occasioned a thrill in my whole system. We had these magnificent objects before us the rest of the way to Berne, from which city also they are in plain view.

The road, as we drew near the town, was lined by side-walks, and avenues of fine trees, and no garden-path could be in better condition. It was a source of complaint, before the revolution, that the Bernese neglected the roads in their conquered territories, while they kept those in their own immediate vicinity in the highest state of repair. Concerning the first part of the charge I shall be mute; but nothing is probably more true than the last.

We entered the gates of this venerable seat of aristocracy in the shape of the *Bürgerschaft*, just as the sun was setting, and drove to le Faucon, one of its best and most frequented inns, which, like most other best and most frequented inns, was so full as to render us less comfortable than was desirable.

Letter IV.

D EAR ———,

Berne is, assuredly, both a picturesque and a beautiful town. It stands on a peninsula formed by the windings of the Aar, and as this river has dug for itself a channel near, or quite a hundred feet below the surface of the adjoining country, the place appears to lie on an eminence, while, in fact, it is rather lower than the level of most of the great valley of the canton. The history of this city is the history of the canton, and, in some measure, it is the history of the Helvetic Confederation.

The whole of this mountainous region, after the breaking up of the kingdom of Burgundy—not the duchy, which, in comparison, was quite a modern state—this portion of Switzerland fell into the hands of divers great barons, or petty princes, among the most powerful of whom was the house of Hapsbourg. These counts of Hapsbourg were strictly of Swiss origin, and they are the source of the present house of Austria, though through the female line. The country immediately around Berne was granted by this family to one of its great nobles, as an independent sovereignty, about the year 1200, and, for a time, it was known as the duchy of Zæringue, or Zæringen. This state was of short duration, however, for as early as the thirteenth century, Berne was ruled by its own burghers.

The origin and character of the peculiar aristocracy which so long governed this canton and its dependencies, and which still governs the canton* proper, shall detain you from more agreeable matter but a moment. But I have promised to point out any thing peculiar in the polity of foreign states, and there is very little general knowledge in America of the real condition

---

* This was true in 1828, or at the date of the letter. In 1831, there was a change of system, which will be alluded to in its proper place.

of Switzerland, if I can judge of my own complete ignorance on the subject, previously to visiting the country.

The city of Berne was built on its present site on account of its facilities for defence. The great depth of the bed of the Aar, and its singular curvature, cause the place to be completely encircled with an admirable natural ditch, with the exception of a neck of land of no great width. A wall thrown across the latter, and the construction of houses of solid stone work along the brow of the precipices that overhang the stream, made it, at a period when the use of artillery was unknown, at once a fortified town.

In the middle ages industry was always fain to take refuge within good substantial walls. The lawlessness of the times, the predatory violence of the barons, whose castles dotted the surface of nearly all Europe, and the manner in which right was made to yield to might, rendered such protection indispensable to the growth of civilization. Berne became one of those cities of refuge to commerce and the arts, though always on a scale suited to the condition and wants of a region like that of Switzerland, and, in the course of half a century, many of the neighbouring nobles, even, were glad to associate themselves with the powerful fraternity of citizens which sprung up behind the defences of the Aar, and to enrol themselves in the list of burghers, in order to find protection against others of their *caste*, who were too strong to be resisted.

Such, in brief, was the origin of the city of Berne. She extended her limits gradually around her walls, this year swallowing up one *seigneurie* and the next another, until she reached something like her present extent of territory. Not content with these acquisitions, however, she engaged in war, and the country of Vaud, as it was then called, together with that of Argovie, were both conquered, and held as dependencies until the French revolution, when each was rendered independent and made a separate canton. There are sad blots in the escutcheon of liberty, one of her votaries holding men, and another entire states in bondage!

All this time, the government of Berne was in the *Bürgerschaft*, or the body of the burghers, a class of citizens who correspond with our own freemen, as they existed before the formation of the present constitution, and when the "freedom of a city" carried with it a political right. As these burghers were comparatively few, and the right was hereditary, the government of the canton is strictly an aristocracy. The rights of the *Bürgerschaft* may be acquired; they are even openly bought at the present time. Of all the expedients to deposit and maintain power and privileges in the hands of a few, that of these open aristocracies is the most ingenious, and the least likely to give way, if they who reap the benefits know how to moderate their desires. The whole secret is in wisely graduating exactions.

Berne is not rich enough, and has too little call for taxation, to render its aristocracy particularly oppressive. Perhaps it is the most just and the most moderate of all the governments of this form, that have existed in modern times; in short, it may be considered as the very *beau idéal* of exclusion. The laws are said to be well executed, the police is vigorous and equitable, while the sinecures are scarcely worth quarrelling about. It is true that certain families have filled particular employments for ages, but this is a matter of far less importance to the public at large, than to a few ambitious individuals. There is no marine, no army, no representation to create expense, and, on the whole, the public gets on probably quite as well as it can hope to get on, until education shall be more diffused, and more avenues are opened to personal enterprise. One of the withering effects of exclusion is the dread of inquiry, and thought is shackled to suppress it; a policy that is certain to retard civilization, and to keep the poor uncomfortable. Berne is obnoxious to this charge, in common with every other state that is not really free; for mere lessons in obedience, and homilies on submission and patience, like those taught in the European governments that affect to instruct, are not to be confounded with the liberal education which, by setting the spirit free, arouses the latent energies of character.

Although the political aristocracy of Berne is strictly that of the Burghers, there are several noble families of great antiquity and of long continued political importance in the canton. The Erlachs have been celebrated in the Confederation for five hundred years: an Erlach leading his countrymen against the bands of Austria in the fourteenth century, and an Erlach head-ing the forces of the canton against the French invasion at the close of the eighteenth. The Swiss nobility are supposed to derive their rank from some of the sovereigns, the emperor in particular; though there are, as usual, one or two, I believe, who pretend to be older than the rest of mankind. There is no more valid objection to a family cherishing recollections like these, than there is in an honest exultation at the greatness of living relatives. I believe, when kept in due bounds, that they serve to make men better; and God forbid the day should ever arrive in America, when the noble acts of the ancestor shall cease to be the subject of felicitation with the descendant. All that common sense and the most fastidious principles require is care, in fostering such feelings, that what is properly a sentiment, be not converted into a narrow and injurious prejudice. Were I a Swiss, I should be proud of being an Erlach; but, being an Erlach, I should think I acted as best became an Erlach, in giving every one of my fellows an absolute and equal participation in all my political rights. It strikes me, that there is no chivalry in refusing a "clear field and no favour" in politics, as well as in all other honourable competition. Exclusion may muster some arguments on the score of that branch of worldly prudence that is sometimes yclept selfishness, but to set it up like an antique to be admired, on the pedestal of chivalry, is downright delusion! There is not a particle of the truly noble in any thing but fair play. What meaner advantage can be taken in the race of greatness, than to start for the goal in possession of "the track," merely because we have been favoured by the accident of birth.

The notions that are generally entertained of republics are too often vague and untrue, as I fancy you will confess, after reading over this imperfect account of the polity of Berne. You will always remember, however, that this canton no longer holds Vaud and Argovie in vassalage, though something like such a state of things still exists in Schwytz, the very focus of Helvetic freedom. But liberty, half the time, means no more than national independence. Even among ourselves, what errors are prevalent on the subject of the institutions. Nine out of ten of our worthy *Bürgerschaft*, more especially of the erudite and accomplished class that comprises the talents, decency, and property of the country, (according to their own account of the matter,) will swear to you that civil and religious liberty are guaranteed by the federal constitution, when, so far as that instrument is concerned, the twenty-four states may establish twenty-four different religions as soon as they please, and the civil liberty of the citizen may be legally put at the disposal of an aristocracy far narrower than that of Berne. I do not know that it would be contrary to the federal constitution, even, for an American state to hold a colony, or a conquered territory. I will put an hypothetical case. The nation is at war. New York raises an army and a fleet, independently of her contributions to the common cause, and takes an island from the enemy. Would not that conquest become hers?—and has not a state all right to regulate its own polity, provided it bears the chameleon-like hue of a republic? Had Massachusetts, for instance, chosen to govern Maine in this manner, what is there in the federal institutions to forbid it?

Letter V.

M. Y DEAR——,

One hears a great deal of the magnificent mountains of Switzerland, while too little is said of the rare beauty of its pastoral lowlands, if any thing can be called low in a country which lies two thousand feet above the sea. Putting the Alps and the Jura (both of which in fact form prominent objects in most of the views from this canton) entirely out of the question, Berne would be in the centre of one of the most lovely landscapes in Europe. The country is broken, but cultivated like a garden, and so well wooded as to resemble a vast park. There are many hedges too, a feature that is usually wanting in the continental picturesque.

Of the city itself, you have already some idea. Though so well situated for defence before the use of artillery, the place is commanded by heights that would render walls and bastions now of no great use. The latter, therefore, have been wisely converted into public promenades, and most beautiful they are, in every particular. Although the Alps are not necessary to render the views from them pleasant, yet there they are to add a background of sublimity to a foreground of surpassing loveliness.

The *Platteform* is the place of most resort, and, though small, and ornamented in the ancient formal style, it is a charming spot. It overhangs the river, on the side of the town next the Oberland, and is supported by a wall more than a hundred feet high. The roofs of the houses in a small suburb, that has crept along the margin of the stream, lie at a dizzy depth beneath, and the incessant murmuring of the Aar, broken and foaming over rocks, ascends as from a cavern. There is a sort of miracle, too, to lend a charm to the spot. A horse is said to have leaped over the battlements, a century or two since, and the rider to have escaped with life!

A little rivulet glides, in a stream large enough to turn a mill,

1. Bern, with the Alps of the Oberland *Switzerland*, 32–33

11. The Valley of Lauterbrunnen *Switzerland*, 48–50

III. Thun, with the Bernese Alps *Switzerland*, 43–44, 130–31

IV. The Jungfrau *Switzerland*, 50, 65

through a sort of trunk, in the middle of the principal street, supplying water for all the purposes of cleanliness, and as a safeguard against fires. This current, which is kept covered with planks, is swift and limpid, and I saw no sufficient reason why its water might not be drunk.

The town abounds in arcades, a good defence against the snow, but they are so low as to be gloomy. It is, I believe, entirely built of stone, much of which is hewn and of a good colour. Altogether, including the lower town, or that which hugs the Aar at the base of the hills, it may contain some seventeen thousand souls.

We have not been idle since our arrival. Although less than a fortnight has passed, we have visited most of the surrounding villages, besides settling ourselves down in a country-house, for the next three months. We are in one of the pretty, little, retired villas that dot the landscape, and at the distance of only half a mile from the town. The sinuous Aar glances between us, but it has burrowed so low in the earth, that no part of it is visible until we stand on its very banks. Graceful footpaths wind among the fields, which are little encumbered with fences or even hedges, and we have roads as narrow and as good as those which one sees in pleasure grounds. The *calèche* is housed; and in its place, I have hired a good roomy Swiss vehicle, that, at need, will carry us all, without having recourse to either dickey or rumble. Our team is composed of two strong cattle, which have, at least, the virtues of going up hill steadily, and down the declivities with surety, two indispensable requisites in a Swiss team. To these we have added a *char-à-banc*, for the purpose of running in and out of town with a single horse. The *char-à-banc* has four low wheels, with a seat placed sideways between them, in such a manner as to allow the traveller to get in or out, while the horse is moving. It will carry three in comfort, though the crab-like movement is disagreeable, until one gets to be accustomed to it.

Our house is about as large as one of the ordinary boxes of Manhattan island. It is built of stone, and, on the whole, is sufficiently comfortable. We found both house and furniture faultlessly neat. The place had just been occupied by the Spanish Minister, but it is the property of the Count Portales of Neuchâtel, who is another Monsieur Tonson as regards landed estate, his name meeting you at every turn. A farm-house is attached to the property, which is in charge of a highly respectable man, who is a favourable specimen of the Swiss yeomanry, and from whom, I am quite willing to confess, I have derived a fund of useful information on the subject of the usages and laws of his country. He is of the *Bürgerschaft*, and a captain of militia, besides being a moderate aristocrat.

Agriculture in this part of Switzerland is conducted much as it is in other countries, most of the common grains and roots being cultivated; but it is quite a different affair among the mountains, which are necessarily in pasture land or meadows; and large portions of which are the common property of the communes. The word Alp means a mountain pasture. The vast piles of granite which heave their colossal tops into the skies, in this region, are covered with verdure, in despite of the everlasting fields of ice which repose in chill sublimity among their upper valleys; nothing being sweeter or more delicate than their grasses. As the only available means of turning most of these extensive cattle-ranges to profit is through the dairy, every one is permitted to turn on a certain number of cows, and the cheese and butter being all made in common, by dairy men and dairy women who pass the grazing season among the clouds, it is found necessary to establish each particular cow's character for milk, in order to make a just partition of the yield. This is done periodically, by good judges, the results being duly registered. At the end of the summer the accounts are examined, and each individual receives his proper portion, according to the properties of his beasts.

In some of the mountainous parts of the country, the inhabitants, though, like our own rude borderers, much attached to their wild abodes, fare but badly, as they raise little or no grain, and, notwithstanding their herds, are not particularly rich in meats. The introduction of the potatoe, within the last thirty years, has greatly meliorated their condition, and they are said to be gradually getting the better of a hard fortune. While making one of our little excursions in the neighbourhood last week, I counted one hundred and twenty-nine gleaners in a field of less than six acres. A *gens d'armes*, who was passing, told us that they came from the Oberland, and that all the grain they consumed was obtained in this manner. He added that seven hundred had passed his beat in a week! These poor people are compelled to substitute potatoes and cheese for bread. The harvest was nearly in, and this conversation took place on the first of August. As the city of Berne itself lies in a valley on a huge mountain, or at an elevation of some eighteen hundred feet above the sea, this may be considered in pretty good season.

The day after meeting this herd of gleaners, who, by-the-way, were of all ages and both sexes, we went to Hindelbank to see a celebrated monument in the village church. The history of this monument has been often told, but it is so touchingly beautiful that it will bear to be repeated.

Hindelbank is no more than a sequestered and insignificant hamlet, at the distance of two leagues from Berne. The church, also, is positively one of the very smallest and humblest of all the parish churches I remember to have seen in Europe. Small as it is, however, it contains the tomb of the Erlachs, whose principal residence is at a short distance from the village. A German artist, of the name of Nahl, was employed to execute something for this distinguished family, and, while engaged in the work, he took up his residence in the house of the parish priest, whose name was Langhans. The good pastor had been recently married, and tradition hath it,—I hope justly, though I have seen sufficient greatly to distrust the poetry of these irresponsible annals,—that his young wife was eminently beautiful. She died at the birth of her first child, and while the sculptor was yet an inmate of the family. Touched by the sorrow of his host, and inspired by the virtues and beauty of the deceased, Nahl struck out the idea of this monument at a heat, and executed it on the spot, as a homage to friendship and connubial worth; looking to the Erlachs alone for the vulgar dross through which genius too commonly receives its impulses.

We saw the *château* of the Erlachs, at a little distance on our right, before reaching the village. It is a house of no great size, but is historical on account of its connexion with this ancient family. The humble little church was readily opened, and we entered, filled with expectation. A large, laboured, and magnificent, but I think tasteless monument, nearly covered one side of the building. It was richly wrought in marbles of different colours, but was confused and meretricious, wanting certainly the simplicity that belongs to every thing of this nature that is truly admirable. I had come to the spot, without particularly attending to the history of the pastor's family, expecting to see a piece of sculpture of rare merit, without exactly knowing what. At that moment I knew nothing of the Erlachs' having a tomb at Hindelbank, and seeing nothing but an exceedingly rustic and plain village church, which was nearly half occupied by this laboured work of art, quite naturally supposed this was the object of our excursion. I was already endeavouring to dissect the confused details, in order to find out the grain of wheat among the heaps of tares, when I was called to the rest of the party.

The sexton had ascended a little platform, at the head of the church, which seemed to be covered with boards thrown loosely on the joists. Raising one or two of these, the real monument was immediately beneath our eyes. An ordinary flat tombstone, with armorial bearings and inscription, lay at the depth of about six inches below the floor. The idea was that of the grave giving up its dead for judgment. The stone was rent longitudinally in twain, until near the head, where a fragment was so broken as to expose the faces and busts of those who were summoned to the resurrection. The child lies tranquilly on the bosom of its mother, as if its innocence were passive, while the countenance of the latter is beaming with holy joy. One hand is a little raised, as if reverently greeting her Redeemer. The sculpture is equal to the thought, and the artist, probably from the circumstance of moulding the features after death, while he has preserved the beauty of a fine symmetry, has imparted to them a look entirely suited to the mystery of the grave. These things too often savour of conceit; and after the momentary feeling of wonder, into which, perhaps, you have been surprised, is a little abated, the mind turns with greater pleasure to the more severe models of classic taste. Such is not the case with this extraordinary monument. It grows upon you by study, and its rare simplicity is quite as remarkable as the boldness and poetry of the conception. Even the material, perishable and plain as it is, helps to sustain the interest; for it betrays the poverty which could not restrain, though it might trammel genius. There it lay, in noble contrast to the more ostentatious sorrow of the Erlachs! I would not have changed it into marble if I could, although it is no more than the common friable sandstone of the adjoining hills, of a grayish-blue colour, and of which half the houses in Berne are constructed.

I have heard it said that the thought of this monument is not original. For this I will not vouch; but I think it has all the appearance of being produced under the pure inspiration of the imagination, quickened by strong and generous feeling. One seldom sees or hears a particularly clever thing, without setting about hunting for the original; ideas which are the most natural and beautiful usually striking us with the force of old acquaintances, on account of their fitness and truth.

There is a monument in Westminster Abbey, in which Death, in the form of a skeleton, appears opening the gates of a tomb, ready to strike his victim. This is a conceit of Roubilliac, and nothing but a conceit. The cumbrous allegory of this work can no more compare with the sublime and evangelical thought of Nahl, than the laboured couplets of Racine can sustain a parallel with the vigorous images of Shakspeare. No work of art—no, not even the Apollo—ever produced so strong an effect on me as this monument, which—because the most exquisite blending of natural sentiment with a supernatural and revealed future— I take to be the most sublime production of its kind, in the world. It was the grave giving up its dead. The details are sufficiently good.

We passed Hofwyl on our return, venturing near the buildings. Mr. Fellenberg was met on horseback; but having no other business than curiosity, and no letters, I did not conceive myself authorized to intrude. The farm appeared extensive, and under good cultivation; but not better, we thought, than that on which we resided.

Coming from France, we were struck with the physical differences between the French and the Swiss. Among seventy-four whom we met on the road this day, fifty-eight had light hair, or hair that had once been light, though in many cases it had changed to a dark auburn. In France, the proportion would certainly have been the other way. The Bernese are, in truth, Germans; speaking a dialect of the German language, and possessing most of the customs and characteristics of the Teutonic race. Yet the real Germans are little liked by their brethren!

I have discovered a mountain! Windham and his friend Pococke merely discovered a valley, a thing that might well lie concealed from the eye, and into which a man might blunder in the dark; but it has been my better fortune to discover a glacier that is a good deal whiter, and quite as high as the clouds. There is an elevated field near la Lorraine, (our country house,) on which P[aul] has just been initiated into the mysteries of flying a kite. I have been his instructer; and a few days since, while engaged in this aerial occupation, with eyes fixed on the heavens, the aforesaid discovery was made. A glittering peak appeared through a vista in the hills, in nearly an eastern direction, distant several points of the compass from the range of the Oberland, which is in plain view from this place towards the south-east. It was to be seen only from one spot, and at that precise spot I happened to turn a glance in the right direction, and the wonder was achieved. I mention the fact, because no one in the vicinity had ever heard of a glacier being visible in that quarter; nor could I gain credit for the discovery, until the unbelievers were confronted by ocular evidence. Judging by the maps and the compass, this peak must be the summit of the Titlis, which lies on the line between the cantons of Unterwalden and Uri, and some fifty miles from Berne. What must be the character of a country, in which the fact of a beautiful glacier like this being visible, is either overlooked by the nearest inhabitants, or has been forgotten! In America, we should travel hundreds of miles to get a glimpse at this single sight.

At Berne, from which city, as well as from every eminence in its vicinity, the entire range of the Oberland lifts its white peaks constantly before the eye, the appearance of a single glacier, more or less, is a matter of no interest. The spectators assembled on the occasion merely nodded assent, quietly admitting that I had really discovered a mountain.

It is at all times a very difficult thing to convey vivid, and, at the same time, accurate impressions of grand scenery by the use of words. When the person to whom the communication is made has seen objects that have a general similarity to those described, the task certainly becomes less difficult, for he who speaks or writes may illustrate his meaning by familiar comparisons; but who in America, that has never left America, can have a just idea of the scenery of this region? A Swiss would readily comprehend a description of vast masses of granite capped with eternal snow, for such objects are constantly before his eyes; but to those who have never looked upon such a magnificent spectacle, written accounts, when they come near their climax, fall as much short of the intention as words are less substantial than things. With a full consciousness of this deficiency in my craft, I shall attempt to give you some notion of the two grandest aspects that the Alps, when seen from this place, assume; for it seems a species of poetical treason to write of Switzerland and be silent on what are certainly two of its most decided sublimities.

One of these appearances is often alluded to, but I do not remember to have ever heard the other mentioned. The first is produced by the setting sun, whose rays, of a cloudless evening, are the parents of hues and changes of a singularly lovely character. For many minutes the lustre of the glacier slowly retires, and is gradually succeeded by a tint of rose colour, which, falling on so luminous a body, produces a sort of "roseate light;" the whole of the vast range becoming mellowed and subdued to indescribable softness. This appearance gradually increases in intensity, varying on different evenings, however, according to the state of the atmosphere. At the very moment, perhaps, when the eye is resting most eagerly on this extraordinary view, the light vanishes. No scenic change is more sudden than that which follows. All the forms remain unaltered, but so varied in hue, as to look like the ghosts of mountains. You see the same vast range of eternal snow, but you see it ghastly and spectral. You fancy that the spirits of the Alps are ranging themselves before you. Watching the peaks for a few minutes longer, the light slowly departs. The spectres, like the magnified images of the phantasmagoria, grow more and more faint, less and less material, until swallowed in the firmament. What renders all this more thrillingly exquisite is, the circumstance that these changes do not occur until after evening has fallen on the lower world, giving to the whole the air of nature sporting, in the upper regions, with some of her spare and detached materials.

This sight is far from uncommon. It is seen during the summer, at least, in greater or less perfection, as often as twice or thrice a week. The other is much less frequent; for, though a constant spectator when the atmosphere was favourable, it was never my fortune to witness it but twice; and even on these occasions only one of them is entitled to come within the description I am about to attempt.

It is necessary to tell you that the Aar flows toward Berne in a north-west direction, through a valley of some width, and several leagues in length. To this fact the Bernese are indebted for their view of the Oberland Alps, which stretch themselves exactly across the mouth of the gorge, at the distance of forty miles in an air line. These giants are supported by a row of outposts, any one of which, of itself, would be a spectacle in another country. One in particular, is distinguished by its form, which is that of a cone. It is nearly in a line with the Jung Frau,* the virgin queen of the Oberland. This mountain is called the Niesen. It stands some eight or ten miles in advance of the mighty range, though to the eye, at Berne, all these accessories appear to be tumbled without order, at the very feet of their principals. The height of the Niesen is given by Ebel, at 5584 French, or nearly 6000 English feet, above the lake of Thun, on whose margin it stands; and at 7340 French, or nearly 8000 English feet above the sea. In short, it is rather higher than the highest peak of our own White Mountains. The Jung Frau rises directly behind this mass, rather more than a mile nearer to heaven.

The day, on the occasion to which I allude, was clouded, and as a great deal of mist was clinging to all the smaller mountains, the lower atmosphere was much charged with vapour. The cap of the Niesen was quite hid, and a wide streak of watery clouds lay along the whole of the summits of the nearer range, leaving, however, their brown sides misty but visible. In short, the Niesen and its immediate neighbours looked like any other range of noble mountains, whose heads were hid in the clouds. I think the vapour must have caused a good deal of refraction, for above these clouds rose the whole of the Oberland Alps to an altitude which certainly seemed even greater than usual. Every peak and all the majestic formation was perfectly visible, though the whole range appeared to be severed from the earth, and to float in air. The line of communication was veiled, and while all below was watery, or enfeebled by mist, the glaciers

---

* Jung Frau, or the virgin; (pronounced Yoong Frow.) The mountain is thus called, because it has never been scaled.

threw back the fierce light of the sun with powerful splendour. The separation from the lower world was made the more complete, from the contrast between the sombre hues beneath and the calm but bright magnificence above. One had some difficulty in imagining that the two could be parts of the same orb. The effect of the whole was to create a picture of which I can give no other idea, than by saying it resembled a glimpse, through the windows of heaven, at such a gorgeous but chastened grandeur, as the imagination might conceive to suit the place. There were moments when the spectral aspect just mentioned, dimmed the lustre of the snows, without injuring their forms, and no language can do justice to the sublimity of the effect. It was impossible to look at them without religious awe; and, irreverent though it may seem, I could hardly persuade myself I was not gazing at some of the sublime mysteries that lie beyond the grave.

A fortnight passed in contemplating such spectacles at the distance of sixteen leagues, has increased the desire to penetrate nearer to the wonders; and it has been determined that as many of our party who are of an age to enjoy the excursion, shall quit this place in a day or two for the Oberland.

We have opened a communication with the keeper of a circulating library, and are devouring all the works on this country that can be had; for to say truth, beyond some vague notions concerning Tell, and a few leading historical facts, the American usually has as crude opinions of Switzerland as the Swiss has of America.

Among other books, I have laid my hands, by accident, on the work of a recent French traveller in the United States. We read little other than English books at home, and are much given to declaiming against English travellers for their unfairness; but, judging from this specimen of Gallic opinion, our ancient allies rate us quite as low as our quondam fellow subjects. A perusal of the work in question has led me to inquire further into the matter, and I am now studying one or two German writers on the same interesting subject. I must say that, thus far, I find little to feed national vanity, and I begin to fear (what I have suspected ever since the first six months in Europe) that we are under an awkward delusion respecting the manner in which the rest of Christendom regards that civilization touching which we are so sensitive. It is some time since I have made the discovery that "the name of an American is *not* a passport all over Europe," but, on the other hand, that, where it conveys any very distinct notions at all, it usually conveys such as are any thing but flattering or agreeable. Few nations are so much the dupes of oily tongues as our own, and so overwhelming is the force of popular opinion, that the native writers shrink from exposing the truth, lest they should be confounded with the detractors. Then, how few Americans really know any thing of the better opinion of Europe on such a point? I shall pursue the *trail* on which I have fallen, and you will probably hear more of this, before these letters are brought to a close.

Letter VI.

My DEAR ———,

We left la Lorraine in good season, and travelled along the course of the Aar, over an excellent road, and through a most beautiful country, for two hours and a half, when we arrived at Thun.* The view of the higher Alps was concealed by the formation and proximity of the lower mountains, and the scenery had some resemblance to that of the better parts of England. We saw excellent cattle, substantial farm houses, with projecting roofs and of Swiss architecture, and everywhere an appearance of comfort and abundance. A small country house, near the river, of an exterior and size but little, if any, superior to that we had just left, was pointed out as the abode of the Grand-duchess Anna. This lady is a daughter of the late, and a sister of the present Duke of Saxe Coburg. She is, of course, also, a sister of Prince Leopold of Saxe Coburg. When young, she was married to the Grand-duke Constantine, from whom she was divorced, when she retired to this valley, where she is said to pass her time more tranquilly than while living in the splendour of the imperial court. These accidental *rencontres* with royalty are of more frequent occurrence in Europe than is commonly believed in America. Members of the reigning families are often met on the high-ways, the present peaceful condition of the world favouring their natural wish to visit countries other than their own.

Thun presented a picturesque appearance as we approached. A small *château*, built, one might almost fancy, to adorn a landscape, stands on a hill, overlooking the place, and breaking its outline. The houses are clustered together at no great distance from the shores of a lake of the same name, and the Aar, which flows out of it, winds its way among the narrow

* Or Thoun; pronounced Toon.

and thronged streets, like some busy tradesman bustling through a crowd.

We here got the first view of a really Swiss lake. This of Thun is much smaller than that of Neuchâtel, but it has all the characteristics of grand scenery, islands, in general, rather belonging to the beautiful than to the sublime. Promontories, headlands, points, bays, churches, castles, and villages line its shores, the whole being enclosed in a frame of granite that is worthy of belting an ocean.

This being the height of the season, and the Oberland the very heart's core of Switzerland, the town was well filled with travellers. There are always a number of boats in waiting to cross the lake, and it is usual to take a guide at this point. The first are under regulations, like hackney coaches, the prices being established by law. It is a pity the care of the canton did not extend a little farther, and obtain the model of a good boat, with orders to construct all that are made for the public service on the same plan. Those in use are clumsy, awkward skiffs, that are, by far, too much out of water, and which neither row fast nor make good weather when there is much wind. The Swiss lakes are so deep, and the air is so apt to plunge from the high valleys which surround them, that one frequently encounters waves of sufficient magnitude to make the qualities of a boat a matter of some moment. The flat bottom is well enough, but the upper works are out of all proportion, and more hold of the water is necessary to keep them head to wind in a stiff breeze. The Thun craft have a little table in the centre, under an awning, the passengers being seated in the centre of the boat. This is probably the best arrangement that could be made. Women as well as men row; one of the former obtaining no small notoriety for her pretty face, soon after the late peace, under the name of *la belle batelìere*.

We engaged a guide, ordered a boat, and proceeded. It is the fashion to decry the indifference of manner which one meets in the service of an American inn; but, while I admit that the charge is too often merited, I do not remember a stronger specimen of American nonchalance, than we had this day of Swiss nonchalance, at the inn of Thun. We were served, it is true, and that is all that can be said. I should tremble for free institutions, if I thought there is any necessary connexion between rudeness and liberty. But Berne republicanism is farther removed from democracy than it is removed from despotism,* and the fault must be imputed, I believe, to the circumstance of the landlord's enjoying a monopoly by his situation and by the absence of enterprise. Monopolies and an absence of enterprise have little in common with real liberty. Our food, with the requisite covers, were brought into the boat, and we took a lunch by the way.

We had to contend with a swift current in the Aar, for the distance of half a mile, after which we got into the lake. The day was fine, the wind fair, and our two oarsmen and one oarswoman, who, by-the-way, was *not la belle batelière*, being full of nerve, if not of skill, we got across the field of blue water with sufficient rapidity. Rudolph, the guide, proved to be an intelligent man of his class, and I believe nothing was lost through his omissions.

The direction of this well known little lake is from the southeast to the north-west, and our course was from the former towards the latter point. Most of the northern shore is a precipitous mountain, though there are spots of sufficient breadth to receive a few farms, and, here and there, a rude hamlet. The site of one of the latter, that had been swept away or buried in a land-slip, was shown to us. But a single cottage was saved. We passed another village that is called the Village of Fools; its inhabitants being supposed to be less gifted with brains than their neighbours. To me they had the air of being extremely poor, a calamity which often induces heavier accusations than that of mere folly. Most of the hamlets lie low, near the water's edge, and all of them have a gloomy air that nearly confounds them with the brown rock. They are, however, exquisitely rustic, and admirably suited to their situation.

The southern shore is gayer. A wide valley or two opens on this side, and the mountains are more insulated and distinct. I speak only of the immediate foreground, for, when fairly on the lake of Thun, the whole visible horizon is limited by a view of the minor Alps. One of the most celebrated of the Swiss monuments adorns this side of the lake. It is the castle of Spietz, which is well placed to help the picturesque. It is seen only in

* This was written in 1828.

the distance, however, the passages being made by the northern shore; but it may be questioned if the traveller loses any thing by the fact. The principal tower of this edifice is said to be as old as the ninth century, and the hold is believed to have been a favourite residence of one of the sovereigns of that kingdom of Burgundy, which once included all the western part of what is now Switzerland; a kingdom which, to my shame be it said, I never heard named, until the late acquaintance with the circulating library at Berne. Our knowledge is much like the recollections of the aged, who can recall the events of the last few years, and whose memories then take a backward leap to the period of youth. We read of the present, and of that past which relates more immediately to present things, when we make an enormous stride into the annals of the ancients, stepping over the diademed heads of hundreds of sovereigns, of whose empires, even, we scarcely ever make mention. We Americans are exceedingly provoked if an unlucky wight of an European happen to call Massachusetts a town, or Kennebunk a state; and yet how many of us can enumerate the names of the twenty-two cantons of Switzerland, or of the thirty-eight states of Germany, or even of the ten Italian governments? Did you ever hear of such a kingdom as that of Austrasia? I shall confess I never did, until I passed the ruins of a palace of its monarchs, when one could do no less than inquire to whom it had belonged? That those who direct the affairs of Europe are ignorant, and culpably ignorant, of America, is true; for they seem determined to learn nothing unless they can learn that which is in conformity with their own particular prognostics and wishes; but, after making a reasonable allowance for the rapidity of changes among us, for the small *visible* importance of our annals—I say *visible*, for I believe Christendom, in the end, is to feel the full influence of our facts—and for the necessary poverty of the literature, I do not know that, in reference to those classes to whom intelligence of this sort is usually confined, we have much the advantage of the old hemisphere in this respect. It is true we *do* know English history, while few Englishmen know any thing of our history beyond its leading facts; but, at least, we ought to remember and admit our ignorance as to all the rest of Europe.

I believe the *château* of Spietz has passed into the family of Erlach. It is truly an appropriate abode for the descendants of such a stock, surrounded, as it is, by a nature as grand, and yet as fair, as the recollections which attach to the venerable name. I sincerely hope that its present possessor is a liberal, (while he is above the cant and hypocrisy of those who are willing to concede rights to their fellow creatures merely that they may be included in the number, and who would willingly, if possible, stop with their own particular class,) as every real gentleman should be.

When about two thirds of the distance across the lake, we caught a glimpse of the peak of the Jung Frau, resting like a silvery mass above the lower range of mountains, which overhung the water in a massive wall of perhaps two thousand feet in height. I know nothing that gives a more vivid, or a more imposing idea of the vast elevation of these glaciers, than to see them in this manner, out-topping huge mountains, at whose very base, as it were, the eye is looking up at the wondrous pile. The day had become clouded, and we caught this glimpse of the peak at a favourable moment, when, resembling a fragment of another orb, it was throwing back a flood of frozen effulgence; for even the sun's rays seem chilled, when reflected from these masses of eternal snow.

We were three hours in going from Thun to Neuhaus, which, in literal conformity with its name, is but a solitary dwelling. It has a small artificial port, that has been formed by casting stones loosely into the lake in a line nearly parallel with its bank. Behind this little primitive mole lay a crowded fleet of clumsy boats, the crews of which were lounging about the strand, in waiting for passengers. The former, as usual, were of both sexes. One boat, with a freight of English, was coming out of port as we entered. *Chars*, and carriages of a larger size, were in readiness, and, in a few minutes, we were all seated in one of the latter, with orders to push forward to the bases of those mountains, which had so long been tantalizing us with their glories in the distance. I believe the carriages are in some way regulated by the police, for we were transferred from the boat to the vehicle without noise or contention. By eating *en route* one is enabled to get along a great deal faster than would otherwise prove the case, and, aided by the promptitude of the guides, boatmen, and coachmen, a journey through that part of the Oberland in which there are wheel roads, is very soon effected.

We soon entered and passed the village of Unterséen, which has a thoroughly Swiss, and, consequently, a truly picturesque character. We then inclined to the south, leaving Interlachen on our left, and plunged into a dark gorge. Every step heightened the interest, which resembled that we felt in passing the Jura, though increased by the increasing magnificence of the scenery, and sustained with the freshness of novelty, even after the experience of that exciting day. A noble torrent foamed on our left, while a mountain frowned on the right, in many places within reach of the whip. Every thing seemed appropriate, and on an Alpine scale. In a few miles we came to a point where the valley, or gorge, for it was scarcely more, divided into two parts, one inclining still further to the south, and the other diverging eastwardly. Each had its torrent, and each its wildness and beauty, though the first evidently was of the most savage aspect. We turned into this, ascending gradually, burying ourselves, as we then thought, in the very mysteries of the Alps. We soon caught a view of a thread of spray falling from an immense height into the narrow opening before us, and presently we stopped at the door of a very comfortably looking inn. We were in the celebrated valley of Lauterbrunnen, and such had been the rapidity of our course, so great was the change, and so strangely and wildly picturesque the place, that I do not remember ever to have felt so strong a sensation of breathless enchantment as at that moment.

Lauterbrunnen is commonly thought to be the most intrinsically Swiss, of all the inhabited valleys of Switzerland. It certainly strikes the novice with more of wonder and delight than any other that I know; but our tastes change and improve in matters of scenery as in other things, and the same objects, seen a second time, and after frequent occasions of comparison, do not always produce the same relative impressions.

We walked to the waterfall, which was the celebrated Staubbach, (Torrent or Fall of Dust,) and at a short distance from the inn. It contained as much water as would turn a large mill, and fell over the face of a stupendous rock, itself an imposing object, seen as it then was by twilight, beetling above the narrow valley. The perpendicular, or lower fall, is said to be eight hundred feet. About a third of the distance, the fluid descends towards the eye in a sort of thick spray; it then seems to be broken into falling mist, until it touches a projection in the mountain, where it resumes the more palpable character of the element, and descends, washing the base of the rock, to the spectator, flowing past him in a limpid current. It is well named, for so ethereal or dust-like is one of its sections, that once or twice it appeared about to sail away like a cloud, in the duskiness of the evening, on the wings of the wind.

I despair of making you see Lauterbrunnen through the medium of the mind's eye; still you shall have the elements of this remarkable valley, to combine in such a picture as your own imagination can draw.

Standing at the foot of the Staubbach, you have in the near ground a hamlet of truly rustic peculiarities; scanty, but beautifully verdant meadows, a little church, and the inn. The latter is merely for summer use, and, though Swissish in exterior, might be spared from the view. It has three stories, and twelve small windows in front;—too much like a hotel for the picturesque; but it is scarcely observed amid the stupendous objects around it. The valley may possibly be half a mile in width, in an air line, though it does not seem to be nearly so much. One of its sides, that of the Staubbach, is little other than a rampart of ragged rocks; but the other is composed of a sort of verdant *débris*, that admits of herbage, and even of some little cultivation, though still so steep in the main as to require great care in descending. The whole valley, and the whole of this mountain side, are dotted with those perfectly rural objects, châlets, or small dark picturesque barns of larch, such as you have often seen in engravings. I counted one hundred and fifty-eight of them, from the windows of the inn. Towards Interlachen, or in the direction we had come, a huge mountain lay directly athwart the entrance of the valley, appearing to close it entirely; though we pigmies, by following the torrents, had stolen around its base; and, in the other, or the opposite direction, was one of those awfully mysterious and grand views that are occasionally seen in Switzerland, which present a strange and chaotic assemblage of the sublimest natural objects, thrown together in a way to leave even more to the imagination than is actually presented to the eye.

We walked a mile or two up the valley, in the latter direction. At that hour, dim twilight, it was not difficult to fancy we were approaching a spot which Omnipotence had not yet reduced to order and usefulness. We looked out of our own straitened valley, through a gorge, into a sort of mountain basin, that was formed by the higher Alps. Glaciers bounded the view, and torrents were seen tumbling into the chaos beneath, looking chill and wild. The whole gradually disappeared with the waning light.

At no great distance from the inn, there is a huge mountain-abutment, in the shape of a dark rock, which cannot be less than a thousand or fifteen hundred feet in perpendicular height above the level of the valley. While standing at a window, gazing at this black pile, whose summit was hid in mist, the latter floated away, and there lay the well known peak of the Jung Frau directly behind and over it, glittering gloriously in the sun! The height and proximity of the nearer rock caused this glimpse to give us a more imposing idea of the virgin glacier than any view of it which we had yet enjoyed.

By-the-way, the long merited name of the Jung Frau is in danger of being lost; for there appears to be more settled designs this season of overcoming her frozen and hitherto unattainable bosom than ever. Several parties of English amateurs have attempted to ascend; but they do little more than follow where the guides lead, and publish magnificent books afterwards. A gentleman of Soleure, however, was said to have got as high as eleven thousand feet the day before our arrival. He was driven back by a snow storm. These several attempts have touched the pride of the chamois hunters, and there is a rumour in the valleys that the Jung Frau will shortly cease to be a Jung Frau at all. The end will show.

The inn was alive at an early hour next morning, and as these Swiss mountain abodes are little more than boxes of larch, they rattle like drums, or rather like our own shingle palaces. We heard the reveillée beaten by the feet of divers busy travellers. By half past 6 A.M. we had breakfasted and were in the saddle. W[illiam] and myself were mounted in the usual manner; but the two ladies were seated sideways, within a low circular support for the back, without saddle horns, and with both feet resting on a narrow board suspended like a stirrup. There was a guide to each of their horses, who were charged with their safety, and who were to return with the cattle after we should get as far as Meyringen, on the other side of the Great and Little Scheidecks. The road led up the valley as far as the "Torrent of Dust," when it turned and descended to that other torrent, which tumbles through the centre of the valley. The clock struck seven as we passed the church, and, although we were only at the 5th of August, the rays of the sun had not got any lower into this huge ravine than halfway down the Staubbach.

The ascent commenced immediately on quitting the stream; for the surface of the valley is merely the *débris* of mountains, less precipitous than common, and fertilized by time. The path lay directly up the side of the acclivity, and, although it ran in short zig-zags, there were places in which we were not ashamed to cling to the manes. The slightest pull on the rein was certain to produce a dead halt. Two American gentlemen* were descending this very pass a few days later, when one of their horses made a false step, and, rolling heels over head for a great distance, he actually broke his neck. As no one thinks of *descending* without dismounting, the loss of the poor beast was the extent of the damage.

We were forty minutes in climbing to the brow of the first acclivity, where we landed on an inclined plane, dotted with châlets, and carpeted with a beautiful green sward; or on what is strictly an "Alp." This romantic mountain pasture contained also several inhabited cottages. Our route lay through meadows of short but sweet grasses; and little girls came out to meet us, every ten or fifteen rods, with offerings of roses, cherries on their branches, and strawberries in the leaves; a species of picturesque mendacity, which, while it did not perhaps adorn, did not absolutely disfigure the character of the scenery. I parted with a crown, in *batz* and *half-batz*, before we fairly got rid of the pretty little pastoral beggars. These children very uniformly had light hair; fair, oval faces; and not unfrequently dark, sparkling eyes, on which, I am sorry to add, a *batz* invariably produced a very lively impression. Many had the promise of

* Messrs. R[ay] and L[ow], of New York.

actual beauty; but he who looked abroad on the gray and frosted piles among which they dwelt, felt it was a beauty doomed to be nipped in the bud.

Lauterbrunnen, seen from this spot, appeared merely a ravine. The river and houses had, as it were, sunk into the earth, and the line of the valley was to be traced only by a wide crevice between the piles in which this celebrated hamlet was confined. The rock over which the Staubbach falls proved to be only the base of a huge mountain, that towered above it to the elevation of a lesser Alp. We traced the windings of the torrent down its steep side for more than a mile, dashing among rocks, or gliding through groves of firs; here a glancing rapid, and there a brawling brook, until, reaching the margin of the precipice, it leaped off, and was lost, a silvery thread, in the abyss. A great deal of that which we had looked up to with awe the day before, we now looked down upon with surprise, realizing the trite truth, that every thing has two sides.

After gradually ascending for some time among these meadows, the path turned at right angles to its former direction, running nearly parallel to the valley of Lauterbrunnen, and in a direct line for the Jung Frau. The summit of the latter was bright, unclouded, and apparently within a mile. It was only when the eye attempted to detect details that we were made entirely sensible of the deception. We ascended diagonally for an hour, and yet the glittering mass underwent no apparent change of form or distance. The whole of our discoveries were limited to ascertaining that a portion of the real surface was visible among the frozen snow, and that what in the distance had seemed all glacier was, in truth, partly rock.

We soon reached a point where nearly every trace of the valley was lost. Nothing remained but a fissure, across which it seemed easy to hurl a stone, so closely did the opposing piles seem to be incorporated. On the other hand, objects at a distance not only came into view, but appeared to be at our feet. Unterséen, Interlachen, and the Aar were among them, while the side of the mountain in their rear formed the background of the picture. I can only compare the sensation of command I felt in that elastic air, and at this elevation, to that which one experiences when he is mounted on a horse whose tread and muscle give assurance of uncommon power. I felt as if riding a mountain.

Snow was lying in spots on the opposite hills considerably below us, and on our side of the valley, at no great distance above us. Of course, the exposure had some influence on this feature of the scene. The immense mass of rock, over whose dark top I had caught a view of the Jung Frau the previous evening, now showed its brown head nearly on our own level, forming, truly, no more than the abutment to the tower above, as I have already described it to be.

We were three hours, after gaining the Alp of the pretty beggars, before we reached the châlet of the Wengern, where travellers usually rest. Here we refreshed ourselves with mountain cheer, of which milk, cheese, and bread are the staples.

From this spot the whole summit of the Jung Frau on one side, and that its best, is visible from the commencement of the snow to its peak. The mountain, which had so long been exciting wonder and expectation from a distance, was now directly before us, and we stood gazing at its magnitude, its shining sides, its mysteries which were no longer concealed, and even its naked rocks, with pure delight. Noble neighbours flanked it, and to the right lay one of those awful glens that are large enough to hold a small canton, in which ice, rocks, ravines, and waterfalls are blended in a confusion that no pen can perfectly describe—a picturesque chaos.

We were separated from what might be called the base of the mountain (you will remember we were nearly, if not quite, seven thousand English feet in the air ourselves) by what appeared to be a hollow of no great width or depth, but which, in fact, would be called a valley in another place. I felt the boyish ambition to cross it, and for the first time to stand on the snow of the Upper Alps. Five minutes of severe exercise convinced me it would cause too much delay, and the attempt was reluctantly abandoned.

A short time before reaching the châlet a sound proceeded from the mountain which was not unlike that produced by the falling of one of our own high trees in the forest, though altogether on a more imposing scale. It came from the glen, already mentioned, which is, in truth, the termination of the valley of

Lauterbrunnen, and was accompanied by a long reverberation. This was an avalanche. While at the châlet, on passing along the faces of the three mountains—the Jung Frau, the Monch, and the Eiger—we heard twenty, several of which we saw. These avalanches, as you will readily imagine, are of as many different forms and characters as can be assumed by falling snow under the vicissitudes of the season, and amid the wild formations of the Alps. Sometimes they are of fresh snow, that has accumulated in huge balls, which come down with their own weight, or are broken off by the oscillations of the air; at other times superior pressure drives them from their seats; the melting of the thaws, and the passage of rills of water produce others. In short, all the causes that can so easily be imagined, combine to force the frozen element from its aeries into the valleys.

Once or twice the sound we heard was like the mutterings of a distant storm, and we tried to fancy it a mountain turning in its lair. A mountain groaning is very expressive.

My eye was fixed on the side of the Jung Frau, when I saw a speck of snow start out of a mass which formed a sort of precipice, leaving a very small hole, not larger in appearance than a beehive. The report came soon after. It was equal to what a horseman's pistol would produce in a good echo. The snow glided downward two or three hundred feet, and lodged. All heard the report, though no one saw this little avalanche but myself. I was in the act of pointing out the spot to my companions, when a quantity of dusty snow shot out of the same little hole, followed by a stream that covered an inclined plane, which seemed to be of the extent of ten or twelve acres. The constant roaring convinced us the affair was not to end here. The stream forced its way through a narrow gorge in the rocks, and reappeared, tumbling perpendicularly two hundred feet more on another inclined plane. Crossing this, it became hid again; but soon issued by another rocky gorge on a third plane, down which it slid to the verge of the green pastures; for, at this season the grass grows beneath the very drippings of the glaciers.

This was a picturesque avalanche to the eye, though the sound came so direct, that it was like the noise produced by snow falling from a house, differing only in degree. The size of the stream was so much reduced in passing the gorges, that it bore a strong resemblance to the Staubbach, and according to the best estimate I could make, its whole descent was not short of a thousand feet. The hole out of which all this mass of snow issued, and which literally covered acres, did not appear to have more capacity than a large oven! We shook our heads, after examining it, and began to form better estimates of heights and distances among the Alps.

On quitting the châlet we inclined to the left; and soon after turning the point of the Wengern, or rather of the Little Scheideck, we began to descend. Here we got a view of the valley of Grindelwald, the object of the day's ride. It lay in a basin of pasture-land, surrounded, of course, by huge mountains, and its broken surface was dotted with cottages and châlets, as indeed was the side of the Great Scheideck opposite to us, up which lay our path for the next day. There was a church, but scarcely a village. We also got a glimpse of one of the glaciers, or a place where the ice descends from the frozen fields above, through gorges in the Alps, to the level of the inhabited vallies.

The descent was rough, rapid, and not entirely without danger, though very far from being as precipitate as that which leads into the valley of Lauterbrunnen. As a matter of course, one can get neither on nor off a mountain, here, without labour and some hazard; especially females. The guides, however, were very attentive to their charges, and W[illiam] and myself blundered down as well as we could. We trusted to our cattle, usually the wisest thing, and reached the valley in safety.

Letter VII.

D<small>EAR</small> ———,

Grindelwald has little in common with Lauterbrunnen, with the exception of the rural looking abodes, and picturesque châlets. It did not strike us at first with the wonder and admiration with which we had gazed at its neighbour; though its beauties grew on the eye, and it at least possessed the merit of having a totally distinct character. Its two glaciers alone would suffice to render it a place of resort, had it not other attractions of a high order.

These glaciers have been compared to seas suddenly congealed. The comparison is fanciful, and it may be sufficiently exact for those who, not being familiar with the ocean, have no very distinct notions about its true appearance; but it must not be understood too literally. The surface of a glacier has none of the rolling regularity of billows, though, in places where swift and conflicting currents meet, one does sometimes see the water tossed into little pyramidal waves which do strongly resemble the frozen surface of the glaciers, though they are never on so grand and imposing a scale. Still the favourite comparison is sufficiently exact to answer all the purposes of poetic description.

Seen from the inn, the glaciers of Grindelwald are apt at first to disappoint the traveller. The magnitude of the mountains diminishes the apparent size of all other objects, and it requires practice with these, as with other things, to form a true estimate of their dimensions. Before I had left the place, the very vastness of these immense fields of ice filled me with wonder. In order that you should have accurate ideas of what they are, it will be necessary to explain.

You are to imagine, in the first place, that all Switzerland, with Savoy, and indeed the Tyrol, and other adjoining countries, lies on a huge mountain. They all have their valleys, it is true, but these valleys are more elevated than even the hills of the lower regions: Thus Berne, which lies in a valley, is at the height of eighteen hundred feet above the sea; Interlachen is higher than Berne; and Grindelwald, as you approach the Upper Alps, more elevated still. Though this formation is continued to the very highest peaks, which are separated from each other by their valleys, yet, towards the apexes of the great mountains, there is less confusion in the arrangement—the last ascents usually towering many thousand feet in distinct but neighbouring piles, that admit of different names and peculiar features. These highest peaks also run in ranges, and, as a consequence of all, there is a vast upper plain, or a succession of connected valleys, out of which the summits shoot in a variety of forms—some conical, others more broken, and all sublime—that extends for a hundred miles. These plains or upper valleys are, of course, covered with eternal snow. I do not say that it is literally possible to find the extent I have mentioned in one continued field of ice, for valleys break the continuity in some portion of the range, and occasionally a barrier of rock interposes; but it is known that these glaciers are of very great extent. They are frequently traversed, from one inhabited valley to another, and histories of the perils of these journeys have been published, which have the interest of dangerous sea voyages. The snow falls in avalanches, from the peaks, and there is a constant accession to the masses, which, if they do not increase, as certainly do not diminish. There are writers who affirm that the glaciers add to their power by their own cold, and that, in time, without the intervention of some new natural phenomenon, they will eventually extend themselves downward into the valleys that lie on the next level beneath, overcoming vegetation and destroying life. A succession of cold summers might certainly extend the boundaries of the glaciers, but it is scarcely possible that the heat of the sun can be finally overcome in this manner. There must be a limit, somewhere, to the increase of the ice, and it is almost certain that these limits have been attained during the centuries that the present physical formation of Switzerland is known to have existed. Local circumstances may have induced local changes, but, as a whole, the contest between heat and cold ought to be set down as producing exactly equal effects.

Here and there the ice has forced itself through gorges in the higher peaks, towards the inhabited valleys. These gorges are the natural outlets through which the water that flows from the heat of the sun (for it is not always freezing, even in the higher valleys) finds a passage. The ice is undermined by the currents beneath, and large blocks slide downward, until they reach the end of the inclined plane in the inferior valley, where their descent is necessarily arrested. In the course of time, the piles increase until that equilibrium state is attained in which there ceases to be any very material augmentation or lessening of the masses. In this manner the glaciers of Grindelwald have had their origin. Their terminations are sudden, presenting walls of ice, twenty or thirty feet high, out of which gush torrents full grown at the birth. The meadows are verdant to the very edge of the ice, and we gathered strawberries within a few yards of it.

The distance from the lower end of the lower glacier, (they are called the upper and lower, from their relative positions in the valley,) to the plain of ice above, may be half a mile, and the width of the gorge through which it finds its way, seems to be less than half that distance.

There formerly stood a small chapel on a point of rock near the margin of the upper valley, and in the gorge itself, where the chamois hunters and those who attempted to pass to the other side of the great range, could offer up prayers for their safety. This chapel disappeared—for a succession of two or three severe winters could do greater marvels than swallow up a small pile of stones—and (a certain evidence of the manner in which these lower spurs of ice are fed) the bell found its way down to the meadows, and is now exhibited in the church of Grindelwald.

It is not an easy matter to walk on the surface of those parts of the glaciers which lie on the inclined planes, or between the gorges and the fields. The fissures between the broken masses are of a depth and width that render it far easier to enter than to get out of them. There is a tradition, however, of a hunter who fell into one, and who effected his escape, with a broken limb I believe, through the vaults which are formed by the passage of the water beneath. The thing seems possible, but the odds must be greatly against its safe achievement.

We found at Grindelwald another fir house, of the drumhead tightness and sound. The fare was reasonably good, and the beds clean. Here we had a specimen of mountain music, a choir of Grindelwald damsels frequenting the inn for the entertainment of travellers. They sung in German—mountain German too—and in good time, if not with good taste. The notes were wild, the throats powerful, the chords not bad, and the words detestable, without alluding to their meaning, however, for of that we knew nothing.

We asked for the *Ranz des Vaches*, as a matter of course, and now learned, for the first time, that there are nearly as many songs and airs which go by that name, as there are valleys in Switzerland. Grindelwald has its own *Ranz des Vaches*, and with that we were favoured. I like it less than some of the others since heard.

We have had a glorious spectacle this evening, in the Eiger, partly covered with mist. Mist—mist—mist;—give me mist, for scenery. Natural objects are as much aided by a little of their obscurity and indistinctness as the moral beauties of man are magnified by abstaining from a too impertinent investigation. I have met with views in which curiosity was so far whetted as to cause me to desire the veil might be altogether removed; but I scarce remember one over which I did not wish it partially drawn again after the eye had been fully satisfied. A strong sunlight is less displeasing in low latitudes and warm climates, where the luxury of the atmosphere accords with its heated glow; but in high latitudes, or in elevated places, it is too apt to give a bald and meagre appearance to the rocks and pastures. For such places, there is nothing like a partial covering of vapour.

The guide met us the following morning with an ominous shake of the head. The established barometer of Grindelwald, or, the Wetterhorn,* had its top concealed in clouds. This was a certain token of rain, an event that seemed likely enough to occur, as the whole firmament had a most sinister and watery look. Notwithstanding the omens, however, we were all in the saddle by six, on our way to the next celebrated valley of the Oberland, or that of Meyringen.

We made a little *détour*, to visit the upper glacier. It is smaller and less broken than the lower, but has the same general fea-

* Weather-peak.

tures. The ascent commenced soon after quitting this spot, and
our progress was cheered by some glimpses of the sun.

In accompanying us along these mountain paths, you are not
to suppose we are toiling through vulgar roads, with bridges,
and ditches, and ruts, and all the other attendants of a highway.
So far from this, we are often moving on the turf; or, if there
is a beaten path, as is most commonly the case, it must be remembered that it winds prettily through pasture land, and
meadows, and not unfrequently among flowers, which are singularly delicate in these high regions. A broom with its handle
stuck in the earth, is a sign that a field must not be crossed; and
a rail with one end laid on the ground, and the other next the
path placed in a crotch, is a hint not to diverge from the proper
route. Even these admonishing marks occur only in particular
places, to protect a meadow, shorn like velvet perhaps; at all
other times the sole motive to keep the track being the certainty
it is the shortest way. Fences there are none, or next to none;
for a few imperfect barriers are occasionally seen in the valleys.

The ascent of the Great Scheideck is not at all difficult,
though long and high. In about an hour after quitting the inn
we reached a spot that commanded a view of the plains of ice
above the upper glacier, and behind the Eiger, the Mettenberg,
and the Wetterhorn, or of those boundless frozen fields so
lately mentioned. It was a glorious glimpse, and it contrasted
strangely with other portions of the picture. By looking down
into the valley, and excluding the sight of the mountain, all was
placid, verdant, and rural. The imagination could scarcely form
images which, of themselves, presented stronger affinity to our
ideas of rustic repose, simplicity, and peace. To be sure, it was
necessary to forget that the Corydons and Floras of the vale
were speculating on the picturesque, and that the whole district
was in the market of admiration; but so very beautiful is the
scene, that it was not difficult to draw the veil before this enemy
of the romantic. By turning the head a little, every thing like
life, or vegetation, or the rural was shut out, and the eye rested
on a waste of snow that transported us at once to the remotest
regions of the globe. The edges of the glacier were exposed.
Those which we saw could not be less than a hundred feet in
thickness. In some places they are said to be of three hundred,

or even of much greater depth. An enormous bird was sailing at a vast height over the chill and silent fields of ice, and we tried to fancy it a *lämmergeyer*.

The pass of the Great Scheideck is not quite as high as that of the Little Scheideck, though by the time we had reached the chalet we were again nearly seven thousand feet in the air. It is broader, and obtains its name by the greater expanse of its bosom. We made a close acquaintance with the Wetterhorn, while ascending, it being our nearest mountain. It did not improve in its barometrical symptoms, and shortly after quitting the chalet its prognostics were realized, by the commencement of rain. Degenerated mist ceases to aid the picturesque. We were driven to our cloaks and umbrellas, and all sense of sublimity was lost in downright discomfort. Our feelings had become so *blasés* that we could not rouse sufficient *touzy-mouzy* to again enjoy a soaking. We reached the inn, whence travellers diverge to the celebrated glacier of Rosenlaui, wet, fagged, and glad to be housed.

Warm fires—it was the 6th of August—refreshments, and dry clothes, put everybody in good humour again. But the relentless rain would not admit of our going to the glacier. After several hours detention we were compelled to make the most of the time in order to reach Meyringen before night-fall.

When we left the inn (another mountain-house that is closed in winter) the rain had ceased, and the delightful mists had come out again, like boys to play, rising along the sides of the mountains, and rolling like billows out of every glen. It appeared, too, as if the recent rain had set all the Swiss *jets d'eau* in motion, for little cascades were shooting out of fifty caverns. Some of these falls were, beyond a question, permanent, as their streams were larger than that of the Staubbach, nor were their descents much less. You will understand how easy it is to have a cascade in Switzerland, when you remember that vast bodies of snow lie eternally on the mountains, at an elevation which does not preclude melting in summer; and that the water is compelled to find its way down rocky precipices, some two or three thousand feet, in the best way it can. A perpendicular fall of a hundred fathoms is, consequently, a very common occurrence. We saw six or seven of this height to-day, besides all the little temporary spouts that owed their ephemeral existence to the last rain.

We got a view of the Rosenlaui, at a distance; and, though but a glimpse, we felt satisfied the guide was right when he pronounced it to be better worth seeing than either of the glaciers of Grindelwald.

On reaching the chalet we had also obtained a sight of the rampart of rocks which bounds the other side of the valley of Meyringen. It is not unlike the Hudson river palisades, though higher, browner, and alive with cascades. Volumes of mist were now rising out of the yawning gulf which we could perceive lay between us and this long line of mountains; but no other sign of a valley was visible until we reached its brow, on the side next to Grindelwald. W[illiam] was a little in advance as we trotted towards the point, on reaching which he tossed his whip and gave a shout. We knew this to be a sign that his young spirits were strongly excited, and, hurrying on, beheld one of the loveliest landscapes in nature.

Unlike Lauterbrunnen and Grindelwald, the valley of Meyringen has a perfectly even surface, resembling a river bottom in America. It is, in truth, a long flat, bounded by nearly perpendicular rocks, and wearing the cultivated appearance of pleasure grounds. The marked difference in character between these three contiguous valleys, forms one of the charms of a visit to the Oberland. The first is a savage glen on a grand scale, relieved by an art admirably adapted to its wildness; the second is pastoral, and of a totally different form; the last rustic, but with an air of association and advancement, though seated in the centre of a nature that is always grand and stern. There was a village here, and a church, whose conical spire resembled a slender extinguisher. The mist was stirring, softening all, and keeping curiosity alive. The guides looked up to us with honest exultation, as they heard our expressions of delight, while we stood, as it were, suspended over this beautiful view, for the whole lay like a map at our feet; and Rudolph Wünster complacently reminded us, he had foretold that the best was yet to come. Best it was not of itself; but aided by the mist, we had seen nothing of mere landscape to compare with it, since the glorious day of the Val Travers. The lake of Brientz bounded the view in the direction of Thun.

We had been riding on the banks of a torrent since quitting the inn; a stream which, I believe, flows from the Rosenlaui, receiving tribute, however, from every foaming water-spout by the way. This stream, a clear, brawling, sparkling brook of the largest class, or what would be called a river were it not for its brief course, tumbles suddenly off the last pitch of the mountain (that on which we stood) into the valley. This fall is deservedly one of the most celebrated of Switzerland. It is called the Reichenbach, or the Rich Fall, a name it well deserves, the volume of its water, and its varied aspects, rendering it one of the *richest* cascades, to use the German term, I remember to have seen. We made our way to its margin, the ladies being compelled to use *chaises à porteur*, on account of the wet grass, however, more than on account of the difficulties of the approach.

Quitting the fall, we mounted, and descended slowly to the level of the plain. Here, W[illiam] and myself committed our companions to the care of the guides, and trotted briskly on towards the village, to prepare fires and order supper. We crossed a spot where a torrent had ravaged the valley, in despite of walls to limit its course, and entered the village.

In half an hour, everybody was comfortably seated around a good fire, looking back with calm satisfaction at the sights, and glories, (not our own, but those of nature,) and fatigues of the day. The men and horses were discharged, and we retired.

Our next movement, at six in the morning, was on wheels, which took us down the valley to Brientz, a village on the shores of the lake. The Aar, which rises among the glaciers, flows past Meyringen, through the lakes of Brientz and Thun, washing the walls of Berne. Although distant more than forty miles from la Lorraine, the sight of this stream rendered some of the party impatient to return to those we had left behind; and we took oars, without delay, for Interlachen, breakfasting in the boat.

We cast longing eyes at the Giesbach, a cascade of singular beauty which falls into the lake, but could not spare the time necessary to visit it. The passage down the blue and glancing Aar to Interlachen was pretty, and helped to hurry us along. Here we took a carriage and drove to Neuhaus without stopping. While in front of the gorge that leads to Lauterbrunnen, we cast curious looks up at the Jung Frau, a magnificent object from the valley. We saw the spot on the Wengern Alp, or Little Scheideck, near the chalet; but it appeared low and humble amid the icy piles that overshadowed it.

The romantic situation of the village, and a desire for a little tea, a beverage that does not comport with boating, induced us to stop at Unterséen. Nothing can be more romantic than this town, both by situation and in its construction. Here we had more singing girls, who gave us better chords than the choir of Grindelwald, and another *Ranz des Vaches*.

The wind was fair, and, in despite of awkward handling and an awkward sail, we made a short run across the Lake of Thun,* whose *château*, churches, and towers, appeared singularly picturesque as we again entered the Aar. Our own carriage was in waiting, and at six in the evening we alighted at the door of la Lorraine.

This little tour, of rather more than a hundred miles, has been through the very heart of Swiss scenery. The traveller who has not seen it has missed some of the most striking objects of this magnificent country, though he has not yet beheld a moiety of that which is wonderful and worthy to be visited.

The Oberland, though belonging to Berne, has political franchises which place it in a better situation than the other dependencies of the great canton. It contains about 17,000 inhabitants, who in general have a healthy and athletic appearance. The women, in particular, are fair and comely, and appear robust, without coarseness. Their voices, like those of all who dwell in cold countries, are soft and musical; and it is said the men make good and faithful followers, and that they never entirely lose the frankness of mountaineers. As a race they differ essentially from all around them, and their origin is ascribed, oddly enough for their situation, to a colony of Swedes! Most of the male attendants of the taverns, however, were not the product of the region, but mere *speculators*, tempted by money to pass the summer in the mountains. These little pecuniary circumstances are sad drawbacks on the picturesque; for in such a country one could wish to meet with nothing that is not indigenous, wine excepted.

* Or Thoun.

Letter VIII.

M<small>Y DEAR</small>————,

I gazed back at the Alps, the day succeeding our return, with renewed interest. Places that I now knew to be naked rock seemed white with snow, and, as they covered vast surfaces, a better idea of distances and magnitude was obtained, by observing how completely they were swallowed up in the glittering masses. The peak of the Wengern—not the spot at which we crossed, but a summit a few hundred feet higher—thrust its brown head up from the confused multitude of mountains that were grouped around the footstool of the Jung Frau, and enabled me still better to appreciate the enormous size of the virgin pile. There are peaks which are higher than the Jung Frau; but no mountain near it has the same breadth and sublimity. Indeed, the variety of forms help to make up that sum of glory which is spread before the spectator who sees the range from a distance.

We have been occupied in examining Berne and its environs for the last few days. Among other things, the places of interments have attracted our attention. The principal enclosure is subdivided into spaces for graves, which are marked off by little black posts at the head and foot. Those which have been used have a larger post in the centre, with a brass plate let into a circular tablet near the top, on which is the inscription. Occasionally the latter is written on paper, enclosed in glass; and sometimes it appears in white paint on the wood. But the brass plates predominate. In one or two instances we saw printed verses within the glass. A very few monuments were of stone. Most of these, however, had the inscriptions engraved on the brass plates, which were let into the stone. Many of the tablets were protected by a little roof *à la Suisse*, a precaution, absurd and minute as it appeared, that was very necessary for the paper memorials, some of which were already illegible. The centre poles are about five feet high, and are painted white and black, after the manner of a barber's pole! We saw a few faded wreaths, and here and there a grave was ornamented with living roses. Some were complete beds of what is vulgarly called "everlasting," or what the French more prettily term "*immortelle*." The effect of the whole was odd, and when the evening sun fell athwart the plates, the glittering of the brass caused the array to look like so many armed spectres keeping ward over the silent company beneath. This churchyard arrangement exists within two leagues of the monument of Madame Langhans!

Curiosity, in an idle moment, drew us into the high quarries, where all the building stone is procured for the town. The view was westward, embracing the opening of Val Travers, the course of the Aar, and much of the fine country in the great valley of that river. During the drive back, I counted the proportion of light haired people again, including all whom we met or passed. The whole number was one hundred and ten. Of these ninety-seven had hair of the different shades that make auburn, from the very light brown to the very fair. None had red hair, and scarcely any black. In France, I still think the proportion would have been the other way.

In another of our excursions, we rode through a valley that might have passed for one in Otsego, were it not for the cottages, and something like a *château*, on the spur of a mountain. The elevation was not materially greater than that of our own valleys, which reach, as you know, to twelve or thirteen hundred feet. Our base is well enough; but we are sadly deficient in superstructure. There was, notwithstanding, the same general character, even to the stumps. I counted twenty-three labourers in a single hay-field, on that occasion, of whom sixteen were women. This did not savour of Otsego. Notwithstanding their exposure, these women are far better looking than those who do field labour in the lower countries.

We have also seen the Alps by moonlight, for the first time. Their hue changed from the spectral look of twilight, already described, to a faint rose colour. These transitions add greatly to the pleasure of a residence in their neighbourhood.

What shall I say of those unseemly appendages, the *goîtres*? They are seen by thousands; nay, few people here are absolutely free from swellings in the glands of the throat, and it is quite usual to see them of hideous size. Of course, you know they are attributed to the water and the climate. The water of la Lorraine deposits a fine granular substance that looks like loaf sugar partially dissolved, or like the finest particles of salt. As yet we are all hangable, which is really more than can be said of all the Swiss, unless they are to be suspended by the heels. They tell a pleasant story of a stranger entering a church in the Valais, the very focus of *goîtreism*, during service. The congregation betrayed improper curiosity; and the pastor, after a sharp reproach for their want of civilization, reminded them it was not the fault of the poor man, "if he had no *goître!*" They treat the disease lightly here, and say it is not difficult to arrest in the commencement. Were it not for the idea, I am far from certain that *tant soit peu de goître* would not embellish some female throats in our own country.

I must again tell you that drunkenness is by no means an exclusively American vice, as some pretend. Believe me, dear ———, men, women, and children drink too much in various other countries. Here I have seen a good deal of it, even among the females. I met one of the latter staggering drunk in the road, as lately as yesterday. On the whole, I repeat for the eleventh time, that I have come to the conclusion there is less of this degrading practice at home, among the native population, than in any other country I have yet visited. Certainly much less than there is in either England or France.

We have just had a visit from two old acquaintances—Manhattanese. They tell me a good many of our people are wandering among the mountains, though they are the first we have seen. There is a list of arrivals published daily in Berne; and in one of them I found the name of Captain C———, of the Navy; and that of Mr. O., an old and intimate friend, whom it was vexatious to miss in a strange land. Mr. and Mrs. G———, of New York, are also somewhere in the cantons. Our numbers increase, and with them our abuse; for it is not an uncommon thing to see, written in English in the travellers' books kept by law at all the inns, pasquinades on America, opposite the American names. What a state of feeling it betrays, when a traveller cannot write his name, in compliance with a law of the country in which he happens to be, without calling down upon himself anathemas of this kind! I have a register of twenty-three of these gratuitous injuries. What renders them less excusable, is the fact that they who are guilty of the impropriety would probably think twice before they performed the act in the presence of the party wronged. These intended insults are, consequently, so many registers of their own meanness. Let the truth be said; I have never seen one, unless in the case of an American, or one that was not written in English! Straws show which way the wind blows.

This disposition, in our kinsmen, to deride and abuse America, is observed and freely commented on by the people of the continent, who are far from holding us themselves in the highest respect. Meinherr W[alther], the respectable tenant of the farm attached to the house we occupy, laughingly related a little occurrence the other day, which is of a piece with all the rest, though certainly better bred. "It would seem," he said, "*que messieurs les Anglais n'aiment pas trop les Américains.*" I demanded his reasons for thinking so? He then told me an English gentleman had come to the farm, a day or two before, and inquired if he had found la Lorraine? On being answered in the affirmative, he announced himself as a friend of the family which had occupied the house the preceding summer, and expressed a strong desire to see it. He was told it was inhabited, but no doubt it would be shown to him with pleasure. "Oh no doubt," answered the other; "I presume they are English, and I shall have no difficulty in making myself understood." "None in the world; for, although not English, the whole family speak the English language: they are Americans." "Americans!"—and after a moment's hesitation the Englishman beat a retreat. "These Englishmen dislike each other so much as to look the other way when they meet," said my observant and honest *bourgeois:* "this gentleman, however, *was* willing to encounter a countryman to see the house; but he could not encounter an American."

We were laughing at this little affair, when a neighbour of Meinherr W[alther] joined us. Continuing the subject, he observed that he had understood there was a strong antipathy to the Germans in America; an antipathy which grew out of the employment of the Hessian and Brunswick troops during the war of the revolution. The idea was entirely new to me, and I would not admit the fact. Our neighbour assured us he had heard many Germans affirm it was so. I told him that "conscience was father to the thought;" that there were few in America who did not know how to distinguish between the governments of Europe and their victims; and that we were so accustomed to see foreigners there was not sufficient jealousy of them for our own good. It was easy to perceive that my statement did not produce conviction.

In reflecting on this matter, I find some causes for the existence of the notion. The expressions "You Hessian!" and "The Hessian!" as terms of reproach, have come down to us from those who probably did detest the Hessians heartily; and, although rarely heard now, they were quite familiar in my boyhood. Then the American of the common class has a most patriotic contempt for all foreigners, believing himself (and generally he has right on his side, so far as his own *caste* is concerned) much superior in intellect and moral qualities to the European emigrant. When such a state of feeling exists, it is not likely the party most interested will long remain in ignorance of it. By some such means has the German arrived at the conclusion that he is disliked in America, and ignorant of any other reason, he has jumped back to the war of the revolution in search of one. He is not altogether wrong, perhaps, though far from being strictly right.

I have tried the baths which are on the banks of the river above the town. They are entirely constructed of wood, and, though not rich, are clean and sufficiently convenient. I paid twenty cents for a warm bath, covered with linen, with soap, hot towels in profusion, and a hot linen dressing gown, in short, quite *à la française*. This is the cheapest bathing I have yet seen. By-the-way, is there such a thing as a good bath to be had, out of private houses, in all America? It has never been my good fortune to meet with one.

While looking at the bears of Berne, to-day, I met Mr. [John], and Lady [Charlotte Denison]. They were sight-hunting, like all their countrymen and countrywomen in summer, he being on his second, and she on her first visit to Switzerland. He has been in America; and we chatted a little about our want of mountains, a failing that the truest Yankee must admit. "I wonder," said our namesake and kinsman, Captain [Cooper], of the

Navy, to me one day, "if there is any such thing as grand scenery in the United States?" The idea had occurred to him suddenly, after his mind's eye had run over the coasts of the Mediterranean, the Indies, and Brazil; and he seemed forcibly struck with our deficiency in this particular. He was right: we have beautiful scenery in abundance, but scarcely any that is grand. The Hudson itself, unrivalled as it is by any European river, possesses in an eminent degree all the characteristics of beauty, with scarcely one that belongs to the magnificent.

We have determined on another excursion, and my next letter shall furnish you with the details.

Letter IX.

M Y DEAR————,

We left la Lorraine on Monday, the 25th of August, at eight o'clock in the morning, in our own carriage. The route chosen was that to Soleure, which led us diagonally across the great plain of the Aar to the foot of the Jura. The country and the roads grew less *exclusive* as we receded from the focus of Swiss aristocracy, and, by consequence, rather more common-place.

Near a hamlet called Fraubrunnen, we passed a granite monument erected to commemorate the defeat of a body of English free-lancers, in 1376. Society is materially changed since the English went to Switzerland as mercenaries!

At the distance of about a mile from Soleure, a lad of fifteen made an attempt to stop the carriage, by drawing a rope across the road. After a short parley with the coachman, we were permitted to pass. We had been mistaken for the first of a wedding party, (there being three or four vehicles in sight in the rear,) and we were told that it was a custom for the boys to extort tribute from the *nouveaux mariés* in this manner. A little farther in advance we passed the main body of the young pirates, who, by way of atonement, gave us a salvo of artillery, from a gun of the size of a horseman's pistol.

We entered Soleure by a bridge across the Aar, and through gates and walls of hewn stone. The town has about 4000 inhabitants; and, as it is eminently of the Romish persuasion, it has a goodly number of churches and convents. One of the former has some pretensions. It is said to be among the best specimens of Swiss architecture; but Swiss architecture, like American, is never particularly imposing, and rarely even beautiful, except in its cottages. The towers, turrets, and walls, however, give the place a picturesque air, that is not out of keeping with the interior, which is rather massive and sombre. They boast of the prison, as keeping the condemned without recourse to chains or drags, while they admit it is not well aired. We have long

done all this in America, and aired the prisons in the bargain. I
have somewhere heard that there is a dispute on the score of
antiquity, between Soleure and Treves, each claiming to be the
oldest town in Europe. There are some towers here which are
said to be, and which probably are, Roman; for the Romans
occupied the whole of this valley, from the lake of Geneva to
the Rhine, as their principal highway into Germany, and vestiges of their dominion are by no means uncommon. But Rome
itself will not establish the claim of remote antiquity, Treves
bearing the pretending inscription of, "Before Rome existed,
Treves was." Whichever may be the oldest, Treves was, and is
likely to continue to be, by far the most important place. Soleure, however, is not to be despised, as it was once the capital
of the kings of Burgundy, of the second race.

Apart from the Roman towers, I saw no great evidences of
remote antiquity in Soleure. It had many vestiges of the middle
ages, and there was still an air of monastic seclusion in the
streets, which was not unsuited to that gloomy period. The
lower windows are secured by iron grates; but this is a custom
which prevails, more or less, in all the countries of Europe,
south of the Rhine.

We left Soleure after our *goûter*. The road now ran parallel to
the Jura, and at no great distance from their feet. It was quite
level, for we did not quit the plain; but we had fine views of the
elevated land on our left. There were several well placed little
châteaux on the lower spurs of the mountains, and, here and
there, was a ruin. You will understand that we entered the canton of Soleure a short time before reaching its capital. This canton is rigidly Catholic, and our Protestant eyes began to imagine
there was a change for the worse in neatness and comfort. Soleure being almost as aristocratic as Berne, as good luck would
have it, the fact could not be attributed to democracy. Formerly
it was the *ne plus ultra* of Swiss exclusiveness, but the institutions
have been a good deal modified since the French revolution.

A falling tower or two, with a few flanking walls in the same
condition, a little on our left, and as usual at the foot of the
mountains, were pointed out to us as the ruins of a hunting seat
of King Pepin! Crosses occurred very frequently. We were
commenting on this fact—for they had been lost since we quitted France, where they are fast coming in fashion again under

the pious Charles—when they suddenly disappeared. Presently we met our old acquaintance, the bear of Bernė, stuck upon a post. On inquiry, we found that we were crossing a narrow projection of the great canton, which, like Prussia, is a little apt to thrust its territory in among its neighbours. We soon re-entered Soleure, and met the crosses again, at every turn.

The country people and the houses had scarcely what could be called a Swiss character. They resembled those of Franche Comté more than those of the other parts of Switzerland we had seen. The agriculture, apparently, was not bad; and we now began to see a system of irrigation which is far more perfect than any I have ever yet met with. It is both simple and scientific, and must be eminently beneficial.

The women we passed this afternoon wore a new costume, in which red petticoats, black bodies, and white caps prevailed. But there are as many costumes in even this little canton as there are in Berne. None of them are pretty, except on paper; and yet even the ugliest of them all, worn by the ugliest woman, helps to make up the sum of national peculiarities; and helps the picturesque, also, unless you happen to be very true sighted, or too near.

We looked into two little chapels, which are or were attached to convents, by the way side, and which are left open for the benefit of the piously disposed. We lived adjoining a convent at Paris; but, notwithstanding the tendencies of the court, and the disposition of Charles X., French religion does not appear to be of the true water, whether inclining to superstition or not. It is worn too much like the clothes, or as a matter of fashion and expediency. Even fanaticism itself commands our respect, when it is hearty. At Paris, I never could perceive any portion of the picturesque which belongs to the Romish rites, nor defer for a moment to their superstitions, which always had more or less of the taint of a popular philosophy. The only thing of the sort that awakened the feelings of reverence and respect, were the calm reproofs of some six or eight grave female faces, among an acquaintance of some six or seven hundred; and the earnest, meek, unwearied self-devotion of the admirable *Sœurs de Charité*. Here, however, we began to find some of the poetry of this peculiar sect, and those outward signs of devotion, which if they are not make-weights in achieving the great end of existence, serve singularly to adorn a landscape. Hitherto, as memory has carried me back some five-and-twenty years to Spain, I have been disappointed in this particular; but I now began to entertain strong hopes for Italy.

We had a delightful afternoon. The evening was serene; and the glades among the Jura were soft and inviting. Through one wide opening, we were told, led the road to Basle. Although we travelled with the map before us, uncertain whither to go, we turned away from a town which lay too much in the great world for our present humour, and just as night set in, we entered the dilapidated gates of a small, crowded, and French-looking place called Olten. This town is also said to have the remains of walls built by the Romans. Our day's work was about thirty miles, the whole route being through a perfectly level country.

At six in the morning, we were again on the highway. The Aar was once more crossed by a covered wooden bridge, quite *à l'Américain*, though I suspect our own are, in truth, merely *à la Suisse*, and inclined more to the eastward. Through an opening in the hills, we got a glimpse of Aarberg, a town of Berne, which was once a Roman station, and is now the only fortified place in Switzerland, unless Geneva can be called one. The effect of this perspective glimpse of towers and ramparts was pretty; but less pretty than that we obtained, almost at the same moment, of a little white *château*, on a spur of the Jura, around and above which my beloved mists were beginning to creep, under the influence of the sun.

The houses are chiefly of stone, rough cast, and still French rather than Swiss; nor are they particularly neat. Crosses and little chapels by the way side constantly occur. We entered one of the latter, which was about sixteen feet long by ten in width, and which contained a goodly company of thirteen images of saints and virgins, besides sundry pictures. Votive offerings, in the shape of arms, hands, noses, and other portions of the human frame, abounded; and, as the whole were manufactured with more zeal than skill, the chapel looked like a coarse and well filled toy-shop, in which the dolls were full grown. I cannot say that all this aided the picturesque, the want of taste more than counterbalancing the magnitude and simplicity of the faith.

At the distance of about a mile from Aarau, we passed a post with the arms of Argovie, a sign that we had entered the next canton. In all other respects, the transition was as quiet as it would have been from one of our own states to another. It is true, we had passports in our pockets; but, the authorities of Berne excepted, no one in Switzerland had asked to see them.

The town of Aarau looked well in the distance, and the suburbs were rather better built than common. Water, in a swift current, runs through the centre of the streets, as at Berne. One provident burgher had turned it to account, by erecting a wheel of six or eight feet in diameter. The power thus obtained was applied to various domestic purposes. Just at the moment we passed, it was turning a coffee-roaster!

We breakfasted at Aarau and proceeded, the town offering nothing peculiar to attract us. There were several *châteaux*, some in ruins, and others still inhabited, in plain view as we pursued our course. All were prettily placed, and they added greatly to the interest of the day. They were rudely constructed, but were strong in material, and stronger still by position. That of Wildeck was the most conspicuous.

We drove into the court of a large modern building, that stood near the highway, shortly after passing the latter *château*, and alighted. We were now at the baths of Schinznach, perhaps the most fashionable place of resort of the kind in Switzerland. They stand near the Aar, at the foot of a low mountain called the Wülpelsberg. As our object was this mountain, after ordering a *goûter*, to keep both the landlord and ourselves in good humour, we hastened to ascend it.

A pretty, dark wood of larches and birches covers the hill side. The ascent is by an easy, winding path, which runs, nearly the whole distance, beneath the shade of the trees. A carriage might be driven to the summit, which lies about three hundred feet above the river, on the northern side; but it is a precipitous terrace on the three others. The shape of the little platform on top is that of an irregular quadrangle, of about one hundred feet by two hundred; the greatest extent being from north to south. At the southern extremity, rises a plain, massive, stone tower, and attached to it is a plainer wing; in which, in fact, the tower is partially buried. The whole is dilapidated, but less so than one might expect. This ruin is about eighty or ninety feet in one direction, and from seventy to eighty in the other. The workmanship is not at all superior to what is seen in our own country breweries, and other similar rustic edifices, but more massive. The interior was quite rude, though one apartment, probably the ancient Ritter Saal, or Knights' Hall, still retained its carved ceiling, the wood of which was black as ink with smoke and time. Two petards are mounted at the windows of an upper chamber, probably relicks of a past age. The family which tenanted the room or two that are still habitable could tell us nothing of their history, nor could the guide.

Such is the castle of Habsbourg, in the nineteenth century, the cradle of the House of Austria, and the architectural predecessor of Schœnbrunnen! The village lies on the declivity, a little to the north-east, near enough for the serfs to be summoned by a conch or a cow bell. I counted eighteen thatched roofs in the hamlet. There is no church.

The ruins of divers holds belonging to this family are seen in Switzerland, castles that it built or acquired with its growing power; but this is understood to be *the* Habsbourg, whence the name and race are derived. The castle was built, according to Ebel, in 1020; but the family did not become princely until the succeeding century; if, indeed, until a still later period. Compared with others of their own time and country, the possessors of this hold, in the eleventh century, were doubtless important and civilized personages; compared with those who now live, they would fall far behind ordinary country gentlemen; the relative position with their contemporaries excepted. This relative position, however, makes the scale of worldly grandeur.

You know, of course, that the male line of the family of Habsbourg ceased with Charles VI.; and that by the marriage of his daughter, Maria Theresa, with Francis of Lorraine, the present emperor is, in truth, directly derived from another stock. Still there is probably not a Catholic prince in Europe who is not descended from the ancient owners of, and the dwellers in, this little ruin; and not many, if any, Protestant; for, as Dogberry says, "'fore God, they are both of a tale."

What a chain of events is connected by the historical links between the castle of Habsbourg and the present condition of the Austrian empire!—between the times when the local baron rode forth to a foray, in unscoured armour, and with the other shabby appliances of rustic chivalry about him, and those in which his descendants occupy all the thrones of Europe! The well meaning, but impolitic, Joseph II. is said to have remarked, after steadily looking at this ruin, "truly, we have not always been great lords." If sovereigns would as steadily look forward with the same reflection, the world would be greatly the gainers. The present princes of Austria are, in general, simple, kind hearted, and upright men, and have probably as little reason to deprecate either view as any of their rank; but they labour, among us freemen, under an opprobrium which more properly belongs to the false policy that has endeavoured to raise up, in the centre of Europe, an empire of discordant materials to counteract the power of Russia and France. Happier would it be for all concerned, did the perversity and prejudices of men admit of a reorganization of territory, and to none more fortunate than to those who are now required equally to rule over the Slav and the Italian, the Roman and the Hun.

The view from the little natural platform, on which the ruin of Habsbourg stands, is extensive. To the north it reaches far beyond the Rhine, into what is called the Black Forest, which, like the New Forest of England, is no longer a forest at all. There are some remains of the former, however; though the name applies to that which was, rather than to that which is. Nearer to the eye is the site of a Roman station that was of more importance than any in Switzerland, where the Aar, and the Limmat, and the Reuss meet, before pouring their united tribute into the Rhine; and three other ruined castles were in view.

Shortly after quitting Schinznach, we passed a small compactly built town on the Aar, called Brugg, where Zimmerman was born. A little farther was the Roman station named, of which few or no remains are visible. There are, however, the ruins of an abbey of some note, and sundry legends of the middle ages. The place is now called Kœnigsfeld, or Kingsfield, a name derived from the circumstance that one of the emperors was murdered here. We crossed the Reuss, and, inclining eastward, left the plain of the Aar, and entered the valley of the Limmat, which, just at this point, is dwindled into a narrow defile. After penetrating a short distance, we reached Baden; not *the* Baden of which you have heard, but a little town of the same name. The word means baths. Thus the Grand-duke of Baden is the Grand-duke of Baths, and *his* town, Baden-Baden, as it is called to distinguish it from *this* Baden, is the "Baths of Baths."

Baden was also a Roman station, and has some Roman remains. It is still walled; and the ruins of a castle, which are nearly as large as the place itself, cover a rocky eminence that overlooks it in a way to excite admiration. It has its local legends as well as all of them, and we mounted the height to examine it, thinking ourselves well rewarded for the trouble. It had been a citadel, however, rather than a baronial hold. The Congress which made the peace of 1714, or that which succeeded the long war of the Spanish succession, was held at Baden. It met in the town hall, a room of some size; and we were shown the window at which Prince Eugene proclaimed the result of its labours. The steeple of the church was a queer looking object, covered with tiles of five different colours. This peculiarity reminded us of our own rainbow capitol, where the red of the bricks, the green of the blinds, the black of the iron, and the white of the marble, assembled within twenty-five feet by forty, leave nothing more to be desired.*

The baths of this town were used by the Romans, and are still frequented by the people of the country. The place itself contains less than two hundred buildings, squeezed into a narrow defile, that is still more straitened by the Limmat, which glances under the windows of the houses.

We now took a northern direction again, crossing the low mountains which lie between the Limmat and the Rhine. The country no longer seemed Swiss, even the peasantry having a more German and less distinctive air. Hats with a single cock, breeches open at the knees and shining like dark leather, and buttons as large as dollars began to make their appearance.

---

* The rears of the nine houses which form the terrace of La Fayette Place, New York, and which have marble fronts, are actually painted seven different colours! The writer has enumerated forty-seven different hues on the buildings of this town; hues that are not incorporated with the material, and which are not the fruits of time, but which are chiefly artificial, the offspring of invention, and proofs of an advanced stage of society. Phidias was a mere pretender, or he would have discovered the use of mosaics, in embellishing his statues.

Evening was drawing near, as, descending the hills, we caught a glimpse of a short reach in the Rhine. The first sensation was that of disappointment, for the stream did not seem to be larger than the Limmat. We soon came to the last inclined plane that descends to the margin of the water, where we entered, by a massive gate, a gloomy village, of a single precipitous street, and made our way down the dusky avenue, to a covered bridge. The hotel was on the other side of the river, but we were refused admittance. Recrossing, and toiling up the ascent, we were again denied. Nothing remained but to try the inn at the bridge once more, or to proceed. This time we were more successful, though compelled to submit to be ill lodged.

Secure of a covering for our heads, I found leisure to examine the localities. The inn stood literally in the stream, or so near it, that the water flowed directly beneath our windows, and we heard its murmurs while seated at table. The river here is not wide; I should say about six hundred feet; but it flows with a volume and a majesty of current that render it imposing. The water is blue, but not turbid, being nearer to the tint of the ocean, than to that of the torrents near the glaciers.

A huge tower, a hundred feet high, stands close by the inn. This spot was once occupied by a castle, and I presume there has been a bridge or a ferry here from time immemorial. The command of such a pass, made a man a baron in the middle ages, for by the aid of tolls and robberies, he was pretty certain to become rich.

I ought to say that we were now in Germany, and in the territories of the Grand-duke of Baden, this portion of the empire being formerly known as Suabia. The town on the Swiss side of the river is called Kaiserstuhl, or Emperor's seat; the good Franz being called a *Kaiser*, a corruption of Cæsar, in the vernacular of his lieges. *Stuhl* speaks for itself; being pronounced like our own stool. They who speak English, by a little attention to sounds, can soon acquire a very respectable travelling German.

Letter X.

D<small>E A R</small> ———,

There is one little canton of the Swiss Confederation that lies altogether on the north of the Rhine. Thither we next proceeded, quitting our hotel of the bridge with the appearance of the sun. The road took us through a level and uninteresting country, in which the signs of Swiss neatness, in a great measure, disappeared. We passed through a point of the canton of Zurich, which also crosses the river, and came to a spot where three posts marked the contiguity of Baden, Zurich, and Schaffhausen, the last being the canton just mentioned. We first entered it at this spot.

Quitting the carriage we went through a wood, and by a winding path, down a declivity, until we reached a point that commanded a view of the river and of the much-talked-of cataract. On its left bank, high, and overhanging the stream, stood a rustic *château*. On its right were mills and forges. A few well placed rocks, holding a tree or two, broke the current near the middle, the whole volume rushing down a steep rapid, rather than tumbling, for a distance of one or two hundred yards, within which space, the entire descent is about seventy feet. It is a broken, irregular, and foaming fall, that has more need of rocks and height, than of water, to make it grand. When the Mohawk is full, I think the Cohoos the most imposing of the two, though, at other times, the advantage is altogether with the falls of the Rhine. It is a defect with most great cataracts, that the accessaries are seldom on a scale commensurate with the principal feature. In the case of a deep and swift river, of a mile in width, tumbling perpendicularly one hundred and fifty feet, like the Niagara, the minor faults may be overlooked, in the single stupendous phenomenon; but in smaller falls, the defect is sooner observed. For this reason, I think, we experience more pleasure in visiting mountain cascades, than in viewing a cataract like this of the Rhine.

A single tower stands on a sandy point below .the fall, and is so situated, owing to a bend in the river, as to be nearly in its front. Here a room is fitted up as a camera-obscura, and a beautiful picture is produced, which has the unusual merit of motion. The sound also being on the ear, the illusion is perfect. After all, the real cataract is better than its image. I think we left the falls of the Rhine a little disappointed, although I was the only one of the party who had seen Niagara, and [Mrs. Cooper], the only one, besides myself, who had ever seen the Cohoos. But we had just been among mountain torrents, and glaciers, and the edge had been taken off our sensations. I remember to have been more struck by the Cohoos, the first time it was seen, than by Niagara itself. I attribute this unusual effect to the circumstance, that the first was visited when a boy at college, and the second, after having passed years at sea, and having become accustomed to the sight of water in its turbulence. Niagara, however, like every thing truly sublime, grows upon the senses, and, in the end, certainly stands without a rival. Its grandeur overshadows accessaries. Lights and shadows embellish ordinary landscapes, but of what consequence is it to the awful sublimity of an eclipse, that there is a cloud or two, more or less, within the visible horizon?

We walked to the town of Schaffhausen, where we got a late breakfast. Schaffhausen (or Boat-houses) stands at what we call a "portage." It was once strongly fortified, for obvious purposes, but a community, instead of a baron, has been the consequence. The little territory has swelled out to the extent of some fifteen miles by eight, with a population of rather more than 20,000 souls. Picot says that, previously to 1798, its government was "*aristo-démocratique*," a polity with which I am unacquainted; but which, I presume, means that the aristocrats ruled, while the democrats *thought they* ruled; a state of things, perhaps, more usual than desirable. The whole science of government, in what are called free states, is getting to be reduced to a strife in mistification, in which the great secret is to persuade the governed that he is in fact the governor; a political hallucination which has the same effect on tax-paying that absolution has on sin.

The town is quaint, crowded, and small. Here we first saw houses painted with designs on the exterior. The ancient walls and towers, from which the place has sadly fallen away, give it, notwithstanding, a very picturesque appearance.

We recrossed the Rhine, by a bridge in the town itself, and entered the canton of Zurich. The road followed the river, keeping the stream in view most of the way, though occasionally it plunged into a wood. After a few miles, however, we came out upon the banks of the stream, which remained in sight all the rest of the day.

This was a delightful afternoon. Convents appeared on the margin of the Rhine, surrounded by vineyards and fine farms, and here and there a ruined castle tottered on the tall cliffs of the opposite shore. We got a view of a fortress on a high rock, called Hohentwiel, in Wurtemburg, for portions of this little kingdom were in sight. It is said to be 2000 feet above the Rhine! One of the convents had a large stone barn, built in the form of a cross. We were now in the canton of Thurgovie. At an inn, opposite to the little town of Stein, the coachman demanded time to feed, leaving us the option of remaining at a tavern, of crossing the bridge to Stein, or of walking ahead. We chose the latter.

Our walk led us six or eight miles along the shore of the lower lake of Constance, which we reached soon after quitting the inn. It was a fine evening, and we all enjoyed it greatly.

I ought to have sooner said, that we encountered to-day a new species of beggars. They were sturdy, well-dressed young men, who trotted alongside of the carriage with a stubbornness that did as much credit to their legs as to their perseverance. Astonished to find mendicity in such good coats, we refused to give, but without effect, until W[illiam], provoked at seeing a silk handkerchief in one of the extended hats, imitated their action, and began to beg in his turn. This drove off a party of three, who probably set us down as being quite as queer and inexplicable as we thought them. W[illiam] was indignant, and bitterly nicknamed them *amateurs voyageurs;* for they all appeared to be travellers like ourselves, the circumstance of their going on foot being nothing uncommon in Switzerland. Had we understood the usages of the country, we should have felt less surprise.

There is a custom among the young mechanics of Germany, after having served a certain apprenticeship in their own towns, to travel from place to place, and even from country to country, in order to get new notions of their crafts, and to see the world. While on these professional pilgrimages, they are permitted to beg, by general sufferance. Thus W[illiam] was not so far out of the way, in styling them *voyageurs amateurs*.

As the day declined, we came to the village of Steckborn, where we were overtaken by the carriage. The road now descended quite to the level of the water, and we had a delightful drive, under some cultivated heights, crowned with *châteaux;* the lake, its opposite shore, and its islands spreading themselves on the other hand. This fine sheet of water, which is called the Lower Lake, or the Zellersee, from the town of Zell, on its banks, is connected with the upper lake by the Rhine, which flows through them both. The island, which is called Reichenau, is three miles long, and more than one wide; has three villages, and supports sixteen hundred inhabitants. It is covered with vineyards of good repute, and there is a fine looking ruin of a castle at the eastern extremity. We were still gazing at this pleasing object, when the day closed, and for an hour longer we journeyed in the dark. At length we were suddenly stopped by a gate. On looking out, I found that we were passing beneath a solitary tower, that stood in a meadow. This was a frontier, and we were re-entering Germany through a gate! We now began to understand precisely where we were. This gate was within a hundred yards of the spot where John Huss was burned. In a few minutes we passed another gate, in a wall, and entered the city of Constance. Twenty or thirty drummers were beating the tatoo in a wide street, and profiting by the hint, we sought *l'aigle d'or*, and hastened to our beds, after a fatiguing day's work.

The long journey of the preceding day did not prevent us from rising early, and going out to look at the town. Alas! how changed. Constance has long ceased to be the Constance of gothic times. Its population has dwindled to less than 5000, and there are few remains of the magnificence by which it was adorned, during its celebrated council, which, you may remember, lasted from 1414 to 1418; emperors, popes, and potentates of all degrees, being among its members.

The town stands at the foot of the lake, where the Rhine darts out towards the Zellersee. The site is low, and perfectly level, but the position is not without beauties. The view of the lake is perfectly unobstructed, and there is something novel and exciting in finding such a body of water in the interior of Europe, with coasts that belong to different kingdoms. We shrug our shoulders at Shakspeare's ignorance, in representing a shipwreck as occurring on the coast of Bohemia; but I shall take care hereafter, to inquire if the thing may not be possible, for vessels may certainly be wrecked on the coasts of Baden, Wurtemburg, Bavaria, Switzerland, and Austria out of the Mediterranean; all these states touching the lake of Constance. The Bodensee is about forty-five miles in length, and twelve wide: or large enough to drown all the sailors Shakspeare ever imagined.

The walls of the town are insignificant in the way of defence, and the ditch is nearly filled. The houses, as usual, are of stone, rough cast, nor did I see any that denoted former opulence. There is a garrison of a thousand men, Badenois; the place though south of the Rhine, being in Germany, and subject to the Grand-duke of Baden. The principal street, though short, is very wide.

But our object was the great council. It was held in a building near the water, the lower part of which is now used as a warehouse. The hall above is about two hundred feet long by rather more than one hundred wide. Its roof is upheld by very plain wooden columns. But it was hung with tapestry for the occasion, and a ceiling of carved wood is said to have been introduced. As now seen, the room resembles a vast loft in a warehouse. At one corner is partitioned off a common sized apartment, in which we were shown the chairs used by the emperor and the pope. It is pretended these chairs stand exactly where they did during the council; a queer position certainly, for they are not central as to any thing. They are on a little platform, which is still covered with tapestry, and there is also a canopy of the same workmanship. They have probably been removed for security to this room; greater changes having been made during the last four hundred years. I never see any of these European relics without comparing them with America. Here have these two chairs most probably been kept since a period antecedent to the discovery of our continent! You may remember the orange tree referred to in a former letter.* The chair of the pope has the place of honour, the right; but it is the smallest and the lowest, though the most highly ornamented. Both are arm-chairs, a distinction of some importance, even now, among princes.

In this room is a model of the cell in which Huss was so long confined. It is made in imitation of stone, though really of wood, and is but three feet wide, by about ten long, and between seven and eight high; narrow lodgings, even for a schismatic. The true cell was in the convent of the Dominicans, a part of which, converted into a manufactory, is still standing on an island in the Rhine, within the limits of the town. The window of the copy was taken from the real cell; it is a sort of loop-hole; the door is also the true door. There were a few bricks on which he had cut some letters. They showed his Bible, too, well filled with annotations. The chair that is said to have been allowed him is a curious specimen of gothic taste, the father of sin being carved on its back, in the shape of a demon's head, with talons, strangely enough relieved by flowers. Perhaps it was intended that the paths of sin should appear filled with flowers. The allegory did not hold good as to Huss, who, though a condemned sinner in the eyes of his judges, had any thing but a pleasant road to travel.

There were other curious remains in this place, but as every town in Europe has something of the sort, you must excuse my enumerating any more. At the cathedral, an edifice of some grandeur, we were shown the stone on which Huss is said to have stood while receiving his sentence. "Tell Sigismund, I cannot break my faith with God, as he hath broken his faith with me." There is a lively interest about the fate of this sturdy martyr, which has enticed me into details that you may find unreasonable. Among other curiosities that we saw, was a flail well filled with spikes; an appropriate weapon, that had been used by some peasant in his struggles to release himself and his country from bondage. I would rather own that flail than the celebrated armour of Godfrey of Bouillon!

---

* The writer saw an orange-tree *in a tub*, at Versailles, in 1826, which bore the date of 1425, or sixty-eight years before the discovery of America!

The lake, aided by a calm and lovely day, offered a soft and serene picture. A dozen large craft were floating lazily on its bosom, with their sails disposed in the most picturesque forms. They carry a single square sail, with a great hoist; and this had its yard a-cockbill, that a clue hauled up, and another the canvass in the brails. The effect was exactly that which a painter would most wish to produce. Many of the boats were loaded with lumber from the mountains of the Tyrol, bound seaward. We returned to *l'aigle d'or* to breakfast on the fish of the Boden-see, which proved to be firm and good. At this house, and at Schaffhausen, we had no napkins with our meals, an event, on the continent of Europe, to be recorded.

We took our departure before eleven, following the southern shore, through Thurgovie. At first we only saw the lake in the distance, but we approached it in the afternoon, so close as literally to lave the wheels in its waters. A more pleasing drive can scarcely be imagined. A glorious day, the broad expanse of the water, villages on low points, a fine country, and a background that began to resume the characteristics of Switzerland. There was a noble grouping of mountains toward the head of the lake, and, since the previous day, our eyes had been occasionally treated with distant glimpses of snow-clad hills; the first we had seen of them since quitting Berne. For miles this day, we rode through a forest of apple trees. We could see the towns and castles of the other shore, and, in some instances, the smaller towers of *Schlösser** in Wurtemburg were quite apparent.

The costume of Thurgovie is very different from any we had yet seen. Two women, whom we met on the road, wore small caps that just covered the crown of the head, of which one was silver, and the other of gold. Of course, these ornaments were rather superficial. We saw oxen harnessed, in all respects, like horses, with collars, breechings, and cruppers. I also observed a peculiarity I do not remember ever to have before seen, in the wagons, which had all four of the wheels very nearly of the same size.

We entered the canton of St. Gall at a place called Steinach, though we were not yet quite done with Thurgovie, which met us again at Horn, an insulated village of the latter territory. All

* Castles.

these changes of political boundaries are quietly effected, no one asking for passports, the guard at the gate of Constance excepted, and custom-house officers are quite unknown.

At Roschach we stopped for an hour. It is a pretty little town, with a port, a brisk trade for this part of the world, and in the midst of most enchanting scenery. Here we saw a Bodensee steamboat, which is a prodigy in its way. It reminded me, in its construction, of some of the schooners that I had seen on Ontario and Erie, when serving on those western waters twenty years ago, which were built in barnyards, hauled to the water by oxen, and which sailed, haw and gee, as it were by instinct. A great number of lazy craft were in the offing; while the high mountain which rose behind the town was arable to its summit, having woods, meadows, houses, and vineyards spread over its broad bosom. Here and there a small *château* too was seated on the lofty green acclivity.

The drive to Rheineck was beautiful. The children had healthful, smiling faces; and we were evidently getting off the beaten track of travellers, a luxury you cannot appreciate until you visit a region like Switzerland, and find cockneyisms invading the sanctuary.

All these places are historical in a small way. A ruined castle, not far from Rheineck, was connected with the wars of Appenzell and St. Gall, having been destroyed by the people of the former country. I will not ask you, clever and learned as you are, if you have read any epics on this struggle; but, be candid and answer, did you ever hear of such countries before? They were powers long ere your boasted America was known, and, in a small way certainly, are powers still. In extent, population, and wealth, they are about equal to a New York county. Still, each is one of the twenty-two confederated states of Switzerland, and, as such, entitled to your respect and affection. St. Gall, however, being the sixth canton in extent of territory, and the fourth in population, is rather more important than most of its neighbours. It contains Appenzell in its bosom, the latter being literally embraced by the possessions of the former. It has one hundred and thirty thousand souls, and is rich in manufactures as well as in soil.

Rheineck is the chief town of the Rhinthal, and is well placed on the banks of the river, at no great distance from the spot where it enters the lake, although the latter is not visible. It is a secluded, rural-looking town, though not wanting in industry. The tavern at which we stopped reminded me of one of the old fashioned, quiet, Dutch inns that once existed on the Mohawk; and which were as much superior to their noisy, tobacco-chewing, whisky-drinking, dirty, Yankee successors, as cleanliness, stability, and sour-crout can be superior to a system in which a day may commence with a settlement, and end with a removal. How loathsome is a state of society that reduces the feelings of neighbourhood, religion, veneration for the past, hopes for the future, country, kindred, and friends, to the level of a speculation! The locusts of Egypt do not bring such a blight on a land, as the passage of a swarm of these restless, soulless, shiftless, and yet for ever *shifting*, creatures, who do not stay long enough in a place to love any thing but themselves, and who invariably treat the best affections as they would deal with a bale of goods, or a drove of cattle on its way to the shambles. These are not the men who, by manly enterprise and bold conceptions, convert the wilderness into a garden, but reptiles that wander in their footsteps, swagger of their own exploits, come and go incessantly, and, like the rolling stone, gather no moss.

We hurried down to the river, and, profiting by the return of a hay-boat, crossed into the Vorarlberg. Our advent in Austria attracted no attention, though a *gens d'armes* was visible, a custom-house stared us in the face, and the double-headed eagle stood guard on his roost, near the ferry. But there is little in this secluded spot to excite distrust, or alarm cupidity. After taking a short walk in the emperor's dominions, we recrossed to Switzerland unmolested.

Girls were seated under trees tambouring muslin. The ladies examined some of their work, and pronounced it to be common, coarse shawls; but the Swiss wrought muslins have a great reputation. What a thing is civilization! This cotton was probably grown in the wilds of America; was shipped to Rotterdam; thence transported up the long windings of the Rhine to some neighbouring manufactory; is here in the hands of peasant girls beneath the shade of the paternal vine; may return by the path it came, and yet be seen fluttering in our own mountain breezes!

We have reached a new order of architecture; for Switzerland, though so distinct and peculiar, has as great a variety in its ordinary works of art, as in its nature. Like the *Ranz des Vaches*, there is a costume and a distinct style of building for nearly every canton, with the exception of those which lose their peculiarities in their frontier locations. Here, one side of the Rhine is as primitive as the other, and the houses are strikingly quaint. A description of one shall be written, with the model before my eyes in a little inn directly opposite the window.

The building is of three low stories, of which the first is on a level with the ground. The upper or the third story projects four or five feet. It is the principal floor. The lower stories have eight small windows, or are *all* window, with the exception of the corners of the building and the window frames. Each window has six panes of hexagonal glass. One window is omitted in the centre of the upper story. On this empty space is painted a vine, an emblem of the uses of the house. Between the *rows* of the windows a sort of entablature is marked off in paint, which is filled with pithy German verses, in honour of good cheer and good morals. At one end of this entablature is a *bon vivant* with his pipe and glass, and at the other a man holding the bridle of an ass, which is drinking, not wine, but water at a fountain. The figures are much smaller than life. Each corner has a pilaster. The back ground is common stucco, and the only colour of the paint that of reddish brick-dust. The lower story is unornamented. This is by no means a good specimen; for we have seen fifty much more elaborate within the last day or two, but never under circumstances that admitted of so close a survey.

This opening of the Rhinthal is a lovely spot. The hills, or rather mountains, appear to be cultivated to their summits, and are dotted with habitations, from the *château* to the chalet. A great many churches, also, appear picturesquely perched on beautiful sites. Globular or balloon-shaped steeples are getting to be so common that I almost fancy we are farther east than the truth will warrant, some of them actually looking mosque-like.

A raft floated down the Rhine this afternoon, managed by two men. It had come seventy miles. The wonder is, that these waters are so little used. I do not think we have yet seen twenty boats, skiffs excepted, on this great river. The lake, it is true, was pretty well garnished with canvass, but not in the way it might be, and would be with us. The mistaken policy of giving employment, by means of accidental imperfections, pervades Europe; ay, even England. Why is there no canal around the falls of the Rhine? Parallel to the stream, and moving in its direction, we have passed huge wagons, with six, and eight, and ten horses, buried in harness, with great brass plates, some of which we were told had come from the Tyrol, and might have been going to Basle, or possibly to America; for such things do happen. Our inn, besides being so comfortable, and clean, and good, proved also to be unusually cheap. There is a satisfaction, in finding that a grasping cupidity has not penetrated to a spot like this, that has no connexion with the purse.

We departed again, with the dawn. The Rhinthal proved to be a broad valley, and the Rhine itself, at this point, a wide and shallow stream. It no longer flowed with the steady majesty we had so much admired below the lake, though it was much too wide to be termed a torrent; sand banks and beds of gravel occasionally appeared in the centre of the stream, and, except in velocity, its character was altogether changed. Even the colour of the water was more like that of the mountain streams than the cerulean blue of the ocean. From Schaffhausen to Constance, its course had been west; it now flowed north; and for half the distance between Kaiserstuhl to Schaffhausen its direction had been south. As we were ascending its current, of course our own route was always towards the opposite points of the compass.

The river flows through wide flats, winding from one side of the valley to the other, the low land being covered with maize, hemp, meadows and orchards, and the hill sides with vineyards. Little other grain was visible. The girls were tambouring in the morning air, under the apple trees. They were very generally pretty, and of more delicate forms than the Oberland beauties. Oxen and horses were frequently harnessed side by side; and the wagon wheels continued to be of the same size, or so nearly so as to render the difference nearly imperceptible.

We reached Altstetten to breakfast. It is a quaint, small, and old town, at the foot of the Am Stoss, with many of the painted houses I have described, and wide, wooden arcades in the principal street. Here we encountered a serious difficulty; we could not make ourselves understood. Our German was by no means classical; and English, Italian, and French, were all Hebrew to the good people of the inn. The coachman was from one of the Bernese valleys, and spoke habitually as pure a patois as heart could wish. But even *his* patois would not do; for the patois of the district would own no fellowship with that of this linguist.

In this dilemma I was thrown upon the language of nature. It was not difficult to make the hostess understand that we wished to eat. *Café*, as good luck will have it, like "revolution," is a word of general use in these luxurious times. So far, all was well—but "*what* would we eat?" We were sufficiently hungry to eat any thing; but how was one to express "any thing" by signs? It might be interpreted so easily into "every thing!" In this crisis I bethought me of a long neglected art, and crowed like a cock. The shrill scientific strain had hardly reached the ear of the good woman before it was answered by such a peal of laughter as none but village lungs could raise. W[illiam], who is an admirable mimic, ran after the convulsed party, (two or three girls had been anxiously awaiting the result,) and began quite successfully to cackle like a hen. He was answered by screams that I think must have fairly ascended the Am Stoss. In due time, we had a broiled fowl, an omelette, and boiled eggs; but to the last moment none of the 'women-kind' could look at us without hearty bursts of merriment. To be sure it was droll enough to hear hunger bursting out spontaneously, in these paroxysms of natural eloquence.

We left the inn on foot, the coachman deeming it necessary to hire horses to drag the empty carriage up the mountain; his own finding it work enough to drag themselves after it. It was the steepest ascent I ever encountered on a highway, for so great a distance. The road was very good, but of a matter-of-fact kind that did not condescend to make material sinuosities. We were more than two hours in walking to the summit. The views were extremely fine from various points of the ascent. The valley of the Rhine was visible far away; Altstetten lay at our feet; in Austria were villages, baths, churches, and *châteaux*, as usual; and our own mountain side was dotted with cottages. The Vorarlberg presented a sublime grouping of dark, stately mountains, with retiring valleys, up which the eye penetrated leagues.

Most of the road we had travelled that morning, lay like a line beneath the Swiss hills. The fields near us were verdant, enclosed, and neat.

Beggars had been a blot on the scenery for the last day or two; nor did it appear that they asked so much from necessity as in the way of speculation, for they often laughed in our faces when refused. We had paused, to rest ourselves, on the side of this mountain, when two or three children came scrambling from a cottage, on the usual errand. The oldest could not have been five, and the youngest was scarcely two years old. The last was an infant of rare beauty; fair, with the eyes of an angel, and perfectly golden hair. She literally wore no covering but an apron. The little cherub plaintively lisped, as she approached, as near as we could understand, "pity, pity." I put a small piece of coin into the extended hand, when she immediately raised the other, with her "pity, pity."* We gave each a trifle, and away they scampered, screaming with delight. The cottage from which these little beggars came was extremely neat, had a comfortable air, and the mother witnessed all that passed from a window. The parent that initiates her daughters thus early in the arts of mercenary entreaty, is in great danger of seeing them in later life the victims of their own practices. Indeed, the reflecting and intelligent Swiss admit that the great influx of strangers is rapidly demoralizing the country, particularly that portion of it which is best formed by nature to foster the higher moral qualities. Men are so constructed that they will turn the picturesque into profit, and even women too.

We met a wagoner driving down one of the steepest pitches of this mountain, on a quick trot, fast asleep in his wagon. One wheel, it is true, was locked; but such is the force of habit that neither the master nor his cattle seemed in the least to mind the descent.

At the summit of the Am Stoss is a small chapel and an inn. The former, I believe, is to commemorate a victory, and the latter is pretty sure to catch all the travellers who ascend. Here, an entirely new scene burst upon us. In the valley most of the

---

* Greater acquaintance with the German has since shown me that the little thing merely uttered the common entreaty of "*bitte, bitte*," or "pray do."

objects already mentioned were still visible, while before us lay a prospect unlike any thing we had yet seen.

We were on a sort of elevated plain, or vale, that was sprinkled with cottages of a truly Swiss aspect, treeless and almost shrubless, and which was shorn as close as scythe could cut, and which it did not seem that the ploughshare had ever stirred. I dare say the latter fact is not so; but I can only compare the whole to the appearance of freshly mown lawns, divided by rustic fences, and dotted with rural habitations, that seemed to be placed without any order in the middle of delicate meadows. So "shaven and shorn" a region I never before witnessed. The distant hills had some wood, it is true; but I question if there were twenty stunted trees in sight in the two or three square leagues of the table land. Comparing the effect of quitting the orchards and fertility of the Rhinthal to all this nakedness, it was like going from a *ballet* to a meeting of the Shakers.

After trotting over an excellent road, through this exquisite nakedness, for two miles, we reached a little ascent. Here we took leave of the Vorarlberg mountains, and caught a near look at Gais, the village which gives its name to the district. I ought to have said that we entered the canton of Appenzell, near the chapel at the summit of the Am Stoss.

Gais lies in one of the little dales, into which the country now became broken. A livelier bit of still life is not often seen. There may be a hundred houses scattered over the lawn-like meadows, with no great attention to regularity. They are of various colours, and the church was spacious and white. Every thing was as neat as Brugg itself. Naked earth was nowhere visible, the narrow road and a few winding footpaths excepted.

No cattle—no trees—no grain—scarcely any shrubs—for miles. Nothing but meadows as closely cut as velvet, houses that looked like large boxes laid carelessly on enormous grass carpets, and a road that was just wide enough, and quite good enough, for a park.

After passing Gais, the country became more broken, and we began to descend. Trees now reappeared, especially the apple. Here and there was a hedge. At Teufen we saw another remarkable village; the houses being quaint and of various colours, as well as faultlessly neat. In the gable of one I counted six rows of little windows, none much larger than those of a coach. Pea-green, white, and lead colour, were the favourite hues. Tinted Manhattan! how art thou shamed and outdone by this nameless hamlet!

All the cattle were most probably on the upper pastures at this season, the whole region here appearing to be meadow.

After quitting Teufen, we descended rapidly by a wild ravine; but before entering it from one point there was a distant glimpse of the lake of Constance. St. Gall was now re-entered by its own appropriate valley; and we were again transferred into an entirely new region. These sudden transitions are sometimes nearly magical, and always pleasant, no country offering greater variety of scenery, or a greater variety of artificial objects, in spaces so small. The town of St. Gall was seated in a rich bottom. There was an air of wealth about it which took us by surprise, the suburbs giving every evidence of an extensive industry. The environs abounded with manufacturing establishments, and the green acclivities were covered with fine muslins, bleaching. The place seemed much larger than Constance. It contains, in fact, about ten thousand inhabitants. In short, in this retired valley, we found a town with more of the appearance of business than any we had yet seen in Switzerland, not even excepting Berne. It is a neat little city, surrounded by ancient walls, the ditches of which are converted into gardens.

St. Gall, a town and canton, derives its political existence from a holy hermit of this name, who was a Scot. In the seventh century, Pepin de Héristal, Mayor of the Palace, in France, founded an abbey which was called after the anchorite. This abbey pretended to have been the repository of learning for three centuries, during that long and dark period when kings and nobles sometimes deemed it a disgrace to know how to read and write. Its library was one of the largest extant, and we are said to be indebted to its riches for the works of several of the Latin authors. At a later day, the children of the emperors and of the neighbouring princes were sent here to be educated. Towards the year 1200, however, St. Gall lost its character for learning, through the cupidity and ambition of its abbots, who had become little territorial sovereigns, wielding the sword on favourable occasions. They have left behind them warlike names, even in this warlike region. The abbots having been raised to the dignity of princes of the empire, this sort of government continued, with the usual quantum of victories, defeats, rebellions, and other pious abominations, until the great political changes of 1798, when their temporal authority was overthrown. The monastery itself was entirely suppressed, by the obstinacy of its abbot, in 1805.

The town of St. Gall was at first a dependency of the abbey, owing its origin to the crumbs which fell from the rich man's table. In process of time, its people, serfs of course in that age, purchased their freedom from the monks, obtained franchises from the emperors, and became burghers. They had a bad neighbourhood with the monks, and matters proceeded to such extremities, that about two centuries since they built a high wall between the abbey edifices and the town, most probably to keep the holy celibates at home at night. Previously to this, the burghers had made an alliance with the Swiss cantons, and were in fact, if not by legal right, independent of the abbots. At the close of the seventeenth century, this independence was formally acknowledged by treaty.

I have given you this little outline of clerical history, as curious in itself, and because it contains the same elements as the history of all the little religious governments of Switzerland, of which formerly there were several, that have left behind them deep impressions of their origin.

We visited the deserted buildings of the abbey, passing through the celebrated wall, which is still standing. The church is large, highly ornamented, and in good repair. It is a cathedral, I believe; at any rate, there is a bishop, who passes his time between this place and the Grisons. The altars of the church are more elaborated than any we have yet seen, not excepting those of Belgium, though wanting in the fine pictures of the latter country. Cherubs, in high relief, abound, the walls looking fairly alive with them. There are pictures, too, but none I believe of much reputation.

All this has taken us by surprise, for we expected neither the evidences of industry, nor those of the ancient magnificence of the monks. We did not enter the deserted monastery.

On leaving St. Gall, we journeyed down the valley, crossing a stupendous bridge, that would have done credit to the environs of Paris, and re-entered Appenzell. The drive for the remainder of the day was through a pastoral and manufacturing district, cattle reappearing, but still no signs of grain. We ascended a little, and reached Herisau, one of the capitals of the canton, just as the day closed. I say, one of the capitals, for several of the Swiss cantons, while they have but a single vote in the national Diet, are subdivided into entirely distinct governments within themselves. Appenzell is of the number, being divided into the Protestant and Catholic districts, or *Rhodes*, as they are technically termed. The first is the wealthiest, the most industrious, and the most populous; the latter being purely—I might say eminently—pastoral. Both polities are pure democracies, the people enacting the laws in their original assemblies. This system, however, has some checks, but no balances—you know my theory on the important distinction between the two—in the councils, which exercise a species of veto. In the Protestant *Rhode*, all males of sixteen have a voice, and in the Catholic, all males of eighteen! This is surpassing our own country, where precocity is rather rife, and boys get to be men with surprising facility. In a community of 50,000 mountaineers, in the centre of Europe, where every musket counts, and where the interests to be controlled are chiefly confined to the pasture and the dairy, this arrangement, however, may do well enough.

Herisau is a neat and striking little town, in which there is a mixture of the ancient and of the modern Swiss architectures. Manufactures aided by a fire have been parents to the latter. You may form some idea of the former, by the following description of our inn, which is strictly of the old school.

We occupy the principal floor, to reach which we have ascended two low flights of steps. Our parlour is seven feet high, twenty long, and fifteen wide. There are seven windows, all on one side, and each window has six panes of glass. The outside shutters rise, like coach-blinds. That part of the room is covered with curtains; for, luckily, they manufacture cotton here.

I have observed several houses to-day, with six windows in the gables, these gables being usually the front of the building. The arrangement of one of them was as follows. There is a single window in the apex, or garret; then came a row of three, and a row of five. These are all within the roof. A row of seven, and one of nine were in the frame, and a row of eight was in the stone-work of the foundation. The whole height from the ground to the pinnacle of the roof, might have been forty-two or three feet.

The public square of Herisau, like that of Gais, is exceedingly neat and pleasing. Two ruins appeared on hills near the former place, but they promised little.

We did not leave Herisau until after seven, on account of rain. The road led us through an undulating mountain-region, descending, however, on the whole. We soon reached the frontier of this little republic, once more entering its grasping neighbour, St. Gall. Cattle were more numerous, and here and there we saw the signs of grain. The ancient county of Tockembourg (at present in St. Gall) was the next district, and the country ceased to be as peculiar as that lately traversed. It is of another kind, altogether, and yet in almost any other part of the world, even this valley would be deemed very remarkable.

We met, this morning, four different parties of W[illiam]'s *amateur* beggars. All of them had knapsacks stuffed to overflowing, and they were, in general, sleek, well fed, and sturdy. Begging, whatever may be its temporary conveniences, is but a questionable mode of commencing life.

We reached Lichtensteig to breakfast. It is well placed in a very pretty valley, and has a convent, with a *château* at a little distance. Bleaching grounds and manufactories are seen in all these villages. "Very pretty," too, in Switzerland, you will remember, means something more than common. Indeed, when fairly among the mountains, there is scarcely a spot in the whole country that has not something remarkable, for if you even happen to find yourself in a common-place "bit," nine times in ten the eye may get a distant look at snow-clad summits, and the wild grandeur of the Alps.

The people of the inn manifested unusual interest in us, when they discovered we were Americans. Some of their friends had emigrated. They told us that the Catholics and Protestants of the village use the same building, resorting to it at different hours. A woman here gains about eighteen cents a day by embroidering, and yet the superior wealth and comfort enjoyed in the manufacturing districts, over those which are purely agricultural, is visible at a glance.

The valley of Watwyl is beautiful, the village very neat and flourishing; and there are, as usual, a convent and a *château;*

charming accessaries to the landscape; especially to those who merely trot through the place. The castle is said to be the only one which still takes rank in the Tockembourg, where formerly there were nineteen. That at Lichtensteig is probably converted into a manufactory, a fate that has befallen half the *châteaux* of the continent, and is still likely to befall the other half. We have not yet seen a *château* in the course of construction in all our travels, nor even a great private hotel, in any town! Royal residences alone form exceptions to the rule. Does not this prove that "the age of bargaining is come?"—and yet there are men so blind to the signs of the times, that they wish to see the civil institutions which have come down to us through the oppressions of feudality, renewed even in countries where more modern facts have gotten the ascendancy. Men of this perverted state of feeling exist even in our own land, where potent and majestic facts are dragging opinions after them, wriggling and reluctant, like tails dangling to kites. But selfishness is obliged to wear a mask, and new combinations are becoming necessary to enable the few to make the most of the many.

At the end of the valley of Watwyl, we had to obtain an extra horse for the mountain. While waiting its appearance, melodious female voices were heard, repeating *aves*, on different keys. Presently three women appeared, coming down the road, and counting their beads, each taking up the prayer in turn. They were on a short pilgrimage to some neighbouring shrine. Such a group added greatly to the charms of a country, which has always appeared to me like a vast natural altar, reared expressly in honour of God.

After toiling up a heavy ascent, and crossing a mountain top, we came to a point on the opposite side, which commanded a view, that I took the pains to describe on the spot, with the top of the carriage for a desk. I give it you, as a specimen of that admixture of the wild and the beautiful that so constantly occurs in Switzerland.

Fields and woods, diversified like a park, covered the broad mountain side, or the foreground of the picture, to the level of the valley. A rich and wide bottom spread itself beneath. The lake of Zurich stretched far away to the right, and on the left, gigantic mountains raised their summits into the regions of eternal snow. Every thing was on a scale of commensurate breadth and sublimity. The opposite side of the valley was a long range of magnificent Alps, holding on their broad breasts hamlets, cottages, and fields, with a noble background of hoary peaks. Fleecy clouds rested here and there, on the masses of verdure, rendering the deep hue of the larches more lustrous and dark. The town of Rapperschwyl, which resembles a quaint ragged castle, was in relief against the lake, and churches, villages, and isolated dwellings were sprinkled profusely on every side, far and near. In the immediate foreground, a monastery was seated on a high green spur of the mountain, overlooking all these glories with religious calm.

As we descended, the view opened toward the south, and the glen opposite expanded to a deep but broad valley, which contains the canton and town of Glarus. A mountain near it was girt by a belt of vapour, at half its height, the upper edge of the mist being drawn as truly as if cut by a knife. It looked like a halo encircling the moon. Objects constantly grew more and more distinct, until skiffs that at first had been swallowed by distance, assumed the appearance of specks, then of birds, and finally were seen skimming the water. In the end, we distinguished the blades of their oars flashing in the sun.

Here, for the first time, our eyes were greeted with the sight of that famous little state which has given its name to the Confederation, the mountains opposite forming the northern boundary of Schwytz,* which comes to the shores of the lake.

At the foot of the descent, we passed Usnach, a walled village, when the remainder of our day's drive lay on the margin of the water. We hurried on, and stopped at a very good inn, the Paon, just without the gates of Rapperschwyl.

---

* Or, Schweitz; or, Schwitz; pronounced Schweitz, as in height.

Letter XI.

D EAR ———,

I walked into Rapperschwyl alone, next morning, at an early hour. The position and external appearance of this little town are very remarkable. It stands on a small elevated peninsula, and its narrow limits have blended *château*, towers, churches, houses, and walls together, in a way to give to the whole the air of one huge and quaint edifice. It was formerly the residence of a sovereign count, and the disparity between the warlike and baronial, and the more humble and useful, is very apparent; though both are on a scale suited to the simple habits of mountaineers. Straitened as it is for room, there is a tolerably large square in the centre, most probably an ancient *place d'armes*.

The lake of Zurich is divided into what are called the upper and lower lakes, the former being much the largest. This division is produced by the peninsula of Rapperschwyl, and by a long tongue of low land which projects halfway across the water, or at least a mile, directly opposite. Ebel had informed me that Leopold of Austria caused a bridge to be made connecting these two points, in 1358; and my eyes had told me, in descending the mountain the previous evening, that this bridge, or a successor, still existed. I walked through the town, therefore, taking the direction to the water.

A toll was demanded at the end of the bridge. This ancient structure—ancient after the fashion of vineyards, in which the vines are periodically renewed—this ancient structure occupies the second rank in the gradations of bridge building; the first, I take it, being the common American expedient of laying logs on sleepers. It is made of low bents, or framed gallowses, with three rows of sleepers, and planks that are kept in their places by string-pieces well pinned down. With a slight exception, there is no railing, and the whole is only twelve feet wide. The bridge is not straight, but it forms two obtuse angles, having probably been made to vary from the true line on account of the depth of the water. Three hundred yards from the gate are a pier and a small chapel, both of stone; and just at this place is the bit of railing alluded to. At this spot one may be said to take "his departure," and to go forth on the lake. Carriages and wagons do pass this ticklish affair; but one can believe that even a man might not relish it in a gale of wind. As the water is not deep, I presume the waves never actually break over it; still, twelve feet, and no bulwarks, make a narrow beam for a craft a mile long!

I walked to the opposite shore, at my usual gait, in seventeen minutes and a half, and returned in seventeen; from which I infer that the length of this bridge a little exceeds 5000 feet. Ebel makes it 1800 paces, which is equal to 5400 of our feet, or a little more than a mile. On reaching the southern shore, I first touched the soil of Schwytz.

It was Sunday, the last day of August. The morning was fair, and bland, and calm, as became a Christian Sabbath. The bells were tolling for early mass, in twenty glens, and along the whole village-lined shore. Peasants and their wives were hurrying past, in rustic finery. Most of the men wore flowers and vine-leaves in their hats, from which I inferred they were going to a *fête*, until I discovered a faded *gobea* in my own travelling cap, a piece of pastoral coquetry, for which I was indebted to one of my companions.

Mist lay before all the mountains to the south, rendering them mysterious and mighty. The vapour was just rising along the whole shore of Schwytz, too, unveiling villages, pastures, cottages, and dark forests, as it ascended, and forming exquisite transitions of light and shadow. The whole western side of the lake and valley was already illuminated by the sun, looking bright and cheerful; a gay panorama, that included a thousand objects, beautiful alike in nature and art. The towers of Rapperschwyl were soft and sunny. I counted twelve of them, grouped together, in the small peninsula.

After this little pilgrimage to the cradle of Helvetic liberty, I returned to the Paon, in an excellent humour to enjoy a break-fast that would have done credit to an American kitchen. In passing, I observed a little artificial port at Rapperschwyl, made of piles. The buildings along the north-west shore of the lake, were now all visible beneath the vapour, and as they blended with the glassy lake, and were snowy white, they looked like a thousand sloops becalmed.

The day was so glorious, and the scenery opened so finely, as the mists ascended, that, impatient to enjoy it, we all left the Paon, on foot, leaving orders for the carriage to follow. A short walk transferred us from the canton of St. Gall to that of Zurich. At the distance of a mile or two, Rapperschwyl showed itself in a new aspect. The houses and all the lower buildings were hid by an intervening swell of the land, and nothing was visible but the old castle, the church,—in Europe the houses of God are always taller than the houses of men,—and the towers of the town walls. The side of the eminence next us was dark and green, lying in shadow, while the outline above was tinged, like a halo, with the rays of the sun. These pictures, if less imposing than the more magnificent glaciers and terrific valleys of the upper Alps, abide more fondly with the memory.

By this time the whole of the Schwytz shore was uncovered, and we saw it, pasture above pasture, cottage climbing over cottage, to the elevation of I know not how many thousand feet. The exquisite transparency of the air, out of which every thing like vapour appeared to have ascended, enabled us to discern very distant objects with great fidelity, and helped greatly to increase our satisfaction.

All that the lakes of Switzerland need to render them faultlessly beautiful, is islands. They differ so much from each other, as to fill up the sum of all that such landscapes require, with this exception. Here and there an island is met with, it is true, but they are usually insignificant, and not well placed; nor is there anywhere an approach, in the most remote degree, to what may be called a grouping of islands. In this respect, Lake George is as much before all its Swiss competitors, as it is behind most of them in every other particular, that of the transparency of its water excepted. The lake of Zurich is better off than common, however, having an island or two. One of them enjoys the advantage of some historical associations. It is called Ufnau, and it lay directly opposite to us, when about a league from Rapperschwyl, at a spot where the lake is said to be three miles wide. There is a ruined tower on it, but the effect is lost amidst the multitude of finer things.

Our road lay altogether along the lake. The shore is an irregular acclivity, covered with villages, farms, vineyards, orchards, and churches, and even the experience of my worthy friend and connexion, Mr. McAdam, could scarcely produce a better wheel-track. You are to recollect that roads in this country literally help a view, being neither straight nor wide. About a league from Rapperschwyl, we drove for some distance along a sort of natural terrace, overhanging the water. I can give you no just idea of the charms of the entire scene at this particular spot. The shore of Schwytz, lined with white villages, churches, and cottages, formed the opposite coast. The lake was like a mirror, and some twenty large boats, with high square sails, this with the yard a-cockbill, that with one clew up, another with the halyards not half home, and all looking lubberly and picturesque, were silently stealing along, before a gentle north air that seemed too ethereal to descend to the surface of the water. At this moment, the tones of a dozen mournful bells issued out of the glens of Schwytz, some so faint in distance, as to sound like Æolian harps, reaching the ear at intervals only, borne along in swells by the passing air. The effect of these bells, sending their melancholy notes out of mountains, and across the water, added to the day, and its solemn calm, was to convert the whole scene into a vast and sublime tabernacle!

We passed, at Zolliken, near Zurich, a vineyard, of which it is said there exist records to prove it has borne the vine five hundred years. Like the bridge, you will readily suppose that the materials have been often renewed. One is sometimes startled at the antiquity which renders objects of this sort respectable in Europe. At Küznacht, the words, "Boston, North America," on a tablet let into the outer wall of a church, caught our eyes. It was an inscription to the memory of a young traveller, who had been drowned in the lake, near this spot. His body had been found and interred here.

We entered Zurich, after a very delightful drive of some eighteen or twenty miles, through ramparts of verdure, which appeared admirably in keeping with the landscape, whatever may be their efficiency in the way of defence. After being dragged back and forth, through narrow and clean streets, but of very unequal surfaces, we found shelter at last in an inn that stood literally on the margin of the port.

The Limmat, the outlet of the lake, glances through the

centre of the town, the separate parts of which are connected by bridges wider than the streets. The head of the river is opened like a fan, and across the upper part piles have been driven to designate the limits of the port. As this expedient can have no effect in breaking the waves, and is quite idle in a military sense, unless resorted to for the purposes of revenue, I am ignorant of its uses. It may, however, avail something against floating ice, in the spring. An ancient square tower rises out of the water, in the centre of the little port. It was probably erected for defence, but is now a prison.

Zurich has about 15,000 inhabitants, and is one of the wealthiest and most important of the Swiss towns. Its manufactures are respectable, and the people have an air of ease and comfort. The canton is the seventh in extent, and the second in population. The latter fact is not difficult to be believed, for I scarcely remember a portion of the earth in which rural habitations more abound. The whole lake-shore is a hamlet. The history of the population of this little country exhibits some remarkable changes. According to Picot, (received authority, I believe,) the canton contained in 1610, 143,990 souls, and in 1634, only 86,621. War and pestilence had wrought the difference. Famine—a scourge America has never known since its earliest days—cut down the people again, between the years 1678 and 1700. This evil has frequently reduced the numbers, not so much by deaths, however, as by compelled emigration. The present population is about 180,000.

The history of Zurich greatly resembles that of Berne. The city ruled the country, and certain families of burghers ruled the city. This system has been modified, however, the French revolution having let in a flood of light upon the rest of Europe. At present, it is the fashion to make all men equal "before the law," as it is called, though all men are very far from being equal in *making* the laws. Formerly, the great were openly exempt from taxes; now *all* are taxed, in name; but as the rich exclusively make the laws, they contrive to arrange the matter in a way to make the poor pay as much as possible. I have told you, for instance, how at Paris a bottle of wine, which costs six sous, pays just the same duty as the bottle which costs six francs; one being taxed eighty per cent., and the other four per cent. Wine being a necessary in these countries, bread and wine forming the two first articles of consumption with all classes, the policy may be understood. The pretence is, that if wine were cheaper, the labourers would drink too much! I do not say Zurich is obnoxious to this reproach, for the Swiss aristocracies are more mild and just than common, sheer necessity compelling moderation; but it is necessary to admonish you against being deceived by names. All men, let it be understood, therefore, under the new liberalism of Europe, are absolutely equal before the law; each paying just five sous duty, a bottle, on his wine!

Zurich is much less aristocratical than Berne. The people are mostly Protestant; though there are two small districts of Papists. The learning, industry, and general character of this canton have long been respectable; and, without pretending to know more than may be gathered by a mere passer-by, I should say that there is no falling off in the two latter, at least. You will recollect that I have promised to give you little more than can be gleaned in this imperfect manner; for we Americans generally travel through Europe "unknowing and unknown."

In one thing I cannot be mistaken. The water under our windows was as limpid and pure as that of our own Otsego. The lively perch were swimming about, looking as much like the perch at home as one pea is like another. W[illiam], in his *amor patriæ*, cast a line, but in vain, to get a nearer view of them.

I have already told you that we have a Swiss foundation, too, in our own hills; Zurich, Berne, and Geneva, lying all at about the elevation of your native valley. We merely want a granite formation, and superstructures that mount two miles into the air, with the usual accessaries, to be another Switzerland. Until some convulsion of nature produce the change, however, we shall remain most probably just as we are.

Letter XII.

MY DEAR ————,

We left Zurich next morning, before breakfast, in a fog, which completely limited the view until we had crossed the Albis, a high and frequented mountain pass, that lies between the lakes of Zurich and Zug. Ebel extols the view; but I am mute. This time my beloved mists had the best of it, practically demonstrating that there is no earthly good without its attendant alloy. We ate an inexcusably poor breakfast on the summit.

In descending, there were some exceedingly pretty glimpses, including the lake and canton of Zug—I say the canton, for the latter is so small, that it comes very well in at a glance. We passed an old convent and entered this little state, the smallest in the Confederation, at the distance of a mile or two from its capital. Its population is less than fifteen thousand, and its size somewhat smaller than that of a common New York township, containing about twenty-five square miles. Even this little region, one of the oldest cantons, had the aristocratic form of government, until the French revolution—the country, containing some ten or twelve thousand souls, being subject to the city, which contains two. The religion is Catholic.

The town of Zug stands on the lake shore, and is rendered a pretty object in the distant view by its walls and towers, which were constructed to resist the ancient modes of warfare. As we approached it, the children rushed out to beg; sturdy young rogues who deem earning a penny in this manner a sort of pastime. One lad officiously offered to place the *sabot* beneath the wheel; but, after a moment of parley with the coachman, he dropped the iron, and walked surlily on. On inquiry, I found he had been notified there would be no pay. *Point d'argent, point de Suisse.* We could not help laughing at the coincidence; though the same result would be just as likely to follow the same circumstances in France or Italy. In England, habitual deference would have got the better of cupidity, though the lesson would be remembered; and in America pride, and perhaps principle, would have carried the lad through with his self-assumed job.

At Zug we quitted the carriage, with orders for it to proceed to Lucerne. We then engaged a guide, and took a boat for Art. The shore was well lined with *batteaux*, fitted as those already described on the Oberland waters, with established prices, and other conveniences. The delay did not exceed twenty minutes. A collation, which had been ordered "for the good of the house," was taken into the boat, and eaten by the way.

We were nearly three hours in going to Art, with as many oars. The lake is pretty; but by no means so singularly beautiful and wild as those we had before crossed. Our guide proved to be intelligent, and a little of a wag. He was a staunch defender of the new system. Among other things, he told us, with evident satisfaction, there was but one man in his canton who wrote *de* before his name; at the same time, he appeared to be fully aware of the important truth that perfection is hopeless, and that too much must not be asked of democracy. In short, he had, as is commonly the case, much more practical common sense, on all these subjects, than those who claim to be exclusively the salt of the earth. Those who think themselves set apart for the sole enjoyment of the good things of this world, forget that this state of being is merely a part of a great whole; that a superior Intelligence directs all; that this divine Intelligence has established equitable laws, and implanted in every man a consciousness of right and wrong, which enables the lowest in the scale to appreciate innate justice, and which makes every man, in some degree, critical in matters that touch his own welfare. Education and habit, it is true, may blunt or pervert this natural faculty; but, as prosperity is notoriously more apt than adversity to lead the heart astray, I have never yet been in a country in which what are called the lower orders have not clearer and sounder views than their betters of the great principles which ought to predominate in the control of human affairs. I speak of classes, and not of individuals, of course; nor do I believe that any condition of slavery, however abject, ever extinguishes this perception of simple truths, which has been implanted by God for his own great ends. The ability to express is not always commensurate with the ability to conceive; and, as to what are called popular excesses and violence, they are commonly the results of systems which deprive masses of the power to act in any other manner than by an appeal to their force. Bodies of men may be misled, certainly, and even justice when administered violently becomes dangerous; but in all such cases it will be found that a sentiment of right lies at the bottom of even the mistaken impulses of the majority. What sense of right, on the other hand, can accompany those who throw firebrands into masses with a view to profit by their excesses; who hurry a people on to madness in order to benefit themselves, through the reaction, by a return to power; who, in short, deceive, excite, and combine, in order to betray, that they and theirs may profit by the frauds? The latter was the course of the European aristocracy during the French revolution, most of the abominations of which, I believe, are now attributed by coolheaded and impartial men to their secret agents. Majorities may certainly oppress as well as minorities; but the former, having the conviction of their force, rarely do so for their own security.

Art is a small village, at the head of the lake of Zug, in the canton of Schwyz, or Schweitz. Of course, we had now reached the very focus of Swiss independence, and were, in truth, drawing near the scenes of Tell's memorable exploits. We ordered horses for the ladies, and proceeded ahead, on foot, towards the ruins of Goldau. The walk, for a mile, was along an excellent carriage road, and through meadows of exquisite delicacy and verdure, among fruit trees and all the other accompaniments of rural beauty. I can cite to you nothing with which to compare the neatness and velvet-like softness of the fields, but those of door-yards in our prettiest villages; for, in the way of agriculture on a great scale, we have nothing that is comparable. The English lawns are not neater, and their herbage did not appear to me to be as lively and choice. Figure to yourself the chill that came over our delight, at passing through such a vale, when we found its loveliness blasted by piles of rock, earth, and stones, that had fallen across it, in one overwhelming mass, burying hamlets, houses, churches, fields, and owners. Of this extraordinary catastrophe I shall have occasion to speak hereafter.

At Goldau, which stands on the site of a buried hamlet of the same name, we left the carriage road, diverging, by a bridle path, into the fields. Here we were overtaken by the horses, and the ladies were placed in the usual well-protected seats. W[illiam] and myself continued on foot. We had been much amused at Art with a species of pious flirtation, between the landlady and two capuchins, whom she was treating to some of the creature comforts of her well supplied larder. This woman wore a muslin frill, by way of apology for a cap, which, the colour excepted, exactly resembled a cock's comb. The hair was all drawn back from her forehead and temples, to form a foundation for this singular ornament of the head. We found this, however, to be the prevailing fashion here. When will it reach Broadway, *viâ la rue Vivienne?* One of the capuchins in question came up with the horses, and I profited by his good humour to get into discourse with him. All the cantons of this part of the Confederation are Catholic, and this brother was one of a fraternity which dwells habitually in the valley, but which keeps an outpost on the side of the Righi, at a spot where there is a chapel dedicated to *Notre Dame des Neiges*—Our Lady of the Snows!—There is at least poetry in the Popish names; nor can a pious intention be denied those who formed an establishment like this. My companion was one of the three who, just then, were on duty on the mountain, and we had the prospect of his company as far as his abode.

At first, the ascent was gradual, the path leading through meadows and copses of wood, in a way to render it pleasant. This lasted for some time, during which I walked ahead with the monk. At length he suddenly excused himself, by saying that the hour had arrived when he was obliged to attend to his periodical devotions. Taking out a breviary, to work he went, by beginning to mutter the usual Latin prayers. W[illiam] and myself, observing that we had a sharp pitch of the mountain in front, pushed vigorously ahead without looking behind us, for several minutes. Though resolute and active, downright want of breath ere long compelled us both to stop.

The path here actually ascended by a species of stairs, made by placing logs and stones among the rocks, in a way to render them secure. Each step was very broad, and some of them were disagreeably high. There were a good many landings, and of course the direction varied from time to time. We had come to a halt, on a projecting spur, of our natural ladder, and the scene was now so thoroughly Swiss that it merits a more minute description.

There had been a shower while we were on the lake, and the mists were rising from the forests and clinging about the sides of the mountains. We got but partial glimpses through the openings at the distant view, though these constantly varied like a moving panorama, besides being really beautiful in themselves. Among the other floating objects was the pretty little lake of Lowerz, with its rocky island and ruined tower. Directly beneath us lay the meadows and copses through which the path meandered down to the desolation of Goldau. The party below had been detained by meeting some return horses from the mountain, the guides choosing to change the cattle. They were now coming on, however, in a line through the meadows, with the bareheaded capuchin bringing up the rear, still at his *aves* and *paters*. The relieved horses were disappearing in a thicket, on their way back, and a drove of cows was winding its way down the steps beneath us, followed by six or seven dairy-men, having their tubs and milking stools strapped to their shoulders. It was the day when the mountain pastures were abandoned for those in the valley. One sturdy broad-backed fellow closed the procession with a live calf on his shoulders. The mildness of the day, the hue, (for evening was not distant,) the play of the mists, the smoking forests, and the dark verdure of the meadows, contributed to render this one of the most exquisite rural scenes imaginable. You may form some opinion of the scale of the whole picture by getting an idea of the size of this mountain. Three thousand cows alone are pastured on it during the summer; there are numerous flocks of sheep besides. This being the first day of September, most of them were descending by the different paths which communicate with the valleys. That we were on was one of the least frequented by the herdsmen and shepherds.

We were by no means done with our stairs, which seemed fairly to lead to heaven. At length, after being nearly out of breath, heated, and with parched mouths, W[illiam] and myself reached a little tavern that was well filled with shepherds, cowherds, and calf-carriers, on their way down. Delicious water spouted from a fountain a little farther on, and I hurried to it, with a feeling of thirst that I scarcely remember to have suffered before. Fearful of drinking, I put my wrists under the stream. So great and sudden was the effect, that I was actually quitting the spot, when W[illiam] reminded me that I had not tasted the water! One or two swallows sufficed. It may be more pleasant to drink on such occasions; but the other is by far the safest course, and it is equally efficacious in slaking thirst.

We now had a delightfully cool walk through a wood of larches; the whole party overtaking us, with the exception of the monk, who joined the cowherds at the inn to slake his thirst in a less heretical manner. Quitting the wood, we entered some meadows, always ascending; but the labour seemed light after that we had just gone through. At length we came to a cluster of eight or ten buildings, among which are several inns, and the *hospice*, with the little chapel of "Our Lady of the Snows." This hamlet is in a sort of dale, though perfectly level ground is scarcely found this side the great staircase, being surrounded with pastures and meadows. As we passed the *hospice*, two monks looked at us through the windows; these, with the one left behind among the calf-carriers, composed the fraternity that inhabited the building. They pass the winter here, and offer succour to all who want it; but scarcely any besides the shepherds ever approach the spot after autumn. The *hospice* dates from 1689; but the inns have been set up since the rage for travelling has become so general. The baths are abandoned, I believe, in winter. This place is much resorted to on Sundays and holydays by the mountaineers, and the 8th of September is a great festival, in honour of the birth of Mary. Other *fêtes*, of a more rustic character, are kept on this vast and pleasant mountain, which attract large concourses of spectators.

We stopped at an inn. The crowds on the summit frequently drive travellers here in summer, in quest of lodgings. By advice of the guide, we betook ourselves to refreshments; to my surprise, he ordered tea for himself, and we followed his example. This man told me he could undergo more fatigue, aided by this stimulant, than by any other. The practice of taking tea, as a restorative, after a hard day's work in the mountains, is, I find, very general; but, although we take it constantly, as a national usage, I was not aware that its consumption had got to be so common on the European continent.

The path was always upward, after leaving the *hospice*,

though there was no very severe ascent. It led through pastures, and nearly in a direct line. W[illiam] and myself pressed on, nor did an inscription, in memory of some Saxon prince, cut on the living rock, tempt us to halt. Before us lay a broad reach of pastures on an inclined plane, the azure of the heavens bounding its upper margin. Thither then we eagerly held our way, leaving guides, horses, and companions far behind. Twenty times, during the afternoon, I had been reminded of the Pilgrim's Progress, by the rocks, marshes, burdens, and weary ascents, and it now appeared as if the end of our labours, like his, was to be heaven. Upward then we urged, until, without the smallest sense of fatigue, we stood on the very verge of that line which for half an hour had lain before us, bounded by air!

For myself, I can fairly say, that, the occasion of a total eclipse of the sun excepted, I never felt so deep a sentiment of admiration and awe, as at that exquisite moment. So greatly did reality exceed the pictures we had formed, that the surprise was as complete as if nothing had been expected. The first effect was really bewildering, leaving behind it a vague sensation, that the eye had strangely assembled the rarest elements of scenery, which were floating before it, without order, in pure wantonness. To this feeling, the indefinite form of the lake of Lucerne greatly contributed, for it stretches out its numerous arms in so many different directions, as, at first, to appear like water in the unreal forms of the fancy. Volumes of mist were rolling swiftly along it, at the height of about two thousand feet above its surface, and of as many below ourselves, allowing us to look through the openings, in a way to aid the illusion.

The party came up in time to enjoy the effects of the vapour before it blew entirely away. We were at the point which is called the Righi Staffel, and I can describe the position no better, than by likening it to the roof of a shed, placing the spectator on its upper edge. The entire mountain is near thirty miles in circumference at its base, standing like an advanced bastion of the Alpine range, separated from all others, and the place we occupied was more than 4000 feet above the adjoining lakes, and about 5500 above the sea.

The manner in which Lucerne coquetted with us, before the vapour drove away, was indescribably beautiful. This town, which is surrounded by ancient walls, that are bristling with towers, and which contains many striking objects in its churches and other edifices, was actually several leagues distant, though it appeared nearly beneath the eye. But why speak of one object, when there were a thousand? Of towns, there were Küsnacht, Sarnen, Lucerne; and villages without number. The blue of the water, too, imbedded, as it was, in dark mountains, was alone sufficient to make an uncommon landscape. It was of the colour of the skies in the old Italian paintings, which every one from the northern regions is ready to pronounce preposterous, but which was certainly seen here, in the other element, and to a degree almost to cause us to believe we had made acquaintance with a new nature.

As we did not choose to stay at the inn which has been erected near this enchanting spot, with the bald head of the mountain at no great distance, and in plain view, we pressed forward for the Righi Kulm, or head. Having still a little time to look about us, however, the guide led us to a place at which the water had made a passage through the rocks, and where a stone dropped in the orifice above, found its way out at the side, several hundred feet down the high perpendicular wall which forms this face of the mountain. As you are so familiar with the state of New York, before quitting the Righi Staffel, I may give you some idea of the nature of its view by telling you that it is not unlike that from the terrace of the Pine Orchard, with the material difference, however, of the spectator being twice as high above the adjoining country, and three times higher above tide. The Righi is nearly naked of trees, too, at this elevation; the mountain is better placed, standing more forward from the great ranges; the atmosphere has that visible transparency which one observes in the most limpid water, and which great artists sometimes succeed in throwing around a landscape, while the country seen from the Kaatskill, will bear no comparison, in either natural objects or artificial accessaries, with those which cover the whole face of the land in the region I am describing.

I very well know that these comparisons are little likely to find favour among patriots, in a country in which it is permitted to say with impunity what one will of the institutions, the work of man, and for which men are or ought to be responsible; but where it is *lèse majesté* to whisper aught against the perfection of natural objects, unless some plausible connexion can be made out between them and democracy. American *bon ton*, in these matters, is of a singularly delicate texture, polite patriotism spreading its mantle before even the cats and dogs, when it will suffer those sturdy truths, which form the true glory of the nation, to defend themselves in the best manner they can. Thank God! they are strong enough to go alone. At the risk, however, of being set down as one spoiled by travelling,—a dire calamity!—and of certain defeat, should it ever be my ill luck to be put in the way of preferment by a "regular nomination," I now tell you the Pine Orchard will compare with the Righi, only as the Kaatskill will compare with the falls of Trenton, and that the Hudson, unrivalled as a river and in the softer landscape scenery, bears some such resemblance to the lake of the Four Cantons, in the grand and the sublime, as the Falls of the Canada do to those of the Niagara.

After viewing the fissure in the rocks, which threatens another land-slip at no distant day, we left the edge of the precipice, and followed a circuitous path which led to the summit. Here, although no longer taken by surprise, we enjoyed a still more extended and magnificent prospect. The mountain rises like a cone, from the shores of Zug preserving this form for nearly half a circle, when it joins the more irregular and huge mass already alluded to, and up one of whose sides we had been climbing. At the extreme northern end, or that which overhangs the lake just mentioned, the conical form is preserved, even above the inclined plane of the Staffel, until it reaches the height of near 5000 feet above the neighbour-waters, and of more than 6000 feet above the sea.

The summit of the Righi Kulm may contain three or four acres, on a slightly inclined plane, the irregular section of an irregular cone. There are a lodging house *à la Suisse*, stables, a cross that is visible at a great distance from below, and an elevated platform, whence the most extended view can be obtained. This spot is without tree or shrub, but it is sufficiently well covered with grass.

Most views lose in the detail what they gain in extent, by climbing mountains. After the first feeling of satisfaction at commanding so many objects with the eye is abated, the more critical amateur misses those minuter points of beauty which we come most to love, and which are lost for the want of the profile in bird's eye prospects. In Switzerland, however, this remark is less true than elsewhere; the grand scale of its nature rendering a mountain, even when reversed, a mountain still. As most of the country is in high relief, the shadows remain distinct, and little is lost, or rather that which remains is so palpable and bold, that the minuter parts are not missed. In the view from the Righi, towards the north and north-west, it is true, this remark is not quite infallible, for in that direction the eye is limited only by distance, the country being generally broken, but comparatively low. Even this wide sweep of vision, however, helps to make up the sublime, being map-like, distinct, and in remarkable contrast to the magnificent confusion of Alpine peaks in the opposite points of the compass.

The lake of Zug, being the nearest, is the most conspicuous sheet of water that is seen from the Righi Kulm. Over the dark blue expanse of this oval basin, the spectator seems literally to hang, as if suspended in a balloon. There is a spot, in particular, from which it appears as if one might almost leap into the lake, and nowhere is its southern shore visible immediately beneath the mountain. Art and its lovely valley, the desolation of Goldau, and the vast chasm in the mountain itself whence the ruin came, the little lake of Lowerz, the town of Schwytz, were ranged along the left. Behind them rose mountains in a crowd and confusion that render description hopeless. I leave your imagination to body out the thousand grand or picturesque forms in which these granite piles lift their bald heads, for in that quarter few were covered with snow.

I cannot tell you how many lakes are visible from the Righi Kulm. I counted thirteen; besides which the lakes of Zurich and Lucerne peep out, from behind the mountains, in no less than six different places, each basin looking like a separate body of water. Then there are many rivers, drawn through rich meadows in blue winding lines. Everywhere the waters were dark as ultramarine. Of towns, and churches, and towers, it is almost commonplace to speak, on such an occasion. They dotted the panorama, however, in all directions; for it was not possible to look into one of the many valleys which opened around us like a spreading fan, without their meeting the eye.

I presume you think you have now obtained some just impressions of the view from the Righi. So far from this, I have yet scarcely alluded to its leading, its most wonderful feature. The things mentioned, beyond a question, are the first to strike the eye, and for a time they occupy the attention; but the most sublime beauties of this elevated stand are to be found in the aspect of the high Alps. These peaks are clustered all along the southern horizon, looking hoary, grim, and awful; a congress of earthly giants. They are seen distinctly only at short intervals, in the morning and evening. Frequently they are shut up in a gloom adapted to their chill mysteries, and then again parts appear, as whirlwinds and mists drive past. At such moments they truly seem the region of storms.

Amid the stern group, it is possible to distinguish the Jung Frau, and all her majestic neighbourhood; the Titlis, my Bernese discovery; and a hundred more that I could not name, if I would. I believe none of the great southern range of the Alps, including Mont Blanc and Monte Rosa, came into the view. They are excluded by the great height of the nearer line of the Oberland.

We found a good many travellers on the Kulm, mostly Germans. Every one was too much occupied with himself, however, and with the great objects of the ascent, to waste the time in intercourse. The guide-books speak of the fearful nature of the precipices, and of getting down on the hands and knees to look over their brows; but I cannot say we were so humbled; for though imposing and grand, I found no difficulty in standing near the verge, and of sustaining my female companions there. As for W[illiam], he went skipping and bounding along the outer edge of the plane, in a manner so goat-like that I was compelled to check him. Steadiness in such situations is, I believe, purely physical, and of course hereditary. The father of W[illiam] was remarkable for this property, and had he been a Swiss, he would have made a notorious chamois hunter.

The Righi Kulm was the scene of a melancholy event, not a great while since. A German—a Prussian I believe—ascended with his wife. From some cause or other, (insanity, most probably,) the poor man took it into his head to leap off. It would seem that he announced his intention, for the screams and entreaties of his wife induced the guide to interfere. After a severe struggle, the German got away, and effected his purpose. The first fall is estimated at about eight hundred feet; and when the body was sought, by torch light, it was found necessary to throw it down another precipice before it could be brought to a path.

The house was crowded, and although there is a private parlour or two they were occupied, and we were obliged to take a table in the general eating room. Most of the company were quiet and well behaved; but there were three or four German swaggerers who were sufficiently disagreeable. These gentry, students I believe, talked loud and dogmatically, filled the air with smoke, and, in walking, stamped like horses. I think they were the *ne plus ultra* of vulgar self-importance.

The night was windy, but it was cheered by a misty moon. I walked out alone, to enjoy the novelty of so unusual a situation. We seemed to be raised in the air, on an elevated platform, for the gales to beat against. The views were dim and extraordinary, but, at moments, of singular wildness. Once or twice, during the night, I awoke with a sort of sensation of flying; nor do I think it impossible that the house may yet slide off, from its giddy perch, before the high winds that prevail here in autumn. In such a case, it would probably be found floating in one of the lakes.

We were up early, of course, and enjoyed the rising of the sun. The mists were soon stirred, and the clouds began to float between us and the lower world. One, in particular, came sailing on our own level, and presently the whole summit was wrapt in vapour. The feeling, as you may suppose, was much like that of being in a heavy fog. For a few moments we could not see across the Kulm. Then it blew away, and we saw the vapour flying towards the Alps. We had some exquisite glimpses through the mist at the lakes, and once or twice the whole line of the Upper Alps stood out in noble relief from the horizon. The mountains appeared to have come nearer to us, and were more awful than ever. Every minute, however, changed the appearance of objects, until the sun prevailed, when the day shone forth, fair and genial.

Letter XIII.

MY DEAR———,

The ladies determined to descend on foot, and we left the inn immediately after breakfast. Just before the door of the house at the Staffel, the guide took the way over the brow of the precipice, in a manner that looked very much like jumping down it. We found, notwithstanding, a good and, at that season, a sufficiently secure path. It is not always without danger, however; for, a few hundred feet down the mountain, he showed us a spot where he had slipped the previous spring. He had slidden, on the frozen snow, to the very edge of a precipice, whence a fall would have been destruction. He saved himself by the point of his iron-shod walking staff, and was rescued from the perilous situation by the aid of his companions.

The descent was very pleasant, and far from difficult. At first, there were a few sharp declivities, but we soon reached the meadows that lie along the bases of the mountain. A party of pilgrims, from *Notre Dame des Neiges*, passed us, chanting the *aves* alternately, the male and female voices harmonizing sweetly as usual. We made a short halt at a chalet that stands on a terrace, where we got some milk, and whence we had a fine and more earthly view of the two lakes, than that from the Kulm. This would be a lovely spot for a summer retreat.

On our left, as we passed through some extensive meadows, the top of a small *château*, quite in ruins, showed itself from out a copse. This had been one of the holds held by Gessler, who had several in the mountains. To this place he was coming when killed by Tell. The latter event occurred lower down, at a spot where a good carriage-road now passes from Art, around the base of the Righi, and by the shores of the lake of Zug, leading to Küsnacht and Lucerne. It is called the *chemin creux*,* (or, as we should term it in America, the dug-way,) from the

---

* In German, *die hohle Gasse*.

circumstance of the path being cut between two banks. Tell took the *bailli* at a disadvantage, in this narrow defile, protected himself by a thicket. He killed him outright by an arrow. History, which too often trespasses on the grounds of a sister muse, puts a fine speech into the mouth of the mountaineer, but these things are generally done in a very quiet manner, and without much parade of sentiment. It is singular so little is known of Tell. Some writers affect to doubt whether such a man ever existed. But his birth seems to be certain, though a mystery still hangs over his death. One version of it says he was drowned in trying to save a child. He does not appear to have been more than a resolute mountaineer, who was willing to risk his life for liberty. Tell was one of the conspirators of the Grütli, but not a chief. Walter Furst, Werner Stauffach, and Arnold de Melchthal were the three leaders, each of whom brought with him, to the celebrated meadow, ten followers. Independence was not so much the object of these patriots, as relief from the tyranny of subordinates, and private grievances lay at the bottom of their zeal. Their measures were precipitated by the affair at the *chemin creux*, and the revolt commenced immediately. Its success has led to the establishment of the present Swiss Confederacy.

Gessler was killed the 18th Nov. 1307, and yet here is the same little hollow pass in the road, in which the deed was done! The castle was taken and destroyed, in January, 1308, and there stands its weather-beaten towers, much as they were left by the assailants; but it is now doubted whether Tell ever lived, and no one can say, certainly, where or how he died! The life of a man, truly, makes but a point in the march of time, his own hands rearing monuments that outlast his memory!

We reached Küsnacht, after a charming walk of three hours and a half. Here we discharged the guide, and took a boat for Lucerne. The course lay down a deep bay, when, turning a head-land, we proceeded by the main lake to its foot. A worse boat could not have invented, there being no very sensible difference between its bottom, and the "top-hamper" of the wooden canopy. Sometimes our movement was very crab-like, and once I really thought we were about to try the sailing qualities of the roof. I am inclined to think it was just the worst craft in Switzerland, for most of the rest had awnings, and did go bow foremost. But we could get no other.

We passed two or three very small rocky islands, quite near the shore. Notwithstanding the awkwardness of the navigation, it proved to be a pleasant row, and we entered the port of Lucerne, which is the river Reuss, in safety, and in pretty good season. For the latter advantage, we were somewhat indebted to a fine breeze, that sent us along, for the last hour, in a very "will ye, nill ye" fashion.

Ordering dinner, we hastened to see the sights. One is a wounded lion, carved in the living rock, after a model by Thorwaldsen, and erected in honour of those Swiss guards who were cut to pieces at the taking of the Tuileries, in 1792. The keeper was a survivor of that bloody day, and he discharged his duty with the courtesy of an attendant upon kings. As a work of art, this lion is justly extolled, though I think it inferior to one of the two celebrated animals of Canova. Thorwaldsen is usually more successful, on the whole, with the grand than with the beautiful, while with Canova the reverse was notoriously the fact. Yet, in this instance, the modeller of Venuses, and Hebes, and Magdalens, appears to have stepped out of his usual track, and to have struggled successfully with his great competitor.

There is at Lucerne a raised map of Switzerland, on an extensive scale, which is well worthy of being seen. It nearly fills a large hall, and the mountains, glaciers, lakes, villages, roads, paths, ay, even the chalets, (meaning the traveller's chalets,) are designated with singular beauty and truth. It is the work of many industrious years, and quite a treasure in its way. These maps are now common enough, especially in Germany, but this, besides having the great merits of a size and an accuracy that surpass all others, is said to have been the first of the kind. I traced our different excursions by it with great satisfaction, and, with the closest scrutiny, could detect no essential error. Of course, an infinity of detail is wanting, though there is even more of this than one would be apt to imagine. Having all Switzerland in a room, I was enabled to satisfy myself that my own discovery was really the Titlis.

One of the bridges of Lucerne (covered of course) has a dance of Death painted beneath its roof, like the celebrated painting, on the same subject, at Basle. It is a miserable conceit, and only valuable as a relic of another age, and of a different state of manners.

The walls of Lucerne enclose a good deal of empty space. Like those of Zug, and many other Swiss towns, they are picturesque, being well garnished with towers, ornaments of a landscape that can hardly be misplaced, or so constructed as not to embellish the view, but which have become quite useless in modern warfare, except as against a *coup de main*, having been built in the fourteenth century.

We went to bed with a sense of fatigue hitherto unknown in all our rambles. I rose, on the following morning, with a stiffness about the muscles of the legs, which I had never before experienced, and glad enough was I to see the carriage draw up. W[illiam], on the other hand, left us on foot, taking the celebrated valley of Entlibuch, in his way to la Lorraine.

Our road now lay by the open country, and, though always through a beautiful district, it offered little, except in the neatness and architecture of the dwellings, of a very interesting kind. We passed the lake of Sempach, on whose banks, in 1386, was fought one of the great battles that assured the liberties of this country. On this occasion, 1400 of the Swiss were opposed to 6000 of the Austrian chivalry. The latter dismounted, and, forming a phalanx that was thought impenetrable, stood with their lances presented, to receive the assault. The Swiss placed themselves in column, presenting an angle, and charged. They were repulsed by a wall of iron. At this crisis, when the Austrians were beginning to open, in order to surround them, Arnold de Winkelried, a gentleman of Unterwalden, called to his companions to protect his wife and children. He then rushed forward, and, being of great size and strength, he seized the ends of as many lances as his arms could embrace, and as he fell, pierced by their points, he drew his enemies down with him. By this opening, his countrymen penetrated, throwing the heavily-armed Austrians into confusion.

This is the Swiss account of the matter, and, numbers excepted, it is probably true in all its leading points. There are certain great events embalmed in history that it will not do to question, and which, even when false, it is unwise to disturb, as they are so many incentives to noble deeds. The early ages of Switzerland, moreover, show great self-devotion in her people, and I believe this act of Winkelried rests on much better authority than the affair of Tell and the apple.

We stopped to take a *goûter* in the middle of the day, and such a *goûter* I never before essayed. We asked for a fruit tart, and (odours and nosegays!) they gave us one made of onions; which the landlady maintained was a very good fruit, in its way. Of course, we ate exactly as much of it as we wished.

There were fewer farm-houses this day than usual; though the husbandry seemed good and the country rich. As we approached Argovie again, the system of irrigation reappeared. We passed an ancient *château;* got another peep of Aarberg, through the hills, but from a side directly opposite to that whence we had first beheld it; had a beautiful glimpse of a *château*, seated on the side of the Jura; met the Aar, soon after, against whose current fifteen men were pulling a boat; and made our halt at Langenthal, for the night, in sufficient season to fill the vacuum that the onions had not occupied.

A fine village and a beautiful country, though quite level. We were again in the great valley of the Aar, you will remember, or in the district that separates the Jura from the Alps. We stopped at an inn which was the very *beau idéal* of rural comfort. The landlord was a hearty, well fed countryman; I dare say a magistrate of some kind or other; civil without servility, kind, obliging, and disposed to do all we wanted without fuss or the appearance of venality. In short, he was the exact counterpart of a respectable New England inn-keeper; a happy mixture of what a freeman ought to be, with what one of his calling finds it for his interest to become. As I walked like a horse with the spring-halt, he good naturedly inquired if I had received a hurt. Touching the calf of a leg, I merely answered, "Righi Berg." The laugh that followed was hearty and good humoured, and seemed to be mingled with honest exultation at the triumph of his mountains. It was contagious, and a merrier acquaintance was never commenced. We had delicious tea, a good supper, and as excellent beds as can be made with feathers—a material that ought to be declared contraband of sleep. We were served in our own room by a daughter of the inn-keeper, who by her intelligence and decency also strongly reminded us of home.

There are many manufactories at Langenthal, and near it, though in the canton of Lucerne, is a convent of monks. The latter are Dominicans, and we were told there were thirty-three of them. This place is in a corner of Berne, and but a mile or two from the boundaries of Lucerne, Soleure, and Argovie.

On our way from Langenthal, we saw the first *garde champêtre* that had been met in Switzerland. There are plenty of *gens d'armes* in Berne; light men, commonly, with fusees slung at the back, wearing brown uniforms, shackos, and swords; soldiers in reality, though less military in their mien than those of France. We are too much in the practice of confounding the substance with the shadow, on all these matters, in America. It is the fashion to say that we have had a good training in liberty through our English descent. I believe the pretension to be singularly unfounded. It is true, that some of the great principles of English law accustom the subject to the exercise of certain rights, and create a disposition to defend them. But where do not similar feelings exist, as respects some immunity or other? There is no despotism so strong, that it is not obliged to respect usages, whatever may be the authority of the monarch, on paper. The great difference between England and the other nations of Europe, in this respect, has arisen from the fact that her rights are admitted in theory, while those of the continent have existed more as concessions from the monarch. England, too, has had more of them; and the institution of juries, in particular, has caused an admixture of authority that, beyond a question, and in despite of gross abuses, has given tone and confidence to the subject. Still, as many fallacies and defects have followed this system of immunities, perhaps, as positive benefits. Take, as an example, the high-sounding privilege that "every man's house is his castle." This has a big appearance; and, in a state of society in which arrests in civil cases were liable to be abused by power, it may possibly have been some protection against practical tyranny; but, admitting the principles that the debtor ought to be made to pay, and that his person must be seized in order to proceed against his effects, on what sound notion of right and wrong is a law to be defended which enables him who owes, to bar his door and laugh at his creditor through a window? If a debtor ought to pay, and if service of process be necessary to bring him into court, it is rank nonsense to call this evasion of the right by a word as sacred as that of liberty. English jurisprudence and English liberty abound with these contradictions, many of which have descended to America, as heir-looms.

One of the consequences of considering mere franchises as political liberty, is a confusion between cause and effect, and prejudices like these which exist against a *gensdarmerie*. Political liberty does not exist in the nature of particular ordinances, but in the fact that the mass of a community, in the last resort, holds the power of making such municipal regulations and of doing all great and sovereign acts, as may comport with their current necessities. A state that set up a dictator, so long as its people retain the practical means of resuming their authority, would, in principle, be freer than that which should establish a republic, with a limited constituency, and a provision against change. Democracies may submit to martial law, without losing any part of their democratic character, so long as they retain the right to recall the act. Thus may a democracy commission *gens d'armes* to execute its most familiar ordinances, without in the least impairing its political pretension. Laws are enacted to be executed; and if a man with a gun on his shoulder be necessary to their execution, it surely is no sign that liberty is on the wane that such agents are employed, but just the contrary,* by proving that the people are determined their will shall be enforced. Liberty does not mean license, either through franchises or

---

* In England there is a government of what is called three estates—or, of King, Lords, and Commons. Here are three distinct elements, admitted into the very organization of the system. The king and the peers hold powers that are hereditary;—the commons, at first, did represent that portion of the community below the lords, which in fact knew enough, or cared enough, about government, to take any great interest in its management. But the king, besides a power to make peace and war, and to create peers, and to dispose of all dignities and places; besides administering justice by his deputies, and executing all the laws through his agents, had also legislative authority co-ordinate with that of Parliament. His veto was absolute. It is scarcely necessary to add, that under such a system, the king literally governed, checked, according to circumstances, by the Parliament. The peers were few, and though addicted to rebellion and conspiracies, they were effectually managed by attainders and the axe. So long as the monarch could make and unmake them at pleasure, and the commons were poor, impotent, and ignorant, both were virtually his tools. He reigned and governed; reigned, in virtue of his birthright, and governed all the better, perhaps, by this machinery of a spurious liberty.

This state of things was gradually changed by the progress of society. A succession of feeble and corrupt princes, too, concurred to assist the natural tendencies of events, which is generally to strengthen political aristocracies at

through disorders, but an abiding authority, in the body of a nation, to adapt their laws to their necessities.

We passed by Hindelbank, on our way home, (for so we term

---

the expense of the sovereign. After wresting power, little by little, from the Stuarts, the last of that family was finally set aside, the aristocracy profiting by a religious excitement to effect its ends. The constitution, as it now stands, was established in the reign of his successor, though subsequent ages have greatly developed its latent principle, which has tended from the first to convert the government to an oligarchy. The result is no secret. The King of England is permitted to do but one official act, except through the agency of his ministers, and, under the liabilities of ministerial responsibility. This one act, is a power to name his ministers. This power, however, would still leave him a monarch, were it real. It is notoriously unreal, the king having been reduced to be a mere parliamentary echo. Practically, he is compelled to respect the pleasure of the two houses, before he can even name those who are called his advisers.

The power to dissolve Parliament is available only to the faction of his ministry, which, as a matter of course, wields it solely for its own ends. If it can get a majority by a dissolution, well; if not, the alternative is resignation; the pleasure and judgment of the king himself counting for nothing.

In such a state of things the exercise of the veto becomes useless. So long as the ministry, which in fact alone can use it, is in the majority, it would not be likely to be called for—certainly not in any question of gravity—and, when in a minority, it is compelled to make way for successors, who would be of the same manner of thinking as Parliament. A dissolution might postpone, but it could not change these results. It might, possibly, a little modify them as to forms. Hence then, arises the fact, that political contests in England, are actively carried on *in the legislative bodies;* for these in truth decide on the character and complexion of the administration; and the fact, that nearly a century has elapsed, since any king of England has been known to use the co-ordinate power, which, by the old theory of the constitution, he was thought to possess in legislation, by resorting to the veto. In these later times, even his right to dissolve Parliament, twice in succession, has been pronounced unconstitutional. It was done by Mr. Pitt, and successfully, but with the moral certainty that he was sustained by the nation, and, what was of more account, with a belief that he must prevail in obtaining majorities, through the great influence of the patronage he wielded. The test of power, it will be seen, rests always in the fact of parliamentary majorities, the assumed prerogative of the king counting for nothing. In short, in the face of a majority, the royal authority is rendered null, or as if it did not exist. The indirection by which the aristocracy rules in no manner impeaches the result, since with these results are connected the entire action and efficiency of the government. The state of things is exactly reversed from what it was in the days of Elizabeth, who governed *through her Parliament;* whereas Parliament now governs *through the king.* There can be no question, that England has made much nearer approaches to

the temporary abodes in which we dwell, in these distant countries,) and cast many longing glances at the little rural church,
that contains the admirable monument of Madame Langhans.

---

liberty than formerly, by this change, for, while the sway of a limited constituency which, in itself, is controlled by a body of great landholders, is not true
political liberty, it has at least the machinery of a free state, is compelled to
promulgate the opinions of a free state—opinions, that, like drops of water,
will, in time, wear away even the rock—and is certain to raise up a powerful
body of dissentients which, in the end, may become in very fact the political
and governing majority itself. In such a state of society, therefore, if all that is
extorted from the prince be not really gain to the people, it has that appearance, accustoming men to reflect on their rights, and eventually securing a
still nearer approach to the eternal principles of natural justice, which, in
truth, contain the essence of political liberty.

Let us now look at America. Here, the sovereignty of the people, or of a
popular constituency, is both avowed and maintained. All political power is
expressly, periodically, and practically, representative; not representative, as
is pretended by the English writers and declaimers on constitutional law, or
on the principle that all power of this nature, whether derived from descent
or not, is a trust, and to be exercised for the benefit of the whole; but representative on this general and just principle, representative in form, and representative by the constant recurrence to the constituency for fresh authority; in
short, representative in fact. The judiciaries are no practical exception to this
rule, for they perform no original acts of government, are purely interpreters
of the law on principles which the other representatives may alter at will, and
discharge their trusts under such responsibilities as to render abuses very un-
likely to occur. They, too, are practically representative, through the fact that
the constituency has retained a power to set them aside, or to modify their
organization, and their trusts, at pleasure.

These facts are true, both as respects the states, and as it respects the Federal government. It follows that every trust committed to each branch of the
government is to be literally exercised by that particular branch, *and by no
other*, else is the fundamental law violated not only in its letter, *but in its most
vital principle*. For the legislative branches to pretend to check the executive
branch, in such a polity, in the exercise of its legitimate functions, is not liberty
in any shape, since it is a direct attack, not on the incumbent, (though such
may be its pretended object,) but on the rights of the constituents, who have
chosen to make this distribution of power, as well as to select the different
agents. No truth can be clearer than the fact, that the delegate who exceeds
his authority, trespasses on that of his principal. Now, while Parliament may
wrest power from the king, who is representative only by a powerless theory,
in the interests of the nation, and consequently in those of liberty, the American Legislature that wrests authority from an American Executive, or in any
manner impedes the exercise of his constitutional trusts, invades the rights of
a common superior. There is not even the excuse of a defective and otherwise

In another hour, we alighted at la Lorraine, after a delightful excursion of eleven days, during which we had scarcely an hour of really bad weather, an advantage of rare occurrence in Swit-

---

irremediable organization for such a step, the constituencies having especially reserved to themselves the means of making all necessary changes.

These truths, so evident by the very organization and condition of society, and so unanswerably proved by the letter of the constitution, become still more apparent, when we reflect on the consequences of their violation. Not only do the people gain, in effect, by the invasions of Parliament on the authority of the crown, but harmony in the action of government, an indispensable requisite to peace at home and dignity abroad, is preserved by the right to dictate to the King whom he shall choose for his ministers. A continued collision between the legislative and executive powers of the state cannot exist in England, since the latter must be made to conform to the former. Before the revolution means were found to make Parliament conform to the will of the king; since the revolution, means have been found to make the king conform to the will of Parliament. But here, the reverse is exactly the case. In England, ministerial conflicts are necessarily legislative conflicts; here, they are decided by the people, *and ought to be conducted only before the people*. The American legislator, who suffers any considerations of effecting a change in the incumbency of the executive, in any manner, to influence even his public speeches, abuses his situation, (though the rights of debate are protected,) for he is not delegated to effect any such purpose, nor can he, *as a legislator*, be instrumental in producing such an end, without a complete perversion of the governing principle of the institutions, which infers that the *represented* are to impart their tone to the *representatives*, and not to receive it from them!

Abuses of this sort in debate, and performed by indirection, are perhaps inseparable from human frailties. But surely we have not yet reached the pass, when, under the pretence of liberty (!) one portion of a branch of the government can step out of its sphere, with impunity, and sit in judgment on the conduct of another branch of the government, by overt acts, as was the fact in the celebrated resolution of the Senate, during the session of 1833–4! It matters nothing whether the President had or had not exceeded his powers, in the act which led to this vote. If the Senate be suffered openly to assume the power of censuring him when he is wrong, the time is not distant, when, to effect the ends of party, he will be censured when he is right. The consequences of a continuance of such a practice, *and, unless firmly put down in the outset, a practice it will become*, will be a confusion and a want of harmony among the several powers of the state, against which the constitution has provided no remedy, and which, in the end, will of necessity, lead to further innovations, as a protection from its own abuses, and thus ultimately transfer from the constituent to the representative, an authority that is inherently necessary to liberty. The school-boy use of the epithet tyranny can delude no honest and reflecting American, on these essential points. The very act which may be, and is essential to liberty, as government is instituted in England, zerland, more especially among the mountains. Rain, indeed, is almost the only drawback on the pleasures of a summer residence in the cantons.

---

becomes a most dangerous usurpation, as government is instituted here. There is, moreover, no necessity for any such interference on the part of the legislature, the constitution having provided the judiciary, as the guardian of all law, whether fundamental or merely ministerial, reserving the *people* as arbiters in the last resort. There is but a single pretence for this legislative interference, and that is one which infers a radical defect in the most radical feature of the government, viz. an incompetency in the constituency to discharge the duties which this very constituency has imposed on itself.

The same truths apply to the use of the veto. It may be liberty in England to repress the exercise of the veto power in the crown, as separated from parliamentary majorities: while, with parliamentary majorities it clearly becomes unnecessary. But in America, *the veto is instituted in the interests of liberty*. The greatest power, and, of necessity, the power most to be apprehended in this country, is that of Congress. The veto is given to the Executive, therefore, that, as a representative of the entire constituency, he may check the greatest power of the state in the exercise of its authority. The fact that he is only one man, and that Congress is composed of many men, gives additional grounds for sustaining him in the discharge of a duty so delicate, since, it is notorious, that in a really free state, there is far more danger to be apprehended from bodies of men, than from individuals. Our own history abounds with instances of the Executives shrinking from the responsibility of doing their duties, on the one hand, and of legislative innovations on the other.

Each measure is to be judged by its separate merits, as a matter of course, but I speak here of the abstract question. To accuse the Executive of setting up his will arbitrarily against that of the numerous bodies which compose the two houses of Congress, without reference to the merits or demerits of his reasons, and idly to compare his wholesome authority with the nominal authority of which Parliament has stripped the king, thereby centring, in fact, all the powers of the state in one of its branches, is to quarrel with one of the most salutary of the expedients which have been devised to prevent this very accumulation of trusts here, and to assail one of the most wholesome checks provided by the constitution.

The popular reasoning and popular feeling, too, on these important questions, among what are called the enlightened classes, go to show what I think must strike every man who has lived much out of his own country, or how very far opinion is behind facts. While the facts of this case are so peculiarly American, or, to express myself with greater accuracy, *would* have been American, had not the constitution been so rudely violated, both in its spirit and in its letter, the opinions that have been uttered have been very generally English.

I am aware that these are bold opinions to utter in a country where the mass has become so consolidated that it has no longer any integral parts; where the individual is fast losing his individuality in the common identity; and where, in a political sense, the only public is the *public servant!*

Letter XIV.

DEAR———,

The Swiss certainly surpass us in courtesy of manner when speaking of the sisterhood of cantons. I do not remember to have seen a coarse allusion, a discourteous expression, or a sneer of any kind, in the remarks which frequently occur in the journals, concerning the measures of their neighbours. I was much amused the other day, at finding the people termed "The honourable public" in a proclamation. "The praise-worthy canton of ———," "The respectable canton," "The honourable canton," are very usual modes of designating a sister state. In America we presume on our common parentage, fraternity, and identified existence, and too often treat each other with a homely familiarity, there being in truth less real difference (there is abundance of imaginary) between a skipper of Kennebunk and a planter of the Arkansas, than there frequently is to be found between two Swiss peasants whose cottages may be seen in the same valley.

After staying three days at la Lorraine, to "set our house in order," we left Berne, once more, for Thun. This time we took the left bank of the Aar, and were highly gratified with the views it presented. More *châteaux*, or rather more country houses, appeared than in the former excursions, and as the eagerness for the grander scenery abates, we begin to find a thousand new beauties in the common landscapes. Those parts of Switzerland which are not absolutely among the mountains, may vie with the best portions of most other countries in simple rural scenery, possessing, also, in addition to the ordinary features of all such views, the advantage of having a frame-work of the Jura, or of the Alps, or, as often happens, of both. In our drive to Thun, the southern background of the charmingly rural country through which we travelled, was the brown side of the Stockhorn, a mountain that rises above the lake of Thun five thousand feet, or one-fourth higher than the highest peak of the Kaatskills, and nearly seven thousand above the sea. Behind this, again, hovered the silvery peak of the Blümlis Alp, radiant, pure, and shining like a glory.

The approach to Thun, on this side of the river, is much finer than that on the other. We crossed a wide plain, keeping the picturesque, little, old *château* directly before us, like a lighthouse, and swept round the walls, nearly half a mile, before we reached a gate. These walls are built of small stones, rough-cast; and, as they are embattled, and are well relieved by little circular towers, they, at least, help the scenery, which, I believe, is their chief merit. It is scarcely possible to fortify a town in Switzerland against the attacks of modern warfare, so many commanding positions lying near them all. Here and there, an exception is to be found; but the true policy of this country is to meet the enemy at the threshold. The whole region is a great natural bastion; and France or Austria will be sure to offer succour, perhaps compel its acceptance, in the event of invasion by either party. The Swiss, however, have seen Russian battalions pouring through their defiles. The Confederation has been formed and will be kept together more by outward pressure than by any natural cohesion. Could Savoy, Nice, the Tyrol, and the Vorarlberg be added to its territory, it would make a power quite capable of taking care of itself, and one altogether unique, by the conformation of the land, and the rustic habits of its people. As it is, "*les honorables cantons*" would be sadly troubled to make head against a vigorous combination, like that which partitioned Poland.

For the second time, we were treated with so much indifference, to give it a soft term, at the principal inn, that we left the house for *la Croix Blanche*. The guide, who was already engaged, manifested a good deal of surprise at this movement, intimating that we were quitting the genteelest house in the place. He was given to understand that less gentility and more civility would suit us better. The change proved a good experiment, in the latter important particular, at least; though the good people of *la Croix Blanche* seemed quite as much surprised as the guide himself, at finding English who were willing to favour them with their custom. You know we usually pass for English on the continent of Europe; and I have long since given up the attempt to explain. In France, however, one gets on pretty well, by observing that he came from the country to which the French gave independence some fifty years since. So completely are the French persuaded of the efficacy of their interference in the revolution, that when I asked an intelligent French friend to name the battles in which their troops were engaged, the answer was, "*Mais dans toutes les batailles, n'est-ce pas!*" France is much too rich in victories to trespass on our small claims to glory.

At Thun, I parted from the rest of my fellow travellers, who returned home, while, provided with a walking staff, (an ashen pole, six feet in length, and shod with iron,) and accompanied by the guide, who carried my knapsack, I took oars again for Neuhaus. I had engaged a boat for myself, and was just "shoving off," when a proposition was made by an Englishman to be of the party, with his wife and daughter. It would have been uncivil to refuse, and I consented. The wife was quiet and simple; but the husband was a thorough John Bull, who appeared to regard even the peak of the Jung Frau with sullen contempt, as if there were better things in its way in England. When I occasionally pointed out a strong feature in the view, his manner of assenting seemed to say, "it was pretty well for Switzerland;" and once when I drew his attention to a singularly beautiful effect produced by the sun on a mountain top, he muttered a reply, and immediately began to tell me how cheap mutton was in Herefordshire. His wife, a meek-looking little woman, appeared to acquiesce in all he said from habit; but I thought she turned longing eyes towards the mountains, and I make no doubt that their visit to Switzerland is owing to her secret admiration of nature. He probably takes his revenge for the trouble she has given him by dilating constantly, when they are alone, on the excellence of the *côtelettes* they might be quietly eating at home.

I was not sorry to get rid of my male companion at Neuhaus. He conscientiously offered to pay his fair proportion of the price of the boat; but, provoked at his mutton, I declined accepting his money, a little *en grand seigneur*. He was evidently both surprised and mortified, when, to relieve him, I took back half of that which had just been given to the boatmen. We parted civilly, and I was honoured with a stare, and a profound bow; for indifference to money is certain to command respect in England. We had not got five rods from the party, before the guide whispered that the Englishman had not paid enough, his share coming to three-fifths instead of one-half. He had been mortified at my folly in refusing to take any thing at first, and almost as much grieved at my ignorance, in not knowing better how to balance accounts. These little touches of national character are amusing enough—but, I know not how it is, the littlenesses one meets with among these sublime mountains occasion more disgust than they do in tamer countries!

The afternoon was fine, and I determined to pass the remainder of the day in exploring the valley, which lies between the lakes of Thun and Brienz, and which is very properly named Interlachen, (between lakes.) To avoid the crowd of travellers who frequent the inn at this place, I took a room at Unterseen for the night. They who throng baths, lodging houses, and fashionable places of resort, in a country like Switzerland, are usually ill qualified to enjoy its beauties, and I avoid them as so many blemishes. It is almost *primâ facie* evidence of unfitness for the scenery, to be caught in such a situation. Having secured a quiet room, I sallied forth, attended by the guide, a veteran who had passed his life in such service, relieved of his knapsack. As we walked onward, the old man began to converse, and I encouraged him, in order to come at the kernel as quickly as possible. In the outset, I discovered that he held democracy almost as cheap as a *parvenu* who had completely forgotten the struggles of his own probation. In speaking of the popular cantons, he observed that men like himself were permitted to have a voice in public affairs. This, certainly, was a home thrust, and it was an argument that I was forced to laugh at, in spite of a determination to discuss the matter gravely. German was his mother tongue; and I inquired how he liked the Germans? "Not as well as the French," was his answer. "But the French overran the country, and carried away all your treasure, and otherwise much abused Switzerland!" "All very true; but then the soldiers treated us better than the Germans. In the houses they were polite to the women, and they can live on a little bread and an onion. *Monsir*, a German will eat as much as three Frenchmen." There was no resisting the latter argument, especially in a country where half the population rarely taste meat.

This feeling towards the French, as a people, is very general in the countries they have invaded. I have not been in Spain since the last war; but many who have, tell me the French are often more esteemed by the people of the country than their English allies. Here, the preference is generally given to the French troops, over the Germans and Russians, the people distinguishing very properly between the acts of those who lead and of those who merely follow. All this, however, is no more than a very common consequence between manner and matter. No great body of men was probably ever more wanting in the first principles of morality than the armies of the French revolution, and yet, retaining the *suaviter* of the national character as it then existed, they were enabled to turn it to better account than probably would have been the case with more honesty and less tact.

We walked to the mouth of the vast gorge which leads towards Lauterbrunnen, and ascended a little hill, called the Rügen, which stands nearly before the entrance. I say a hill, for so it seemed to the eye amid the grandeur by which it was surrounded; but on ascending it, it proved to be in fact a mountain nearly as high as our own "Vision."

I was well rewarded for the trouble, by a noble panorama. The Wengern Alp appeared low in the throng of giants by which it was overtopped, and I could hardly persuade myself it was really the mountain, whence the lower world had looked so distant and diminutive. Behind it, the peaks of the Jung Frau and of the two Eigers, were glittering in the heavens, under the light of a setting sun, whose rays seemed to fall frozen from their snowy sides.

Near this little mountain is a ruin and a meadow, where the peasants have been accustomed to keep their rural games. A *fête* of this nature is spoken of in connexion with Mad. de Stäel, who was present; but what is Mad. de Stäel herself, much less her humours, in competition with the sublime altar that God has here reared in his own honour! I observed larches near thirty feet high growing on the crumbling walls.

The lake of Brienz is about as long as the Otsego, is materially wider, though much less indented by bays. Here the resemblance ceases. Instead of being *surrounded* by hills, some five or six hundred feet high, it is *imbedded* among mountains that divide the clouds. These masses are often nearly perpendicular, though chalets cling to their precipices, and rich water-falls stream down their sides. An island or two would make it perfect.

A female voice, singing an English air, was heard in the thicket as we returned. Presently we met a pretty young English girl in the narrow path, her bonnet dangling from a finger, like one who was out on a careless evening stroll near her paternal abode. The party to which she belonged was not far behind. Her notes ceased as I came in view, and the bow I made in passing was disregarded. She mistook me for an Englishman, and did not dare observe this simple act of civility—nay, of human feeling—even in Switzerland, lest I might not be of precisely as elevated a class as herself "at home." Had I been mistaken for a continental European, the case would have been different; though it may be questioned, had my real origin been known, whether I should have escaped without a frown.

These *rencontres* of travellers are rarely agreeable. The presence of strangers who appear to be engaged in *low-country pursuits*, mid such scenery, produces on me the impression of an unpicturesque irreverence for nature. I had just left a spot, too, where a young Swiss had been in beautiful keeping with the scenery. There is a small meadow in a dale near the ruin. The last rays of the sun were streaming across it, and a pretty peasant girl, with dishevelled hair, was raking together the scanty crop of grass. She was entirely alone, and seemed as innocent and as contented as she evidently felt secure. After all, she might have been out speculating on the picturesque, a suspicion that rudely obtruded itself when we met the English party.

As we descended the little mountain, several boats were seen pulling towards our own strand, and the evening, as the English say, was truly delicious. I had forgot to tell you that I clambered into the ruined tower, where I frightened two black-looking and most ill-omened birds from their roosts. I hope no evil will come of it!

These mountains sometimes produce sudden and startling effects. This evening, while retiring to bed, and after the candle was extinguished, I was struck with the sombre appearance of the night. Going to a window, all seemed dark and gloomy, when, raising my eyes gradually to the zenith in quest of a star, I found they had been ranging along the side of the black pile which frowns upon Unterseen. The night, in fact, was clear and cloudless.

The next morning found me on the way to Interlachen before the shops were open. While sauntering in front of the great gorge, in waiting for the guide, and looking at its noble mysteries, the honest old fellow came up, big with the intelligence that the hunters and guides of Grindelwald were in earnest in an intention to scale the Jung Frau; and that the attempt was to be made within a day or two. So many strangers were disposed to undertake the adventure, he added, that these mountaineers were incited to anticipate them, for the honour of Helvetia. It will give you some notion of the scale of Alpine nature, as well as of the purity of the atmosphere at this elevation, when I tell you that this morning, though distant from the spot more than three leagues, perhaps three and a half, I distinctly saw the little oven-shaped hole in the snow, whence the avalanche which has already been described had issued! I could not perceive that it seemed any smaller than when viewed from the Wengern Alp. It is possible, however, that more snow may have fallen from the same spot since our passage of the mountain; for I observed that a rock on the Wengern itself, which was then covered, was now bare.

The valley of Interlachen is ornamented by some as fine walnuts as I remember to have seen. Most of the fashionables were not out of their beds in the great lodging house, only two or three drowsy looking domestics being afoot. I did meet two young ladies, however, walking beneath the fine trees; though they appeared to be communicating secrets rather than admiring nature, as the tongue of one was in earnest motion, and the eyes of both were riveted on the ground—just in the way one would expect a soul-absorbing confidence to be given and received.

The boatmen were ready, and in half an hour we were on the lake of Brienz. There are no vineyards nor grain on the precipitous mountains by which it is surrounded; though Alpine pastures cover many of their sides, extending, in a few instances, quite to the summits.

Brienz stands immediately beneath a mountain, a perilous position in Switzerland, as has been proved by its own disasters. As the boat approached I counted one hundred and twenty brown roofs, besides the church, which is of stone, and which stands on a high rock a little without the cluster of houses. Several of the cascades that had been seen in August were now dry, the snows that supplied them having entirely melted. A torrent runs through the village, which, four years before, had swept away a house or two, drowning the inhabitants. Accidents from lightning, *sacs d'eau*, raging torrents, landslips, or rather falling rocks, and avalanches, are the regular Swiss calamities. To this may be added hail. I do not remember to have told you that there are companies of mutual assurance against the effects of hail, in some parts of Europe, and in this country in particular! This is a pass of circumspection to which we have not yet reached; though I believe we have something like it against losses from horse-thieves! On the whole, our companies argue the most advanced stage of civilization.

The boatmen pointed out a wall near the shore that rose about three feet above the surface of the lake, and said they had passed over it with their boat this very summer. They speak of the present as being both a warm and a dry season, both of which are great advantages in Swiss travelling.

We left Brienz on foot, passing the extensive *débris* of two wide torrents soon after quitting the place. At one of them I was told a village had been entirely swept away, and children had been saved of whose parentage nothing was known; the latter bearing the name of the village. One of our boatmen was descended from this unknown stock. After all, he is only in the condition of nine-tenths of mankind, in being ignorant of his ancestry.

We soon left the highway, beginning to ascend through broken pastures, among which cottages were plentifully scattered. After passing a rude little hamlet, from which there was a fine view down the lake, the ascent became more rapid. We next entered the woods, and took the mountain *en corniche*, by a very good bridle-path. A place was passed, where the face of an overhanging rock had fallen across the route, covering six or seven acres below with fragments; still it was not easy to trace the spot on the precipice above, whence the vast masses had come. A valley may be filled, or ruined here, and the mountain from which the desolation descended shall stand, apparently, as undiminished in magnitude, as it is unconscious of the ruin it has produced. From this point, where I stopped to rest, a part of the lake came beautifully into the view, and three brilliant waterfalls were in sight, leaping from precipices of dizzy height. Even the rushing sound of one came to us very distinctly across the broad valley. It descended about 700 feet, jumping playfully from shelf to shelf. The whole plain beneath was covered with dark barns, or chalets, of which I counted three hundred.

The ascent was gradual and easy, the path running beneath the shades of beeches, which we found very grateful, the day being warm, and the labour, though not severe, nearly constant. *Débris* abounded, but trees were growing among them all; a sure sign that ages had gone by since their fall.

At length a point on the mountain was reached, that commanded a view of Meyringen, with the whole of its rich bottom. Unfortunately there was no mist, and the scene was less enchanting than when first beheld. The edge of novelty, moreover, was taken off, and I found myself growing critical and fastidious: perhaps it would be better to say, more reasonable, and less hasty in my tastes: less under the influence of surprise and wonder, and more under that of the faculties of the mind. Travelling is an art, as well as another, and the experienced traveller has some such advantage over him who is setting up the business, as the connoisseur has over the mere tyro, in the fine arts. I had ceased to hunt for drapery, and fingers, and noses, and the other accessaries of the picture, to look more for expression and the thought.

The Aar brawled immediately beneath the point of rock just mentioned. Its bed had been nearly filled with *débris* washed down by the Alpbach, a torrent on the other side of the valley, and its waters were finding their way past it, through fifty little temporary channels, that they were as busy as ants in cutting for themselves. An unsightly swamp was likely to be the consequence. All this was lost to the eye, however, in travelling by the road beneath.

Here we struck off, nearly at right angles, toward the summit of the Brunig,* which is the name of the pass. It took us just

* Or, Brüning.

twenty minutes more to reach the pastures and meadows, that lie in the gorge, between two high mountains, which, quite luckily, it was not necessary to scale. The place was retired and pretty, vast fragments of rock being scattered among the verdant grass, as if the spot had formerly been a field of battle, where mountains had discharged their artillery at each other.

The descent now commenced, or rather we ceased to ascend. Soon after, I met our old acquaintance, the bear, carved on a stone, a sign I was once more on the borders of the great canton. At this point we entered the territory of Unterwald, the country of Winkelried, and one of the little districts that originally resisted the power of Austria. There are a few chalets, or rather cottages, on the pass, and at one of them I obtained a draught of milk, so delicious, that it will be remembered long after many a gorgeous banquet will be forgotten. Keeping in view the homely hospitality of the American woods, I scarcely dared offer to pay for it, in a place that looked so romantic and unsophisticated, but, sooth to say, the money did not come amiss. I believe, as a rule, that the Swiss may be considered, very generally, as sufficiently civilized to be paid. One knows that these things depend on the frequency of the demands, and, on the whole, he who has the means to pay is commonly all the better off for being required to pay; yet the act of constantly filling the palm appears singularly out of place amid this wild and magnificent scenery, where one could wish no coin were current, but that which has been stamped in the mint of nature.

While on the subject of money, it may be well to let you understand something of the *matériel* of this country. In the first place, having no banks, there is no paper in circulation; the bankers are principally dealers in exchanges, though I presume they lend money too, making their profits in the difference between what they pay and what they receive. Each canton has the power of striking its own money, and each canton, I believe, does; though many of the smaller limit their issues to the very lowest denominations of coin. The old French crown, which has almost entirely been superseded in France itself by the five-franc piece, is very common here, having, as I understand, a small additional value in Switzerland. The old *Louis d'or*, of twenty-four francs value, is to be had also, and is the most convenient for travellers. Most of the cantons issue crowns, or four-franc pieces, and gold coins corresponding to the *Louis* and double *Louis d'or* in value, but they are not very abundant. Many of the smaller coins will not pass out of their own cantons, while in many of the cantons even the base German coins are taken. The French money passes all over Europe, I should say, England alone excepted. The Swiss franc has the value of a franc and a half French, a circumstance that frequently misleads strangers who come from France. When the rent of la Lorraine was named to me in francs, I thought it particularly low; but when the payment in advance was made, as is usual with strangers, I had reason to think it particularly high.

On quitting the frontier house of Berne, the milk-money of which has induced a digression that you may find out of place, we proceeded through the meadows and pasture lands as before. I observed a quick, anxious look about the eyes of the guide, as we walked briskly forward, but without in the least suspecting the cause. A few minutes, however, sufficed to explain it. We mounted a little ascent, and came to a small chapel that stood on the edge of a precipice, and at a point where the path plunged suddenly into the valleys of the two Unterwaldens. Of course there was a view.

You have read so much already of surprises and of the effects of extraordinary and unexpected scenery, that I almost fear to recur to the subject. But the truth will not be said unless I tell you this was *the* surprise, before all others. In most of the previous cases something extraordinary had been expected, and, although the fact so much exceeded expectation in this instance, nothing of very uncommon beauty had been looked for. I knew the Brünig was a celebrated pass, and that much had been written about its beauties; but I had thought its reputation was derived from the views on the side of Meyringen and the Oberland, which would certainly be highly esteemed in any other country, but with which, by comparison, I had been a little disappointed. I now discovered that the Brünig had charms of an entirely new description, and that its northern aspect is immeasurably the finest.

As soon as the delight of being so completely astonished had a little subsided, I quitted the path, and took a seat beneath the shade of a tree, that stood on the very verge of the precipice, to enjoy the scene more at leisure. The whole picture was in one long, straitened valley, that expanded a little however in the distance, and which was bounded north by the savage Pilatus, and the smiling Righi. The near view embraced the village, meadows, and lake of Lungern. The latter, looking blue and dark, laved the side of one of the most exquisitely rural mountains eye ever beheld; the whole of its broad breast being in verdant pastures or meadows, and teeming with brown chalets. This foreground lay on a terrace, a league or two in length, and half a league wide, several hundreds of feet beneath the spot where I had seated myself, and as many above the more distant lake and the plains of Stantz and Sarnen, which formed the background. Great depth was given to the whole by this accidental formation; and yet the atmosphere was so pure as scarcely to leave the outlines of a cottage indistinct.

The alluring tints of this view were among its most extraordinary beauties; for while the mountain appeared to cast a deep shadow athwart the lake, the water playfully threw its cerulean hue upward against the mountain. There was indeed a rare bluish tint cast athwart the whole valley, so unusual as scarcely to seem natural, and yet so soft as to produce none but the most agreeable effects. It was not unlike that vivid, unnatural atmosphere we find in some of the old Italian paintings, already mentioned, and in which the ultramarine has stood after the other colours have faded. In the midst of it all the verdure was exquisitely delicate, the colours of which I speak seeming to exist in the two fluids of air and water, and to temper rather than alter those of other objects.

The lake of Lungern is about a league in length, and the descent to the level of that of Sarnen, at its northern end, is so sudden and rapid as to give it the appearance of being dammed. This is literally the fact, though nature has been the workman. The district is at this moment engaged in cutting a tunnel through the rocks, with a view to lower the surface of the pretty little basin, by which means it is calculated that a thousand acres of excellent meadow will be obtained. I exclaimed against this innovation on the picturesque when it was told me; but, after all, the banks of the lake are so precipitous, and the water so deep, that less injury will be done to the view than might at first be supposed. At all events the case is hopeless, if the inhabitants of this valley see a plausible reason for anticipating, from the experiment, so large an addition to their meadows. In their eyes, a cheese is a more beautiful object than a lake or a rock; and such, I apprehend, is the governing rule for the appreciation of the sublime and beautiful among the mass of mankind everywhere. A love of the picturesque, unhappily, does not depend on the first wants of nature, while the love of bread and cheese does.

I complained to the guide that Ebel had not done justice to the Brünig. Hereupon the old man broke out into a philippic against all books, gazetteers, and maps, intimating pretty plainly that the word guide should never be compounded with any other, if the traveller did not wish to be misled. He illustrated his position by admitting that, although he had passed through the cantons a hundred times, if compelled to compress his knowledge in a book, he should make but a bad hand of it. I have certainly found a good many mistakes in Ebel; but, on the whole, it is one of the most accurate works of the kind I know.

In descending from the high place into the inhabited world, the mind was rudely recalled to the failings and wants of mortality by a little girl, who scampered across a meadow towards a gate, which she succeeded in shutting just in time to ask something for opening it again as we arrived. At Lungern we halted a moment to refresh ourselves. This place is Catholic, as indeed are all the Forest Cantons, or the four little states that were the nucleus of Swiss *independence*—not of Swiss *liberty*, you will remember; the distinction being all-important. The churchyard was glittering with little gilded iron *headstones*, (excuse the bull,) many of which were ornamented with miniatures of the deceased. Thus a man and his wife would appear side by side, on a plate let into the iron, which was usually a good deal wrought. On some of these plates I counted not less than six or eight very unsophisticated miniatures, which probably represented the dead of an entire family. Some were quite faded with age, and others, again, were fresh and tawdry.

The road lay along the eastern shore of the lake, and a most beautiful path it was. As we came to the northern extremity of this exquisite sheet of water, the manner of its formation was completely visible. A fall of part of a mountain has literally dammed the upper valley; and the water, after accumulating to a certain height, flows over the lowest part of the broken and uneven rocks, into the next level beneath. The good peasants, therefore, are rather restoring nature to what she originally was, than innovating on her laws, by cutting their tunnel.

From this point we got a view of the valley of ober Walden, or Upper Walden—this canton being subdivided into two of those communities that our nullifiers, with so much emphasis, call independent and sovereign states—*imperium in imperio*—which are termed the Upper and the Lower Walden. Lungern is merely a part of the former. In extent, Unterwalden, for such is the cantonal name, is the thirteenth of the twenty-two sisters, and in population the twentieth. It is in the very heart of the Confederation, and the entire population may be about twenty thousand souls, who are pretty nearly divided between the two great internal powers. The governments of both are essentially democratic, though that of Lower Unterwald being more sophisticated than its sister, while it is pure and integral in the source of its power, has the most practical checks. In this half-canton the citizen is admitted to his political rights at the age of eighteen. The laws are all passed in original assemblies of the people, which, after all, in numbers do not exceed many of our own town-meetings. We have very many townships that contain ten thousand inhabitants, and Upper Unterwalden has not more than nine thousand. Boston, previously to its incorporation as a city, you will remember, contained more than fifty thousand.

These little communities have many primitive fundamental laws. Thus, in Lower Unterwalden the pain of death is pronounced only by what is called the "Council of Blood," which is composed of the Simple Council, or a body formed for other objects, of certain magistrates and counsellors, and of all the citizens who have attained the age of thirty years.

There are very sonorous titles in this little country, which has stadtholders and counsellors without number. I should think the principle of rotation in office of little practical utility here, for one does not very well see where so small a population is to find incumbents for so many places. In such a state of society one would soon tire of political salutation. The people are very generally pastoral, and of the simplest habits, by necessity, as well perhaps as by inclination. They are rigid Catholics; and the fact is often cited as a proof that the religion of Rome is not necessarily opposed to the most extended political liberty. No very conclusive argument is to be drawn, either in favour of or against any particular system, by the example of communities situated like these. Unterwalden has been an independent country since the thirteenth century; but it would surely be absurd to look into the local institutions for the means which have enabled a people so weak to maintain for so long a time their separate sovereignty, while so many powerful states have been overrun, parcelled, or destroyed in the interval. Switzerland itself exists as a distinct Confederation by the common consent of her neighbours, and the preservation of the particular rights of its several parts have been the consequence of an imperious necessity, heightened by the prejudices of origin and even of religion, rather than from any especial merit in the institutions, or in the people. The country has not been worth the cost of conquest, sufficing barely to give an humble subsistence to the inhabitants, and possessing no other political value than that of a frontier; a character it is probably better able to preserve inviolate as a neutral, than as a dependant. It is not improbable, however, that the religion of these small cantons may indirectly have been instrumental in maintaining their independence of each other, and that personal liberty is the boon accorded as a reward for the sacrifice; for a great and enduring sacrifice it is, in the Swiss, to maintain the confederated form of government, as a moment's reflection will show.

For a nation of limited extent, and tolerably identified interests, the confederated form possesses scarcely an advantage, while it necessarily brings with it many peculiar disadvantages. Diversity of laws, want of unity, embarrassments in the currency, the frequent recurrence of frontiers, organized means for internal dissensions, and a variety of similar sources of evil are, beyond a doubt, the ordinary price that is paid for the confederated form of government. This is proved by Germany, by our own early experience, and is daily felt in Switzerland. These evils are even materially increased in this Confederacy by its diminutive size, and by the great number of its members. All the liberal and enlightened Swiss, with whom I have conversed, admit that the present system is imperfect. Most of them, it is true, are opposed to consolidation, for the inhabitants of the towns object to having their policy brought down to the level of that of the mere mountaineers; but they desire a Union, like our own, in place of the Confederation: a central government, that, for certain common objects, can act directly on the people, without the interference of agents, who derive their authority from a different source. In short, it may be said, that, in Switzerland, there is a constant natural tendency, dependent on the force of their true interests, to unite more closely, but which is violently and successfully resisted by the mere strength of habits and prejudices. The great, affluent, and populous communities are all of the reformed religion; Zurich, Berne, Basle, Schaffhausen, Vaud, Neuchâtel, and Geneva, being essentially Protestant cantons. These seven states contain nearly, if not quite half, of the entire population of Switzerland, and probably much more than half its wealth. Appenzell, St. Gall, the Grisons, Argovie, and Thurgovie, are nearly equally divided between the two churches; and it follows, that a consolidation, or a very intimate union even would give a preponderance to the Protestant interest. In addition, Catholicism avoids discussion, and it would be a part of its natural policy to keep its folds as distinct as possible from all others. I infer from these facts, that the church of Rome would find sufficient motives for permitting the simple mountaineers of the Forest Cantons to maintain their democracy, on condition that they will insulate the church. General deductions are never to be drawn from particular facts. The political tendencies of the Romish church, or proofs of its spiritual liberality, are not to be sought in these remote and little important communities, overshadowed, as they are, by the greater influence of their powerful Protestant neighbours, but in those great countries where it is uncontrolled, and can independently carry out its real policy. At Tockenburg, we were told, the two sects use the same building; and I have witnessed a similar toleration at Berne. Yet at Rome itself, notwithstanding the great importance of travellers to that decaying town, the Protestants receive it as an act of grace that they are permitted to worship God after their own forms, at all!

The most purely democratical cantons, beyond a question, are Catholic cantons. Still their democracy is the result of accidental circumstances, rather than of principles; for some of these very states rule dependencies, peopled by their relatives, friends, and neighbours, as political vassals.* Freedom is obtained by two great processes. In the one case, the facts precede opinion; in the other, opinion precedes the facts. The first is always the safest, and generally the most abiding; the latter, the most elevating and ennobling. English liberty, and, by obvious connexion, our own, has the former origin; French, Spanish, German, and Portuguese liberty, whatever there may be of it, has the latter. We enjoy the advantage of antiquity, and, consequently, of a greater degree of advancement; but, I think it will be found, in the end, that the latter will be the most consistent, since, if they have not commenced in a way to ensure moderation and safety, they have attacked the citadel of prejudice, and will not be so liable to run into contradictions between fact and opinion, by walking backwards; moving one way, while their eyes are cast along another. Nothing strikes the foreigner more unpleasantly, on visiting America, if we can credit their own accounts, than finding us *practising* on one set of principles, and *talking* and *feeling* under the influence of its converse!

The Catholic cantons of Switzerland are probably democratic, because they had no available substitute for the prince they set aside, when they rejected the house of Habsbourg. A community of herdsmen could not furnish a prince, and they quietly settled down into that form of government which was the most easy of attainment, and the most natural to their condition. So far from the circumstance of their being Catholic proving any thing in favour of the political liberality of Catholicism, their church itself is, in a great degree, owing to the want of a true spirit of liberty. Religious toleration is an inevitable consequence of political liberty, and, in point of fact, the reformation was at first proscribed among them. Had their political condition originated in principles instead of fortuitous and unavoidable circumstances, its first care would have been to secure liberty of conscience. Education is greatly neglected, moreover, and superstitions are made to take the place of higher motives. All this shows that true liberty has no abode here. Catholicism may have deferred to facts that are too potent for its direct efforts, but, in so doing, it has taken care to keep

* Schwytz seceded, temporarily, from the Confederation, in 1832, to maintain this unjust supremacy.

opinion in leading-strings, and to render civil liberty a lure to its own views, rather than a frank associate.

I stopped at a church by the way-side, that is named after the celebrated St. Nicholas de Flüe. It shows equally great devotion to sect, and to superstition. There are six altars, and a richness of decoration altogether beyond what one would expect in a country so poor and simple. The portico has some attempts at paintings, *al fresco*, although they may possibly be in oil, for I did not examine them minutely. The graves had the same head-irons, and little portraits, as those of Lungern. But I do not remember to have seen, anywhere else, one mark of Catholic discipline that is to be met with here. The water-table of the church was fairly lined with human skulls; a grinning and grim array!

I remarked, as we came down the valley, crosses erected on nearly all the conspicuous heights. The effect of these memorials of the passion of Christ was both deep and touching, and, at times, they were singularly admonitory. While the eye was, perhaps, studying the brown side of a precipice, seeking to analyze its parts, it would slowly rise to the summit, where, resting, for an instant, on a ragged outline of rock, drawn, as they all are, in strong relief, against a pure sky, faint thread-like lines would issue out of the void, until they stood distinctly poised on the highest peak, emblems of the most sublime mystery that has been presented to the human mind. I saw a dozen in the course of the day, all looking like so many grateful signs of mercy that had descended from heaven.

We reached Sarnen, the capital of the Upper Unterwald, *ob Wald*, or *ob dem Wald*, in Swiss German, in very good season, having come from Brienz on foot, a distance of some twenty miles. After securing a room at the principal inn, which was kept by some great statesman or other, I profited by an hour or two of day-light, to look at the place.

Sarnen is a capital in every respect suitable to the country. On a little height, near the town, once stood the castle of the bailiff of the house of Habsbourg, he who caused the eyes of Arnold de Melchthal's father to be put out. A terrace on this spot is now, and has been for ages, consecrated to the meetings of the *Landsgemeinde*, or convocations of the people; the original assembly in which the nation convenes. Here also, is the place where the population collect to shoot at the mark; an amusement, or rather a discipline, that is national. The rifle is truly a Swiss weapon, for in defending their rocky passes, it is the most efficient that can be employed. Every district has a place for the sharpshooters to assemble, and a round target, about as large as the head of a hogshead, with circles in paint, is to be seen near every hamlet. There is also often a house, for protection in bad weather.

The view from the Landenberg is pretty, overlooking the village, and the broad meadows, amid which it is seated. I counted one hundred and fifty roofs in the *bourg*. The town-hall, or state-house, is a square stone building, with six windows in a row. It is not unlike a better sort of country court-house in America. I examined the council halls, which are plain and business-like. One of them is decorated with paintings of the fathers of the republic, of a most unsophisticated perspective and colouring. The artists had been particularly fortunate in delineating the beards. One portrait of St. Nicholas de Flüe, however, was really good, being the offering of an errant son of the canton in modern times. Most of the houses have the shingles kept in their places by heavy stones, *à la Suisse*, and take, as a specimen of rustic simplicity, the fact that some women were breaking flax in the vestibule of the church.

The Righi and Mount Pilatus limited the sight towards the north, while the mountains of the Oberland rose above the pass of the Brunig, in the south. The near view was that of an extensive plain, surrounded by stern and lofty Alps.

The inn was crowded, travellers arriving from the Righi, and Lucerne, until night. We all supped in a common room, and among the rest was a party of French, who conversed in bad English, with an evident desire to display. I gathered from their discourse, that they had lately been travelling in England. Mistaking me for an Islander, they began to compliment the country in a way that alarmed my modesty, and forced from me a disclaimer. The effect of my saying I was not an Englishman, was sufficiently ludicrous. At first, they seemed to doubt it, as they were pleased to express it, on account of the purity of my pronunciation; but, on receiving a grave protestation of the truth of what they had been told, coupled with the fact, that I had never even put foot in England, until I had reached my present stature, and that eight or nine months, at different periods, within twenty years, made the extent of all the time I had ever passed in the island, admiration became coupled with envy. I was cross-questioned, closely as good breeding would at all permit, as to the manner in which I had acquired the language. "Perhaps, *Monsieur's* father or mother was English?" "Neither; nor grandfathers nor grandmothers, for many generations." "*Monsieur* may have been aided by some similarity in the construction of his native tongue to the English?" "There is some resemblance, certainly." A pause followed, in expectation that they were about to be told what that country was. I continued mute. "*Monsieur* must have commenced learning the language very early?" "I have spoken it from childhood." "It is a great advantage." "In the country in which I was born and educated, we all learn the English in childhood." *De grands yeux*, and looks of distrust. Thinking it time to retreat, I wished them good night, in bad French, and hurried off. As my passport was in my pocket, and these good democrats trouble no one with their police regulations, I escaped without detection. The most curious part of this little occurrence was the fact, that all this time, "great and glorious" America, and the "twelve millions," were no more thought of, than you would think of a trading factory on the coast of Africa, in enumerating the countries that speak French!

When an Englishman speaks of his countrymen, meaning the people of the nation, he says in a lordly way, the English, or Englishmen; but the Scot is obliged to bring himself in under the denomination of "Britons," "the British," or "British subjects." In like manner, when a European makes an allusion to the civilized world, he invariably says, "Europe," as in "European civilization," "European reputation," "European intelligence." America is never dreamt of. I have several times observed looks of surprise, when I have spoken of "Christendom," in making similar allusions. Whatever may be the case on grave occasions, the European, in his ordinary discourse, does not appear to admit the western hemisphere at all within the pale of his civilization.

Letter XV.

M Y DEAR ———,

The following morning, I proceeded to Stantz, the capital of the other Unterwalden, before breakfast. I had met, higher in the valley, a diminutive of the Schwytz cap already mentioned, but here the costume was entirely changed; the girls having the hair clubbed behind, and decorated with red ribands, while the matrons had the club ornamented with white *rosettes*. Many of the latter seemed to have literally pulled their hair out by the roots, in the effort to draw it tightly back into this club, or ball. I saw four, who certainly had not a hundred fibres left among them all, and one was actually bald, with the exception of the back of the head, where there was a dirty *rosette*, attached to some down. A few wore flat straw hats also, and I still saw one or two of the cocks' combs. The guide was of opinion that the frost had killed the hair at the roots, in the case of the bald ladies!

The noble Arnold de Winkelried has a statue in the square, in which he is represented embracing the heads of the Austrian lances. The town is both larger and more modern than Sarnen, and the principal church, taste apart, is quite as fine and as magnificent as any thing we are accustomed to see at home.

At breakfast we were an Englishman, a Scot, an Irishman, and myself. The three first were in the same party, while my plate was put near them, but on a different napkin. I was much amused by my neighbours, who were complete illustrations of their several countries. The Englishman was magisterial and authoritative; the Scot, close, wily, and acute; the Irishman, garrulous, eager, funny, and warm-hearted. The two last took little notice of me, but the first watched all my movements narrowly, and, as I travelled with a guide to myself, he was apparently disposed to open some communications between us. I really think I should have been honoured with some act of civility or other, had I not made the unlucky mistake of offering

v. The Upper Cascade of the Reichenbach *Switzerland*, 63

vi. The Valley of Grindelwald *Switzerland*, 55–59

vii. Castle of Spietz, Lake of Thun *Switzerland*, 45–47

VIII. Statue of Arnold von Winkelreid, at Stantz *Switzerland*, 150

him a piece of toast from my stores, when he had been calling in vain for a fresh supply from the kitchen. The offer was coldly declined, and from that moment, I was set down as "a nobody," or "a shoving fellow," and of course cut. I ought, in justice, however, to add, that an Englishman of station would have understood the civility, and met it in a better spirit. It is only the class who live, as it were, between wind and water, daily exposed to intrusions on their gentility, who are so wary of their privileges. Still, as the latter is by far the most numerous class, the trait just described, has really become national. Good breeding is so unobtrusive, so little apt to indulge in display at every plausible opening, that it is no wonder common minds, acting under a common training, should not always know when mere natural feeling is to be permitted to assert its rights.

I left my three cousins murdering French with the innkeeper, and getting into a *char*, took the way to Stanzstad. The road lay across a perfect plain, or rather through a basin in the mountains. The Rotzberg stood on our left, crowned by a ruin, but, though actually nine hundred feet high, it looked like a mere hillock by the side of the piles that enclose the valley.

Stanzstad is placed on the side of one of those arms which render the lake of Lucerne so beautiful. To the right was the route into the main sheet of water; opposite, a deep bay, with Winkel at its head; and on the left, another, that leads to Alpnach. To these must be added the bend towards Lucerne, and the long, narrow arm that conducts to Küsnacht. There is a point on the lake near Stanzstad, where its waters may be seen retiring in five different directions. The main lake itself is as irregular and beautiful as these deep bays. Its first course is north; then, by a narrow pass, it flows west, headed by a false lake; then north again through another pass; thence westerly by a most graceful curvature that keeps the curiosity always alive. As the foot is approached, one does not know, among so many windings, which is the main lake, and which are the bays, for the latter are actually larger than the former. The distance from Lucerne to Fluelen, embracing the whole of the direct route, is about twenty-three miles.

While a boat was preparing at Stanzstad, I praised the beauty of the lake to my old guide. He assented, for not only all the lakes but all Switzerland was beautiful in his eyes; but the lake of Zurich was more—it was superb, *"toujours des vignes."* I thought the precipitous rocks of Lucerne, with their Alpine pastures, finer even than the vineyards of Zurich; but, like my Frenchman of Val Travers, the old fellow drew a critical distinction between the *beau* and the *pittoresque*. "Handsome is that handsome does," was clearly an axiom with both.

My barge, as usual, was of the most primitive mould. The crew consisted of a man, his wife, and their daughter; quite a family affair. I stepped into it with confidence, however; firstly, because I knew I could swim across the lake, at need; secondly, because I knew the boat, being of light wood, could not very well sink; and thirdly, because the lake was so calm as to resemble a glittering mirror. Here, then, were all the elements of courage necessary to trust oneself on a lake that has had rather a bad reputation for its frolics, ever since the time the Swiss hero leaped to shore on Tellen's Platte.

Stanzstad consists of two or three houses, all that were left from a conflagration during the war of 1798, and an old tower that is placed near the water, and which dates from the thirteenth century. Quitting the port, the family trio were requested to pull out into the centre of the lake, where its five arms would stretch themselves before me, when it would be time enough to determine whither we would proceed. On reaching this point we lay on our oars, with all the inviting reaches of this eccentric sheet of water fairly open. While I was dissecting natural beauties, as undecided as a connoisseur in the Circassian market at Stamboul, the old guide very deliberately told off on his fingers, the different prices to the different havens, leaving me to choose between them. The whole thing was reduced to a purely Swiss calculation, or it was six francs worth of the picturesque against seven.

I had been at Lucerne and at Küsnacht; but the broad breast of the Righi lay invitingly warm and sunny within a league of me. Whilst gazing wistfully at the isolated cone, the melancholy sounds of a deep-toned bell came chiming over the placid lake from the bight of Küsnacht. It seemed to invite me to return; and certainly more delicious music was seldom heard. The effect produced by these bells, as they send their voices athwart the water, among the solemn rocks and mountains of Switzerland, is indescribably sweet and soothing. I could have spent hours in listening. The sounds soon ceased, however, when I desired that the ladies would be so obliging as to pull up under the Righi and thence take the direction to Brunnen, a village in the canton of Schwytz, some three or four hours' row up the lake.

As we glided along under the mountain, the guide pointed to a precipice, high against the Righi, whence there had been a fall of rocks which reached the lake, some ten or twelve years before. A similar fall, farther up the lake, had caused the water to overflow a part of the town of Lucerne, though fifteen or eighteen miles distant, doing material damage. In building among these grand flights of nature, one has to study the dangers of a position well, or he may find himself, his dwelling, and his estate, sudden sacrifices to the sublime and beautiful. Avalanches, land-slips, falling-rocks, *sacs d'eau*, torrents and their long progeny of evils, abound throughout all the valleys. It is not sufficient that your dwelling stand in a broad valley, or on a plain, apparently removed from danger; for the cracking of a glacier, fifty miles off, may possibly bring down a deluge on your security. This is not altogether a poetical account of the matter; for the dangers are much more frequent and serious than a stranger would be apt to suppose. The site of one of these local accidents, of a very singular character, was pointed out to me just before we reached the place where the fall of rock had occurred.

The village of Weggis stands on the base of the Righi, near a point where the mountain descends to the lake at an angle smaller than common. The melted snows and rains had entered the crevices of the rocks above, until, in process of time, they converted a considerable internal stratum of the mountain into a bed of mud. Had the cohesion of the superior part of the pile been broken, a land-fall would have occurred; but such not being the case, the immense weight forced the mud through openings in the rock to the surface, whence it flowed down the declivity into the lake. The progress of this extraordinary avalanche was slow, like that of lava, but irresistible. It left the earth completely covered for the height of many feet, sweeping before it every vestige of the labours of man that was abandoned to its course. There was time, however, to save nearly every thing but the earth itself, and its fruits, the peasants actually removing most of their houses. The ruin was not very extensive, but it was very thorough.

Soon after passing Fiznau, we went through a streight inclining southward, and came abreast of a small territory lying on a spur of the Righi, which rises here nearly four thousand feet above the surface of the lake. The whole district is on the mountain side; nor did it appear to me, in passing, that there was an acre of really level land from its base to the summit. It seemed, however, to be fertile, and well covered with fruit trees, a southern exposure being very favourable to the growth of the latter. The houses, of which I counted fifty, were nearly buried in trees, and there were a good many evidences of industry. The books told me that some attention was also paid to the manufacture of silk. This district is called Gersau, and, although it is now a part of Schwytz, for the four centuries that preceded the invasion of 1798, it formed an independent republic. Its width, along the shore of the lake, is less than three miles, and, up the inclined plane, its greatest length scarcely reached five. Here, then, was a state of less than ten thousand acres of land! The objects of exportation, and indeed of production, in this country are butter, cheese, skins, wool, and fruit. The entire population in 1798, or at the close of its independent existence, was fifteen hundred souls. This, and San Marino, in Italy, were the two smallest civilized communities in the world. The latter is still nominally independent, having foreign relations, which, as I understand the matter, was, on paper at least, formerly the case with Gersau, it forming neither a canton nor a part of a canton, previously to the era named. There was, however, a species of permanent alliance with the Confederation that reduced it, in fact, to a condition of political dependency. This country contained twenty family names, and all males of sixteen voted in the *Landsgemeinde*. The people chose every other year a *Landamman*, or president, a statholder, a secretary of state, a treasurer, and nine counsellors! A family must have been in a very bad way that had not one of its members in office.

It was intensely hot as we rowed past this territory, the sun beating on its side in a way to explain the secret of its fruits. Indeed the whole country was nothing but a natural wall to raise apples, and pears, and plums, and figs, and almonds against. Small as it was, I was heartily glad to be rid of it, and to reach the end of the Righi, or a point where the rays, by passing into a vast amphitheatre in the mountains which contains the village of Schwytz, were no longer thrown back upon us by reflection. Soon after we put into the port of Brunnen.

The position of this village is beautiful, it lying exactly at the principal bend in the lake, where it commands a view in both directions. Towards the west lay the basin over which we had just rowed; and towards the south the lake stretched away, for seven or eight miles, between huge and nearly perpendicular piles, to Fluelen, in Uri, or, in fact, to the base of the St. Gothard.

The day still continued placid, and after taking some refreshment I determined to go to Fluelen, and thence, by the Devil's Bridge, into the Grisons. A new contract was entered into with the family of oars, and we proceeded. Just as we were quitting the shore, a young German student came running down to beg a passage. He was admitted, and we steered towards the Grütli. The lake now presented a most lovely picture; not a breath of air was stirring, and boats were stealing athwart its glassy surface in a dozen different directions. The mountains were sombre and grand, more particularly around that deep reach of the lake into which we were penetrating, the scene of Tell's danger and escape. A heavy barge, filled with merchandise for Italy, and impelled by some thirty large oars, was sweeping on, nearly abreast of us, crowded with a hundred passengers, and lumbered with piles of boxes. Altogether it was a most enchanting scene, and as inviting by its repose as by the admixture of the soft with the sublime. A crowd of romantic recollections, moreover, were hovering about all the prominent points of the landscape.

Within a few minutes, however, a fresh air began to blow in our favour, and we set the sail. Our course now became easy and rapid, and we were soon abreast of the Grütli. Anxious to profit by the breeze, I determined not to land; for the place really offered no other inducement than a little extra enthusiasm. This I endeavoured, as far as possible, to feel in the boat. The Grütli is evidently a fragment, of some sixty or a hundred acres, that has fallen from a mountain. Its surface is sufficiently smooth to be cropped as a meadow, and, lying between the lake and the rocks, it offered a good point of rendezvous for conspirators (patriots before they were sure of success) who lived on different sides of the water. For such a purpose the place was both convenient and secluded. Tradition, I presume, does not pretend to point out the precise spot where Walter Furst met his two associates; but as three men who had got together to plot a revolt would be quite likely to stand reasonably close to each other, you will perceive that I might have wasted a month in endeavouring to determine the *locus in quo*, had I been bent on the discovery.

We soon met a boat that was pulling hard against the breeze. Her crew called to us, and said that we should be compelled to return, as a wind peculiar to this lake had already struck it on the other side of the Achsenberg. My German companion now told me that the watermen at Brunnen had predicted the same thing. Our family party seemed disturbed; but as we still had a fair and a fine breeze, I kept the boat's head towards the gulf of Fluelen.

I had been told a good deal, and had read a good deal, about the dangers of this part of the lake of Lucerne, which is sometimes called the *Lac d' Uri*. A row-boat is rarely in great danger, in narrow waters, if it can be kept out of breakers; and seeing nothing to be apprehended from this source, in spite of the toppling qualities of our *batteau*, I could not perceive a sufficient reason for abandoning the attempt. It would have been out of all rule, moreover, to desert a fair breeze. We shot swiftly ahead, and Tellen's Platte was fairly in view, when the sail suddenly flapped. The wind appeared to have glanced upward like a bird, and to have left the lake in an instant. The women looked appalled, resuming their oars with great reluctance. I ordered the sail lowered, and the mast to be struck. This was scarcely done, when we heard a noise like that of strong currents of air rushing through leaves, and, at the next moment, we felt the new breeze. It appeared to press almost perpendicularly on the water, forming an opposing current only along its immediate surface. Besides being adverse, it was much fresher than the wind we had lost.

I saw that my half-and-half crew was not only unequal to, but indisposed to the contest. The heavy barge, which we had already passed, now came up, sustained by her momentum; but even she began to hesitate, and to incline towards the eastern shore. Taking the hint, I sheered our boat over in the same direction, and we soon got under the beetling rocks. A heavy swell was fast getting up, and I looked for a place where we might at least hold on; for going ahead any farther began to be worse than doubtful. We succeeded in getting to a rock where there was barely footing for one person. The man jumped on it with the boat's painter, and held us fast for a few minutes, but the heaving and setting of the water increased so much as to render it no easy matter to keep our egg-shell from hopping up alongside of him. The whole shore was a wall of rock from three thousand to six thousand feet high, and, although there were meadows and even cottages hanging over our heads in the upper regions, the foundation of the pile was nearly perpendicular. Here and there were spots, however, where one might land, as at Tellen's Platte; and in some instances there were narrow strands, under the cliffs. The barge was sheering in towards one of the latter, to attain which a hundred hands were struggling at her sweeps. She withstood the action of the waves, aided by her great weight, and finally succeeded.

I thought we might possibly do as much, and was certain that we could not safely continue where we were, and taking the fourth oar myself, the man was ordered to jump aboard, and to shove off. With my aid, we were enabled to hold our own, and that was all. The seas beginning to break, and the wind to increase in power, I reluctantly gave up the point. The boat's head was thrown quickly round, the frail machine tottering, suspended on the crest of a sea for an instant, but righted, luckily, with its bow towards Brunnen.

My German companion "made big eyes" during these little manœuvres, and he stared with all his might at the waves over which we were careering; the boat, by this time, fairly flying, without showing an inch of canvass. "*Mein Gott—mein Gott!*" he ejaculated; and he seemed to think my involuntary laugh a species of marine blasphemy. He had been a little disposed towards *touzy-mouzy* at the sight of the Grütli and Tellen's Platte, but it all fled before the flaw. As for the amiable family of water-fowl, they appeared to think this much the pleasantest part of their day's work; though I saw well enough that there were certain misgivings among them about the forthcoming *honorarium*.

Of danger there was none; but this touch of the quality of the lake of Lucerne was sufficient to satisfy me that very serious difficulties may be encountered on its waters, more particularly in the clumsy boats in use. The natural resort against danger would be the very course we took, because we could take no other: that of running before the wind. Owing to its shape, the lake is certain to furnish a lee in a few minutes, let a boat be in what part of it she might. Gessler, it is to be presumed, was not much of a sailor. Landing, between Brunnen and Fluelen, during a storm, except in particular spots, would be out of the question; nor can the shore at such times be approached, without some hazard, anywhere. Parties of females, in particular, would always do well to respect the opinions of the weather given by the boatmen. This is a point on which their honesty may be implicitly trusted; and even men might do worse than by confiding in their faith and local knowledge. I had felt disposed to smile at the predictions of the soothsayers before the adverse wind came; but in the end there was reason to respect their prescience.

On landing again at Brunnen, we proceeded towards Schwytz, on foot. The natural basin in which this town stands is very beautiful, and highly cultivated. The town itself, the heart's core of Helvetia, is neat, much ornamented by fruit trees, and its houses are chiefly in stone, whitened. Behind it stand two bald rocks of vast height, which are called the Mitres, (*Mythen*,) from their shape, and probably from the circumstance that among the hills in their rear, has stood for ages, and still stands, one of the most frequented shrines of Europe, under the government of a mitred abbot; the Benedictine convent of Einsiedeln.

Without stopping in the town of Schwytz, we took a path through the meadows that soon brought us into the road to Goldau. In coming from Brunnen to the outlet of the lake of

Lowerz, we turned the eastern extremity of the Righi. The little sheet of water just mentioned is less than three miles in length, by a little more than one in breadth, and on its southern side it washes the base of the mountain, leaving sufficient room for an excellent carriage road, however, to wind along its banks. The ground is low at the outlet, which flows through the beautiful meadows of the district into the lake of the Four Cantons, or that of Lucerne. The outlet is called Seewen, and a hamlet near it bears the same name. Here I stopped to view the scene, and to rest myself. The ruins of Goldau, the Rossberg, and the pile of the Righi lay directly before me, across the water, at the distance of a league. Beckoning to a peasant who was mowing in a field near by, I inquired if he had witnessed the fall of the Rossberg? This man was at work, at the moment of the catastrophe, within a few yards of the very spot where we then stood. He described the noise as being sufficiently terrifying, but as less loud than one would suppose. A dense cloud of dust spread itself across the valley of Goldau, and up the side of the Rossberg, a distance of two miles or more, and he saw fire shooting through the air. From the appearance of the latter, the first impression in Schwytz had been, that there was a volcanic eruption; but it was afterwards known that the fire came from some lime-kilns that had been burning on the mountain. The fall of the Rossberg was owing to water passing through crevices of the mountain, and forming an enormous layer of mud, off of which the huge superincumbent mass had slid, like a ship when she is launched. It differed from the accident at Weggis only in the fact of the strata of the mountain separating, and by the greater magnitude of the phenomenon. The mud was driven downward by the enormous pressure with great impetuosity, and most of it, finding an outlet in that direction, was forced, in the twinkling of an eye, as it were, into the other end of the lake. Here it literally formed nearly a thousand acres of land! What an idea this fact gives us of the magnificent scale on which the works of nature are displayed in this country. One has difficulty in believing in such an event; but the meadow tells its own tale. The depth of the lake, in general, is about fifty feet; but the water was more shallow at its upper end, where this extraordinary change occurred.

The sudden entrance of so much earth, as you will readily

suppose, compelled as sudden an exit of an equal quantity of water. My informant described the first effect of this phenomenon to be a nearly perpendicular barrier of water, which stretched across the head of the lake, and which was the first feature of the catastrophe that he distinctly understood. Comprehending the nature of this danger, he had just time to run from the eminence where we were standing, and on which he had then been at work, into the street of the hamlet, and to bring up a little brother of his, who was playing before his own door. This was hardly done, when the wave reached the eastern shore, and poured its volume against the base of the Righi, and through the low pass of the Seewen. A great deal of the force of this wave must have been broken by the mountain, which is quite precipitous here, and the recoil of the water no doubt helped to diminish the violence of the succeeding shocks. Still the torrent that broke over the low ground washed all before it, including several houses, taking its course by the bed of the Seewen into the lake of Lucerne. There were three great waves, after which the water gradually subsided. I believe no lives were lost, a circumstance that must have been owing to the fact that the water escaped from the lake, chiefly on the reflux, the side of the mountain receiving the principal shock.

The walk along the lake shore was charming, and I loitered by the way like a truant school-boy. There are two small islands, of which, one, a little rocky mound, contains the ruins of a small baronial hold, that tradition gives to the old tyrants of the country, or to the bailiffs of the house of Habsbourg. A peasant, who was at work opposite this island, pointed to a low wall on it, which he said was part of a small chapel, that had been swept away by the water. He added that the wave completely covered the summit of a tower that was still standing, visible proofs of the passage of the water remaining on the stones. I computed the height of the rock above the water to be about twenty-five feet, and that of the tower above the rocks, forty-five. This would give seventy feet for the height of the wave above the surface of the lake. There is nothing like this seen on the ocean, but as, in this case, the water was violently and suddenly displaced, it does not follow that there was a "trough," as in gales at sea.

The hamlet of Lowerz stands at the western end of the lake, which lies in a north-west and south-east direction, and a little out of the course of the destruction. Its church, houses, and meadows mostly escaped, though the latter are more or less sprinkled with fragments of rock. The made ground lies directly behind it, and it was either in coarse grass, or in rude meadows, that had been recently cut, haystacks being profusely scattered over its whole surface.

Here the road ascended, and skirted the scene of desolation, passing the site of Goldau, or past a hamlet that is called New Goldau. This is the place where we took to the fields, in our ascent of the Righi, and I had now entered it from an exactly opposite direction. I ordered supper and a bed, determining to pass the night on the spot.

About ten, a noisy party of some thirsty *porteurs de chaises* came down the Righi, and invaded the inn. They had been up with the Grand-duchess Helena, the wife of the Grand-duke Michael, of Russia, and having probably been well paid for their toil, seemed disposed to make a night of it. I was right glad when they were all well filled with sour wine.

It was a chill, foggy morning when I rose, and the air suited the dreary aspect of the neighbouring desolation. New Goldau is a very humble commencement, containing merely the inn and a parsonage, with a chapel annexed. The priest was at matins, surrounded by a congregation of a dozen women and children. Opposite the temporary chapel, which is now in a sort of cellar, is the foundation of a new church. I got into conversation with the *curé* when he came out, and gleaned from him, and from the different people about the inn, as many facts relating to the fall of the mountain, as I could obtain. After breakfast, we proceeded on the same errand, directly across the ruin to the foot of the Rossberg. As this catastrophe is so truly Swiss, I shall now endeavour to give you a more distinct idea of it.

Imagine a valley bounded on its east and west sides by two lakes, and on its north and south by lofty mountains. The distance between the lakes is about two miles; and that from mountain to mountain, in the nearest point, is a little more than one. The southern mountain (the Righi) is a sharp acclivity; the northern rises more gradually, admitting of cultivation and meadows to its summit. The side of the latter mountain, which is the Rossberg, presents an inclined plane, at an angle of about thirty degrees, judging by the eye; being nearly or quite a league in length. The summit is given by Ebel as being 3516 French feet above the level of the lake of Zug. The whole southern surface was dotted with cottages, many of which still stand within a few yards of the line of the ruin. The extreme summit of the Rossberg is represented as having been a mass of rock, that projected at more than a right angle with its inclined surface, and which, of course, a little overhung its own base, in the direction of the valley. This accidental formation is believed to have been the chief cause of the disaster.

A fracture in the rock, running directly up the mountain in a straight line, marks the eastern limits of the fall. It has left a precipice the whole distance, varying from eighty to one hundred and twenty feet in height. This, of course, was the average depth of the sliding mass, though its thickness gradually diminished towards its western margin, where it seemed shaved off to an edge, in consequence of the mountain's receding northward. The width of this frightful track is about a thousand feet. Admitting that the length is only ten thousand, the width one thousand, and the average depth but forty feet, we get 400,000,000 cubic feet of matter, as the mass that was set in motion, on this dire occasion. Judging by the eye, I should think this calculation to be materially within the truth. By allowing an average depth of eighty feet, the mass, of course, is doubled. A better sort of Manhattanese dwelling contains about sixty thousand cubic feet. Assuming that the matter displaced by the fall of the Rossberg was 600,000,000 cubic feet, we get the result of a mass equal to the cubic contents of ten thousand of our largest dwellings. This number of dwellings of that size, would, perhaps, be quite as great an amount of matter as is actually contained in all the buildings of the town,* so that you have to imagine all the edifices of New York converted into solid bodies, and then cast, in a single minute, into a valley and lake, with a superficies of less than two thousand acres, in order to have some idea of the desolation produced by the fall of this mountain. Ebel estimates the size of the chasm left by the falling

* This was written in 1828.

fragments at nearly double that I have here given, but I think he has not allowed enough for the irregularity of its form.

The upper stratum of the entire side of the mountain, within the limits named, has been forced from its bed, from its summit to its base. The resistance, as the matter became piled in the valley, has thrown off fragments of the summit obliquely; and there are rocks as large as small buildings now lying near Goldau, which must have been projected through the air a distance of at least two miles. I have little doubt, notwithstanding, that most of the destruction has been done, by the superior matter forcing the inferior before it. The buildings of Goldau which lay near the extremity of the ruin, are said to have been *shoved* from their places, though subsequently overwhelmed. The priest estimated the depth of the *débris*, on the site of the present road, at about thirty feet. There are places in the valley, however, where its depth cannot be less than two hundred.

Near the base of the mountain is a sort of oasis in the desert. It is a little spot, of clayish meadow land, that has escaped the fall of rocks, and which is fenced and mowed.Whether it is the miserable remains of the original meadow, or whether it is a portion of meadow that slid from the mountain, I cannot say, but quite probably it is the latter. It is covered with a wiry grass. Pools of water exist all over the ruin, which altogether looks fresh, although the accident occurred in 1806. At the base of the Righi are detached rocks scattered about the meadows, that were hurled a good deal in advance of the mass. This place looks like a battle ground, where Milton's angels had contended.

After passing an hour amid this desolation, I mounted the Rossberg, for some distance, and stood on the verge of the precipice left by the fall. The view of the ruin beneath was frightful, and it was in strange contrast with the exquisite loveliness of the meadows that closely embrace its sides.

Four hundred and thirty-three of the inhabitants of the mountain and valley perished on this occasion; but to these must be added sixteen residents of other parts of the canton, and eight travellers. The latter were a bridal party, about to ascend the Righi. One or two gentlemen of their company were so far in the rear as to escape. These heard the rending of the rocks; and the last they saw of their friends, the latter had stopped and were looking up at the Rossberg, the sounds having evidently attracted their attention too. In the next minute they were buried beneath the ruins! The noise had previously alarmed some of the residents, of whom seventy-four escaped by flight. Those who lived on the mountain, by taking lateral directions, had to run but five hundred feet in order to be safe. Ebel estimates the pecuniary loss at a little more than half a million of dollars.

A person might have stood unscathed at the verge of the line of ruin, on the mountain; but, below, the air must have been momentarily filled with flying fragments. There is a house still standing on the western side of the track, or on that which is the least regularly marked, in fearful proximity to the *débris*.

Quitting this scene of devastation we took our way diagonally up the mountain, by a footpath that led us among cottages, copses, and pastures. One village, with a church, was passed; but the broad breasts of these Alps are uniformly peopled like the valleys, except in those cases in which the elevation, the inclination, or the sterility forbid the abodes of man. The latter scarcely ever occurs on the sides of mountains that are not mere piles of rock. We had beautiful views of the meadows towards Schwytz, and the eye completely overlooked the ground which had been made in the lake. The village of Lowerz did not entirely escape, as I had thought on passing it; for the guide now told me that the body of its church had been blown down by the concussion of the air, while its tower was left standing! Such a thing might have occurred, especially if the current of air happened to be well saturated with rocks, as was most probably the case.

After a steady ascent for an hour, we entered the high road, and, continuing to mount, soon reached a place called Rothenthurm. Here is a tower of some size, which was probably built to guard the pass, for it stands on the brow of the ascent, and on one of the principal entrances to the Forest Cantons. I gladly ordered a *char-à-banc*, a vehicle that has a great variety of forms, the ancient *char* having degenerated to carriages of different modes of construction. In this instance, it turned out to be a regular one-horse wagon. The country now became open, high, and broken. I scarcely remember a less inviting district in all

Switzerland, than that through which I passed during the next hour or two. We got a distant glimpse of the lake of Egeri, and the spot where the battle of Morgarten was fought. There was, also, some sharp fighting with the French, in 1798, near this spot. A great deal of peat was cutting along the road, and I passed a hamlet of chalets, that were designed to hold it, when dried. The houses were vulgar, and, in short, the whole scene was as little Swiss, as if it had been one of those half-deserted, exhausted settlements, of our own frontiers, in which none but the shiftless and improvident remain.

The road was pretty good, however, and I was surprised to find a neat and well built stone bridge thrown across a ravine. At this spot we overtook a party of pilgrims proceeding towards the shrine, where it was supposed many thousands would soon be collected, to assist at a solemn triennial ceremony. There were thirty-two in this company; two thirds females; and they had come from Alsace, or more than a hundred miles, to be present on this great occasion. A few were barefoot, and all prayed aloud, without ceasing, one repeating after the other. Deeper voices were heard in the rear, and another party, of sixteen, mostly men, ascended a knoll in the road, advancing towards the shrine in the same manner. The effect of these little processions, and the beautiful blending of prayers, was singularly touching.

After walking the horse some distance, to enjoy the intonations of these piously disposed travellers, we trotted on, and were soon on an eminence that commanded a view of the place to which they were going. The whole country had a naked appearance, rather than the shorn look so often described, and which, while it gives a meagre air to a landscape, renders it pleasing by its quaintness. Here, though there was not absolute sterility, there was a want of the opposite quality, that left an impression of dreariness. In the midst of such scenery, and in a sort of large amphitheatre formed by ragged mountains, towards the south and west, stood a vast pile of buildings, that has the reputation of a general resemblance to St. Peter's at Rome, although greatly inferior in magnitude, style, and material. There were ranges of conventual buildings grouped together and attached to the church, like the palace of the Vatican; the church itself; and a substitute for the celebrated circular colonnades, in two rows of cells, that are used as shops for the sale of images, and other similar articles of ecclesiastical traffic.

As these edifices occupy a conspicuous site, on a side hill, they strike the eye imposingly, in that poor and inhospitable region. About a hundred houses, all or nearly all of which are taverns for the accommodation of pilgrims, were clustered together, in a more humble position, and lower in the valley, as became the menials of the shrine. The village was neat, and, as we drove through it, it was plain enough that its people subsisted chiefly by administering to the superstitions, or to the bodily wants of the pilgrims. Nearly every house, besides being a tavern, was also devoted to the trade just mentioned, and large preparations were making to reap a fruitful harvest from the approaching festival.

Letter XVI.

D<small>EAR</small> ———,

I took a room at the Ox, the best inn, and hastened towards the abbey. As I can scarcely recall a day of stronger or more varied sensations than this, it may be well to give you a brief history of the causes which have brought the shrine of Einsiedeln into so much repute.

A hermit* of great sanctity lived near the spot many centuries since. This man was murdered, and respect for his memory induced a religious community to establish themselves around his cell. On the occasion of a consecration of a chapel, the bishop, it is affirmed, was anticipated by angels, who performed the rite to heavenly music, at midnight. This event at once brought our Lady of the Hermits, as she is called, into high request, and from that day to this, or for nine centuries, Mary of Einsiedeln has been a favourite with pilgrims of all the surrounding nations. Other traditions are also connected with the principal miracle. The Saviour is stated to have visited the shrine dedicated to his mother, in the human form. There is a copious fountain before the church, which has fourteen spouts, and at one of these (which is not known) he is believed to have drunk. He also left a complete impression of his hand on a silver plate; but the French removed both impression and plate at the time of their invasion; for it would have been the greater miracle of the two had they left any thing formed of the precious metals behind them.

Einsiedeln, unlike Loretto, has never been much frequented by the great. There is an unction about Italy, in such matters, with which it is nearly vain to hope to compete; and the difficulty of access and the proximity of heresy may have aided in diverting the current of pilgrimage. But, at the present time, Einsiedeln has probably more votaries than the shrine of the

* He is said to have been a contemporary of Charlemagne, and a member of the house of Hohenzollern, which is now seated on the throne of Prussia.

Roman States, though they certainly are of a greatly inferior quality. It has struck me that this particular species of devotion, or, indeed, most of those ancient observances of the church of Rome, which depend more on tradition than on doctrine and revelation, are fast falling into disrepute with all classes of society but its two extremes; the princes and the peasants; superstition, it would seem, being as much the companion of very high as of very low fortunes. In the latter case, it is the result of ignorance, and of a misery that seeks all modes of relief: and, in the former, of that innate sense of unworthiness, which renders every man conscious of his own inability to control high events, and secretly disposes him to lean on a supernatural power. That they do not place their reliance on more rational aids, is, probably, in both cases, the fault of education, little more being taught to princes than the accomplishments which are useful in maintaining the representation of their rank. Thus they are all linguists, but very rarely logicians. Napoleon himself is said to have believed in his fortune, and to have been much under the influence of superstition; a fact, which, with his education and previous disposition, must be attributed solely to the consciousness of being required to decide on events that belong rather to destiny than to any human will. Thus, you perceive, as "hypocrisy is the homage that vice pays to virtue," I am ready to maintain that superstition is no other than an involuntary admission of our want of the higher attributes of intelligence. Perhaps no man is entirely without it.

At all events, princes and peasants are the two classes who now appear to retain the greatest respect for the ancient superstitions of the Catholic Church. Policy, no doubt, in some measure, influences the first; but I think the world does not give them credit always for a sincerity which, for the reasons named, I believe they oftener feel than is supposed.

Pilgrims were arriving throughout the day, in parties varying from a dozen to a hundred. Their approach was always announced by the untiring repetitions of the prayers, the effect of which, in the distance, especially when male and female voices alternated, was poetical and plaintive. All drank at the fountain, and nearly all at its several spouts, in order to make sure of pressing their lips to the one which is supposed to have been consecrated by the lips of the Saviour. They then invariably entered the building, serious, earnest, and devout, and knelt before the shrine.

The church is large, and almost worthy of being ranked with the cathedrals of Italy. It is a good deal ornamented, having many marble altars, painted ceilings, and much gilding. The shrine is of marble, and it stands quite near the great doors. Iron gratings in front, and on parts of the two sides, permit views of the interior, where the bronzed images of the mother and child are so placed as to receive the rays of a single but strong lamp. Their habiliments resembled pure gold.

When I entered, hundreds of pilgrims were kneeling on the pavement around the grates, keeping their eyes riveted, without an exception, on the dark, mysterious faces within. Many maintained this position for hours, and all appeared to be absorbed in subdued devotion. The light of the church was growing dim with the decline of day, and I walked stealthily around the groups, and through the vaulted aisles, with feelings of reverence, pity, admiration and awe, so blended, that I find it difficult to describe them. I knew that the temple was God's, and that his Spirit was present; I felt persuaded that much devout reliance on his mercy was blended with the superstition I witnessed; and, while my reason showed how fearfully near idolatry these poor people had approached, the mystery of the incarnation never appeared so sublime, and, if I may so express it, so palpable, as at that moment. I believe few men are less under the influence of superstition, or a dread of any sort connected with spiritual agencies than myself, and yet I found it necessary to draw largely on my Protestant insensibilities, in order to gaze at the bronzed countenance of Mary with indifference. Sympathy with the earnest and well-meaning crowd who knelt before her, a belief which, while it rejected so much of the embellishment of their own faith, admitted so much of its substance, and a sense of common inability to penetrate the great secret of the system of the universe, disposed me to be charitable. It was impossible to witness the pain and labour with which these poor people had traversed plains and mountains to reach the shrine, the subdued and imploring air with which they approached the image, and the fixed attitudes of reverence and deprecation, mingled with a strange sentiment of affectionate reliance, that all assumed, without feeling how insignificant shades in creed become, when devotion really occupies the soul. In short, I was in no humour to be critical, and felt strongly disposed to receive every thing as it was offered, and as it wished to appear.

Most of the pilgrims were Germans. A large portion were from the Black Forest, though there were also a good many Alsaciens, and a few Italians in the different groups. Some of the men had noble classical faces; and I can recall one or two, who, bending on the stones with naked knees, heads inclined, and eyes humbly but steadily riveted on the bronzed image, were perfect models of manly submission to an omnipotent and incomprehensible Power. I did not see a comely female among them. Beauty, real and of a high character, is everywhere rare; but that near approach to it, which we receive as its substitute, and which we should be willing to admit is beauty itself, but for the occasional exceptions that serve to raise the standard, and which is so very common in America, is of very unfrequent occurrence in this portion of Europe. A pretty peasant is hardly ever seen, and the costumes which appear so well in prints, are actually neutralized by the want of personal attractions in those who wear them. Nothing could be more wretched in externals than most of the female pilgrims on this occasion, though even they seemed respectable and more human than usual, while grouped around the shrine, in quiet, enduring, earnest devotion.

The twilight was still in the aisles, when a procession of monks entered by a lateral door, and approached the shrine. I had seen one or two of the fraternity gliding among the pillars of the narrow galleries that connect the upper portions of the church, apparently looking down, in watchfulness, at the devotees; but, though picturesque to the eye, their flitting about in this manner had recalled me from more pleasing thoughts, to recollections of monkish craft, and I fancied their presence unseasonable. Now, however, they came in a body, the princely abbot at their head, and began to chant the offices. The delusion was disturbed by this idle parade; for there is usually a want of reverence in the manner of the officials in Catholic worship, that does not at all comport with Protestant humility. They soon withdrew in the same order; and then commenced a scene that was still less in unison with our opinions. The pilgrims pressed forward, offering boxes of beads, images, and other similar articles, to a monk who remained in the shrine; and who, after touching the image with the different objects, returned them to their several owners to be preserved as relics. Nothing could be more business-like than the whole process, which, unfortunately for previous impressions, I mentally compared at the moment to the rapid evolutions of a notorious vender of *galettes* on the *Boulevard St. Martin*, at Paris. Such ludicrous associations make sad inroads on the touching and the beautiful; and I turned away, to stroll up the body of the church, devoured by skepticism. Every altar was crowded, and by this time the light was so dim as to give a shadowy appearance to the images of the edifice, its rich ornaments, its columns, galleries, aisles, and even to the kneeling pilgrims. I took this opportunity, while the last impressions were agreeable, to quit the place, and to return to the inn.

Several bodies of pilgrims had arrived since myself; and at the inn I still heard them repeating their prayers in the streets. As soon as I had dined, I sent for the guide, in order to measure the *étape* for the next day's march. He had hardly entered before the sound of voices in the street drew us to the window, which a party of seventy-four pilgrims was passing. The men walked bareheaded on one side of the road, and the women on the other. The guide shook his head, as if he looked on all this as very wicked. He is an inveterate Protestant, and got himself in difficulty not long since by speaking his sentiments on the subject, a little too freely. According to his account of the matter, it would have been very easy for either of us to gain the honours of martyrdom, by just stepping into the square, and proclaiming our private opinions concerning the divine consecration of the chapel of our Lady of the Hermits. I earnestly advised him to try the experiment; but this he adroitly evaded, by saying he owed it to his character and conscience to see me safe back to Thun. Of course, after this considerate explanation, I did not press the matter. While we were discussing the point, another party passed, barefoot as well as bareheaded.

As we concluded it was the most expedient not to attack the angelic consecration, I settled the affair of the next day's march as fast as possible, and hurried back to the church. The building was now dimly lighted, and the pilgrims still knelt in its gloomy shadows, resembling statues of stone. Many of them had their packs on their backs, like types of their sins. Two females of better appearance than usual were praying at a side altar; but no one else of either sex, of a station above that of a peasant, was in the church, the officials and myself excepted. The books certainly say that men of condition do make this pilgrimage; but if any such were here to-day, they were thoroughly disguised; so completely so, I should think, as to baffle the penetration of even our Lady of the Hermits.

I could not lose three days, at this late season, (Friday, 12th September, 1828,) in order to witness the ceremonies of the succeeding Sunday, and we departed, therefore, on foot, early on the following morning. The road was lined for some distance with "stations," as they are called, or little chapels that usually represent the passions of the Redeemer, in which the pious go through a succession of prayers suited to their own weaknesses,—a common observance in Catholic countries. Pilgrims were still met, every half mile, some coming from the cantons, some from Germany, and some from the Tyrol. One party were carrying their packs on their heads, another were barefooted, and each apparently had some peculiar form of penance.

We also met many boys and girls bearing fruit to the village. As the day proved very warm, it was grateful to cool the palate with plums and pears, while toiling up the sharp and frequent ascents. I had got completely out of my reckoning, though the fact that we were on the broken surface of a mountain was sufficiently evident, not only by its productions, but by the air which bounded the view towards the south; in Switzerland, the landscape being usually in a grand setting of rocks, unless the spectator is on an elevation.

After more than an hour of hard walking, we came to an ascent that was steeper than common. As we drew near the top, I observed the eyes of the guide were getting to be restless, and began to think he was disposed to try a little *Kirschwasser*, for he had just told me there was an inn at the summit, where very good liquor was to be had. I did the old man injustice. He was thinking, altogether in the way of his vocation, of the glory of Switzerland, and of an agreeable surprise that lay before me.

The ascent brought us suddenly to the summit of that mountain which bounds the southern shore of the lake of Zurich, and the region to the north and west of that sheet of water being what may be called a champaign country for the Alps, we were on the threshold of "a view." A few steps brought us to the verge of the declivity, where the eye ranged over a vast reach of country into Germany. We were about two thousand feet above the lake of Zurich, a portion of which lay at our feet, cut by the bridge of Rapperschwyl. The island of Ufnau was also in sight; and the mountain that we had descended on our way from the Tockenberg, lay a little on the left. In short, it was completely the reverse of the picture we had seen on the occasion of passing up the other shore of the lake, as already mentioned in our late excursion.

The road was quite good; but it was a dogged pull directly up the side of the mountain. In the sharpness and length of the ascent, it resembled that of the Am Stoss, though I think the last still entitled to precedence. Luckily, instead of climbing, it was now our agreeable duty to descend, and, after delaying a few minutes to enjoy the scene, we plunged towards the valleys.

The view increased, both in beauty and breadth, as we descended. Nearly all of the lake of Zurich became visible, both shores of which, lined with villages, churches, and cottages, in white, like so many brides, and beautifully relieved by verdure, forming parts of the landscape. Ufnau was so distinct as to permit me to distinguish the chapel, barn, meadow, and crosses. Here and there, a line of deep blue appeared among the undulating swells on the remoter side of the picture, looking like patches of the purest sky. These were lakes, whose names you would not recognise, were you to hear them. Switzerland has three classes of these fresh waters: the lakes that have a reputation for their varying but extraordinary beauties, such as those of Geneva, Lucerne, Zurich, and Constance; the lakes that are smaller in size, though still of very respectable dimensions, and which are known more for their accidental positions in frequented parts of the country, or for battles that have been fought on their banks; and the lakes that, enjoying neither of these advantages, are seldom visited by the traveller, or even named. I write with the map open, and a dozen of these nameless waters lie before me, not one of which have I seen, except in bird's eye glimpses, obtained in the manner just mentioned, from the tops of mountains.

A fountain, in stone, surmounted by an image of Mary, crowned with a gilded glory, stood by the way-side. Delicious water spouted from it, and a boy was in attendance to earn a *batz* by offering a cup. His object, probably, was to lie in wait for the pilgrims, of whom, however, we had seen none for the last hour.

When halfway down the mountain, the guide took a path that diverged from the highway towards the east. It led us through meadows and orchards, and by a most delightful descent to the valley, which we reached near Lachen. I breakfasted in a room that overhung the lake, and the view across the placid water was, as usual, a picture to admire. Looking down from lofty heights astonishes, and, for a time, excites the feelings; but I cling to the opinion, that we most love the views, at which we are accustomed to gaze from the margin of quiet waters, or from the depths of valleys. That picturesque and quaint-looking place, Rapperschwyl, had more of the air of a small walled city, seen from this side, than viewed from the other.

I ordered a *char*, which made its appearance, here, in the shape of a small one-horse phæton, with an apron *à cabriolet*. Though in the very heart of Switzerland, I have not seen a single real *char à banc* since leaving Berne. In our former tour we met very few, from all which I conclude they are not in as general use as is commonly thought.

The road now lay on the margin of a wide marshy district, that was once under water, the lake probably extending, in former ages, thus far. We got pretty views of the convent above Uznach, mentioned in a former letter, of Uznach itself, and of all the long mountain side, by which we had descended. It was pleasant to reverse the picture in this manner, and, to say the truth, Switzerland generally "gives as good as it receives." After journeying for a league or two we stopped to feed the horse, at an inn so near the mountain as to be in shadow at two o'clock! I asked the waiter, who spoke French, for some pears. "*Pois! des petits pois!*" he roared; "why, *monsir*, the *peas* have been gone these six weeks." "I do not ask for '*pois*,' but for '*poires*,' '*des poir-r-es*,'" which are just in season." One would think this explanation sufficient, and that I might have been quietly answered, yes or no;—not at all. My sturdy Swiss very coolly turned upon me, and gave me to understand that the reason he had not comprehended me at first was my very bad pronunciation. "*Fous n'abez bas un bon bronunciashun, Monsir; voilà, pourquoi je ne fous ai bas combris.*" Certes, my French is any thing but faultless, though I have no reason to suppose it worse than that of my castigator, who made a most ludicrous appearance as he reproved me for calling a pear, peas; an offence, by-the-way, of which I was not at all guilty. Now, what would have been thought, if such a thing had occurred in an American inn! As we drove from this school of quantities, the guide, who had been much shocked by his countryman's dogmatism and want of politeness, by way of atonement remarked, that "*ce gasson là n'est bas, pien boli.*"

In another hour we entered the canton of Glaris. These central states are soon traversed, for they are among the smallest of Switzerland, Schwytz being the seventeenth canton in size, and Glaris the sixteenth. The first has also the same rank in population, while the latter ranks even one degree lower. Schwytz contains rather more than thirty thousand souls; but Glaris has less than twenty-five thousand. The entire population of Lucerne, Zug, Schwytz, Unterwalden, Glaris, and Uri, or, of the six cantons that form the territorial nucleus of the Confederation, according to the official enumeration of the Federal Diet, is only 184,300 souls. If we deduct Lucerne, (86,700,) the five remaining cantons do not much surpass, in population, the smallest American state, proverbially minute as we deem our own little sister to be.

Not long after I had escaped from my purist, we met a highly respectable-looking divine in the road. He was walking, though evidently a traveller, accompanied by an ecclesiastic of inferior station. Soon after, an old-fashioned, heavy coach, drawn by four sleek, well-fed clerical-looking horses, with servants, in quaint, old-fashioned liveries, followed. On inquiry, this personage proved to be the Bishop of Coire, (the successor of the princely abbots of St. Gall, in a clerical sense at least,) who was proceeding to Einsiedeln, to take part in the approaching ceremonies. I presume most of the Catholics of this portion of the country are under his ecclesiastical jurisdiction; though those on the other side of the lake of Lucerne are generally connected with German dioceses.

The houses along the road side, and even in Schwytz itself, are less Swissish than they are in Berne. After travelling a league, we turned into an enormous ravine, or valley, and drove to the town of Glaris. I was now in the glen which had lain opposite to us when descending from Herisau, the day we reached Rapperschwyl. The surface of this vast gorge is smooth, and its width is rather more than a mile; but the height and perpendicularity of the mountains give it a straitened appearance. The battle of Naefels was fought near its entrance, under a sublime precipice, worthy to overlook so gallant a struggle. The whole canton, in effect, lies in this valley, and in one or two others of less size, which open into it. There is a good deal of mountain, it is true, but the rocks lie nearer the surface here, than in other parts of Switzerland, and the beautiful Alpine pastures are neither so rich nor so abundant as in the Oberland. The rocky pinnacles that enclose this country vary in height, from seven thousand to more than eleven thousand feet above the level of the Mediterranean. The Linth flows through the principal valley, and washes the skirts of the town. Nowhere is the contrast between the mild verdure of the valleys, and the savage aspect of the mountains, more marked than in Glaris: still the latter nourish vast herds of cattle, which constitute a principal part of the wealth of the canton.

The town, which contains some five or six thousand souls, lies along the Linth, principally in one extended street. This is the place where the cheese so well known in America, the *Schrabzieger*, is made.* The peculiar smell of the cheese was quite strong on approaching the town. It was like meeting with an old acquaintance, and, as I had but an hour to stay, I hastened to one of the places where it is made.

The curds are formed on the mountains, the milk of goats and cows being used indifferently. Indeed, so far as I could hear or see, the cheese, in this respect, differs from no other, except that it is made of the whey left after a churning. When

---

* I never met with one of these cheeses in any part of Europe, Glaris itself excepted; nor did I ever hear an Englishman, German, or Frenchman say that he knew the cheese at all.

formed, the curds are brought down to the valley in bags. I met a wagon loaded with them, as we entered the place. In this state, there is nothing peculiar in the taste, nor does the material seem at all rich, as you can very well imagine. It is pressed as dry as possible, and then put into a mill, resembling a small cider-mill; the one I examined being turned by water. There might have been a hundred weight of curds in this mill, and the wheel was passing over it constantly, with no one to superintend the operation. I presume the consistency of the cheese is owing to this thorough kneading, and the subsequent pressure, though those I questioned pretended that there is a virtue in the particular pastures. The peculiar colour, scent, and flavour are imparted by the herb,* which is grown in the valley, dried, pulverized, and incorporated with the mass in the mill. The odour of the powder was strong, and its taste vegetable, but I liked it less, pure, than in the cheese. The latter is thought to attain perfection in a twelvemonth, though it will keep a long time. I bought a small cheese, and took my leave of the establishment. Out of Glaris, I know no place where the *Schrabzieger* is so often met with as in Broadway. The name, so far as my knowledge extends, is compounded of *zieger*, (goats,) and some local word that means either plant, or the name of a plant. The latter, however, is purely conjecture. *Busch* is shrub, in German, but *schrab* sounds so near it, that I dare say it is some obsolete word of the same signification, although it is no more than fair to repeat to you that this is sheer conjecture.

Glaris has some manufactures, that are conducted in a pastoral and pleasing manner, and in a way greatly to obviate the vices and broken constitutions of a crowded population. I saw an orchard this afternoon, completely covered with pocket handkerchiefs, bleaching on the grass, the sight creating an irresistible desire to blow one's nose!

The town is principally built of stone, rough-cast. The houses have projecting roofs, but, in other respects, are more like the buildings near the Rhine, than those we are accustomed to consider Swiss. Many are painted externally, in designs, one of which was as follows. The basement was quite plain, having two doors, and a single grated window. All this is above ground, you

Trifolium melilot. cærul., or, a blue pansy.

will understand, no people burrowing, I believe, but the Manhattanese, and their humble imitators. The first floor had one large window, also protected by a grate, that had once been gilded; then comes a bit of wall, that was painted to resemble a window, a lion rampant being visible within. The rest of this floor had the common small Swiss windows, or, in other words, was nearly all window. The second floor had two small windows, with a coat of arms between them, bearing the coronet of a count, by which you will perceive the house I am describing was patrician. On the space of wall on one side of the window is a mounted knight, armed *cap-à-pié*, with his lance in the rest, in the act of tilting. On the opposite space, another mounted warrior, without armour, is drawing an arrow to the head. They appear to be opposed to each other, though separated by the windows and the armorial bearings. All the windows have painted ornaments, and a little boy, who forms part of the one nearest the armed knight, is stretching out a hand, as if to seize the head of his lance. The third floor has three windows, well garnished with boys. The fourth has but one real window, but near it is one painted, at which a lady is seated, looking down complacently, and pointing with a finger at the armed knight. The figures are all as large as life. The whole is in colours, and the paintings are far from being as bad as the conceits would give reason to suppose. These are queer ornaments, certainly, for the exterior of a nobleman's dwelling, though it is probable they have some allusion to a material passage in the history of the family. They may possibly refer to the battle of Naefels, in which a few mountaineers defeated the heavily armed troops of Austria.

Opposite this patrician dwelling is an inn, bearing the date of 1609, with a wild man, some twelve or fifteen feet high, painted on the plaster. The colours are quite fresh, and look as if they had been recently retouched.

There is certainly some hazard in a traveller's entering a country and quitting it within six hours, and then pretending to give an account of its habits. I believe my whole visit to the canton of Glaris did not occupy more time than this, and yet I cannot quit the place without protesting against one of its practices. Cattle are slaughtered in the public streets. I saw three sheep and a calf, under the hands of as many butchers, in the very heart of the place. I have seen something like this in French villages, but never before in a capital!

In the evening we returned, by the road we had come, to a point near the battle ground of Naefels, where we crossed the valley; and, following the banks of the foaming Linth, proceeded to Wesen, on the shore of the lake of Wallenstadt, in the canton of St. Gall. The boundary is a canal, which connects the Wallenstadt with the lake of Zurich.

This little inroad into Glaris already seems like a dream. The place is so retired, the mountains are so wild and abrupt, and there is so great an admixture of the savage with the civilized, that it stands distinct and isolated, amid the multitude of images that this fruitful region has supplied.

Letter XVII.

My DEAR————,

By casting a glance at the map, you will perceive that the lakes of Wallenstadt and Zurich lie nearly in an east and west line, a few leagues asunder. The country between them, though some thirteen hundred feet above the level of the sea, has the character of a bottom rather than that of a valley. It is bounded by enormous mountains, it is true, but the streams which descend from them had converted the place into a vast marsh. The Linth having caused most of the mischief, the inhabitants have found means to bring that torrent into complete subjection. This great object has been very ingeniously effected, by turning the current of the stream into the Wallenstadt, where its waters can, at least, do no harm; and by enlarging the channel of communication between the two lakes, which has been converted into a canal.

Wesen is a small town at the western end of the Wallenstadt, between the mountain and the strand. The lake, which is ten miles in length by two in breadth, is deemed to be the most dangerous in Switzerland, and the police regulations for the boats are the most rigorous. In addition to other rules, the watermen are commanded narrowly to consult the weather, to keep the southern shore at certain seasons, and to renew their skiffs once in three years. It never enters into the calculations of these mountaineers, however, to construct boats that can resist a sea, or lay up to the wind! This lake has still another danger, that is more formidable than any which is produced by the weather. Its bed is said to have been raised several feet by the *débris* of the torrents, and the marshes are supposed to be slowly gaining in extent. The country, as a consequence, is getting to be seriously unhealthy.

I had a little fever in the morning, but can hardly attribute it to these marshes, which, after all, are not the Pontine. The heat of the previous day was probably the cause. I took a boat, after

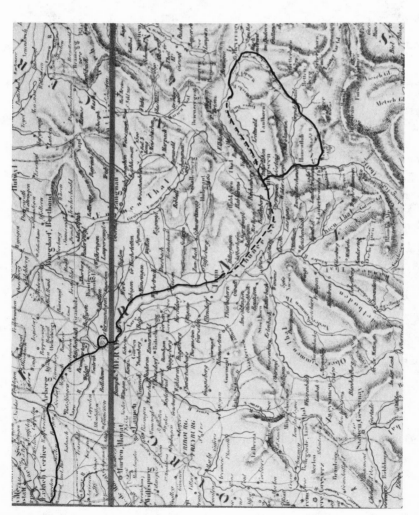

Map 1. Arrival at La Lorraine, Bern (mid-July), and first excursion to the Bernese Oberland (4–10 August): Thun, Unterseen, and around the circle through Lauterbrunnen, Meyringen, Grindelwald, and Interlaken back to Thun and Bern.

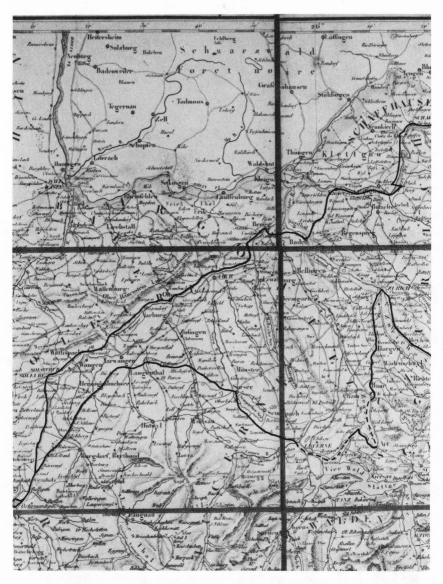

Map 2. Second excursion. To Constance via Schaffhausen and return via Zurich and Lucerne (25 August – 2 September).

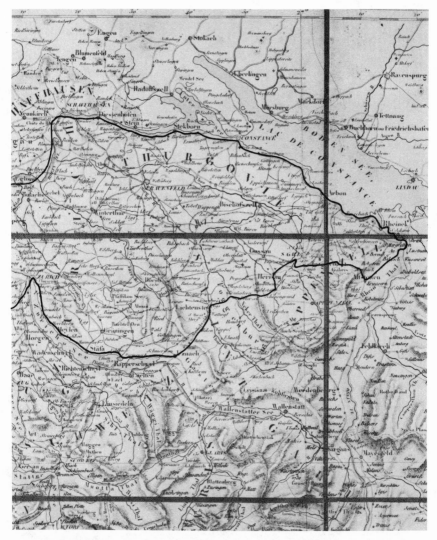

Map 3. Eastern part of second excursion.

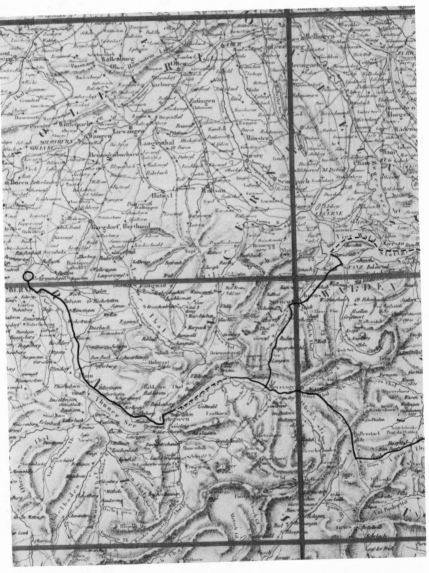

Map 4. Third excursion. To the shrine of Einsiedeln and Wallenstadt via Lake of Lucerene; then to the source of the Rhine following the river south and southwest; then to Meyringen by the St. Gothard Pass and back to Bern (8-19 September).

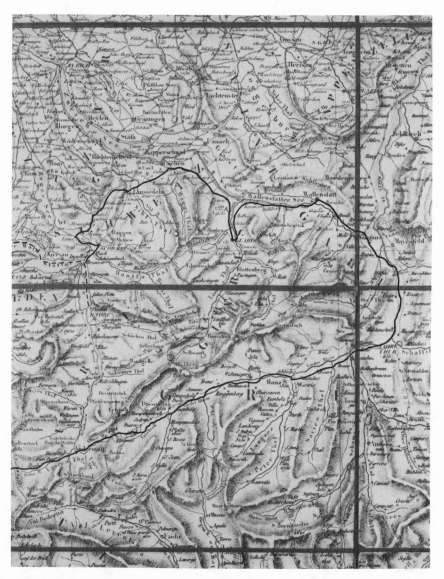

Map 5. Eastern part of third excursion.

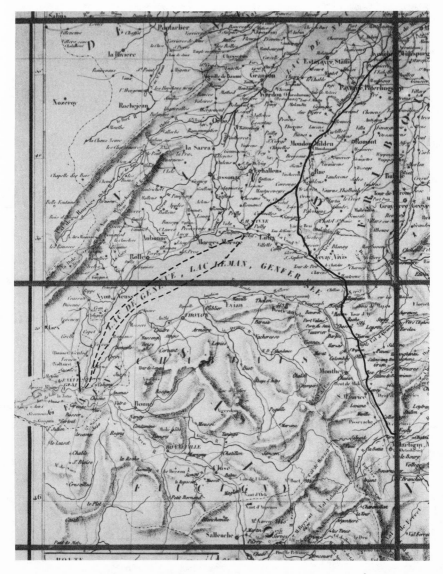

Map 6. Fourth excursion, to Geneva and back to Bern (24 September–1 October).

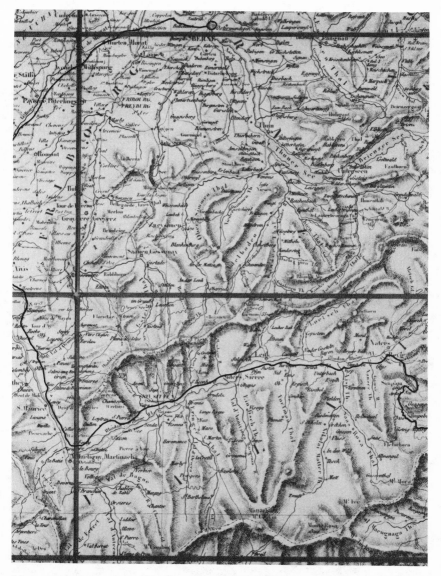

Map 7. Departure for Italy via Martigny and the Rhone valley to Brig, then over the Simplon Pass to Milan (8–14 October). See also Map 6.

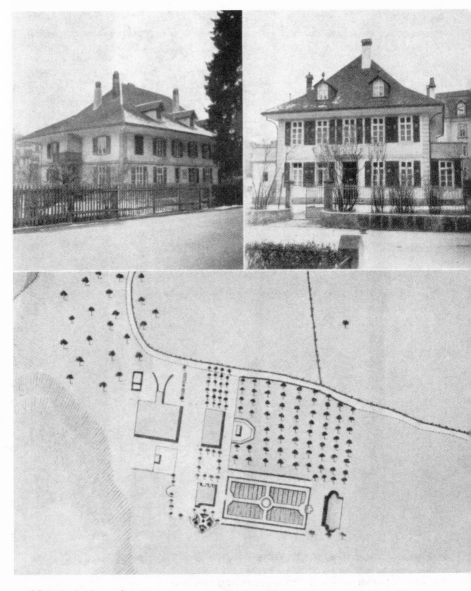

Map 8. La Lorraine
(above left) The former fief-house, presumably occupied by L. G. Walther during Cooper's visit.
(above right) The manorial house occupied by the Coopers, now a kindergarten.
(below) Plan of La Lorraine manorial estate, circa 1800.
© Paul Haupt Berne Publishers.

breakfast, and we rowed to the other extremity of this beautiful sheet of water. Many prefer its scenery to that of the lake of Lucerne, but, I think, unjustly. You may form some idea of its appearance, for yourself, from a very brief description. The dimensions you know. The east and west ends open on low marshy lands of considerable extent—valleys, in fact, that admit of fine views into noble vistas of mountains. The two sides are hedged in by walls of rock, that rise to an average height of six thousand feet above the surface of the lake. You have only to cut down the highest peak of the Catskills (The Round Top) to something like an irregular perpendicularity, add one half more to its elevation, stretch it along the margin of a sheet of perfectly limpid water, on both of its sides, for ten miles, embellish the crags with an occasional cottage, hamlet, or *alp*, build a village or two beneath the beetling precipices, and you will combine the most material elements of the Wallenstadt.

I took but two oars, wishing to prolong the pleasure of the passage, and, the weather being bland as May, we had a delightful pull across this sheet. We kept the northern shore, which has several beautiful waterfalls, and I thought there was no part of this side of the lake, in which a place might not be found, within half a mile, to beach a boat; though the little puff of wind on the Lucerne has convinced me that a formidable swell is soon raised in these deep waters. This lake is said to have nearly a hundred fathoms of soundings. The southern shore possessed several prettily placed hamlets, with churches and towers, that, in the refraction, seemed fairly to float in air above the water.

Wallenstadt is altogether a miserable place. It was formerly walled; but having been burned in the revolution, it has been meanly rebuilt, resembling a dirty French *bourg*, rather than a Swiss village. The valley in which it stands is narrower than that of Wesen, and the land is still marshy; nor do I remember a more wretchedly looking population in Switzerland, than that of Wallenstadt.

I ordered a *char*, which came forth, to all intents and uses, a dearborn. The road was good, and the mountains were magnificent, as usual, but the plain was cold and meagre. The grasses were coarse, the meadows untrimmed, and the agriculture seemed less perfect than common. Alpine pastures appeared to the south, but northward, rocky precipices lined the valley. The ruins of a few picturesque castles, and a church on a rock that was scarcely accessible, a little relieved the dreariness.

At Sargans, a small town that was formerly the residence of a count, the country improved. On a height near the village, stands the castle of the ancient masters of the district. It appears to be still habitable, and workmen were repairing a roof as I passed. It is composed of a single tower, and a *corps de bâtiment* or two, of no great extent, all in the usual rude taste of the mountains. These little lords, after allowing for the differences produced by a more advanced stage of civilization, could not have been better lodged than an American gentleman, who has a spacious country house; still, this Count of Sargans was probably a man of local note, the great communication between Germany and Italy, for this part of Switzerland, lying immediately beneath his tower, and affording plenty of toll. The route you will easily understand. The traveller passed the Rhine at Schaffhausen, and proceeded to Zurich; there he took boat for the head of the lake; then came the portage to the Wallenstadt, the lake, and the valley to the Rhine again, which, owing to its sinuosities, is met at the distance of a few miles from Sargans. The river is ascended, by its southern branch, until the last chain of the Alps is overcome at the Splügen, where the descent to Italy commences. The roads being good for the entire distance, this route is now constantly travelled by post carriages, the only interruption occurring at the Wallenstadt, which must be crossed in boats.

Between the Rhine and Sargans, there is an imperceptible elevation of about twenty feet, the only barrier to the river's flowing into the lake of Wallenstadt. The bed of the stream constantly rising, owing to the *débris* that is washed by its numerous tributaries from the mountains, a change in the direction of the Rhine is an event quite within the limits of possibility. As every valley here necessarily has a stream, even this change would produce no great influence on the river below the lake of Constance; certainly none below the junction of the Aar, which is the common drain of all the waters of all the large Swiss lakes, with the exception of that of Geneva. It is thought the Rhine once flowed by the Wallenstadt, and that its present bed is of modern date. A particle of water that took the route in question would probably reach the sea, assuming equal currents of about two miles the hour, some days sooner than by the present circuitous channel. If we except certain bad consequences in the way of marshes, *voilà tout!*

The modes of agriculture, and the *costumes* appear to undergo sudden changes, as one travels through this valley. At Sargans, every one we met on the road was driving a single horse with a pole, our own equipment; while at Ragatz, a league or two further, it was a single ox in shafts.

There was a fine glimpse down the Rhinthal, from the latter place, including a cream-coloured *château* on the verdant breast of a broad mountain, and a ruin opposite. The first must have been in Germany, which here touches the Rhine. There are also ruins of *châteaux* above Ragatz; indeed, all the minor eminences in this thoroughfare appear to have once been occupied as holds, whence the local *seigneurs*, right noble and loyal, issued to rob the passenger; or, failing of a pious pilgrim, a provident trader, a helpless dame, or a wealthy burgher, to prey on each other.

At Ragatz we abandoned the wagon, the guide shouldered the pack, and we took a footpath which led us up the first pitch of the southern mountain. The ascent was sharp, but not very long. On reaching the summit, we found ourselves among meadows, chalets, and pastures, with a noble background of rock, on the right, that reached the clouds; a deep gorge, through which flowed a torrent, lying along our left. On the other side of this gorge, the country was an open sheep pasture, with a convent seated on the most advanced of the mountain spurs. Our path led us always up the gorge, and at no great distance from it.

As we ascended, I got a glimpse of the Rhine, a broad straggling torrent, half its bed, just at this season, when the waters are low, being naked sands, or piles of gravel. The water was no longer blue, as below the lake of Constance, but of a dull, dun colour.

The gorge, at first, was three or four hundred feet wide; but it gradually narrowed, until the rocks actually closed above the torrent beneath; we had walked several miles, however, before this junction occurred. A little this side the spot where the rocks met, the guide pointed to a small building that was overhanging the precipice, on the other edge of the gorge. It had formerly been used for the purpose of sending articles into and from the ravine. Here we rapidly descended, by a sharp zig-zag, for a distance of several hundred feet. At the bottom of the ravine, we found the celebrated baths of Pfeffers.

This is probably the most extraordinary place of its kind in the world. The breadth of the ravine below is not more than two hundred feet, nor is it a great deal wider at the top. Its direction is nearly east and west, and, on the south side, the rock may be said to be literally perpendicular. I am not certain that the summit does not overhang the base; in particular places this is certainly the fact. On the north it is less steep, but still a precipice. I do not believe that the mouth of this infernal gorge can much exceed three hundred feet, if indeed it is so wide. Ebel gives the exact height of the southern rocks at 664 French, which are about equal to 715 English feet. Even this width gradually diminishes, until the earth actually closes overhead, as already mentioned, in a manner to permit the path to cross a natural bridge. The sun, at midsummer, is first seen here at eleven in the forenoon, and disappears at three.

At the bottom of this semi-subterranean world stands a substantial edifice, capable, at need, of lodging several hundred guests. The baths are the property of the abbey of Pfeffers, a community that dwells in the conventual buildings just alluded to, and the place is much frequented in summer. The season was now over, few coming but such as were attracted by curiosity. The house is of stone, raised on arches, having vaulted rooms on the lower floor. It stands at the foot of the northern precipice, the Tamina flowing between it and the southern. There is a chapel in the centre, as befitteth a monkish ownership, and the kitchens, baths, and offices, are sufficiently sombre to harmonize even with the cowl. In short, the place might very well pass as one expressly designed by nature for monks to delight in.

On entering an enormous vaulted corridore, where six or eight rough-looking fellows were amusing themselves at cards, I was received by a waiter, with the usual ceremonies of the upper world. Passing these, and penetrating deeper into the building, I came to an inner room, where the host, a monk, and one or two of the animal fixtures of the establishment, were occupied in the same way. I cannot describe to you the first effect of this scene. Coming from the mountains, and the mountain air, from the fragrance of the fields and the light of heaven, and plunging into this frightful chasm, to enter the dark, dank, and vaulted rooms, and there to meet with groups like these, had a strong tendency to recall the images of childhood, which, according to American puritanism, associated cards with ungodliness, and a monk with the devil. The Benedictine, sooth to say, had a most hardened and foreordained air, and the mixing up of the cowl in such a picture almost led me to look for the cleft hoof beneath his brown and dirty-looking robe.

After depositing the packs, securing a room, and ordering some "creature-comforts," I took a local guide, and proceeded to the fountain. You are to understand that the natural wildness of this remarkable spot, and the healing qualities of the waters, have no other than an accidental association. The Tamina, a large, well-filled torrent, that is fed by glaciers, has worked its way into a huge fissure of the rocks, out of which it issues but a short distance from the building, and past which it roars to throw its truculent waters into the Rhine, near Ragatz. The hot springs are in no manner connected with this stream. They gush from the rocks that line the sides of the torrent, it is true, and they would be altogether lost in it, had not artificial means been used to lead a part of their water to the dwelling.

We left the house on a narrow platform of planks, that is laid, perhaps, thirty feet above the bed of the stream, and by the side of which the water of the springs is led, through a wooden trunk, to the baths. This ticklish bridge soon crossed the gorge, after which it followed the rocks, being secured to them by the iron clamps that sustain the little aqueduct. After proceeding some distance in this manner, the beetling precipice gradually closing above our heads, and the angry torrent leaping violently from rock to rock beneath, we entered a cavern, the superincumbent mountains actually shutting out the view of the heavens. This is the spot where the path of the upper world crosses the gorge. One enormous rock was completely detached from its native bed, and would have fallen but for the fact of its being caught in the jaws of the gorge; where it had probably been suspended a thousand years, acting as a wedge, to keep the mountains asunder. At this point the width of the gorge is reduced to forty feet, while its height is near two hundred and fifty.

The distance that we walked on this unsophisticated bridge was about a quarter of a mile. The planks were wet occasionally; sometimes there was but one; at some places the overhanging rocks compelled us to bend our heads aside; while at others we were led off to the centre of the gorge, where we were suspended in the air very much like rope-dancers. The overpowering feeling of wonder, and the constant temptation to look about me, contributed to make the excursion any thing but perfectly safe. The roaring torrent, glancing constantly beneath the eye, and stunning the ear with its eternal din, served to make up the sum of the astounding. To a steady head there is no great danger; but a weak one had better avoid the place. The only precaution that I found necessary to take, and a good one it is, was to stand quite still while looking at the different remarkable points of view which presented themselves.

This yawning chasm is sufficiently crooked to keep expectation alive; and the bridge, at first, seemed interminable. Although less than one-half as long by measurement, it is quadruple the length of that of Rapperschwyl in sensations. I was constantly muttering the word "infernal," and, after all, I believe this is the epithet which best describes the place.

The bridge of planks ends at the point where the hot springs gush from the rock, and where, of course, they are first received in the wooden trunk; though there are several outlets, and a great portion of their water is permitted to fall into the Tamina. The local guide affirmed that this gorge might be penetrated six leagues! This may very well be true, for one must remember on how grand a scale nature has wrought in Switzerland. The effects of the play of light, in this gorge, are not the least of its horrible beauties. The guide, perceiving that I was sufficiently firm of foot, ran ahead of me; and the appearance of his form gliding in the air, as it seemed in the distance, now in light and now in deep shadow, served materially to make the spot resemble the entrance of the nether world, with sprites flitting through its sombre passages.

The baths have been frequented many centuries; and places where there were formerly chambers, near the springs themselves, for the purpose of bathing, are distinctly to be traced.

I have described this remarkable spot to you in the simplest manner, for no method can be so certain to give distinct impressions of the place, as that of bringing it to a comparative scale of feet and inches. Fancy for yourself a rocky gorge, or cavern, in which the tallest steeple of America would stand, varying in width from sixty to thirty feet, with a roaring river beneath, the vapours of a hot spring, the play of light and shade, and men running about it, apparently, in mid air, and you will get something like the wild effect of the scene.

On returning to the house, I dined, and, finding nothing to interest me in the species of lower-region society that it contained, to which another dirty-looking Benedictine or two had been added, I wrote up my journal, and forthwith went to bed, in a tolerably comfortable room. This *coucher*, I presume, would have taken place by daylight, had it been my fortune to be a tenant of the upper world; but, as it was, a fowl could scarce have hesitated a moment about going to roost.

The rain fell into the ravine, in torrents, during the night, and I was not without some half-dreaming imaginings of a visit from the Tamina, in at the windows. These chances, however, have all been calculated, no doubt; though I should think a *sac d'eau*, or the rupture of a glacier, might send the bridge, building, monks, cards, wine, grease, dirt, and dank corridores, all in a heap, post-haste, to Ragatz. The great solidity of the edifice has probably some connexion with a dread of freshets.

Letter XVIII.

MY DEAR ——,

Io Pæan! The baths of Pfeffers, in my own unworthy person, have wrought a sudden and right marvellous cure! The case is briefly this: After quitting Einsiedeln, I became conscious of exceeding irritability, accompanied by slight symptoms of fever. At Wesen, the *mal aria* excited unpleasant distrust, and had got to be in bad odour with me, and, though the wonders of the yawning gulf at first diverted my thoughts to other subjects, on retiring to my room to write, all the unpleasant symptoms returned in redoubled force. Throughout the livelong night, I was more or less under the influence of what Dr. Johnson might have described as an earnest cuticular attrition, in which the horny extremities of the fingers were the immediate agents. At length, it flashed upon my mind to try the virtues of the waters. As the manner of using them is of importance in resorting to medicinal springs, I shall give the details for your especial benefit, should you ever be so unfortunate as to suffer in the same way.

A bundle of clothes, taken from the knapsack, including every part of my dress, shoes and travelling cap excepted, was formed by tightly enveloping the articles in a silk handkerchief. With this in my hand I proceeded to the baths, wearing the attire of yesterday; symptoms unabated, irritability increasing, accompanied by vehement objurgatory tendencies. The place of bathing is approached by dark, damp vaults that are quite in unison with the gloomy horrors of the glen, and which singularly predispose the body to enjoy the genial warmth of the water. The baths themselves are spacious, light, and comfortable.

Depositing the bundle in one corner, I undressed in another, performing the act in a careless, *dégagée* manner, that would be likely to lull suspicion, even in one of our own grand inquisitors, who had met with a repulse in inquiring into your private concerns. Having perfectly succeeded in this part of the application, another bundle was made, tightly enveloped in another silk handkerchief. With this in my hand, I plunged into the water, taking care to hold it, by a firm grasp, at the very bottom of the bath, for fully ten minutes. The effect was instantaneous. I felt in a moment as if I had got all the danger under, and from that time the symptoms gradually abated, and finally disappeared.

On quitting the bath, the dry bundle was opened for the first time, its contents applied, and the wetted bundle was removed to another receptacle of still hotter water, where Sir Joseph Banks might have experimented on the affinity between fleas and lobsters to his heart's content. I shall close this report by correcting an error in the number of pilgrms who are said to resort to Einsiedeln, on the occasion of the triennial *fête*. Thirty thousand was the estimate of the guide and of the innkeeper; but, by some calculations into which I have since entered, I am led to believe thirty millions would be nearer the truth.

Apart from these medicinal properties, the waters are truly delicious. The air is scarcely more transparent. They are too warm for comfort, perhaps, when used near their source; but the baths are arranged in a way that gives them time to cool. The water is also constantly flowing both in and out of the bath, by which means it is kept at the same temperature and purity. We have all heard of the effects of the oriental baths; but I can hardly fancy them greater than that which this water produced on me. It removed all sense of fatigue, renovated the spirits, and rendered both body and mind more vigorous and elastic.

The day seemed lowering, and I began to grow weary of the unearthly glen, under the apprehension of passing another night there. Vapours hung over it, and the little light that descended was struggling and dim. A suspicion of the truth, at length, flashed upon me, and, desiring the guide to shoulder his knapsack, I sallied forth, determined, at least, to ascend among the abodes of men. After conquering the zig-zag, the toil of ten minutes, we issued into the day, and saw a reasonable hope of a fine, bright morning. Before quitting the point where the paths separated, a party was met descending, which had come from Ragatz, already, that morning. There was a lady, who was borne in a *chaise à porteurs*.

After following the brow of the gorge a short distance, we

crossed it by the natural bridge, and soon began to ascend by stairs cut in the rock, for a considerable distance. In passing the bridge, we could see into the gorge, where the Tamina was foaming, looking like a fluttering white riband. Its roar scarcely ascended to the ear; though it once reached me, blended with the rustling of the gentle air that stirred the leaves on the mountain.

When we had reached the top of the rude steps, the path turned along the southern, or rather the eastern side of the gorge, towards the great valley. It ran at a little distance from the yawning gulf, but at a much greater elevation. It was the Sabbath, and we met parties of peasants, in their holiday dresses, hurrying to the baths. One party from the latter overtook us on its way to the abbey to attend mass. I was struck by the melody of the voices, which are the softest I have ever heard; in this respect, both sexes being alike.

The day proved to be lovely, and the pastures through which we travelled, even at this late season, were fresh and fragrant. Stimulated by so many favouring circumstances, I hardly touched the earth, giving good reason to the old guide to recall three things to my mind, which he did quite civilly, but in execrable French—viz.: that I had the longest legs, was twenty years the youngest, and did not carry the pack.

We soon reached the abbey, from which the deep intonations of the mass were audible, as we passed. Proceeding a little farther, in order to avoid the appearance of disrespect and of indifference to the rite, I took a seat on a rock, allowing an opportunity to my old comrade to lay aside the knapsack, and to take breath, as well as a little *Kirschwasser*. The half hour passed at this point was one of the most delicious of my life, and you will overlook the prolixity if I stop to relate a few of the reasons.

You know, as a matter of course, that the Swiss Alps are divided into two great chains, the northern and the southern. The first contains the Jung Frau, and her sister giants; the last Mont Blanc, (though not in Switzerland,) Monte Rosa, the St. Bernard, St. Gothard, *cum multis aliis*. There is one point, however, where the two chains are, in a manner, united, and whence the Rhine and Rhone flow between them, the former taking an eastern and the latter a western course. These great rivers, in fact, are the streams which run through the two great dividing valleys. The northern range properly commences at the Dent de Morcles,* in the Valais, and terminates at the precise spot where I had halted. There are, certainly, mountains which are fragments of this chain, farther east and west; but the continuity is broken, and they appear rather as accidents, than as parts of the great harmonious design.

It is not often that the visible effects of the grander phenomena of Swiss scenery are equal to their cause. Thus the views from the great mountain passes are rarely extended, and all that is said of the impulse given to the army of Hannibal by a sight of the plains of Italy must be pure poetry, no point on Mont Cenis, so far as I can learn, offering any such prospect. But here was a termination, in some measure, worthy of the chain, though it was not altogether of the character one might be led to expect.

Three vast vistas divided the view into as many grand and distinct parts. To the left, the valley opened towards the Wallenstadt; in front, the eye followed the windings of the turbid Rhine between the Alps of the Vorarlberg, and some isolated peaks of Switzerland; and, to the right, the landscape receded between noble ranges of mountains, in the direction of the sources of the great stream. All was on an Alpine scale, admitting of an infinity of minor parts.

Immediately beneath, was a deep but beautifully verdant ravine, that melted away in the valley; on the left, the abrupt promontory that held the glittering white edifices of the Abbey, relieved by the humbler, brown tenements of its dependants. On a lower eminence of the same spur, were the ruins of a feudal castle; and near it, but on a separate rock, was seated, in picturesque piety, a modest little chapel, which seemed placed there for secluded devotion. The Rhine, dark and truculent, ravaged the valley, appearing and disappearing at points, capriciously. Beyond one of the prettiest of its reaches, lovely meadows stretched away to the base of the hills, where the little city of Mayensfeld reposed amid fields of grain, orchards, and verdant pastures. Farther to the left, a nameless village peeped

* The Dent de Midi and its neighbours are advanced bastions of Mont Blanc.

out above groves of fruit and nut trees; the opening of a noble
defile, celebrated in the wars of the Grisons, and the wooded
sides of stupendous mountains, forming its background. Above
all, the sharp outlines of naked peaks were drawn, in high relief, against a void of blue, so pure, as to leave the sublimest
impressions of the depth of infinite space.

While I sat gazing at this scene, the solemn tones of church
bells came floating past, on the morning air, modulated by distance, and sounding like aerial music. The chant of the mass,
which occasionally reached me from the Abbey, mingled with
these melancholy chimes, seeming to invite the soul to bow before the Creator of a scene in which sweetness and sublimity
were so eminently mingled.

When the feelings with which I regarded this exquisite spectacle had a little subsided, I turned to my maps and guide books
with a good deal of curiosity, in order to ascertain, if, after having reaped the honour of discovering a mountain, it was not
now to be my good fortune to discover a country! Among the
thirty-eight states of Germany, as it was constituted by the peace
of 1814, least, if not last, stands a certain principality, called
Liechtenstein. According to the scale established by the Diet,
this power, besides covering $2,\frac{45}{100}$ German square miles of
surface, contains 5850 inhabitants, pays seventeen florins of
contribution annually to the treasury, and furnishes fifty-three
men to the army of the Confederation. In fine, it is one of the
most tiny of the many tiny parts into which Europe is politically divided. By way of brushing up my geography, which had
been a good deal deranged by the ambition of Napoleon, I had
faithfully studied the location of all the German States, the
Swiss Cantons, and the new divisions of Italy. Everybody knows
where San Marino is to be found; and as for Monaco, I have
actually been in it; but, by no process of study, or by no inquiry,
could I ascertain where this Liechtenstein is; though its royal
family, according to the *Almanach de Gotha*, contains twenty-five
princes and princesses. If I asked a German, and he pretended
to know, the next of his countrymen to whom I put the question
was certain to change the site to another quarter of the empire.
At length, after chasing it all over Germany, I had been induced to think that Liechtenstein lies on the Rhine, at no great
distance from the very place where I was seated, and in plain

view. I questioned the guide, but he had never heard of such a potentate as the King of Liechtenstein. But then he did not know that the Emperor of Austria was master of some of the distant mountains before us. He thought it was all Switzerland, and, certainly, so far as *appearances* were concerned, he was right enough. After all, I was obliged to abandon the point, and, to this hour, I am as ignorant as ever where Liechtenstein is.*

As we walked round the brow of the mountain, following a winding path, the glimpses of the Rhine were converted into views of miles in extent. The valley also opened more to the south, and villages began to be seen in that direction. The churches became very conspicuous, and nearly every hamlet had a *château*, or a ruin. The ringing of the bells was renewed, and the sounds of one that came from the extreme distance were like those of an Æolian harp. I tore myself from this exquisite spot with reluctance, but the old man began to hint that we were a long distance from a good dinner.

We soon began to descend, though obliquely, but always in the direction of our route, and in just half an hour, we again trod the soil of the valley. A mile further, we crossed the Rhine by a rude wooden bridge, beneath which the water rushes with a rapidity, that requires a steady head to gaze at with indifference. At this spot, the stream has ravaged nearly half the valley, leaving it covered with *débris*. Near the bridge we quitted the canton of St. Gall, and entered that of the Grisons.

The scenery in the valley bore the comparison nobly with that from the hills. It had all the old elements wrought into new combinations. Ruined castles, in particular, became very numerous, reappearing on nearly every favourable position near the valley, a few being even perched on heights that seemed inaccessible, at elevations of four or five hundred feet above the river. Several had evidently been destroyed by fire. There were two hanging over the little town of Haldenstein, (through which we passed,) and four others at the same time were in sight.

The churches, too, are frequently placed on the most pic-

* Luckily, this interesting country has lately been merged in the Austrian empire, sinking accordingly, from its high estate, to the insignificance of a mere province. *Troja fuit!*

turesque sites imaginable. Many stand on rocky projections, high against the mountains, and some in places that appear to be absolutely tenantless. The latter must be chapels for the resort of those who pass the summer months in the Alpine pastures. I also observed a few *châteaux* standing on naked rocks, so blended with the background of forest, as to be drawn from their solitude only by long and steady gazes. You may imagine how much all these accessories contributed to the charms of a grand nature, in which valleys of immense capacity were diminished to the ordinary size, by the magnitude of the piles that enclose them. Notwithstanding the experience I had now enjoyed, it was only when the eye attempted to enter into details, and to penetrate distances, that I became entirely sensible of the magnificent scale on which every thing had been constructed.

We got another one-horse phaeton, and trotted along a good road through this fine scenery, for, to say truth, the baths of Pfeffers had given me such an impulse, that I had emulated some of honest Bunyan's travellers after they got rid of their burdens of sins, and my old companion was fairly overdone. All this time the river did not flow very near us, nor was it often visible, though its course was easily traced by piles of gravel heaped along its banks.

At length, we wound around the ancient walls of Coire, and stopped at an inn without the gates. This little capital is very picturesquely placed, and as it is an old town, with quaint walls and towers, it forms, as a matter of course, a pleasing object to the eye. Internally it is less attractive, though not dirty. The streets are narrow and intricate; the houses of stone, roughcast; and the dress of the people has nothing peculiar. A few elderly men, however, wore the old-fashioned cocked hat, with the three regular corners. It is not unusual for the Swiss and German peasants to wear a hat with a single cock; but Coire being a capital, its burghers are a little more *coquets*.

Coire stands in a sort of gorge, which gradually ascends, growing narrower towards the summit, parts of the town lying on the different acclivities. The castle of the bishop is perched, conspicuously, above the roofs, and there is one tower in the pile, that is completely covered with ivy. It being Sunday, a large portion of the population was without the lower gate, near the inn; for, in truth, there was scarcely room to amuse themselves in the streets. The meadows toward the river were both extensive and rich, nor did the mountains, just here, appear as barren and intractable as some we had passed.

A great deal of cotton, in bales, was on the road, it having probably ascended the Rhine, though some may have come from Italy, by the Splügen. In either case, the carriage by land is a most formidable affair.

I dined at the inn, at what was called a *table d'hôte*, though a German and myself were the only guests. It is not usual to meet with a gentleman better satisfied with himself, than this young traveller. He mistook me for an Englishman, and was, at first, disposed to be courteous; but soon compelling me to explain that I was an American, his manner underwent a material change for the worse. He was from one of the German trading towns, according to his own account of himself,—an explanation, by the way, that was a little supererogatory. Notwithstanding his absurdities, the man was shrewd, and many of his remarks were amusing. I suffered him to persuade me to ascend the Rhine to its source, before he discovered I was an American, for afterwards it was quite apparent he did not care if I went to the devil. I presume he was one of those modern gentlemen, who resent our democracy as a standing injury to their own particular advantages; the instinct of commerce, while it is so keenly alive to the political privileges of the merchant, being dead to the rights of all other interests. The long established reputation of trade for favouring liberty, refers merely to a liberty that will suffice for its own wants; a liberty calculated with a truly mercantile sagacity, and with little reference to any thing but the profits and conveniences of W. G. V. R. & Co.

In the evening we proceeded to Richenau, a place where the Upper and the Lower Rhine unite. The valley gradually narrowed, the river began to flow between banks high enough to confine it,—a fact which reduced its breadth to a fourth of its former size,—and the mountains became more sterile and frowning. Snow reappeared on the higher ranges, or on the peaks which lay behind the most advanced buttresses of the range.

At Richenau we crossed the Rhine, just below the junction, by a covered wooden bridge. The stream was about a hundred and thirty, or a hundred and fifty feet in width. An inn, and a modern looking building, which was called a *Schlöss*,* composed the whole town. This titular *Schlöss* literally toes the highway, has a *porte cochère*, green venetian blinds, and a stuccoed front; in short, it is some such dwelling as one might expect to see at Milan, or Dijon.

At the immediate point of junction, the two branches of the Rhine flow from exactly opposite points of the compass, and, seen from a particular spot, they look like a river, with a current running in two directions! The main stream, however, really comes from the south-west, while the tributary, or lower branch, flows in from the south-east. They were both full and turbid, of nearly equal size, and each had the steady, *whirling*, imposing current, that marks the character of the stream below the lakes.

There is a good deal of passing by the Splügen, the road being excellent and direct. A party of Germans came in from Italy, in the evening, and supped at the same table with me. Two ladies, who belonged to it, were full of *"touzy-mouzy,"* about the terrific beauties of the *via mala*, and they almost tempted me to diverge in that direction. But one cannot see every thing in the same moment, and I went to bed in the resolution to ascend the main stream to its source, according to the advice of the supercilious and perfumed Hamburgher.

* Castle.

Letter XIX.

M<small>Y DEAR</small> ———,

It rained in the night, and the morning proved to be warm and misty. We left the inn after an early breakfast, and proceeded up the principal valley, on foot. The wheel track could not be said to have entirely ceased, but the road had a suspicious resemblance to those unsophisticated highways, over which, and through which, the American settler contrives to jolt and wade for the first eight or ten years that succeed a settlement. We soon got rid of it, however, the guide professing to know a shorter and a more agreeable way. He took a very pleasant footpath, which, after leading us a mile or two through cropped meadows and green pastures, well shaded by trees, degenerated into a dozen downright cowpaths, and finally became so confused as utterly to defy scrutiny. We soon got entirely out of the maze, and kept crossing the fields, with the Rhine, which flowed in a deep ravine on our left, for our only guide. The river being exceedingly crooked, every step was attended by the uncomfortable certainty, that it was as likely to be wrong as to be right. My old companion was finally obliged to confess that he knew no more of the road than he knew of the King of Liechtenstein, and to call a consultation as to the best mode of proceeding.

I was compensated for this dilemma, by an exquisitely beautiful glimpse on our left. It was obtained from a point that commanded a view into the gorge-like valley of the Lower Rhine, through which runs the road to the Splügen. There was a white *château* reposing on a green mountain side, two or three villages and village churches, the latter of a pure white, and gradations of verdure from the liveliest tint of the pasture to the sombre hue of clouds of larches, all so intermingled by position, and so shadowed and varied by mists, as to form an admirable landscape. The beauty of these *bits* are much heightened by the grand accompaniments of the never-failing background of a Swiss picture. I had not yet beheld the contrast between white and green to so great advantage.

What a thing is association! I seldom look at a white wooden edifice with satisfaction. The idea of the perishable nature of the material, and, as an inseparable consequence, of meanness, invariably arises to destroy it. Who ever looks at a model of fine statuary in the clay, or even in the plaster, with the unmingled delight he looks at the same work in the marble? The mind insensibly includes durability among the excellencies, and even the difficulty of the labour helps to compose the sum of the admirable. The view of the ordinary Swiss cottage, constructed of larch, forms an exception to the feeling, perhaps, but this arises from the fitness of the subdued colour of the resin to the thing; to association, which, in this instance, requires extreme simplicity. I am persuaded that the same cottage, painted white, would be found offensive and obtruding. The resin does not exude from any of our northern woods in sufficient quantities to enable us to substitute this appropriate hue for the present meretricious mode of painting, which is a little too apt to make an American landscape look like a Dutch toyshop. White is neat; and there are some situations in which it may be pretty; but, as a standing colour, I think it one of the worst that can be introduced into scenery, unless there happen to be much more than the usual amount of forest verdure.

The guide proposed that we should forthwith return to the inn, and take a fresh departure. To this I objected, well knowing that the Rhine, however winding its course in the end would not deceive us. After passing through several copses, and crossing as many fields, without a sign of a path, we found a wood chopper. This man directed us to ascend the hill on whose side we had been walking, and said that we should there enter the highway. I observed that he was working with a sort of clumsy hatchet, instead of the well formed and well balanced axe that is used in America. From the manner in which he handled this awkward implement, I have no doubt that a skilful chopper at home would do thrice the amount of work in the same time.

We reached the main route, which could scarcely be called a wheel track, at the little village of Trins, a hamlet that was quite sombre enough to suit the most subdued imagination. Here we got a still more lovely view of the objects already described, the mist having parted anew, unveiling, if possible, still finer parts of the valley of the Lower Rhine, or of Domleschg, as it is named.

The country now became quite broken and rude, though always offering interesting objects to the eye. The road rarely took us through the villages or hamlets, which usually lay a little aloof, appearing retired and pastoral. A place called Flims resembled Gaiss a little, having something of its shorn aspect, but without its extreme neatness and gayety. After passing Lax, another village, we got more completely lost than before, in attempting to shorten the distance, by taking a by-way. As the main path—it deserves no better name—follows the sides of the mountains, where most of the villages lie, and the river frequently winds away for half a league, on this occasion we even lost the Rhine itself. The poor old guide looked as if he had blundered into Liechtenstein, at last, and wore a face so rueful, that I could not scold him. I knew the river lay on our left, and, as a matter of course, took that direction. After getting along as well as we could, for a mile or two, we came out upon a valley surrounded by high hills, and obtained a distant view of the river, flowing among low meadows. This was fortunate, for previously it had dashed along through deep ravines, and we had, once or twice, been actually quite near it, without knowing the fact, the broken face of the country preventing us from detecting the buried stream among so many hills and ravines.

On descending to the meadows, we found the road. A small town, on the south side of the river, at the distance of a mile, was in sight, and thither we bent our weary steps. It proved to be Ilantz, which is the first place of sufficient size to be called a town, that stands on the banks of the Rhine. According to Picot, it is also remarkable for being the only town in the world in which the Rhetian language is spoken; a dialect, as far as I can judge by the ear, derived from the Latin, and yet sufficiently distinct from the Italian. The guide, who had often passed this way, told me he could not understand it at all. I was also told that the people of Ilantz, and those of another town in sight, could not comprehend each other! This is worse than the Indian tribes on the prairies, for they are not stationary, and rarely meet except to fight.

But this is the country of languages. Three very distinct tongues are used among the 100,000 souls of the Grisons; viz. the German, the Italian, and this, which is called the Rhetian. The latter, of itself, has several dialects, each so different from the others, as hardly to be considered of the same root.

These Rhetians are said to be derived from a colony of Tuscans, well diluted, however, by inroads of barbarians. If Ilantz be the only town in which their language is still spoken, conquest must have done its work so effectually, as to render it matter of surprise that even this vestige of their origin is left. The guide was for turning the tables on the descendant for the haughty pride of the ancestor, for he clearly considered them as a very inferior people, who spoke a language that nobody could understand. What a condition of society is revealed by these facts! Here are a people who have lived for ages in the same valley, actually in sight of each other, and for three centuries absolutely connected by political ties, without understanding each other's terms!

We did not stop in Ilantz, but at an inn on the north side of the river. I walked as far as the town, crossing the wooden bridge that spans the Rhine, which was swift but no longer turbid, and still a stream of some size, though gradually lessening. The houses of this retired *bourg* were partly Swiss and partly Italian, but I was most struck by the singularly soft voices of the women. They all wore woollen jackets, with buttons, like men, and round woollen hats. Beauty in the sex is scarcely to be looked for here, or, indeed, any where else among mere peasants. There are exceptions, certainly, but they are very rare among adults, though it is quite common to see children as lovely as cherubs. The villages, or hamlets, that lay scattered about on the mountains, appeared to be assemblages of dusky roofs that were almost blended with the brown of the rocks, each having a church, that, in the light of a clouded day, was of a soft and pale white.

I ordered a saddle-horse, and relieving the guide from the pack, he was left to follow, accompanied by the horse-keeper. The country soon became broken, the valley grew narrower, and the hills appeared less verdant and more sterile than below.

About a league from Ilantz, I crossed the Rhine, by a log bridge, a regular *corderoy*, like those first used in the American settlements. Indeed, the whole country now began to assume the air of one of our wild, half-cleared, half-civilized frontier establishments; one that was about to be abandoned for some local cause, rather than one that was steadily improving. The ruins of *châteaux*, which still occasionally occurred, were almost the only objects unsuited to such a scene. These little holds formerly abounded throughout all this region, and they appear to have been mostly destroyed by sudden risings of the people, in their efforts for freedom. A few were burned in the invasion of 1797; for, over the whole of this wild and secluded part of the world, the French, Austrians, and Russians poured their battalions; and the old guide, who was an actor in some of the warlike scenes of that period, frequently pointed out the spot where he had witnessed a skirmish or a combat.

There are more Protestants than Catholics in the Grisons. Ilantz is of the former persuasion; but I was now approaching a district that was quite the reverse. This canton, like Unterwalden and Appenzell, is subdivided into several leagues, as they are called, which are, in fact, so many little states, each of which has its own seat of government, and it might almost be said its own government. Disentis is one of these leagues, and is, or was the seat of a community of Benedictines, who appear to have spread their faith very effectually over the adjacent country. As a consequence of their religious influence, the hill-sides began to teem with churches; crosses reappeared, and the views suddenly became more picturesque. I met large flocks of goats, and herds of cream-coloured, or rather milk-coloured, cows, marching, like well-drilled soldiers, to the hamlets of their owners.

It was an agreeable surprise, on reaching Trons, a village placed at some distance from the Rhine, to find before me a view of singular beauty, and one as peculiar as it was striking. You will understand that the whole of this huge valley is on an inclined plane, down which the Rhine dashes, as best it may, amid rocks and through ravines. The reach before me was a little wider than common, and the ascent was sufficient to spread every object in a way to be seen from its lower extremity, and this the more especially as Trons itself stood on a little eminence. The sun had set, and the shades of evening were rendering objects sombre in the valley, every inch of which seemed shorn to the smoothness of velvet. All the artificial parts of this view were in admirable harmony with its natural character; the cottages being grave and picturesque, the fences light and graceful, and the roads merely bridle-paths. Pale, spectral churches were seated, in the calm of evening, on the sides of the dusky hills, while the buildings of the Abbey of Disentis loomed in the distance, a white and ghostly pile. There stood at their foot a cluster of brown cottages, that just caught the parting light from the west, by which they were blended together in pleasing confusion. It is quite probable that the effect of this view was increased by the dim twilight, but it must at all times be strikingly peculiar. One of the churches had small, white "stations" at the angles of the zig-zag by which it was approached, so many memorials of the sufferings of the Redeemer.

As the night was fast approaching, I urged the jaded beast in order to reach Disentis, while there remained sufficient light to find the way. But the purity of the atmosphere, as usual, had rendered the distances deceptive; and, unable to achieve my object, for half an hour I was in a good deal of uncertainty about keeping the proper course. The paths, it is true, were plain, and most of the distance they ran between low fences that were only five or six feet asunder; but there were many of them, and no one to ask which was the true direction. The abbey was gradually lost in the obscurity; and at length my only guide was the general course of the valley, and a light in a distant window. Keeping the path which pointed towards this polar star, I found, on reaching it, that it was in the first house of the hamlet, (village being too significant a word for this local capital,) and that this house was an inn.

Now commenced the difficulties of communicating with a people who spoke a *patois* known only to themselves. It was easy enough to signify that good care must be taken of the horse, and to intimate that I should like to eat, myself; but as to all else I was again thrown upon the language of nature. The result of an intricate negotiation was a supper of bread and milk. I had been particularly warned, by my Hansetown gentleman at Coire, to beware of the innkeeper of Disentis, whom he pronounced to be a rogue and an atrocious "*écorcheur;*" thus far, however, I had every reason to commend my host, who man-ifested just the sort of unsophisticated desire to please his guest, that might be expected in a mountaineer, at whose door a well-dressed traveller, and, in all humility be it said, a well-behaved traveller from a strange land, had suddenly alighted, and was content to sup on bread and milk. His inability to un-derstand me had given him great uneasiness; but a sudden thought seemed to give him as sudden relief. A boy was des-patched on a message, in a great hurry, with a long injunction in *patois*, and from that moment he appeared to have regained his peace of mind.

In the mean time, excessively fatigued, I managed to get pos-session of a room and a bed. The whole arrangement, including the hollow, drum-like sound of the wooden building, the closets of rooms, the low-post bedstead, the coarse rugs, the cotton sheets, the ill-fitting doors and windows, and the ridgy bed, strongly reminded me of those times, when, a traveller near the skirts of society, I had lodged in similar houses in America.

Just as I was falling asleep, some one, by a vigorous shove, forced open the door, and a man stood by the bedside with a candle in his hand. When one's citadel is stormed in this un-ceremonious manner, he is apt to recur to the use of his mother tongue, if required to speak at all. I had, moreover, fallen into a dose, while musing on the points of resemblance between my present situation and the American frontiers, and, as a very natural consequence, the first impression was that the stranger wished to share my bed. At this, it is scarcely necessary to say, human nature revolted. To the "Who the devil are you, sir?" which involuntarily broke from me under such circumstances, all I got for an answer was "*serviteur*," uttered with great delib-eration, as if my visiter considered the word to be a *shibboleth*. Supposing that the man, an unwashed, unshaven, foul-looking fellow, understood French, I gave him a free translation of my first address, in that language. To all and each of my questions, however, nothing could be got out of him but the single word, "*serviteur*," which he pronounced more and more deliberately each time. This ridiculous scene lasted several minutes before I began to suspect the truth. It would seem that the honest land-lord, distressed at not being able to comprehend my wants, had sent for an interpreter, who happened to be the worthy and sententious individual in question. It is common enough to meet with those who enjoy great reputations, in their own narrow circles, on very small attainments; but this man, who probably passed as a linguist at Disentis, was the first I had ever seen who possessed such an advantage from knowing but one word of a foreign language, and that one, too, far from particularly well.

I was awoke, during the night, once more, but in a less disagreeable manner. In these Swiss villages, which are usually constructed of very inflammable materials, a watch is uniformly kept, against fire. I do not think Disentis contains more than twenty habitations, but it had its watchman. I scarcely recollect sweeter sounds than, half-sleeping, half-waking, I heard from this honest guardian of the night, as he sang the hour, in a language that resembled Italian, (the Rhetian, most probably,) beneath my window.

Letter XX.

M Y DEAR————,

I was up early on the following morning, but no tidings had reached the inn of the guide and horse-keeper. Ordering breakfast, therefore, I walked out to look at objects by daylight. The abbey, a large half-dilapidated stone building, four stories in height, with a spacious church of a better architecture than common, stood a short distance from the inn, higher against the side of the mountain. I ascended to the spot, which commanded a fine view of the adjacent country, though the mountain tops were concealed in fog. A door in the basement, as large as a gate, being open, I entered without ceremony, in hope of meeting a monk, with whom I might, at least, murder the little Latin that a busy and varied life has spared. After penetrating the corridore more than a hundred feet, I heard the sounds of voices in a cell at no great distance. Treading lightly, lest I might interrupt orisons, I had got near the door, when a peal of laughter, in which the light merriment of a woman predominated, rung through the vaulted passage, and I retreated. The community may be suppressed, and the building inhabited by families, for I saw no Benedictine during my stay at Disentis, and I think one is a little apt to meet these pious people, in Switzerland, hanging about the taverns. At any rate, such has been my good fortune, in half a dozen instances, since I entered the cantons. Moreover, the "*serviteur*" of the linguist was the only intelligible word which had greeted my ear since I entered the place.

The Rhine runs on the other side of the valley, at some distance from the hamlet; and I walked across the undulating and shorn meadows to its very banks. It had degenerated into a swift and noisy brook. There was one spot, in particular, at which I thought I might have leaped across; though this was at a point a little narrower than common. A small *château* stood at no great distance, prettily placed on the margin of the stream, the first of a thousand that adorn the long line of its sinuous and rapid course! It was merely a better sort of house enclosed by a wall, with an embattled tower that stands a little apart. I believe it belongs to the "league."

While standing near the inn, the fog whirled away from the opposite mountains, and I got a near view of snow which had quite recently fallen, and, as I thought, of one permanent glacier. Beneath, the view was unobstructed, and I counted no less than nine churches, all white and seated on eminences, in this retired and obscure valley! These were the pale and spectral-looking buildings that had stood out so distinct, in melancholy tranquillity, during the obscurity of the previous twilight.

The morning was more than cool, and I became keenly sensible of being at a considerable elevation. Disentis is about thirty miles from Coire, the road being a constant ascent. Coire, according to my estimate, must be at least fifteen hundred feet above the sea; and Disentis, I should think, more than as high again. This, you will see, therefore, was like sleeping on the highest of the Catskills.

The interpreter, anxious to open amicable relations, was at me again with his eternal "*ser-vi-teur.*" His vocabulary, however, had not improved; but, by means of signs, he succeeded in letting me know that my breakfast was ready. Well it might be, for it was the *refrain* of the supper; in other words, night's milk and bread, as that had been morning's milk and bread.

I had just discussed this frugal repast, when the guide and his companion arrived, both glad enough to find I had not yet scaled the Ober Alp. They pleaded the darkness of the night as the apology for their delay. After allowing them time to refresh, the former intimated that it might be well if we kept nearer together for the remainder of the road, as the map and pocket-compass I carried would probably be useful in the course of the day. This, you will perceive, was just changing our respective functions.

On leaving the hamlet, a high, naked Alp appeared, at the distance of a mile or two, to lie directly across the route. A path led up its side, and I began to think we had arrived at the head of the stream; but, on reaching the point in question, we found that our road led round a rock, entering, by a narrow gorge, another and a still higher valley. As we wound round the base of this hill, the river was heard gushing through a deep ravine, on our left, that was only a few feet in width. To this was the mighty Rhine reduced at last!

A small chapel stood near the bend. The upper valley was narrower and more naked than that below, and it lay at a considerably greater elevation. There were also a few hamlets, but, like the nature itself, they became ruder and wilder as we climbed the gradual ascent. A little grain was growing here, not having ripened yet in this high region. Another valley succeeded, for they now lay in terraces, each raised a little above the other, the steps between them being short acclivities, and each steadily rising also, in itself. At length we reached Jüf, the last, or rather the first, village on the Rhine. It is a cluster of six or eight miserable huts, with a small chapel. I should think it must be deserted in winter; but this may be a mistake, for the guide invariably gave ignorance of the dialect as an excuse for not being able to answer any of my interrogatories. Log barns continued up this deserted valley for some distance farther, but there were no more dwellings.

The Rhine, still a stream large enough to turn a mill, now divided again, the smaller branch coming in from the south, in which direction it was soon seen tumbling down the side of a mountain. We pushed on eastwardly, following the drear and cropped valley, in which vegetation seemed to be nearly done for the season. We passed two cow-herds, descending, and driving before them a drove of two hundred cows of the colour of milk. They had probably taken leave of the upper pastures until the following spring.

A short distance further, and then, indeed, we drew near the end. A huge pile of mountain lay exactly before us, and in a form to leave no hope, this time, of finding a path around its base. It was gray with freshly fallen snow. We reached its foot, in the course of a few minutes, and came to a halt.

A hundred cow-paths covered the head of the valley, and even the sides of the mountains, with a sort of interminable net-work. It was impossible to detect our own road among their mazes. Indeed that along which we had been journeying for the last hour was little more than an ill-trod footpath. The prospect was far from cheering; it blew a gale, was excessively cold, though scarcely past the middle of the day, and, by way of completing the disagreeable, it began to snow. Not a habitation, nor a human being, but our three selves, was in sight, or probably within miles of us. On every side, the one by which we had come excepted, rose steep mountains, and, so far as we could perceive, they all stretched away to the clouds. We knew that we were on the side of the St. Gothard, and near the sources of the Rhine; but this was all we did know. The guide confessed he was fairly at fault again; and, as for the horsekeeper, he had never before been as far from home as Trons.

The Rhine came brawling down the mountain in front; and the guide, at length, ventured to say that the path crossed it, and ascended on the opposite side of the valley. Being mounted, I went ahead to reconnoitre; but the rivulet was scarcely between us, when the old man shouted out to me not to separate from him in a snow-storm, confessing that he was still uncertain as to the direction we ought to take. I now thought it time to act for myself. The map and the compass were produced, and I was not long in deciding to go to the right. A small lake was laid down on the map as lying on the summit of the pass, and I could see nothing that favoured such a formation in the outline of the mountains in front or to the left; while that to the right had, at least, the recommendation of uncertainty, its position not admitting of so close an examination as those of the two others.

Recrossing the Rhine—I must give it this imposing name while there is a drop of water running in it—I took the ascent to the right, telling my companions to follow the footsteps of the horse. I was soon far ahead, and beyond the reach of sound. At times the snow was up to the saddle girths, and at others I found the animal sinking in a marsh. I was compelled to make a considerable *détour* to avoid the latter, at a moment when the guide and horsekeeper were completely out of sight. It was easy for them, however, to follow the tracks of the horse.

It stopped snowing suddenly, and a minute after the sun shed his heat and radiance upon the naked hills. Looking to the opposite side of the valley, it now appeared as if the formation admitted of a passage in that direction. But Italy lay there, and the map telling me to persevere, I took counsel of its wisdom.

After ascending for half an hour, I got a view of a spot above me, a sort of valley of air, that was bounded by high mountains on only two sides. This was encouraging, for it was just the vacuum that would be left by the presence of a small sheet of water. After an hour of vexation, uncertainty, and toil, I reached a point sufficiently high to get a sight of the little blue lake, looking chill and wintry. Making a wide circuit, to avoid the wet ground, I succeeded in reaching its shores, along which lay a well beaten path. The *débris* of the mountains had formed a little island in the lake, and the cabin of some fishermen stood on its banks. There were even a boat, nets, and a few fish forgotten on the shore; but in all other respects the spot seemed the type of solitude.

The guide and his companion came in view, in the distance, and I made a sign of success; it was answered, when I pushed ahead. I had a hint touching my elevation, in the sight of clouds driving before the mouth of the gorge, at a considerable distance below me. After passing the lake, which might have been half or three quarters of a mile long, I came to the other brow of the mountain, and, quite unexpectedly, got a noble view into the celebrated valley of Ursern. On examining the map, I found that the line of the canton of Uri lay at the opposite end of the lake. Adieu, then, to the Grisons!

Glaciers appeared in the distance, towards the west, and also through openings in the nearer mountains, both to the north and to the south. The scene was as suddenly changed as if one were to issue out of a dense and tangled forest into a smiling plain. I had now reached that great nucleus of the Alps where the two principal chains unite, or, to speak more properly perhaps, whence they diverge, leaving the valleys of the Rhine and the Rhone between the respective ranges. By this singular formation, all the great rivers of Switzerland take their rise near the same spot. The course of the Rhine we have seen and followed. That of the Rhone is very similar, merely rising on the other side of the huge centre, and flowing west instead of east. The sources of the Aar are in its near neighbourhood, while the Reuss came down the northern face of the St. Gothard, or the mountain which bounded the valley of Ursern to the south.

The view, as I descended the sharp declivity to the west, was novel as well as fine, and this, too, in a country whose novelty I had begun to think exhausted. The valley is long and narrow, and, while gazing at it from that height, I remember to have likened its shape to that of a corvette's deck, seen from the foretop. You will call this a queer comparison, but it was the first that suggested itself, and is not altogether without truth, though it will probably be of no great use to you.

The country was naked, resembling downs, with the exception that the valley and all the lower mountain pastures were beautifully green, while the more elevated portions of the latter were faded and wintry. All above these again was either gray with the late fall of snow, or absolutely buried beneath the eternal glaciers.

A village lay about midway the length of the valley, near the base of the St. Gothard, and a beautiful object it was, seen from the Ober Alp. It is called *Hospital*, having formerly been used, I believe, as a place of refuge for travellers. The *hospice*, or the present establishment, stands on the summit of the mountain, where, from time to time, there have been several religious charities of this nature. Andermatt did not appear until I had partly descended the declivity, and then it was seen almost beneath me. A high and steep abutment of the St. Gothard rises so near this town as to render it liable to suffer from the descent of avalanches. As a defence, the inhabitants have, for ages, carefully preserved a grove of larches on the side of this precipice, which has hitherto been found sufficient for its object. It is of a triangular form, with one of its angles pointing upwards, and is so placed as not only to break the fall of heavy bodies of snow, but to divide the masses, throwing them off on its two sides. It is now a slight, and seemingly a perishable defence, though the form of the rocks contribute to aid it, for I observed many freshly broken trees, and even stumps that had been left by the axe. I was afterwards told, by an inhabitant, that the contending armies, in 1799, destroyed many of the trees; and that, weakened by this inroad, each successive year has seen a decrease in the number of these all-important sentinels. A few more winters and those that are left may be swept away at a single swoop; when it will become necessary to abandon the town. Such is an Alpine existence!

Andermatt, though in a valley, stands at an elevation of

nearly 5000 feet above tide; the St. Gothard, on whose broad bosom this valley lies, rising as much more above it. It is a singular spot, and well deserving its reputation. The basin amid these savage rocks, I have already told you, was beautifully verdant, and most faithfully cropped. It is bounded on one end by the Ober Alp, or the mountain which I had just descended; on the other by the Furca, a passage that leads into the valley of the Rhone; while to the south rises the last swell of the St. Gothard; and to the north are smaller mountains, bearing local names, detached parts of the same huge mass.

The Reuss, which appears to have four different sources, of which the principal comes down the St. Gothard, near *Hospital*, waters this valley; and, uniting its several streams, finds its way out of it, at the south-east corner, by a pass in the rocks of only a hundred feet in width. The Ursern, for so is the valley called, is seven miles long, and less than one in breadth, even at its widest part. To the eye, in that pure atmosphere, and amid that grand nature, it did not appear to have half these dimensions. When first seen from the Ober Alp, I did not believe it to be more than a third as long as I find, by examining the books, it really is.

The guide and horsekeeper gained on me in the descent, which, part of the way, was ticklish work, and we all came in together. The latter was to be discharged, and having expended all my smaller coin, I gave the former a double Louis to be changed, for the purpose of paying him. After turning the coin over in his hand, for nearly a minute, the old man begged I would give him some silver. He had been silently calculating his own wages, and finding that they were sufficient to absorb this piece, he felt disposed to secure the premium on gold, by accepting it as a part of his own compensation. I set his heart at ease, by showing him a handful; after which he had no further scruples. I may here add, that the established price for a guide, in Switzerland, is six French francs a day, he paying his own expenses.

After a little refreshment, we proceeded to the point where the Reuss finds its way out of the valley, which is at no great distance from the village. We entered a gorge, between frightful rocks, where the river was fretting and struggling as if in a hurry to get in before us. A gloomy cave opened its yawning mouth, and, seeing no other path but the one which led into it, I was about to proceed, when the noise of bells tinkling within caused me to pause. Presently, a train of packhorses and mules came into the valley, on their way to Italy, by the St. Gothard. Allowing them to pass, I went into the hole out of which they had just issued, and found it to be a dark gallery, about two hundred feet long, and of some ten or twelve in height and breadth. As we went through it, the roar of the Reuss, and the rushing of the winds without, sounded as if a league distant. Immediately on quitting this gallery, which, in the dialect of the canton, is called the "Hole of Uri,"* I found myself in the centre of a scene that was one of the most extraordinary I had yet beheld, in this very extraordinary country.

The Reuss was plunging through the bottom of the gorge, a boiling torrent that falls, at an inclination of nearly five and twenty degrees, among broken rocks; the wind was fairly howling through the pass; the rocks literally overhung us, nearly excluding a view of the heavens; and a slight, narrow bridge, of a single arch, spanned the gorge, with a hardihood that caused one to shudder. The infernal din, at first, nearly destroyed all power to analyze the parts of this assemblage of the fearful and the sublime.

After a minute's pause, I walked on the bridge, and, standing in the centre, gazed around me. Its abutments were the living rock; its thickness but a thread; the span of the arch was about eighty feet; its width might have been fifteen; the height, above the Reuss, a hundred; and there was no railing! The wind blew so furiously that I really wished for a rope to hold on by. This was the far-famed Devil's Bridge; *the* Devil's Bridge; for the name and the manner of construction are both quite frequent in mountainous countries. Other bridges may have been built by imps or journeymen, but Beelzebub himself is thought to have had a hand in this.

The road, a mere bridle-path, after crossing the bridge, winds, *en corniche*, along the rocks, and disappears at some distance below, owing to the widening of the gorge. Another train of packhorses was coming up the circuitous route, adding singularly to the beauty of the scene.

* Or sometimes Urnerlock.

IX. The Devil's Bridge *Switzerland*, 212–14

x. Unterseen *Switzerland*, 48, 223–24

xi. The Castle of Chillon, by Moonlight *Switzerland*, 267

XII. The Abbey of Einsiedeln *Switzerland*, 165–66

The St. Gothard is one of the most frequented passes in the Alps. Travellers, it is true, do not cross it as often as they cross by the Simplon and Splügen, for as a carriage-road it is imperfect. Fifteen thousand persons, it is calculated, however, go into Italy, or return by this route, annually. The distance from Fluelen, on the lake of Lucerne, to Bellinzone, near that of Maggiore, is seventy miles, nearly the whole distance being either a continual ascent, or a continual descent. Three hundred packhorses, or mules, cross the mountain, weekly, for a portion of the year.

The cantons of Uri and Tessin, in which the whole of this pass lies, have partly completed an excellent carriage-road, with the hope of attracting some of those who are distributing their money so freely through the country, and of making their commercial communications more perfect. The plan comprises not only a new road, but a new bridge in this gorge; and men, slung in ropes, were then at work blasting rocks, above the present road and bridge, with this object. The new bridge is to be both larger and safer than the present; and I believe that the canton intends to compete, for the honour of its construction, with the ancient bridge-builder. In these later times, the Devil confines his labours to throwing arches across chasms to facilitate the progress of the traveller on a different journey.

I walked down the road a mile or two, and found the scenery wild and extraordinary; but I had evidently approached it in the wrong direction. By ascending, there is a regular gradation of wonders, until the climax is reached at the bridge. Taking this direction, the effect of the dark gallery, and the surprise of issuing out of this chaotic confusion into the soft beauty of the valley, serve to heighten all. Although prepared for the change, I felt, in returning, most of the sensations such transitions must produce on the traveller. The roar of the river is eternal; and my old guide assured me he never was in the gorge, that the winds were not scuffling and howling, just as I then found them.

I left the place with reluctance, though exceedingly fatigued, for its frightful beauties seemed as if they had been produced by a wanton effort of nature, in order to prove what might be done, at need, in the way of the savage and wild. Man, too, had wrought in precisely the manner best adapted to aid these effects; and I question if the new *human* arch and wheel track will be found as picturesque and appropriate as the old mule path, and the *hardiesse* of the father of sin.

Vast herds of goats came into the village towards nightfall. I witnessed the arrival of one, which, after descending the mountain in a body, and crossing a bridge together, separated in two lines, each going its way as orderly as men, without any apparent interference of the goatherds. Three stopped quietly before the door of the inn. A boy called to some loiterers, and they came bounding forward, licking his hands and leaping on him like dogs.

Letter XXI.

D_{EAR} ———,

There was a sharp frost in the night, ice having made of the thickness of a dollar. The winter, or, in other words, the frosts prevail in this elevated valley eight months in the year. When I left the inn at Andermatt the sun had been up more than an hour; but the ice had not given way. This, you will remember, was on the 17th of September.

Hospital, as it is called, is about half a league from Andermatt. There is now no edifice that deserves such a name, but merely a hamlet of some five-and-twenty houses, and a church. A ruined tower contributes to its prettiness. The scene, as I passed the spot, was singularly picturesque. A line of packhorses was just issuing from the "Hole of Uri," and was holding its way steadily and earnestly toward this point, where the road begins seriously to climb the St. Gothard. The next morning, it would be in Italy!

Realp, another hamlet, scarcely deserves even this modest name, containing but three or four houses. The country was totally devoid of trees, and the grass appeared stinted and short. Thus far I proceeded alone; but the guide and a new horsekeeper now overtook me, bringing with them a horse. The pack was already attached to the saddle, and I mounted.

The ascent of the Furca was by no means as precipitate as the descent from the Ober Alp. Indeed it seems to be a rule, dependent on the general geological formation of the country, that the eastern and northern acclivities should be less abrupt than the western and southern. The path up the side of this mountain is not entirely free from danger to those who are mounted, for it frequently runs on the verge of banks, and a misstep of the horse, or the earth's giving way, would ensure a fall. A young Englishman had a leg broken in this manner a short time previously to my ascent. Admonished by his bad luck, I took sufficient care to prevent a similar calamity befalling myself.

The reversed view of the valley was not as fine as that I had first seen. Still it was good, and its interest was much increased by a more intimate knowledge of the localities. More than once I hesitated, on the side of the Furca, about turning back and ascending the St. Gothard; but we had Italy before us for the autumn and winter, and a separation of ten days from my companions was a strong inducement to return to la Lorraine.

A cross announced our arrival near the summit of the pass, which we reached before eleven. The map of Keller gives the height of this spot at 6420 French feet above the sea, which is about equal to 7000 of our English feet.

The view, eastward from the pass, was confined to a vast mountain basin, shaped not unlike an irregular funnel, and its sides were faded Alpine pastures. There was not a tree to be seen, and scarcely a shrub. The last year's snow still lay, in spots shaded from the sun, several feet in depth. The horsekeeper was discharged at the cross; and, seizing the walking-staff, I began to descend the sharp declivity at a pace that extorted a remonstrance from my old companion, who had resumed the pack. He warned me that we were miles from any habitation, and that by going ahead I might get astray; and took occasion to remark, with some pretension of manner, that he now *did* know where he was, and might be of more use than by simply carrying my clothes. This appeal was seconded by the sudden appearance of the summits of the Oberland range, most of which came in view over the tops of the nearest mountains to the westward. The peaks were all glittering in the sun, and I greeted their reappearance as that of old acquaintances. The sides next us were exactly opposite those seen from Berne, and yet it was easy to recognise them all, so little were the great outlines changed. We strained our eyes, in vain, in order to detect a flag on the Jung Frau, which was to be the sign of success, in the event of the chamois hunters of Grindelwald reaching its summit.

After delaying half an hour to gaze at these magnificent mountains, we proceeded. As we descended lower into the funnel, external objects were completely excluded from sight, and the contemplations of those within the treeless basin were not particularly agreeable. A few huts of stone, places of refuge for goatherds, were the only relief to the monotony of withered pastures. Near one of these huts were two or three springs, which, I learned from Ebel, some people affect to call the true sources of the Rhone. The water trickled from them, in a little rill, through the pastures, toward a concealed opening, by which the basin communicates with the great valley westward. I beg pardon of the republic of Valais, for forgetting to mention that we entered its territory on the summit, the line crossing the pass of the Furca nearly at right angles. The cross, I believe, stands on the frontier.

The guide was again left behind, and plunging rather than walking downward, I was brought to a halt by another grand and unexpected sight. The mountain on the right, or the north, of the Furca, is called the Gallenstock, a name, I dare say, that you never heard before, though it rises nearly eleven thousand feet above the level of the tides. The higher parts of this mountain are, of course, covered with snow, wherever the element can lodge. Fields of eternal ice cover the vast valley that lies between it and its northern neighbours; and from this immense reservoir descends, into the lowest part of the basin in which I was travelling, the particular body of ice that is called the glacier of the Rhone. It now lay directly before me, apparently closing all exit from the funnel, except by returning to the Furca.

This glacier is both sublime and beautiful; sublime by its vastness and grandeur, and beautiful in the purity of the element and in its minuter forms. It is, I think, out of all comparison, finer than either of the glaciers of Grindelwald. It also has one feature peculiar to itself. The margin of the field above, where it falls toward the valley, is marked by a high precipice of ice, resembling a wall, the inclined plane of the glacier being supplied from the frozen magazines beneath.

The deserted huts excepted, not a sign of man was visible. I had got so far ahead of the guide as to be out of sight, and took a seat on a stone, at the part of the basin opposite the glacier, near the path which winds around its sides, in fixed contemplation of the magnificent solitude. It was an exquisite moment, for every object that could divert the intensity of admiration was completely excluded from sight. I appeared to be alone with the glacier, enclosed in this cropped and semi-sterile Alpine basin. The spot seemed created for the abode of eternal repose! Occasionally a groan issued from the mountains, produced by the rending of ice: an interruption admirably suited to the solemn spectacle. The tinkling of a shoe against a stone aroused me from a trance of contemplation, and a multitude of thick-coming fancies, and presently a line of travellers came round a projection of the hill-side, following the path that led *from* the valley. They were English, at a glance. I felt disposed to anathematize the restlessness which drives these people, full dressed, and conventional, just as they issue from their assize balls, and county dinners, into every hole and cranny of Europe. This was the impulse of disappointment, and sufficiently unreasonable, since, apart from having quite as good a right to come from England to the glacier of the Rhone, as one has to come from America, the English are observant and bold travellers. No people had greater need of communication with the rest of mankind, than the islanders of 1814, and no people could have turned the advantages gained by the peace, to better account.

There were two ladies and a maid on horseback, two gentlemen afoot, and a guide or two. I rose to hazard a bow to the first,—one runs as much risk of being thought impertinent, as of being thought polite on such occasions—but this time I was answered by a bending of very soft eyes, and, as I suspected, of slightly stubborn dispositions also. There was more of the world about the men, who inquired frankly for news; but I had none to give them, having been nearly a fortnight in the hills. Some small remains of the old profession probably hangs about me, for the elder of the two good naturedly took the trouble to tell me, as a matter of mutual interest, that Sir Herbert Taylor had been made adjutant general! After these material preliminaries were duly disposed of, they inquired if the passage of the Furca was free of snow. Being satisfied on this point, they said the Grimsel was a little ticklish, and we parted. I account this adventure as my second grand discovery, since entering Switzerland. The first is the mountain, of which I have already had occasion to boast; and the other is the valley of the glacier of the Rhone, which I now announce to be a spot sufficiently secluded and without the pale of human conventions, to render it safe to make a bow to English men and English women, with some certainty of meeting with a proper return.

The guide having joined me, we proceeded to the glacier. The Rhone gushes out of the ice, a river at its birth. It may answer the caprice of poetry, to call the little rill that flows from the springs, and which joins the stream below, the true source of the Rhone, but it is like ascribing the force of the tornado to the particles of dust that it raises. To all practical purposes, the Rhone issues from this glacier, from which a thousand drops are derived for one that comes from the springs. It is true that a rill would run through this valley, were the glacier away, and that, receiving the continual contributions of the mountains, it would gradually become a stream; but, as I have just told you, the glacier sends forth a river from the start.

Most of the peculiarities already described in the account of Grindelwald are to be seen here, with the exception that the ice is much purer and whiter. The river runs through a pass so narrow, a short distance below its commencement, that it is impossible this glacier can ever materially extend its limits; at least the basin must be first filled, and this would be the work of centuries; though the ice is said to have formerly thrust itself a few hundred feet lower than it is at present.

We crossed the Rhone by a bridge, a short distance from the glacier, and reached the foot of the Grimsel. The prospect was any thing but agreeable, as I stood looking up its steep side. The Righi, the heaven-ascending stairs excepted, was not anywhere so steep, though certainly much higher. The afternoon sun, too, was beating on the side of the ascent, and there was not a breath of air. The guide manifested what he thought of the matter, by very deliberately taking off the pack, and beginning to strip. When he was ready, we went at it, with all our resolution. In about five minutes, my coat was on my arm; in less than ten, I began to look back wistfully at the glacier, which presented a most invitingly cool aspect. Luckily we got a little snow near the summit, with which to cool our parched mouths, but, from some cause or other, (the heat, perhaps,) this was much the severest ascent I had yet overcome. Once or twice, the throbbing of my heart was so severe, that I thought it would leap out of my mouth; and, as for the old guide, with whom it was a point of honour to refuse all aid in carrying the pack, he consoled himself, at every halt, of which we made fifty, by exclaiming, "*Boint de pagatelle, Monsir!*"

There were two paths, when all our difficulties in the ascent were overcome. One, the safest but the longest, led over the rocky head of the Grimsel, while the other passed under its brow, *en corniche*. The latter leads along the verge of a precipice, where a false step might prove destruction. This spot was now covered with moist snow, to the depth of two feet, and it was not easy to find the path. I made a hasty computation, by which it was shown that if the snow yielded, or either of us slipped, he would probably fall about four hundred feet. It was blind work, and we had to feel our way with the pikes. This was the only spot, apart from the glaciers, that I had seen in Switzerland, which struck me as being at all dangerous for those who travel on foot, and who use ordinary caution.

The Grimsel, like the Ober Alp, has a little blue sheet, which is called the "Lake of the Dead." The pass is not quite as high as the Furca, but more strongly marked by the features that belong to a great elevation. Ebel, however, says that it is rather more than seven thousand English feet above the sea. There is little besides rocks, on the summit, though it is possible for a few goats to live among them. The line between the Valais and Berne runs along this ridge of mountains, and, of course, we re-entered the great canton, at this point. Two little rills trickle from the lake, one of which joins the Rhone, and the other the Aar: it follows that this secluded sheet of water sends tribute equally to the Mediterranean and to the North Sea.

High poles, beacons for the traveller in winter, marked the path, as we descended, by a sort of magnificent natural stairs, to the *hospice*. We found this place half a league below the summit, in a most savage valley, where little else was visible, besides rocks piled on each other in every possible form, and another lake, that has the reputation of being both deep and well filled with fish. The building is of stone, but of no great size. It is, in truth, a rude tavern. Berne being a Protestant canton, unlike most of the Swiss establishments of this nature, the *hospice* of the Grimsel is not connected with a religious community. Ebel gives its elevation above the sea at about six thousand English feet, and, of course, it lies a thousand feet below the pass. The establishment is farmed out, its keeper being obliged to remain in this isolated spot, from March to November.

It was still early, though too late to think of proceeding any further that night, and I wandered about among the rocks, with a strange sensation of dreariness. I was the only traveller who had arrived, and the five or six people who belonged to the place were all busy. The view is limited, little else being visible but granite, which had the appearance of being stored here, in readiness to be used in the construction of mountains, as they might be wanted. In the evening, a large herd of goats collected before the door, with udders so distended, that they caused me to look around for the pastures on which they had been filled.

A party of bustling Germans, from Holstein, arrived a little before sunset. What the honest innkeeper did with them all, I cannot say, but, after a good many misgivings on the subject, I secured a small room to myself. In Europe, I believe no emergency ever compels two men, pretending to be gentlemen, to share the same bed; at least, no such calamity was ever even proposed to me.

We were on the road the next day as the sun lighted the ragged glens. Luckily, all the other travellers were going up the Grimsel, and we had the woods and solitudes of the descent to ourselves, a pleasure that must be enjoyed to be appreciated. The path follows the little stream which runs from the lake, but which soon joins the Aar; at this place, a swift roaring brook. This river has its rise in a glacier on the side of the Finster Aar Horn,* at no great distance from the *hospice*. The descent was quite gradual, and, for the first league, the path was charmingly sequestered. We crossed the Aar several times, on picturesque little stone bridges of single arches, which were quite jewels in their way. They were just the sort of thing that a fine taste would select as ornaments for the rustic scenery of a park, and meeting them here, as it were, in the natural way, caused equally pleasure and surprise. They were designed by a painter, though the man never saw a pencil. Alas! there is not such a bridge as either of these, which ornament a wild, savage, mountain pass, in the whole of matter-of-fact, utility-loving, and picturesque-despising America!

* Black Aar Peak.

I should think that the ascent to the Grimsel, by this road, would give more pleasure than the descent. Still, take it which way you will, there is a gradation of changes at each step, until the extremes complete one of the most striking transitions possible.

After two leagues of delightful march, that appeared more like a morning walk through an open wood, than a journey, we reached Handeck, near the celebrated falls of the Aar. The river plunges into a narrow and deep ravine, taking a new level, like a canal. This cascade, I think justly, has the highest reputation of any in Switzerland. But, beyond its dimensions and general character, description would be very unsatisfactory. The pitch must be some sixty or eighty feet: there is plenty of water for a cascade: the mind is not distracted from its contemplations by other objects, when one is in the ravine: and there is a collateral charm, in a little transverse fall, produced by a smaller stream, that comes in at right angles, and shoots its waters into the same gulf, and at precisely the same point with the Aar. I believe this is an unique incident in the history of waterfalls.

The country became more open as we continued to descend. A singular, low table-mountain stood directly across the end of the principal valley, barely leaving room for the river to flow between it and the lateral rocks. This hill, which, in appearance, resembles a huge artificial mound, we were obliged to cross. It was the work of near an hour, but while we were winding down its lower side by a romantic path, the view towards the lake of Brienz well rewarded me for the toil. Some lines of packhorses increased the beauty of the picture. A railroad may argue greater advancement in civilization, but these classical looking little cavalcades contribute singularly to the picturesque. They are particularly appropriate in a Swiss landscape, and I have never met one without feeling how admirably they are brought in to aid the effect of winding paths, rocky ascents, and deep glens.

At length, we walked into the inn at Meyringen, where I was right glad to obtain rest and refreshment.

Letter XXII.

M_Y DEAR ———,

Two Englishmen were discussing the question of West-India slavery, at another table, in the room where I soon seated myself, at dinner. One was eloquent in his expressions of regret, that no other nation was sufficiently strong to wrest the islands from Great Britain, for the sole object of liberating the negroes. The other reproved this philanthropy, as unpatriotic, reminding his friend that sugar and rum were very good things, in their way; and that England would make a very poor figure without them. He assured the philanthropist, moreover, that the planters consumed so large an amount of the English manufactures, they could not well be spared; and that the liberation of their blacks would infallibly strip them of the ability to buy, by stripping them of the ability to sell. The other was a wholesale religionist, and was for getting rid of the sin by a *coup de main*. This led to a nice dissertation on the nature of sin in general, and on its particular connexion with slavery. In short, the whole dialogue was an amusing exhibition of a zealous and exaggerated philanthropy battering in vain against the flint-like intrenchments of cupidity. The name of America was introduced; but it was soon disposed of as too insignificant to furnish an example, either for good or for evil. The assault ended, as such trials of skill usually end,—he of the sugar and rum, doggedly maintaining his position of the usefulness of the articles, and he of the universal emancipation, virtually objecting that a man's soul was of too much value to be bargained away for toddy.

I left the metaphysicians on the horns of their dilemmas, and got into a *char* for Brienz, where, on arriving, we luckily found the mail boat ready to depart, and we were rowed down to Interlachen in very good season. The sun was still high, and determining to take my old quarters at Unterséen, I lingered for an hour along the road. On reaching the point where the view of the Jung Frau is obtained, we looked with some curiosity for the promised sign of the success of the chamois hunters. Sure enough, a little flag, or what seemed to be a flag not larger than a pocket handkerchief, was fluttering in a smart breeze. To a good eye, it was, at moments, distinctly visible, owing, I presume, to the exceeding purity of the medium. It was evident, by the quickness with which it flapped, and from the certainty the flag must be of some size to be seen so far, that the wind was blowing fresh aloft, though the lakes were reflecting the rays of the sun from their glassy surfaces, like mirrors. The heroes of Grindelwald had triumphed, and the honour of first ascending this virgin mountain was preserved to Switzerland!

Unterséen improves on acquaintance. It is intrinsically a Swiss town in its exterior; but the great inroad of strangers is only too fast altering the character of the people. Men require all the fixed relations of society to keep them within the bounds of good morals, in addition to the general obligations of religion; and a community that is brought incessantly in contact with strangers, inevitably will suffer a diminution of the sense of right. We are all more cautious of deportment in our own houses than when out of them; at home than when abroad; under the responsibilities of an association that is permanent, than under those of a mere passing interview.

An English journal, published at Paris, called Galignani's Messenger, although totally destitute of any fixed character of its own, is the most useful print in Europe. It is chiefly composed of well-selected articles from the best European newspapers, and, as this duty is done with sufficient impartiality and a great deal of tact and experience, I feel persuaded that a constant reader of this paper, who is a cool observer, and who wishes to obtain truths rather than support a system, will get a more accurate idea of what is really going on in Europe from its columns, than in any other manner, except that of being a principal actor in the events themselves. I sat down to a file of this journal the moment the inn was entered, and in half an hour was *au fait* of all that had passed in the civilized world within the last fortnight, and the news of which had had time to reach Unterséen. Among other important occurrences, I had official confirmation that Sir Herbert Taylor was made adjutant general.

Truly, the "twelve millions" are of very little account in the estimation of their fellow Christians! The gentlemen whom I met at the glacier had never supposed it possible I could be any thing but an Englishman, and this, quite likely, because I was not a son of Ham. The papers, however, just then, were dragging us into rather more notice than common, on account of the new tariff, which afforded a singularly good occasion for abuse. I have already told you how strong was the sensation produced in London by this measure—the women, in society, introducing it even as a subject of absorbing interest. By the women, I do not mean those who go into the world merely to see and be seen, but that class of Englishwomen (and a numerous and highly creditable class it is) who reflect on the condition of their country, foresee its hazards, understand its interests, and reason patriotically, at least, if not always fairly, on the means of supporting them. A hundred ludicrous attempts were made to convince me we never could succeed as manufacturers. My argument was the fact that we had succeeded thus far; and that the past was, in this respect, a sufficient pledge for the future. But one who knows England can easily appreciate the extent and nature of her apprehensions on this interesting subject by the tone of the public prints. They have reopened upon us their batteries of blackguardism. This is a peculiar feature in English character, and is worthy to be known. Were the billingsgate confined to us, I could easily imagine that, understanding the mental dependence of the larger portion of the reading community, it was intended for effect in America, where the abuse would be read; but, in point of fact, the same course is observed towards other nations, where the abuse cannot be read, and as respects which it is so many "pearls cast before swine." The practice has excited a good deal of remark, and general disgust. Washington pronounced the English to be the most abusive nation on earth, near fifty years ago; and a remark of this nature, coming from so pure a source, is entitled to profound consideration. As a matter of course, the prints which are the most distinguished for talent are the least addicted to this practice; though there are some in which admirable articles occasionally appear, that do not disdain the alliance with the fishwomen. As a rule, however, I think no summary of English character can ever be complete, without giving a conspicuous place to the national propensity to *blackguard* those who stand in the way of the national interests.

In the present case, Mr. Huskisson is the champion of English rights. In his zeal for the cause, he has gone so far as to delare in Parliament that our Tariff is a violation of the treaty between the two countries! The Times, Courier, and Standard, overwhelm us with the coarsest accusations, and we are loudly menaced with all sorts of calamities. Our most virtuous citizens are stigmatized as being any thing but gentlemen, and occasionally a sweeping paragraph, more especially in the Standard, consigns the whole nation, at one swoop, to the devil!*

I think it would be quite easy to establish the fact of this peculiarity in the English character; but it is not quite so easy to account for it. After adopting various theories, I have come to the opinion it proceeds from the nature of English interests, which, owing to their being extremely artificial, get to be so high wrought, if one may use the expression, that they are constantly liable to be injured by any justifiable measure to which others may resort for their own good. All purely commercial communities have the same tendency to a jealous and ferocious watchfulness of the pocket; and they invariably think it is a sufficient plea for retaliation, that any person or thing invades their interests, without stopping to examine the abstract questions of right and wrong. As in most instances active retaliation

*The most ludicrous result that I have ever observed in connexion with this system of *blackguarding*, which is beyond question a national trait, grew out of the appearance of the cholera, in 1832. The disease first reached the ocean at Hamburgh. After a delay of a few weeks, it suddenly appeared in England. The King of Holland immediately established a quarantine between the infected ports and his own dominions. Thereupon, the Times opened its vocabulary of well-bred epithets. His majesty, who was by no means in favour, on account of his pertinaciously adhering to a treaty that it was inconvenient to England, just at that moment, to respect, was called a "pig-headed Dutchman," a "fellow behind the age," and by a variety of similar gentlemanlike and intellectual names. This lasted a few days, gradually waxing hotter and hotter, when suddenly there was a cessation of abuse. An attentive observer of all that passes around me, I watched curiously for the *dénouement*. A few days later an order in Council appeared, *sotto voce*, rescinding a quarantine *that had actually been laid by the English government against the whole coast of Holland*, which country the cholera had not yet reached, on the appearance of the disease at Hamburgh!

is impossible, and impulses of this sort are usually transient, where interests are constantly fluctuating, for want of efficient remedies, they have recourse to the natural substitute, abuse. We are not guiltless of a leaning to the same vice; and it is quite apparent that the tone of the journals at home is less measured and decent in the commercial than in the planting states. The whole, of course, belongs to a principle inherent in human nature; but the constant jeopardy and engrossing magnitude of commercial interests render them more active as exciting causes.* Men, usually, will fight for their money, and when precluded from defending it in acts, they will not fail to defend it with their tongues. After a time, cause and effect get to be reciprocal; and the public, which at first was treated with vituperation for interested motives, comes at length to be treated with it because it likes it.

England has a double call for vigilance in the extent and factitious nature of all her commercial interests, as well as in the extent and in the conflicting interests of her empire. In America she resists the principle that great rivers are highways, in order to close the St. Lawrence against her neighbours; whilst in Germany she defends it, in order to open the Rhine to her own manufactures. Now a little *blackguarding* can be very conveniently inserted in the crevices of a philosophy that is so loose. I have seen abuse heaped on America, in the English journals, during the last twelve months, for wishing to open the St. Lawrence; and, during the same period, I have seen abuse heaped on Holland for wishing to close the Rhine!

Cui bono?—You will be ready to exclaim; does all this vituperation serve a practical end? It does, and it does not. It disgusts, and it intimidates. When it disgusts, it does harm; when it intimidates, it may help to advance a given end. If constant dropping will wear away a stone, so will constant abuse wear away a character. Few men, even among those who are in situations to judge correctly, think for themselves; and still fewer are in situations to form correct notions of the characters of distinguished

---

* La Fayette once told the writer that he had received more personal abuse from the money-power-government of the last Revolution in France, than from the Restoration, the Empire, the Directory, and all the combinations that had preceded it, united.

individuals, or of foreign nations. They who do know better, usually want a motive to set the matter right; and they who have the motive frequently want the power. This has been affectedly called the "era of good feeling;" but I think it might, with greater truth, be called "the era of blackguarding." Presses are multiplied without number, and although the tyros of the editorial corps commonly commence with moderation, and with a fair desire to be just and dignified, the larger portion are carried away by the torrent of example, yielding to the vitiated tastes created by such aliment. As a proof of what this taste has got to be, we find prints established which, apart from views of pecuniary profit, indulge in unmitigated, motiveless vituperation. Even the stale and hollow pretext of reforming the world by the exposure of vice, a motive that, when pure, cautiously leads one to abstain from personalities, is barefacedly abandoned. In no countries but England and America are journals known that exist by attacks on private character. Does not this argue a national peculiarity common to both countries?

England, by leading the way in liberty, has earlier reached the abuses which would seem to be its necessary concomitants. We have followed closest on her heels, and, although our press is generally in the hands of men less trained and educated than that of England, and its tone consequently is more vulgar, I do not think its vituperation, as yet, by any means, as ferocious.

In France, the reign of the press-ocracy is just commencing; it will advance, sustained by reason and the right, to conquest;* it will become corrupt by success, and, instead of being restrained by the *bon ton* of a country so justly celebrated for its perfect taste in these matters, it will finally pervert that taste, and place vituperation above principle. The press, everywhere, seems doomed first to destroy its enemies, and then, in the wantonness of victory, to destroy itself.

To return to Mr. Huskisson and Free Trade, any impartial man must admit that this gentleman is, at least, a very inconsistent advocate. He broaches a theory that is suspiciously connected with the immediate interests that he represents, and

---

* The writer, perhaps, ought to hesitate about publishing a prediction after its fulfilment; but he refers, with confidence, to his correspondence, of dates even older than 1828, to prove that such were his opinions long before the revolution of 1830.

when reproached with a contradiction between his professions and his practice, he turns to his budget and says, our corn-laws, and duties on tobacco and timber, and a variety of other articles, are indispensable *as revenue*, whereas *you*, virtually released from taxation, are bound to respect certain great principles that we prove to you to be true, but which we are unable to practise on ourselves. He does not *add*, but he must *think*, "and this you are bound to do, although the restraints arising from our wants work an injury to your interests, and the admission of the principle will, in the actual state of things, work a greater, by enabling our long-established manufactures to crush yours, which are yet scarcely able to go alone." If to this reasoning be added the fact that the taxation of Great Britain is the result of an effort to create what may be called an unnatural empire—an effort to extend the sway of an island on the coast of Europe over a large portion of the world—the case made out would seem to be perfect.

The advocates of free trade will contend, however, that the fallacies and contradictions of the English policy do not affect a principle that is based on general reasoning. This is self-evident, for no moral or physical truth can justly be impaired by the errors of those who see fit to advance it. I have no intention to argue the question of free trade with you, but, in alluding to the contents of the English journals, having said so much on the subject, I ask leave to add another word.

The doctrine of free trade, taken as an abstraction, or as a question that merely affects the single isolated interests of commerce, I take it, is true. But this amounts to no more than if one were to say that a man will run easier and faster without shackles, than in shackles. Nations, as respects all their interests, are shackled by circumstances. It is no more true, in fact, that by equal and liberal international laws, you can bring communities up to the same level of wealth and prosperity, than it is true, that, by conceding equal rights, you can bring all the members of the same community up to the same level of wealth and prosperity. Nature, itself, has forbidden the results, in both cases. It is indeed, less true, as respects the former case, for, in theory, it may be possible to reduce all the members of the same community, by a process of elevating and depressing, to a certain medium level; on the Owen system, for example; but, as every nation would have a scale of its own, dependent on its own circumstances, it becomes utterly impracticable as between states. A people must make the most of its own particular circumstances, just as an individual must turn his own advantages to account, in his own particular circle. It is certainly a mistake for a man to be niggardly and mean in his private transactions, sound policy invariably dictating a liberal course as the one best fitted to his own success, and nations ought to consult the same truth, in their intercourse with foreigners; but he who should call in all his neighbours, every time his position enabled him to turn events to account, and bid them participate in his enterprise, on an exactly equal footing, would soon find that he was a much better neighbour than calculator. The people who raise a second quality of wheat had better eat it, and live a little lower, than throw it away, in order to buy a first quality from him who has a better farm. I apprehend, therefore, that all the advocates of free trade have ever established is the fact, that, owing to the thousand and one abuses of bad governments, and to the consequences of immediate pressure, nations have admitted a vast many regulations into their tariffs, which do not even contribute to their own selfish views. But proving the falsity of a fact does not prove the falsity of a principle, and there I leave the matter.

Revenons à nos Suisses. One gets to be physically fatigued by the mere process of sight-seeing, even when it is not accompanied by undue bodily exertion. The constant excitement, the incessant demand on the imagination, and the fatiguing recurrence of novelties, come at last, to weary the body as well as the mind. I was glad enough, therefore, to return to Berne, after this little excursion, and to digest at my leisure, the remarkable features of the various and grand objects that I had just visited. I had now been absent twelve days from my friends, and had passed leisurely over three hundred miles of Switzerland, and among some of its finest valleys. Under the circumstances, I called a halt, or, in other words, issued orders for a return to Berne.

The next morning we again profited by the mail-boat, to cross the lake of Thun. This lovely sheet of water never palls on the eye. I was now crossing it for the fourth time, and, while it astonished me less than at first, I think it pleased me more.

We found a great display of the chivalry of Switzerland at Thun. This country has no regular army, beyond a few companies of local guards, who act as a *gensd'armerie* in one or two of the cantons, but it depends altogether on its militia for defence. You are aware of that blot on the Swiss policy, which admits of the raising of mercenaries in the cantons. This is a public measure, is regulated by treaty, and the Confederation receives an indemnity. By one of the conditions, Switzerland is authorized to withdraw these regiments in the event of her having occasion for them herself. Thus, should the republic declare war against France, the latter country would be obliged (in good faith, at least, whatever its policy might dictate at the moment) to suffer this portion of its force to withdraw from its own to the hostile ranks. There are regiments under these compacts, at this moment,* in France, Spain, Naples, Austria, and Rome. The Monsieur de Watteville, whose corps figured in our last war, is a Bernois, and the Colonel Fischer, who was concerned in the affairs connected with the siege of Fort Erie, is also of the aristocracy of the great canton, a member of his family being one of the *avoyers*† at this moment. This link has, in a slight degree, connected the Swiss with our own history, although the corps of de Watteville was not raised under a treaty, nor was it ever exclusively composed of Swiss. The *sortie* and the attack of Fort Erie, in both of which these mercenaries suffered heavily, have made some impression on the little *coteries* of Berne; and, in one instance, I heard the American *buck-shot* alluded to, with a manner of reproach, as if we were a singularly disreputable people, for presuming to shoot our enemies with lead cast into bullets of a hundred to the pound. But, alas! I am old enough to remember it was a matter of grave reproach against the national character, that, in the war of the revolution, we had the unfairness to *take aim* in battle! What stigma has poor America escaped in her efforts to be happy and free?

I owe it to my own juvenility to state that the latter accusation did not reach my ears during the war itself; but during the first twenty years that succeeded it, as I presume it must have

---

* Since that period, the Swiss have been disbanded in France, and the cantons seriously think of discontinuing the practice.
† There are two *avoyers*, who preside alternately.

reached the ears of every American who was in a situation to know any thing of vulgar English opinion at that period.

A large portion of the chivalry of Switzerland, then, were at Thun, in the shape of her armed citizens. I had a strong desire to review these troops in person, with a natural wish to see how much better they appeared than our own. Luckily they were under arms when we arrived, and, making an arrangement with a coachman, to follow me, I proceeded on foot to the plain where they were collected. Having seen them, I have only to add, that they are as much like our own derided militia as one pea is like another. The wheeling was exactly in the same curvilinear form; there were the same joking and fun; the same profound indifference to orders; and the same submission of the officers to the men. I cannot say that I saw a precise parallel to that celebrated manœuvre of a Philadelphia regiment, in which the music choosing to go by one street, and the colonel by another, the men manifested the true spirit of compromise by taking a third. Recognising my friend the captain, at the end of his platoon, in obedience to an intimation that it would be permitted, I joined him in the march, in order to inquire after my family; and thus, you will see, I have had the honour of serving in the Swiss ranks, for a small part of a campaign. My enlistment, the more especially as I carried the walking pike, excited a good many pleasant remarks among our comrades, and, judging from appearances, deranged the balance of power, as one end of the platoon seemed much inclined to close with the other, during the conference; the men on the extreme right showing a proper republican desire to know what their commander might have to say to a stranger, who wore a travelling cap, and carried a walking pike, in the field.

The carriage did not arrive. On inquiry, I learned that the rogue of a coachman, finding a more numerous, and, consequently, a more profitable fare, had left me on the battle-ground, while he quietly trotted off to Berne by another road. I allude to the fact, because it is rather peculiar to the lower class of Swiss *voituriers*, who eminently illustrate the truth of the doctrine of the uncharitableness of transient associations with our fellow creatures. The *esprit de corps* of the old guide was thoroughly aroused by this piece of perfidy, and, having as yet been of little use besides carrying the pack, he now seemed zealously disposed to illustrate the justice of the canton. He soon obtained another conveyance, in which we proceeded, and, on reaching Berne, while I hurried across the Aar to la Lorraine, he hurried off to the police to hunt up the delinquent. I am happy to say, that each succeeded in his object. I found the little party of Americans, glad to be once more under my protection, and he found the rogue who had so little grace as to prefer fifteen francs to twelve. The old man made an example of him, by demonstrating that honesty is the best policy, and returned triumphant from the halls of justice. He had been advocate, attorney, and witness, and I rewarded him for his zeal, which appeared really honest and disinterested, by an offering of the damages, which amounted to a pretty good day's work for one *of the trade*, who had not regularly read law.

He went his way, and we parted for ever. The freedom and familiarity of a march in the mountains, had created an intimacy that was thus rudely broken, and, in spite of his vile French, great want of *nose*, dogged protestantism, reverence for aristocrats, and relish for *kirschwasser*, I parted from him with the sort of regret one feels in being obliged to throw away an old shoe that has gotten to be easy to the foot. I returned to my distant contemplations of the mountains, which every hour served to persuade me are finest as a whole, and as seen in the distance. Perhaps, however, the effect was now aided by the intimate acquaintance that had been established between us, which allowed the imagination to bring their real dimensions, their magnificent solitudes, and their sublime repose, into a picture drawn at the distance of sixteen leagues.

Letter XXIII.

M Y DEAR————,

A day or two of rest were not misplaced after the late excursion. But a vast deal still remained to be seen, and I have come to the conclusion, that one cannot get a just idea of this extraordinary country short of devoting two entire summers to its study. We were now approaching the close of September, and we had been admonished of the necessity of quitting Switzerland about the middle of October, after which period the weather usually becomes decidedly disagreeable. As there was no time to lose, on the twenty-fourth I again left Berne, accompanied by several of our party, taking the road to Morat.

The country in this direction is like that of the great valley of the Aar, of which I have already spoken so often, though there were fine views of the Alps on our left. The peaks took new forms, as we altered our position, and had more of the appearance of magnificent skeletons, if you can conceive of such a thing, than when seen from la Lorraine.

Morat, (so celebrated for the battle fought beneath its walls, in 1476, between the Swiss and the Burgundians, under their celebrated duke, *Charles le Téméraire,*) presents an interesting picture as it is approached. It has the ancient style of fortifications, like Lucerne; not with your common-place bastions, and angles, and ditches, and half-moons, and glacis, but a good old-fashioned, straight-forward wall, ornamented with square and round towers, an arrow's flight from each other, of which you have seen many a sample in books, and which, by some association that I cannot explain, always recalls to my mind the history of the Bible; Jerusalem and Jericho. The latter was the idea that suggested itself, when I first laid eyes on Morat.

The town is not large, nor does it appear to have changed in this particular for ages, for it has neither passed nor essentially receded from its walls. It stands immediately on the banks of a lake of the same name, that is about five miles long, and rather more than one mile wide. This is positively the least beautiful of all the Swiss waters we have seen, and yet it is far from being ugly. The shores are comparatively low and uninteresting, those opposite to the town being a ridge of cultivated and nearly treeless country, that separates the lake from that of Neuchâtel.

The Romans had a great station, at a place called Avenche, (*Aventicum*,) and some of the Swiss writers are bold enough to surmise that Morat was formerly one of its suburbs, though the two towns are now five miles asunder. *Aventicum* was a place of some size, and of considerable importance beyond a doubt, but, supposing it to have extended as far in the other direction, it would have been twice as large as Rome itself! Morat was probably a suburban village.

The great battle was fought on a plain to the south, and quite near the town. A vast number of the Burgundians perished in the lake and the marshes. This conflict was a sort of Swiss *Cressy*, although modern historians have ingeniously diminished the glory of the confederates, by lessening the number of their adversaries. It was, however, beyond all question, a great and justifiable victory, the latter fact, in itself, being quite glory sufficient. It is true that Morat lies in the heart of the Burgundy of which you and I never heard until so very lately, but that does not seem to be a sufficient apology for the Duke of the Burgundy, of which every one does know something, making an inroad on its inhabitants. For one, I am glad he was flogged. This thing called national pride is a queer sentiment. A French writer of distinction has laboured hard of late, to strip the republicans of the 15th century of a portion of their renown, and the republicans of 1798 treated them and their deeds as if they had been little better than dogs.

The Swiss, shortly after the battle, collected the bones of the dead in an ossuary, which answered the double purpose of a cemetery and a trophy. This ossuary the French destroyed. An attempt so pitiful, has met with a suitable reward: for the battle is now better known to the ordinary traveller, by this act of impotent revenge, than through the history of the event itself. Time was wearing away the recollection of the defeat, and with it certainly every feeling of disgrace that a Frenchman might reasonably entertain, when both are suddenly revived by an indiscretion that was as silly as it was unjust. The Swiss, more recently, have collected the scattered remains, and erected a monument near the ancient ossuary, on the way side, where every one can learn the whole story.

I owe an especial acknowledgment to M. Ebel, for the pleasures of a long walk, up a hill, under a hot sun, in order to see a linden (*tilleul*) which he has written down as being thirty-six feet in diameter. What will not a traveller come, in time, to believe! There we went, dragging our weary limbs after us, to discover that for "*diamètre*," we ought to have read "*circonférence*." I wish the *erratum* had been in *his* book, instead of *mine*. The view of Morat, however, was unique in its way, from the foot of this tree, looking more like Jericho than ever.

The road to Avenche was good, and we were less than an hour in reaching it. At the distance of a mile from the village, (it is no more at present,) we passed the remains of a ruined wall, that swept athwart the plain and up an acclivity in eloquent silence. To this point the ancient *Aventicum* had certainly extended, and there, amid the grass, and fringed with shrubs, lay the masonry of two thousand years! On a height to the left, stood a part of a tower in the wall; of the latter, portions are still fourteen or fifteen feet in thickness, and as many in height.

Aventicum is believed, by some historians, to have been the birthplace of Vespasian. He greatly aided the town, beyond dispute, and his son Titus piously followed his example. Those unheard-of people, *the* Burgundians, a mongrel race of Saxon-Gallico-Swiss, destroyed the place at the close of the third century, setting up their own empire in its stead. The little they spared was finished by the Huns.

Between the breach in the walls through which the highway passes, and the eminence on which Avenche now stands, is a level expanse of meadow, of a mile in width. Near the modern town, stands a solitary Corinthian column, quite forty feet high, with a stork's nest on its summit. Green grain was growing in the nest, (which was old and deserted, a relic on a relic,) and its blades fell prettily in clusters around the shaft. A hint for a new order in architecture might have been taken from its festoons. The storks had long been gone, and a flight of smaller birds were chattering around the place, apparently in waiting for the grain to ripen. A fragment of a rich cornice lay at no great distance, probably a part of the temple to which the column once belonged.

These were strange and unexpected things to meet in Switzerland. We all know that the Romans were once here; but our ideas of this region are so much confined to natural objects and to pastoral habits, that we Americans scarcely associate any thing so classical as Rome and her arts with the country.

Avenche is walled, and we entered it through a strong gateway, a thing of yesterday, having been built probably some three or four centuries, or just before America was discovered. I remember to have surprised an Englishman, a few years since, with a sudden view of the Cohoos.* After gazing at the fall, for a few minutes, he turned and said, "Now, had you told me this was Niagara, I should have gone home with all my expectations realized." So it was with the walls and towers of Avenche; I could have thought them rusty enough for old Rome itself, had the books not told me better. One of the towers, however, is really said to be ancient. We could not stop to hunt up the remains of amphitheatres and aqueducts, both of which, however, actually exist, though so obscurely as to require good eyes and great patience to discover them.

We passed through the town of Avenche (which may contain two or three thousand souls) without stopping, and in another hour we reached Payerne, the end of our day's work. This place has also a wall, and, what is more, a history.

The winter before the last, I happened to make one of a party that was assembled in the apartments of a Russian lady at Paris, on the occasion of a *fête*. But I ought to premise to you, that the native Russians, as is natural, have an exceeding jealousy of the foreigners who, by the policy of the government, are introduced into their civil and military services. Count Capo d'Istria, who, by-the-way, was present, by a regulated demeanor and unusual probity, has rendered himself more acceptable to his adopted fellow subjects; but he stands almost alone in this particular. On the evening in question accident had placed me near a very celebrated Russian, of a most unpronounceable name, who was thoroughly indigenous, both in feelings and by extraction. The General [Jomini] was standing opposite to us,

* The river was full of water at the time.

and, struck by something Italian in his aspect, I inquired of my neighbour who he might be? There had been some little familiarity between the Russian and myself, and his answer was exceedingly frank and explicit. He commenced by describing the General [Jomini] to me, as a soldier of fortune, who had written a book; who had first served Bonaparte, and then served Alexander,—God and mammon; in short, as a regular *point d'argent, point de Suisse* sort of a person, whom the emperor had had the weakness to encourage, to the injury of better men, his natural born lieges. By this time, my Russian was pretty well wrought up, and turning round, by way of climax, he eloquently added—"In short, sir, he comes from a poor, pitiful, dirty little village, in Switzerland, called Payerne."

It must be admitted that the General [Jomini] is justly obnoxious to a large proportion of the latter charge, though it was a little coloured by Russian zeal. Payerne, notwithstanding, was once the abode of royalty, and, what is of far more importance to us moderns, its principal inn is still one of the best in the cantons. The people, however, boast more of a certain princess, called Bertha, than of the excellent quails and of the frank civility of the *aubergiste*.

It is quite out of my power to give you a very particular account of the political relations and family alliances of Queen Bertha, the lady in question. She was, I believe, in some way or other, however, sovereign of *the* Burgundy; and her principal residence, at the time, was on the very spot which gave birth to the General [Jomini]. Gondemar, the last of one dynasty of the rulers of this kingdom, was overthrown by the sons of Clovis, in 534. The conquerors partitioned his states, and imprisoned him for the rest of his days; a fact I had discovered in Picot, in the course of a very desultory reading, and I thought I was fairly rid of this embarrassing point of history. No such thing. A new race sprung up; and this Queen Bertha lived and reigned some time about the year 1100, though I pretend not to be within a century. She founded a convent at Payerne; passed much of her time in it; and rode in a certain saddle, which in no manner invaded the sacred principle of the salic law, it having been quite as well adapted for a man as for a woman. The kingdom, the convent, the palaces, and almost the history itself, is gone, but the saddle remains! How often have I heard you anathematizing old saddles; but here was one of the age of a thousand years, and yet everybody speaks well of it. Long skirts, equivocal riding frocks, and all similar inventions, known to those ladies who, in their equestrian exercises, reverse the axiom of "united we stand, divided we fall," are put to shame by the simple expedient of this saddle, which had a sort of permanent boot for the reception of each of the royal legs. Thus intrenched, as the age of machinery was then remote, she established a distaff on the pommel, and, according to tradition, away she went, spinning along the highway. The proofs of what you have just heard are shown to all unbelievers, in the village church, as Halleck would say, for "ten and six-pence sterling." The tomb of the *spinning Bertha* is also shown in pious proximity to the saddle.

The next day my companions left me for Fribourg, taking the carriage with them, and literally leaving me in the highway. I intrusted a travelling bag to the innkeeper, to be forwarded to Lausanne by some regular conveyance, and went gayly forward, on foot, with the world before me.

The morning was foggy, and I walked fully ten miles before I got a view of any thing beyond the nearest fields, an occasional farm-house, an excellent road, and, now and then, a dog or a cat. The country was, however, nearly a perfect level, and the farm-houses and meadows, of which I did obtain dim glimpses, gave assurance of ease and comfort. I knew by Ebel and the map, two friends whom I never desert, and who rarely desert me, that I was in one of the valleys along which the Romans had continued their line of posts; and I had, moreover, the comfort of knowing that, could it only be seen, I should greatly enjoy the scenery by which I was surrounded.

At ten, the sun dissolved the mists, and they vanished in air almost as suddenly as swallows that are glancing on the wing. When visible, the country greatly resembled one of the thousand valleys of the older parts of our own country, having a small stream meandering through it, with fine farms, beautiful copses of wood, and here and there a village. But, in addition to these accessaries, the heights were occasionally crowned by *châteaux*, or a ruin. Except in the neatness, there was nothing peculiarly Swiss in the scenery, neither the Alps nor the Jura being in sight; but, as I have just said, it might very well have passed for a better sort of American landscape, a few local peculiarities, such as the ruins, the *châteaux*, and the more frequent occurrence of villages, perhaps, excepted.

I walked as far as Lucens, which has a fine old *château* overhanging it, where I got into the carriage of a *voiturier*, who was going to Lausanne. A lively, black-eyed little *Vaudoise* was in possession before me, and, as she seemed disposed to be communicative, we soon fell into an animated discourse. I ought to have sooner said that we were now in Vaud, Payerne lying in that canton.

It was not long before my companion made the usual remark of "*Apparemment, Monsieur est Anglais?*" On being told I was an American, she manifested a good deal of satisfaction, for she wished to learn something of the country, a connexion of her own having gone there to live. Her friend, a female cousin, had written her long accounts of her own wants and embarrassments, as well as some marvels of the novelties and pleasures of her new situation. As is usually the case, she had dwelt chiefly on the exceptions; for of what avail would it be to send intelligence all the way to Europe of every-day matters! But life, I told my little Vaudoise, is made up of every-day things, however unromantic they may be; and he who omits them in his catalogue of agreeables or disagreeables, draws a false picture. "*Mais, Monsieur,*" said the lively woman, "you can scarcely know the use of manufactures in America?"—"And yet we pay some five hundred millions of francs annually for those we import, to say nothing of as much more for those we fabricate." "*C'est étonnant, cela!* My cousin writes me that she has difficulty in even purchasing pins." "Quite likely; one might even find parts of Switzerland where a pin could not be had." "*Où, donc?*" as quick as lightning. "Why, on the top of Mont Blanc, for instance. Do you think there is a spot anywhere on the summits of the Alps in which pins and tape, or even snuff, is to be bought?" "*Assurément, non, Monsieur;* but America is not the Alps." "Nor do pins grow on the prairies. You say your friend has gone to live twenty miles from any town, on the verge of a prairie; that her nearest neighbour lives five miles off, and that she is compelled to send ten miles to a mill." "*Oui; tout cela est vrai.*" "Well, I live in America, too, near a street that contains eight hundred houses, and two hundred shops, where some millions of pins, most probably, are to be had at this very moment, and in a town containing not only more people, but more pins, too, than all the Swiss capitals united." *"Monsieur, plaisante!"* "That is a liberty I should not presume to take with you, *Madame*. We have a vast territory that is fast filling up; but, if people choose to encounter the privations of the frontiers, they should not confound their own situation with the advantages of those who are satisfied to live among their fellow creatures." *"Ah, ma cousine a tort!"* "I dare say, *Madame*, that your cousin has told you no more than the truth; though she has probably not found it necessary to tell you *all* the truth. She has given such an account of America as I should give of Switzerland, were I to write to my friends, for instance, that I had in vain waited for a carriage on the summit of the Grimsel; for, after a delay of six months, not one had appeared." My little Vaudoise laughed, and confessed that she began to understand me, finishing by saying—*"Pourtant, Monsieur, en a trouvée une, sur la grande route, entre Payerne et Lausanne."* *"C'est cela."*

Such is the history of one half of the well-intentioned blunders of the Europeans touching the republic and the "twelve millions." Of the ill-intentioned blunders, the sources are as multiplied as the interests and selfishness of men. The English, in particular, often mislead while stating things that are literally true in themselves, but to which they attach wrong conclusions. When they meet a man of independent mien, tolerably good attire, and more ideas on general subjects than they are accustomed to find, except among men of leisure at home, they jump to the inference that they have fallen in with an American gentleman, and they set to work, as fast as possible, to record his vulgarities—his democratic *crachats*,* and his want of the silverforkisms.

We—meaning the lively little *Vaudoise* and myself—reached Lausanne in good season, where I proceeded forthwith to secure lodgings.

---

* I ought to apologize even for alluding to this disgusting practice. There is no question that it prevails to an inexcusable degree; but it is spoken of, by most of the English writers, with the furious zeal and affectation of *parvenus*.

Letter XXIV.

MY DEAR ———,

The country was still Swiss; but it was Switzerland in an entirely new aspect. The landscape had an air of finish, like a man or a woman in high dress; and the whole region, though equally exquisite and grand in its natural features, seemed far more civilized than most of those through which I had lately been travelling. The view from Lausanne, in particular, was singularly impressed with all these characteristics. The land rises regularly and gradually from the shores of the Leman to a height of probably not less than five or six hundred feet, forming as it ascends a succession of eminences, terraces, and ravine-like swales, that greatly diversifies its surface. Villas, farms, hamlets, and villages abound; nor is wood wanting to relieve the monotony of the fields.

Lausanne itself stands on very broken ground, and there are many sharp ascents and descents in the principal streets. The views down some of the declivities looked like glimpses into a nether world; still it was a pleasing, because a busy, quaint, well placed, and apparently a thriving town. The throng of travellers, too, to whom it owes most of its prosperity, lends it an air more worldly and artificial than it might otherwise possess.

There was unusual bustle about the inn, and all eyes were looking down the hill which commences directly before the door, in the direction of Geneva. I left the servants thus occupied, when I went out to stroll through the place, and found them thus occupied on my return. It is only necessary for a man to look intently, at even vacancy, to find imitators; and I joined the gazers, though I knew not why. *"La voilà!"* soon gave notice of the *dénouement*. Two travelling carriages appeared in the valley, (the word is hardly misapplied, though it was in the heart of the town,) and began to drag their way slowly up the ascent. The foremost had six horses, a sign of royalty on the continent of Europe, and, indeed, I might say everywhere now, this style of travelling having virtually disappeared from England, thanks to the efforts of Mr. McAdam.

There we were, a party of tuft-hunting republicans, as the Quarterly would be apt to insinuate, staring, with all our eyes, at the approach of royalty. I had formerly been a great admirer of the meteor-like passages of Charles X., whom it was my fortune, during the summer of 1827, to meet once or twice a week in his flights between St. Cloud and Paris. His movements had a sublimity about them. The *piqueur*, who appeared to me to have as much as he could do to keep from being run over; the lancers, with their "plump of spears," sailing along on his crupper; the *gardes du corps;* the magnificent carriages, with their eight horses in a foam; and the broken train of liveried attendants, all scampering along the highway, *ventre à terre*, caused these *rencontres* to be both exciting and memorable. I remember, on one occasion, to have met His Most Christian Majesty, when he appeared with six coaches and eight, two *fourgons* and eight, four carriages and six, as many with four, and something like forty mounted attendants, without including the *gardes du corps*, the *cuirassiers*, and the lancers. In that instance he appeared with rather more than three hundred horses, all of which was in perfect good taste, for he was going to attend the races in the *Champ de Mars*.

Speed and a steady movement are absolutely indispensable to the effect of a royal advent. This was fully demonstrated by the snail-like approach of the present party. A crowd collected about the door of the inn, as the travellers drew near, and, supposing, quite reasonably, they would enter the house where they were evidently expected, I took refuge in the wide passage of a building opposite, the door of which was invitingly open, and which happened to be vacant. Exactly before this building the carriage stopped, while two gentlemen, covered with orders, placed themselves in the door, so that I found myself in danger of turning courtier without my consent.

A *chasseur* first lifted a little girl, some three or four years old, from the carriage, putting her in the passage with an air of great respect. The fellow was whiskered and *moustached*, in a way to look like a bear; but there was a smile of gratification, at her pleased look of evident recognition, as he held the pretty child suspended a moment in the air. This little personage was no less a lady than the Grand-duchess Maria, a niece of the Emperor of Russia. Her mother, the Grand-duchess Helena, descended next. She was a fine woman, of some one or two-and-twenty, and, like most of her family, of noble stature and commanding presence. She is a princess of Wurtemburg, and, of course, nearly allied to the family of Great Britain, the members of which she resembles. By this time, I began to suspect that, by aiming to get out of the way, I had got precisely into the spot where I ought not to be. Nothing therefore remained to be done, but to beat a retreat. This I effected in the best manner I could, by making a low reverence, and passing pretty nearly through the centre of the royal party. Apologies would have been as much out of place as I was myself.

Lausanne, I have already told you, lies at an elevation of some five hundred feet above the lake. A public walk, called *Mont Bénon*, commands a charming view, including all the rare objects that surround a sheet of water that Voltaire pronounced to be the finest in Switzerland. "*Mon lac est le premier.*" I shall not say he was right, unless we are to return again to the distinctions between *beau* and *pittoresque*. Still the lake of Geneva is among the finest, if it be not the very finest of them all. It bears, I think, beyond a question, the palm on the score of variety, for though less *bizarre* than that of Lucerne, there are greater extremes of the grand and the pleasing. Its form, as every one knows, is that of a crescent; and, commencing at its outlet, there is a regular gradation from the beautiful to the sublime, as one proceeds towards its head. I do not know that any portion is as beautiful as the most beautiful parts of the lake of Zurich, or any portion as magnificent as most of that of Lucerne, and the Wallenstadt, or even of those of Thun and Brienz; but, as a whole, as has just been said, it certainly has stronger contrasts than any one of them all.

The form of this lake prevents an entire view of it from any single point. One is as well placed at Lausanne, as at any other spot, perhaps, for such a purpose; but, even there, the western end of the sheet is quite concealed from view by the curvature. If the foot of the lake is hid from the eye, its head, on the contrary, lies open before the spectator, and it offers one of the grandest landscapes of this, the noblest of all earthly regions. In that direction, the mountains of Savoy rise like granite ramparts, and the valley of the Rhone retires in the distance, until it is lost in the sublimity of mystery. Whichever way the eye wandered, over the wide range of hill-sides, villages, vineyards, mountains, and blue water, it never failed to return to this one spot, which, on the whole, offers one of the nicest combinations of the great and the enchanting in scenery, of any place within my knowledge.

The port of Lausanne is called Ouchy, a village stretched along the strand, about a mile from the town, and thither I proceeded on the following morning. It is surrounded by small, pleasant country houses, in which was assembled a social Congress, composed of representatives of all the nations in Christendom. Among them were one or two delegates from America. There is a mole, which affords sufficient protection against the west winds; the proximity of the hills prevents the *bise*, or the north gales from having a sufficient sweep here to do any material damage, but the little harbour is nearly open to the south. A few boats, rigged like feluccas, were at anchor behind the mole.

The great business of the day was the entertainment of the Grand-duchess Helena. She had been invited to make the tour of the head of the lake, and the steamboat was about to quit the harbour for that purpose, leaving us travellers to await her return with a most loyal and submissive patience. A crowd had collected, and the boat had hauled alongside of the quay, in readiness to receive her. I threaded the throng for an hour, with a sensation of loneliness that I had not felt in the solitudes of the Alps. There one could at all times commune with a noble nature; while here I was constantly passing strange faces, whose owners were too much filled with their own little concerns to heed the accidental presence of a traveller, more or less. They prevented all enjoyment of the exquisite scenery, without offering any substitute. I began to grow weary of the crowd, when a countenance I had seen before caught my eye. There was a mutual recognition between the Swiss and myself, although we were personally unknown to each other. Still we had dwelt in the same town in another hemisphere, and I had been occasionally one of the small congregation that listened to his *prédications* in French, and our eyes had become accustomed, at least, to each other's faces. This was sufficient for me at such a moment, and I gladly paid my respects to him.

The Grand-duchess interrupted this little meeting, and the crowd pressed about her while she embarked. A very fantastical personage now made his appearance, armed with a boatswain's call, and wearing a sea-cap of red cloth. His dress and action were those of the hero of a melo-drama, and, certainly, they were both unlike those of any other mariner with whom I had ever before met. He proved, however, to be the master of the boat. Under the flourishes of this gentleman, Her Imperial Highness got safe on board the Leman, when the paddles were put in motion, the boat taking the direction of Vévey.

Some of the authorities of Vaud attended the Russian Princess, in full uniform, *and wearing the decorations of foreign orders*. I believe you will do me the justice to allow that my democracy does not often confound the substance with the shadow, but I shall say that I was very unpleasantly struck by this exhibition. That attention should be paid to a respectable member of a royal family, by the authorities of a democracy—and Vaud is virtually democratic—is perfectly proper, and it becomes more peculiarly so when the object of its civilities is a woman. I have no idea that the monarchists or the aristocrats should get the better of us in good manners; nor do I know that there is any thing opposed to republicanism of the purest water, in rewarding a citizen, by personal honours and decorations, so long as the hereditary principle is kept out of sight. We do all this, ourselves, in a different manner, in bestowing swords, and medals, and diplomas, and other distinctions of this nature. The great danger is from abuses, but this is a danger inseparable from humanity, and one to which, after all our ingenious expedients, we are compelled to submit, in matters of much graver moment. But when a nation has once deliberately decided that it will have nothing to do with titles of nobility, and orders of knighthood, in the management of its own particular affairs, and that all its rewards shall be limited to popular favour and ready money, it strikes me as singularly unwise as well as undignified, to permit its highest agents to receive honours of this nature from foreign states. A decoration is clearly worth something, or it is worth nothing. If the latter, a principle is sacrificed without a motive; if the former, a public servant is exposed to the temptation of infidelity, through an agency that has been rejected at home, as unsafe or uncalled for. The Swiss, especially, are pressed upon by so many different foreign interests, that, in their particular case, it appears to me the objection to this practice is even greater than it would be among ourselves.

While on this subject, I will relate an anecdote, for the truth of which I will vouch, and which is, at least, curious, to attach to it no greater importance. During our residence at Paris, we made the acquaintance of the family of B———, people of great respectability and probity. M. B——— is a member of the Legion of Honour, and the subject of decorations was more than once discussed between us. One day he was rather closer than usual in his inquiries touching the usages and opinions of America on political subjects, and on this point, in particular. In answering one of my remarks, he startled me by suddenly observing that I was a much better republican than Mr. ———, naming a countryman of our own, who, though since dead, was formerly a prominent member of the old Federal party; a *native* American, you will keep in mind, and not one of those imported patriots, who come among us in quest of a livelihood, and then set themselves up as organs of public opinion. I was curious to hear in what manner M. B——— knew any thing of Mr. ———, or of his political opinions. The explanation was very simple. They had met by accident, and liking each other's views, the acquaintance had been cultivated. "But, Mr. ——— was a distinguished man in your country?" observed M. B———. "He indisputably was, and deservedly so, in his particular profession, for he had both industry and talent." "He certainly did not like your institutions, and was constantly predicting their overthrow." There was a short pause, when M. B——— continued, laughing—"His son, who was with him, once, in my presence, attributed his disgust to the fact, that public opinion in America would not allow him to wear his *orders*." "Orders! in the name of wonder, what orders could Mr. ——— possibly wear, or possess?" "He had two; *one granted by the King of Prussia*, and the other, if I am not mistaken, *given to him by the King of England, as King of Hanover.*" "*Mais, Monsieur*

B———, this has been a *mauvaise plaisanterie* of the son?" "Not
at all; he showed me the decorations himself, and I assure you, *I
had them both in my own hands.*"

I tell you the fact as it occurred, and I tell you, moreover, that
the years and character of M. B——— forbid all idea of a *mys-
tification.* I have no doubt that what he then told me was literally
true, though he may possibly be mistaken as to the source
whence one of the decorations was derived, as he himself admitted. Now it certainly is not illegal for an American citizen—
not an officer of the general government—to have his coat covered with orders, if he can obtain them; but *why* were these
decorations bestowed on Mr. ———? He was not distinguished
in the arts, in letters, or in war. I can see no other reason than
the fact, that they whose cause he so warmly espoused in
America, by maintaining principles that were in accordance
with their own interests, were desirous of bestowing rewards,
that, it was supposed, might be particularly grateful to such a
mind. It is not at all necessary to believe that the great body of
the political party with which Mr. ——— was connected, meant
revolution and a monarchy, in order to believe this, although,
that many among them did contemplate both, I do not now
entertain the smallest doubt. You know I was educated in the
particular opinions of this political sect; that I had every opportunity of ascertaining their real sentiments; and I cannot but
know, that, while the great majority of them dreamed of no
more than arresting what they believed to be the dangerous
inroads of democracy, some of their leaders aimed at a return,
in principle, to the old system. Of this number, most probably,
was Mr. ———, of whom personally I know nothing, however;
and he had his reward, in two baubles that he did not dare to
exhibit!

It was near evening before the Leman returned and permitted us to embark, when, for the first time, I put foot on its blue
waters. We were soon under way for Geneva, with a company
of some forty or fifty passengers, chiefly English. Before the
night set in we reached a point, where the isolated and magnificent pile of Mont Blanc became visible. Unlike the peaks of
the Oberland, the mountain stands alone, for the array of lesser
summits that are ranged around its footstool, in no degree affects its solitary grandeur.

Our melo-dramatic *schipper* gave us a queer exhibition of his whimsicalities, as darkness drew near. The trips on this lake are usually made by daylight, rendering a compass of no great use, except in thick weather, or in fogs. But we were now compelled to run several hours in the dark, and truly I do not remember so solemn and so fantastic an inauguration of the instrument as was held on this important occasion. Fully half an hour was passed in arranging the binnacle in a line parallel with the keel, a duty that was performed with great parade, and with grimaces that I had never witnessed before, however suitable they might be to the navigation of a lake that is forty miles long, and some six or eight wide. After all this preparation, we steered by the land, which soon drew so near on each side, as to be seen as readily as the banks of one of our own broad rivers.

We were not permitted to enter the port of Geneva at that hour! Little things, like little men, are apt to be fussy and precise. What should we think, for instance, of a regulation which required that a vessel arriving off New York, in the night, should not enter the harbour after nine o'clock? Under such a regulation, a fleet of ships, steamboats, coasters, and oystermen would collect on some occasions, nearly large enough to "hoist-in," as Jack expresses it, the whole republic of Geneva.

There was no resisting the powers that be, and, running to an anchorage, through a dozen felucca-like looking barks, which, in common with ourselves, had been "locked out," our Prince of the Fandangoes brought his craft up in safety. We were landed at a little station without the gates, and, our passports being delivered, and duly examined, we made our way through ravelins and sally-ports, athwart moats, and among ramparts, into the heart of the venerable town of *Calvin* and *Jean Jacques*.

Letter XXV.

M Y DEAR————,

As the American goes through Europe there are certain great landmarks, that never fail to arouse some of his most deeply seated feelings and recollections. England, as a matter of course, most abounds with places of this sort; but the continent, too, is pretty well sprinkled with them. Geneva is one of the number, and I sallied forth into its streets with more curiosity, and (to use a word of great utility at home) excitement,* than I had felt since entering the streets of Paris.

I cannot say that the town either displeased or disappointed me. Enormous sheds, that greatly resemble the things called piazzas,† which are so frequently built in front of our own country taverns, greatly disfigure some of the streets, it is true; but they have their use, I take it for granted, in the "season of snows." I shall not extol their appearance, whatever may be said in behalf of their utility.

This venerable and illustrious little city is built on both sides of the Rhone, and a large portion of it stands on very uneven ground. There are many streets which it is far more agreeable to descend than to climb, and a few are scarcely practicable for carriages. It is pretty well built, though there is little pretension to architecture, the houses being rather solid and spacious than elegant. I saw very few hotels, or *portes cochères*, which I believe are the tests of this *caste* of habitation, though the French prac-

---

* The Americans are among the least excitable people of this earth, though the word is incessantly in their mouths. Thus we have political, religious, and social excitements, in heaps; an impertinent interference with the concerns of others being also sometimes dignified by the same name.

† I believe the word, in this signification, is peculiar to this country, as indeed, in some degree, is the *thing*. *Piazza* is the Italian for "place"or "square." Many of the squares in Italian towns are surrounded by *arcades*, which, having a general resemblance to the American sheds, has probably given rise to the misnomer. A *verandah* is, I believe, properly, an enclosed balcony.

tice of living on floors appears to prevail pretty generally. Some of the houses had the little projecting mirrors so common in Holland, and to which I have already alluded. I was surprised to meet this custom in a town like Geneva, in which the inhabitants have a reputation for taste and intelligence. I have always taken it to be a certain sign of a want of mental resources, no less than of a good tone of manners, when the better sort of the population of a town frequent their windows, or live much under the common eye. This is a rule, I think, that must be pretty generally admitted to be true; for what is there in the vulgar and every-day objects of a street, that can long divert a mind which has stores of its own, or a cultivated taste to resort to, in moments of solitude? Window-gazing, on the score of refinement, is very much on a level with knitting. Now these looking-glasses, while they betoken vacuity of brain, have a sneaking pretension to gentility, by indulging a vulgar curiosity without detection. They may do for boys, but really one gets to have funny thoughts concerning the tastes of the men and women who cause them to be permanently attached to a window-frame. But I am making the accusation too grave, for in Geneva the practice is by no means general, and, I take it for granted, is chiefly confined to a class that it is quite hopeless to expect will become very intellectual, until we get a good deal nearer to the Millennium than we appear to be at present.

The port of Geneva—that sacred receptacle into which it is forbidden to enter after nine o'clock at night—is formed by double rows of piles driven into the mud, within which were, now, snugly anchored, in addition to two steamboats, and a dozen barks, sundry floating wash-houses. As the current is quite swift near the outlet of the lake, these "buck-basket" establishments are capitally placed, to answer the purposes of some one or two hundred busy and voluble dames, who appear to pass a good deal more than all their leisure time in them. In America, though not a little is heard of washing-day, one rarely sees much of it; but, all over the continent of Europe, the washing seems to be done in public, by levies, *en masse*, like a parade of militia. The Seine is alive with interesting groupes of *blanchisseuses;* nor do I know that they, in any manner, impair the picturesque, though I should think the complaints of the wolf to the lamb would find frequent place among them.

We hear a great deal of the system of pensioning on this side of the Atlantic; but I found the grossest instance of this sort of abuse of which I have yet heard, to the scandal of republicanism be it said, lying at anchor in the harbour of Geneva. What do you think of pensioning a steamboat? I was shown one to-day, which I was gravely assured was in this queer predicament, and, what is stranger still, it escapes all sneers and comments, which are chiefly reserved for the parties who pay. The matter, however, is quite easily explained.

A countryman of our own caused the first steamboat to be built on the Leman. His success induced others to form an association, and to put two new boats in motion. With a view to get rid of the opposition of the busy bark of our *compatriot*, they resorted to the old and well-tried expedient of proving that every man has his price, which, as usual, was found to be successful. The original boat, instead of fuming and fretting in hostility to the interests of the aforesaid company, quietly pockets a Napoleon a day, on condition that it shall not incur the risk of being locked out of the port of Geneva. As this boat, like a true annuitant, is likely, on such terms, to prove a long liver, and is not bigger than a nut-shell, it is to be presumed our countryman has driven a good bargain.

Geneva is not only walled, but fortified *secundum artem*, and its ramparts afford very pleasant walks, and some agreeable views. I made their tour, or nearly so, and was well rewarded for my pains. Although Mont Blanc is visible, there is nothing in the way of mountains, however, to compare with the sight of the Oberland, as seen from Berne. The environs are exceedingly pleasant, the whole of both shores of the lake being, for miles, completely covered by country houses and pleasure grounds. There is little of Switzerland in all this; but Geneva has been a canton so short a time that it can hardly be expected to become Swiss in a day.

The intimacy which formerly existed between Mr. Louis Simond, the well known traveller, and a part of my family, induced me to take a carriage, in order to look him up at his country house. We had not got half a mile from the gate, when I was fortunate enough to meet him going into town. On making myself known, we returned to Geneva, and had a long chat about America. He said he remembered New York when it was no larger than Geneva; and he seemed astonished when I told him it had at present eight times the population of this place.* He did not appear to understand how we got on so well; for I soon discovered that he had anticipated a very different career for America. On this subject we had an amicable contest: he rather inclining to the opinion that we were prosperous in spite of our democracy; and I supporting the theory that it was on account of that much despised element in the American system, that our facts were doing so much discredit to the ordinary calculations. I was much struck by the tone of his argument, which betrayed a feeling that is only too common among men of cultivated minds; though it argues, I think, a singularly false philosophy. He appeared to me to confound *taste* with *principles*. Heaven knows if America is to be judged by her tastes, that she will make but an indifferent figure; but a political system is not to be condemned because its votaries chew tobacco, or extolled because they happen to possess *bon ton*. This style of reasoning is much like objecting to a Fourth of July dinner, on account of its want of gentility! Though taste rarely begets money, money, in the end, will beget taste, unfavourable as may be the prospects of such an event to-day. He ended the discussion in a way that surprised me; for he said—"I am afraid to prognosticate with you, as you were the only person who foretold the result of the naval combats in the late war with Great Britain." I probably was not the only true prophet on that occasion, by a good many; but I well remember his laughing at me for these predictions, in 1812, and quoting General Moreau as authority against me. General Moreau was, undeniably, a good soldier; but there is not much vanity in believing myself to be the better sailor of the two.

The books speak of important accessions made to the territory of Geneva, by the treaty of 1814; but when one studies the map, he is disposed to inquire what has become not only of the accessions, but of the canton itself. In extent it is the smallest state but one in the Confederation, Zug being the most minute of the sisterhood. Geneva ranks higher in population, on account of the size of the town, which is the largest in the whole country; Schwytz, Glaris, Schaffhausen, Underwalden, Zug,

* This was eight years since. To-day, including Brooklyn, it is twelve times as large.

and Uri, having each fewer people. The canton is irregular in shape, extending on both sides of the lake; but its greatest length is less than fourteen miles, and its greatest breadth less than seven. The entire population is about 44,000 souls, of which 25,000 live in the town. To these numbers must be added an average of near a thousand strangers. The government is an aristocracy of burghers, mildly administered in most respects; though there are some accusations of religious intolerance. I know nothing of the merits of this unpleasant controversy; but I am inclined to suspect, *from the statements of some, in favour of things as they are*, that it is a struggle between fanaticism and seemliness, and that the apostles would have been sadly puzzled to decide between the parties. As the connexion between civil and religious liberty is intimate, you will understand that, in this hemisphere, faith is usually drilled quite as thoroughly as the troops. In such a state of things, religious *martinets* get to be rather more common than "Great-Hearts" or "Valiants."

The day after my arrival I went to Ferney, the road leading us through a most beautiful country, which is not dotted, but covered by country houses, with their clouds of plantations. The distance is only five miles; but, short as it was, it took us out of Switzerland. The French have erected a noble cross at the frontiers, as it might be, in direct defiance of the heresy of their neighbours. It is new, and has probably been reared in the present pious reign, during which the church has suddenly become renovated, by the agency of a new dispensation of miracles.

Ferney owes its existence, as a village, to Voltaire. It is neater and better built than common; though it has much of the comfortless, out-of-door look of most French villages. The *château*, as the house is called, is a long, narrow, lantern-like building, a little larger than the "Hall" at C[ooperstow]n, were the latter divided equally lengthwise. It has seven windows in front. The grounds are laid out in the formal French style, and are reasonably extensive. An avenue leads to the building; but there is little taste, and, I think, less comfort, in the general arrangement of the place.

Here, as Voltaire used to say, he "shook his wig and powdered the republic," a feat that was less improbable in his time, when wigs were so large and republics so small, than it would be to-day. The view is not particularly fine, for the whole of this shore of the lake is low, and the trees are so thick as to shut out the prospect. "*Mon lac est le premier*," must have alluded to what the lake is, in its finer parts, and not to the particular portion of it which is visible from Ferney.

We entered the house as freely as if it had been an inn. Others were there on the same errand; and, judging from what I saw, I should think the building, at this season of the year more especially, nearly useless as a residence. The rooms are small. In the *salon* are several copies of the old masters, and a picture that is said to be a conceit of the illustrious philosopher. It is a cumbrous allegory, in which the wit is smothered by the elaboration of the design. In charity, we are to believe that the principal idea was conceived in pleasantry; but the vanity of Voltaire was inordinate. His bedroom is decorated by some vile-ly executed prints, and his bedstead is worth just one dollar.

The church, of painful celebrity, is a small edifice that stands on the side of the avenue, and is much better suited to the being who caused it to be erected, than to the Being to whom it was dedicated. "*Deo erexit Voltaire!*" As Dogberry says, "and write God first; for God defend, but God should go before such vil-lains!" This is the homage of a creature to his Creator; of one who could not foresee what a day would bring forth; who could not explain the physical phenomena of his existence; who did not know what life is, or what death will be, to the Intelligence that directs and governs all! As if in bitter contempt of a vanity so besotted, of a presumption so much beyond the bounds of probability, the inscription has been erased, and the place, when I saw it, had been converted into a receptacle for potatoes. The climax was fully worthy of the sentiment.

While speaking of Voltaire, I will advert to a fact of some interest, which I have overlooked, in writing to you from France. He died, as you know, at Paris, in 1779. By his will, the house he owned on the *Quai Voltaire* was to remain untenanted for fifty years from his death,* after which period it was to be

* On the return of the writer to Paris, in 1830, the period set by Voltaire had elapsed. The hotel was opened and repaired; and it is to be presumed the manuscripts had been examined. This occurred in 1829, or during the reign

opened, and certain manuscripts it contained were to be given to the world. The natural conjecture has been, that these manuscripts were written in conformity with the religious and political opinions that he believed would prevail in France in our time. The period for the accomplishment of this great prophecy is at hand; and we shall soon have an opportunity of knowing how far that "*esprit*" which is "*partout*" could carry its possessor into the depths of the unknown future; or what "*Voltaire erexit Deus.*"

Geneva is one great jeweller's shop. It manufactures *bijouterie* for all Christendom, and one can scarcely visit the place without paying tribute. I bought a watch as a pretext for looking at the establishments, which are, however, rather business-like than brilliant. One can buy any amount, and have the articles delivered in Paris, in spite of the double line of custom-house officers. The Genevese relate, with great *gusto*, the following anecdote, which is of recent occurrence. A high functionary of the French government (M. de St. Cricq, I believe) was making a tour of observation along this frontier, when he suddenly diverged from his line of route, and entered Geneva. Without waiting to have his arrival known, he repaired to a manufacturer, and bought jewellery to a considerable amount, on the terms just mentioned, leaving a certain sum in pledge. His purchase effected, he left the place as privately as he had arrived, and returned to Paris, issuing orders to his subordinates to be on the watch for the expected package. A few days later, a stranger demanded permission to be admitted to his *cabinet*. This person entered, and, depositing the jewels, presented his bill for the unpaid balance. The money was honourably forthcoming; and the perplexed minister, who had given especial and most rigid orders for the seizure of the expected trinkets, offered a handsome reward if the agent of the manufacturer would tell him in what manner they had reached Paris. The

of Charles Xth and the Jesuits! Voltaire, his will, his opinions, and his wishes seemed to be forgotten alike; for all that was known of the matter was, that the hotel was no longer closed and uninhabited. If there is no error in the dates, it is probable that the ruling powers forbade the publication. The spasmodic state of religious inquiry, however, has passed, and is succeeded by the decencies of a political expediency; few appearing to trouble themselves about M. de Voltaire, his church, his prophecies, or his apotheosis.

terms were accepted, and, the money being pocketed—"*Monsieur*," said the smuggler, "you were known, and we found means to send the articles across the frontier *in your own baggage.*"* The delay in the delivery had been made merely to conceal the means.

After remaining two days at Geneva, knowing no one, (for this is a place in which to mingle with the world,) I returned in the boat to Lausanne. We had a great many English on board, as usual, and among them was one who, by his discourse, was a Methodist. On inquiry, I found that the people of his sect were supposed to be at the bottom of the great religious schism that existed at Geneva. He was complaining of some interference of the authorities, and exulting in the progress of the good cause in the same breath, and all in a measured, didactic, go-by-rule manner, that strongly reminded me of a large class of our own dogged religionists at home, a class in which, by-the-way, charity is *not* the chiefest of virtues.

We reached Lausanne in good season, and I made arrangements to return to Berne the following day. It is at all times disagreeable to dwell on the knavery one encounters in travelling; but I should do injustice to my theme were I to omit a bit of roguery of which I was the subject on this occasion. A waiter of the inn introduced a fellow who announced himself as one who had a return carriage for Berne. I distinctly made a bargain with him, to take it for the next day. He had left the room, when, suddenly returning, he inquired if I had any objection to a travelling companion. He was told, none in the world, provided he was a respectable man, and there was but one. With this understanding he left me.

The next morning the *voiturier* appeared in quest of my luggage, giving as an excuse for not bringing the carriage to the door, the difficulty of turning in so narrow a street. I followed him to the vehicle, which I found occupied already by four, while two more were expected. The fellow refused to return my effects, and after some altercation proceeded with them, locked up in his vehicle. This bit of rascality occurred in the open street before twenty people, and no one appeared to take any interest in it. I inquired for a magistrate, for the police, for any

* This story was afterwards confirmed to the writer by the chief of the French customs.

one having authority to arrest a proceeding so flagrant;—was sent here and there without finding any one, until I began to perceive that all about the inn were leagued together. It was certainly the most unprovoked and flagrant outrage that I ever knew committed on a traveller; and yet I had absolutely great difficulty in finding any one who would even tell me where a magistrate lived!

Despairing of justice in Lausanne, I obtained another carriage, and proceeded towards Berne. At Payerne, the scoundrel boasted that he had the effects of an Englishman who had cheated him out of his passage-money. But I had faith in the police of the *Bürgerschaft*, and followed quietly on next morning. On reaching la Lorraine, no time was lost in hunting up the rogue, and in bringing him before the authorities. I was without any witness beyond my own allegations, and the magistrate, while he had no difficulty in believing all I told him, frankly acknowledged that he could afford no redress, as the fellow denied every iota of my statements. Here was a dilemma! At length, by dint of cross-examination, the scoundrel began to contradict himself, when, finding that he was fast getting into a scrape, he opened a volley of abuse on the magistrate, which soon settled the matter altogether in my favour. The affair ended by sending the *voiturier* to prison for a fortnight, and by returning me my effects, among which was the journal, from which my letters to you have derived all their facts.

This is the second imposition of the sort I have met with in Switzerland. They are the natural consequences of the transient connexions which exist between those who pass unknown through a country, and those who live by getting all they can out of them. I should be sorry to stigmatize a population for the misconduct of a few; but the connivance of the innkeeper, of his servants, and of all about the inn at Lausanne, on this occasion, was of a character to leave the most unpleasant recollections of the place, and such as I had never before witnessed. It was like the cool roguery that appears in the pages of Gil Blas; and, more than once, I was as much disposed to laugh at, as I was to denounce it.

But this knavish incident has hurried me along the highway a little too fast. I ought to have made a short halt at Avenche, which I took occasion to visit more deliberately, on my way back to Berne. It is said that the walls of the ancient town can be traced for a considerable extent, and that their entire circumference was not less than three miles. This, after all, is not an *enceinte* of any great extent, but it must be remembered that military stations are usually compressed as much as possible, and that the population was crowded into an exceedingly small compass. Rome, itself, would not be deemed a particularly large town, estimated by the space enclosed within its walls, which still exist. It is pretended that the lake of Morat, now distant fully a mile, formerly washed the walls of *Aventicum*. As the country is low, and the lake unusually shallow, this may very well have been true.

I followed the line of the wall, a mouldering pile of bricks and stones, up the ascent that is crowned by the tower mentioned in a former letter. Works of this kind have a uniform character, whether constructed in Italy or among the barbarians. The towers are little bastions to enfilade the curtain of wall, which is commanded, for an arrow's flight, by their greater height and advanced positions. They are almost always open on the side next the town. This of *Aventicum* was very simple, and probably never excited half as much interest, when filled with Roman troops, as it does to-day, a monument of eighteen centuries.

Letter XXVI.

D<small>EAR</small> ———,

The week succeeding my return from Geneva was passed in preparations for a migration southward, travellers usually quitting the mountains like birds, all near the same time. The weather began to give us hints that the season of flight was at hand. As it is my intention to revisit the cantons before returning home, I shall defer most of my general remarks to future letters, and proceed quietly with the simple narrative of our movements.

So many terrible tales are related of Italian roguery, and their postmasters and *vetturini* bear such bad characters, that my great concern, for the last week, had been to obtain a certain and commodious conveyance to Florence. The recent specimen of what one has to expect from chance bargains, awakened all my caution. The owner of the job-horses, used since our arrival at Berne, being extensively engaged as a *voiturier*, and bearing a good name, I struck a bargain with him on this all-important occasion. You would smile to see the "charter-party," that was duly made out between us, every thing being as much *in formâ legis* as if it had been a contract to transport a cargo of teas from China to New York. There was no insurance effected, it is true, but that might be an improvement, also.

The "party of the first part, covenanted to and with the party of the second part," to deliver him safe and sound in the city of Florence within eleven travelling days, *le dit sieur* agreeing to pay so much *per diem*, for all delays that should proceed solely from his own sovereign will and pleasure, as was meet in the premises. I was furnished with four lively little horses, that were attached to my own travelling carriage, and the *voiturier* found a *fourgon*, or baggage-wagon, with another pair of cattle, to convey the domestics and trunks. This was a very excellent arrangement, for, after reserving a few night sacks, the rest of the luggage could be put under lock and key, and there remain, until it was wanted for the *toilette*, in some large town, or was carried off *en masse*, by banditti. As this was our first experiment, in travelling by contract, I watched the result with a good deal of curiosity, although I did not dip at once so far into the practice, as to permit '*le dit sieur*' to be fed as well as transported.*

It was the eighth of October, before we left la Lorraine, and fires had become very acceptable in the evenings. We were much struck, in this as in many other particulars, with the strong resemblance in the climate, to that of our own hills; though I think we have rather the advantage of the Swiss, in the greater duration of the pleasant season. There is no essential difference between the elevation of Geneva and that of C[ooperstow]n, although one lies in 46° 57′, and our own village is in 43°.

We parted from the worthy people of la Lorraine with regret, and many tears were shed among the "women-kind." The family of M. W[alther] had been uniformly kind, frank, and even affectionate; feelings it is so rare for travellers to excite, that they won rapidly on our esteem. The aristocracy of the worthy captain was as mild as I hope my own democracy was reasonable, and I believe our little discussions led to nothing worse than a complete confirmation of each, in his original impressions.

The wind blew cold, and the atmosphere lowered, as we drove through the gloomy streets of Berne. Every thing seemed chill and wintry, and I perceived that we had not commenced our journey a day too soon. As we pushed on towards Morat, the Alps stood ranged along the horizon to the left, looking stormy and grim. I did not like to examine them in that state, for they had the air of friends whose faces had become cold. Although icy and chill, there is nothing repulsive in the ordinary aspect of these sublime objects, which, usually, are inviting

---

* The writer subsequently submitted to this mode of getting along, by way of ascertaining its comparative merits, and would advise no one to resort to it, who has the means of paying for his own dinner. The Bernese *voiturier* turned out to be a respectable man, and his two postilions thoroughly faithful and honest fellows.

rather than otherwise; but, on this day one felt disposed to shudder as he gazed at them. Perhaps the state of the weather aided to produce a part of this impression.

We slept at Payerne, and I owe it to the worthy landlady to say, that we dined on the very best quails I ever tasted. You know the European bird is much smaller than our own, and that it is distinguished from it in several important particulars; the American quail, though not by any means as large, greatly resembling the partridge of this hemisphere.

We had two parties at the inn to-night, that served to interest W[illiam] and myself, who were in the *salle à manger* for half an hour, in the course of the evening. Both were English. One came in a travelling coach, that bore an earl's coronet: and the other, in a travelling chariot, that (an unusual thing in England) had its panels plain. There was a solemn and quiet mystery about the former equipage and all that belonged to it, which, at first, I mistook for *la morgue aristocratique:* even the servants appearing more sulky and dogged than English servants in general, which is saying a good deal for those who have *un si grand talent pour le silence*. But I have since accidentally learned that a heavy family affliction had thrown a gloom over the party. I have noted down the fact, as an admonition against hasty inferences.

The other group was perfectly exquisite. It consisted of two men and a woman, who arrived in a very handsome London-built chariot, that was lackered and varnished till it shone like a mirror. There was no reserve about these gentry, though they too were sulky and dogged, as it might be, just for the satisfaction of the thing. Their *talents pour le silence* were not sufficient to prevent us from overhearing a consultation that took place in the public room, and which almost threw poor W[illiam] into convulsions. They had ordered dinner, and the mooted point was the nature of the fluid with which it would be advisable to wash down the viands. The *carte* was called for, and one of the men rather sneeringly remarked, that it contained the usual list of "washy things." After a useless examination by the gentlemen, it was gallantly determined to leave the matter to the lady, who forthwith decided in favour of brandy! Who these people were, I shall not presume to say, though I think I am quite safe in anticipating your conjecture, and in affirming they were not servants.

We were away with the dawn, and trotted briskly along the beautiful valley so lately described, cheered by the presence of the sun. At Moudon we breakfasted, an event I record, merely to say that we met with bad fare and a heavy bill, a result that has occurred to me, now, three times in the same house.* The *écorcheur* of an innkeeper profits by the circumstance of owning what the French would call *"une auberge inévitable."*

The day became particularly fine after eleven, and we went merrily on our route, diverging from the road to Lausanne, at a hamlet called Carrouge. After proceeding through a pleasant, but open country, for a league or two, we came to a small lake, which lies on the high land that bounds this part of the shores of the Leman, and which is marked on the map of Keller, as being eight hundred feet above the the level of the lake of Wallenstadt. At this point, the road begins to descend; and presently we got a view of the lake of Geneva, and of all those parts of Vaud which lay between us and the Jura. We thought even this prospect charming, but, rolling along the hard even road, the carriage suddenly stopped on the brow of a precipice, where it became necessary to lock the wheels, and where involuntary exclamations of delight burst from the oldest to the youngest among us.

A more ravishing view than that we now beheld can scarcely be imagined. Nearly the whole of the lake was visible. The north shore was studded with towns, towers, castles, and villages, for the distance of thirty miles; the rampart—resembling rocks of Savoy, rose for three or four thousand feet, like walls above the water, and solitary villages were built against their bases, in spots where there scarcely appeared room to place a human foot. The solemn, magnificent gorge, rather than valley, of the Rhone, and the river, glittering like silver among its meadows, were in the distant front, while the immediate foreground was composed of a shore which also had its wall of rocks, its towns laved by the water, its castles, its hamlets half concealed in fruit trees, and its broad mountain bosom, thrown carelessly into terraces, to the elevation of two thousand feet, on

* The writer had the same luck in 1832.

which reposed nearly every object of rural art that can adorn a picture.

In this landscape, we now met, for the first time, the glow of Italian warmth mingled with the severe grandeur of Switzerland. Vévey, which lay nearly at our feet, is celebrated for the mildness of its climate; and all the adjoining shore produces wine and fruits, that are believed properly to belong to a parallel of latitude several degrees lower than the real position of the place. This circumstance is owing to the manner in which the district is sheltered by the mountains, and to a south-western exposure. The sunny character of the scenery struck us as not among the least agreeable of its features. The beauty of the panorama was singularly heightened by the presence of some thirty or forty large barks, with *latine* sails, a rig particularly Italian, and which, to my eye, was redolent of the Mediterranean, a sea I had not beheld for twenty years. They were lying lazily on the glassy lake, as if placed there by Claude himself, to serve as models. By shutting out other objects, so as to look only at the barks, and to make an horizon of the blue element on which they floated, the deception was complete, so far as mere poetry was concerned, though the obtrusive knowledge of the mariner did, indeed, impertinently demonstrate that a Genevese bark is not absolutely a Genoese felucca. But there was enough of lubberly beauty to render the former very fit objects for a landscape; and the wisest way, on such occasions, is to forget all minute knowlege, and to dwell on the general effect, unless, according to the mariner's code, the "minute knowledge" produce most satisfaction.

I shall not affirm that this was the finest view we had yet seen in Switzerland, but I do think it was the most exquisite. It was Goethe compared to Schiller; Milton to Shakspeare; Racine to Corneille. Other places had a grander nature, more awful principals, and altogether sublimer features; but I cannot recall one, in which elements, of themselves noble and imposing, were so admirably blended with extensive, delicate, and faultlessly fine details. Had the architecture and the towns been a little more Italian, and the shipping more finished, this scene would have nobly sustained a comparison with some of the very best on the other side of the Alps.

Fully a mile of rapid descent lay before us, and nearly the whole distance was lined with vineyards, propped in terraces. Honest Caspar, the postilion, who had ridden a dragoon in the wars of Napoleon, and who now rode among the finest natural scenery as unmoved and rigid as he would have sat his horse as a *vidette*, had, notwithstanding, an acquired taste for foraging, and he found means, by the aid of a few of my sous,—which, I verily believe, were laid up against the moths in his own tobacco-box,—to fill our laps with delicious grapes. In this style, then, we went down the declivity, gradually nearing the blue sheet of the Leman, until the carriage rolled along the strand.

Caspar passed Vévey on a trot, with a postilion's *fierté*, issuing from it, on the other side, among vines and fruit trees, by a road as narrow and as good as the best of England. The route led along the margin of the lake for leagues, sometimes descending to the very strand, rising over swells at others, and always obeying the sinuosities of the coast. It was altogether a fairy scene! This was the region of Rousseau; Mèilleurie and St. Gingoulph lying tranquilly on the margin of the glassy lake, beneath the beetling rocks of Savoy, nearly opposite to us.

The vintage had commenced, and, in addition to the raptures of such a scene, and the luxury of such a day, we had the satisfaction of beholding and of sympathizing in the feeling of plenty and merriment that the season always produces. We constantly met wagons bearing tubs of grapes, and men and women were staggering through the vines, all around us, under burdens in which the luscious fruit was piled above the baskets. Honest Caspar foraged, unperceived by the peasant, on one in passing; but discovering that I had observed his ingenuity, he exclaimed, with a postilion's leer, "They are good now, *Monsieur*, but they will be better *tout de suite*." He alluded to the wine.

[Mrs. Cooper] and myself were on the carriage box, and we went through this magical little district with the most profound sense of enjoyment. The feeling was not so much of the "*touzy-mouzy*" order, as one of calm and delighted satisfaction. We seemed to have entered an entirely new country since reaching the brow of the hill; and the suddenness of the change, the luxurious repose of every thing connected with the earth, the sublimity of the nature, the quick succession of objects, and the classical associations, kept us in a state of constant and varying gratification, that would have amounted to excitement, had not the exquisite tranquillity of the picture rendered such an Americanism particularly ill-timed. Perhaps, after all, it would be nearer the truth to say that we *were* in a state of high American feeling, ready to affirm we were furiously excited, while, in fact, it was some such agitation as one feels at listening to a soothing and delicious melody. The rapidity of our uninterrupted passage through this fairy land, no doubt, aided in heightening the enjoyment, which, like all the joys of humanity, might possibly have been lessened by the transit of a single cloud.

Caspar was an old roadster, and I desired him to name the different objects as we proceeded, the highway being so smooth, that the rattling of the carriage was scarcely audible. He discharged the duty without a spark of poetry, but with the intelligence of a postilion, and the brevity of a dragoon. "*Mèilleurie,*" "*St. Gingoulph,*" aided by a gesture with the whip, were sufficient. As the honest fellow went through the different names as regularly as if he had been at roll-call, and I kept the map open before me, I believe we missed nothing that such a flight could bestow. "*Blonay, Meinheer,*" cried the *ci-devant* dragoon, pointing to a picturesque *château*, that stood back, seated on a swell of the verdant mountain-side. "*Châtelard,*" pointing to an isolated, but massive, venerable tower, that topped a little rocky eminence, near by. "*Clarens,*" a village that we almost entered. "*Montreux,*" another, that lay against the pile before us. "*Villeneuve,*" a town across a bay, that was on the strand, and towards which we were wending our way, as fast as four nimble horses could trot. "——— ———!" exclaimed [Mrs. Cooper], as we descended a hill, near the gate of a villa, where stood a gentleman, his hands in his pockets, with the quiet air of one who was before his own door. The individual who had so unexpectedly broken in, on the roll-call of honest Caspar, was a native of New York, and a distant relation of [Mrs. Cooper]'s, whose father having succeeded to the family property and honours, in the mother country, had "gone home," as it used to be expressed, whence, as it now appeared, this member of the family had once more "gone abroad." He showed his taste in the choice of a residence, for it would not be easy to select a more lovely spot between Copenhagen and Naples, than the precise place in which we got this transient glimpse of one, who stood in this peculiar relation to so many of our party. But the whole coast was lined with small country houses, which were continually peeping out from among the shrubbery and fruit trees, at a little distance on our left. On the right, there was room for nothing, the carriage wheels coming frequently within a few yards of the blue lake.

After proceeding in this manner for several miles we diverged a little from the strand, and we next got from among the vines into a place, where the road led through nut trees, and passed down a gentle descent, beneath a beetling cliff, back towards the water. The change from the vines to the freedom of nature helped to keep up the pleasure, and we were just expressing as much, when the towers of an irregular pile glimmered through the foliage, directly before us, and within a hundred yards. "*Chillon!*" cried the indefatigable and methodical Caspar. "*Arrêtez,*" responded your humble servant. The obedient campaigner pulled up directly before the gate of this celebrated castle. But the sun had already disappeared behind the mountain, and Caspar reminded us that a steamboat was in sight, making the best of her way towards Villeneuve, which town had but one inn where it would be at all agreeable to pass the night. At the same time he looked as if his grays would be all the better for a feed, and for a good grooming. Under these circumstances, it was determined to leave this historical hold as one of the objects that we hope to visit at some future day. We could admire its exterior and position, however, without interfering with the wishes of old Caspar. The first is rude, but exceedingly quaint, and the building stands on some rocks that project from the shore, and is almost surrounded by deep water, a single, low, sandy spit, athwart which a short narrow bridge has been built, alone connecting it with the mountain.

The rest of the road was immediately along the lake shore, beneath a high and frowning wall of rock; and we had a trial of speed with the steamboat until we reached the door of the inn. As is often the case, in more important matters, the battle was not to the strong, nor the race to the swift. The boat got in some time before us; but, being obliged to anchor, there being neither port nor quay, we got possession of the best rooms while our unknown competitors were landing. Caspar snapped his fingers, when I told him of our success, and said there was nothing like a good team, let them talk as much as they would about *"bateaux-à-vapeur!"* "Napoleon had no steamboats," said the old dragoon, triumphantly. "Very true; if he had known their use, his fortune might have been different."

I have nothing to say of Villeneuve, unless it be to tell you that my carriage passed the night in the tower of the church, where it was sacrilegiously housed by the people of the stables, for the want of a more profane *remise*.

Letter XXVII.

M̲Y DEAR——————,

Caspar had us all paraded by daylight, and after roll-call, and a cup of *café noir*, we took up the line of march. The road led for a few miles among meadows that are literally as level as a floor, the result of an alluvial formation. The valley at this point must be a league wide; but the great altitude of the rocks that overhang it cause it to appear much narrower. The river was not yet visible. We had hamlets, and churches, and ruins, as usual, and after two hours driving we passed a *bourg* of some size, called Bex. Proceeding onward, the mountains gradually drew nearer to each other, thrusting up two or three of their bald summits to a giddy height, where they stand, like warders of the country, overlooking the entire flank of the advanced range of the Alps. These peaks are called *Dents;* and the one immediately over Bex, *Le Dent de Morcles*, is the commencement of that formation, of which I have already spoken, by which the mountains of the Oberland have been separated from those of Mont Blanc, the two St. Bernards, St. Gothard, Monte Rosa, and all the others on the line of Italy. Its neighbour and twin, *le Dent du Midi*, lies on the opposite side of the Rhone, and is a sort of outlying sentinel, detached from the body of Mont Blanc.

At the distance of a mile or two from Bex, the bases of the mountain approach so near as to leave little more space than is necessary for the passage of the river. The road winds under the brow of a precipice, with barely room enough to get round the rocks. At this point there is a gate, with a few attempts at fortifications, both sides of the stream offering the same facilities for defence, and each having its arched passage. When these two gates are closed, the canton of Valais (which commences here) is literally under lock and key, there being no other entrance to it, by means of a valley, but this. The station is important, as the several passes of the two St. Bernards, and of the Simplon, with indeed those of St. Gothard and the Splügen, are more or less connected with it. A handful of well commanded men, at this pass, would be sufficient to arrest the march of an army.

After going through the gate, we crossed the Rhone by a bridge of a single arch, near the centre of which is a tower. Through another gate in this tower we were compelled to drive, the real entrance into the Valais being precisely at this spot. At the western end of the bridge, the two great roads of the Simplon unite, the one which was constructed by Napoleon, sweeping along the southern shore of the lake, by Savoy, and the other being that we had just travelled. The village of St. Maurice stretches itself along the base of the mountain in a single street; the rear walls of the houses, in many instances, being actually formed of the living rock. At this place Caspar called a halt, and we called for breakfast.

After partaking of the *côtelettes* and the *café au lait*, I walked ahead with [Mrs. Cooper], in order to exercise our limbs. Had we known the hideous objects that we were about to behold, the walk, most probably, would have been postponed. The Valais has long had a painful notoriety for a race of miserable objects called *Crétins*, beings possessing the most disgusting likeness to our species, of which they are physical abortions, but deprived in a great degree of reason. St. Maurice is the portion of the canton most afflicted with this calamity. As we picked our way through the filth of the street, (every thing like Swiss neatness being wanting here,) we saw perhaps twenty of these objects basking in the sun, with goggling, unmeaning eyes, livid, slavering lips, hideous *goîtres*, and every other sign of physical and mental imbecility. It was like running the gauntlet of disgusts; and glad enough we were to issue from such a scene of human misery, into the beauty of the open fields.

I have called the *Crétins* a race; but the expression, perhaps, is not rigidly true, as most of them are the offspring of ordinary parents. This infliction has been attributed to the adjoining marshes; and it is said that by sending the mothers into the mountains before the births, and by keeping the children there for the first few years of their lives, the evil is gradually disappearing. I should think there must be a combination of causes to produce a curse like this, for other countries are marshy, and even other portions of Switzerland, without being subject to this blight on their happiness.

It is probable we were particularly unfortunate on this occasion; for the morning had been quite cold, and most of the *Crétins* had drawn themselves into the sun, which was now beating hot against the walls, basking in its rays being one of their principal enjoyments. Many of them are deaf and dumb, and others make sounds that are as revolting as their aspects. What would become of the soul, and of that reason of which we are so proud, did any accidental concurrence of circumstances permit the formation of a race of such beings! The perpetuation of physical and mental peculiarities cannot be doubted, and it would not be difficult to construct a genealogy for some of the equivocal animals of Africa, through the theories to which such premises give rise. Although the connexion between the material and immaterial is so fearfully intimate in our organization, these very creatures prove that partial separations do occur; and why may not nature, weary with fruitless efforts, in the end decree a final divorce? In creating man in his own image, God endowed him with a portion of his own high intelligence, but not with his outward form. *He* is purely a Spirit, and not a body of matter. They who people Heaven are still nearer to him in this likeness; but there is no good reason to suppose that they possess our physical attributes. The varieties of our own animal genus sufficiently prove that the ends of Providence do not require any absolute animal identity; and the exceptions which so abundantly exist, everywhere, go to show that reason and a certain precise physical formation, at least, are not inseparable.

Picot ascribes a peculiar character to the inhabitants of this canton. *"Les Valaisans,"* he says, *"loin de désirer d'attirer l'attention du monde, sont jaloux de leur obscurité, de leur ignorance et de leur pauvreté même, qu'ils croyent nécessaire à leur bonheur."*—It might not be amiss to effect a little infusion of American blood into them, which, I think, would thoroughly eradicate the latter singularity. Poor wretches! they have not yet learned to term a lust for money, a virtue; the desire to live in a better house than their fellows, ambition; overreaching a neighbour, genius; and the restlessness of covetous desires, energy! Ignoble as they are, however, they braved the legions of Rome in defence of their rights; overthrew their local tyrants with—not the *energy*, for that word has passed behind the counter—but with the resolution of men worthy to be free; and they gave their powerful French invaders nine desperate trials of strength, in 1799, finally yielding to famine, when their little community of less than 80,000 members, had scarcely food enough to keep their bodies and ignoble souls together. Unhappy people!—who, without the desire to be rich, and its attendant excellencies, "energy" and "ambition," were not enabled to remain the masters of your own misery, and the arbiters of your own humble tastes! But Napoleon caused the great road to be made through the middle of their territory; he developed the capabilities of the Simplon, and, as the rich now roll by daily in their coaches, it is to be expected that better desires will be awakened in their breasts, and that they will not for ever remain in ignorance of the interesting and engrossing fact that "the age of bargaining is come."

There is a very ancient and a very curious hermitage near St. Maurice, which stands on a narrow ledge of rock, against the face of a precipice, and where the eye does not readily detect the means of ascending and descending. It is inhabited, notwithstanding, and we were told that the last, or the present, occupant, (I have forgotten which,) had the extraordinary additional merit for his vocation of being blind! After all, such a man, in such a situation, might be safer than one who had all his eyes about him. Trusting to a sense that was as good in the dark as in the light, his occasional *quêtes*, among the inhabitants of the nether world, in search of a cup or a rasher, would be less likely to lead to accidents than if he threaded his way with a bolder foot. I have heard that a certain person, from whom we are both descended, and whose names we have divided very equitably between us, was blind in his old age, but that he persevered in visiting a kinsman, whose property adjoined his own, using a footpath that obliged him to cross a deep stream by a single plank. As these patriarchs lived in the last century, and had the habits of the period, this was a feat our industrious ancestor chose always to perform about midnight, and which he long performed in perfect safety; while his cousin, on the return visits, was compelled to make a *détour* of a mile or two, in order to avoid the danger, and this, too, sometimes under circumstances that rendered the achievement of an extra mile an affair of some moment. Our predecessor in the end, however, like the pitcher that goes too often to the well, lost his life in one of these midnight marches, though not at the point where danger was most to be apprehended.

A little beyond the hermitage we reached a spot that, on a small scale, resembled the desolation of Goldau. The accident was of very recent occurrence, and had been caused by the bursting of what, in the language of the country, is called a *sac d'eau*, one of the many dangers that always impend over a residence among the Alps. A *sac d'eau* is formed by a rapid thaw, and the accidental falling of a mass of ice across the throat of some gorge in the upper regions. The consequence is the collection of a pond of water, which becoming too heavy for the dam, the whole comes down in a body into the valley. In this instance, a stripe of beautiful meadow, near half a mile in width, and extending from the base of the mountains to the Rhone, had been completely covered, to the depth of several feet, with stones that would weigh a pound or two, among which were mixed a great many rocks that might weigh tons. Although no lives were lost, this was truly a national calamity, in a country where a hundred acres of land, more or less, become an object of importance. A woman, who related the particulars, ended by thankfully exclaiming "it was very fortunate it had not taken place in the night, or the inhabitants might have been frightened!" There she lived, in apparent security, within a few yards of the desolation, and just as confident as if millions of cubic feet of ice did not impend over her head, constantly threatening the same danger. But this life of ours is little more than an affair of underwriting, in which men take risks daily, without entering into very nice calculations of the intrinsic value of the premiums they receive.

The carriages, with the rest of the party, overtook us just as we had reached the farther side of the *débris*, when we all went off together, at a round trot. The length of the great valley is about ninety miles; and between the glacier of the Rhone and its entrance into the lake of Geneva, there is a descent of something less than five thousand feet; but as much the greater part of it occurs in the eastern portion of the canton, the road was very nearly a level.

There is a waterfall about halfway between St. Maurice and Martigny, that would admirably suit a Flemish picture. It is very generally known; but I think more on account of its situation near a much frequented road, and to this accidental *Teniersism*, than through any very extraordinary beauty of its own. Among the Swiss cascades, it holds but a secondary place, in my estimation.

At Martigny, the valley inclines to the north-east, turning at right angles to its previous direction. Mont Velan lies directly athwart the head of the first reach, forming a noble termination, as it is seen from Vévey. The road to the Great St. Bernard diverges here to the west, while we bent our faces the other way, without even stopping at Martigny, which is a hamlet of no beauty whatever. A fine old ruin on a rock that overhangs it, however, is a striking object; but our *ci-devant* dragoon assured us his *étape* was nicely measured, and that we must push forward to Sion, or pass the night where we were.

The valley of the Rhone, for a considerable distance beyond Martigny, has the appearance of alluvion, and, most probably, was once the bed of a lake. This must have been the case, however, in the early ages of our orb, for the place has been frequented and known nearly as long as we have any profane accounts of the deeds of men.

I was glad to get rid of the monotony of a dead level, although it was relieved by huge mountains that were rarely five miles asunder, whose spurs abounded with ruined castles, for the sight of some irregular crags, having their tops and edges fringed with the picturesque outlines of walls, battlements, turrets, and towers. The Acropolis does not overhang Athens in a more kingly style, than these rocks frown upon the humbler town of Sion; nor do I believe that the architecture of the former, however pure and classical, is half as picturesque as the quaint little nests that are perched among the crags of the latter. To heighten their beauty, the buildings in question are chiefly ruins, the winged race who formerly inhabited them having, most probably, become extinct.

The valley is much broader at Sion than at any other point, having a breadth of not less than ten miles, and the environs are fertile and charming. It is an ancient town, the bishoprick alone claiming an existence of quite twelve centuries. The Romans were here, however, long before the bishops. The meetings of the local diet are held in one of the quaint-looking edifices mentioned, the highest legislative body of the republic being, in truth, a congress of the representatives of certain *dizains* (thirteen in number) into which the territory is subdivided, much in the same manner as the Grisons are divided into *ligues*. As the canton is rigidly and exclusively Catholic, the Bishop sits in the Diet, where he enjoys, in his own ecclesiastical person, the dignity and the vote of a *dizain*. But I am wandering from the narrative, and encroaching on ground it is my intention to take up more at large hereafter.

We passed the night in this picturesque looking place, among a flight of travellers, like ourselves, destined for Italy, and took our departure the next day with the appearance of the sun. The beauty and fertility of the valley soon vanished, the Rhone occasionally spreading itself, like the Rhine above the lake of Constance, in a way to destroy every vestige of cultivation. What between *sacs d'eau*, torrents, the river, and now and then an avalanche, it is not an easy matter to keep the plain in the condition of a garden. The mountains began to approach each other, and to become more chill and repulsive in aspect. Still men dwelt among their dreary solitudes, cottages and chalets being buried in the glens, or clinging to the cliffs. This was more particularly the fact with the mountains of the northern range. These buildings are sombre, dun-looking abodes, perfectly harmonizing with the bleak character of the nature. Perhaps I began to weary a little, with the constant sight of piles of granite, heaped on each other to the skies; perhaps the season had come with its chill influence and wintry clouds, to add to the feeling of fatigue; but the entire valley of the Rhone was less welcome to me, and the nakedness of its stern rocks had what I shall call a more *unmitigated air* than any others I had seen in Switzerland. The mountains seemed streaked with sterility in a very indescribable way, while the visible altitudes, at least, were not sufficiently great to offer a redeeming grandeur. Still they *are* lofty, and, in any other country, would, of themselves, afford infinite satisfaction during a visit of reasonable duration.

About the middle of the afternoon, the road was seen winding up the side of a mountain that had the look of naked pastures, and a *bourg* appeared clustered beneath it, in the valley.

The first was the commencement of the far-famed Simplon, and the last was the town that stands at its base.

We reached Brig in sufficient season to have made a relay on the mountain, but the horses necessary to reinforce the cavalry of Caspar were not to be had. There was no alternative, and we took rooms for the night, consoling ourselves with a good dinner; the *étapes* of the indomitable dragoon being much better adapted to his own desultory habits of eating and drinking, than to those with which we had enlisted under his orders. This agreeable duty performed, I sallied forth to reconnoitre.

Brig, Brigg, or Brieg, is an inconsiderable town, that lies directly at the foot of the celebrated pass, though the road literally commences at a village at a little distance, called Glys. It is a stronghold of the Jesuits, who have a seminary here, with buildings of more extent than beauty. A stone that is filled with mica is used instead of slate, and the effect is to give a singularly cold and wintry look to the place. The people call it a resemblance of silver, but it did not appear to me that the idea of silver would ever suggest itself in looking at Brig, while one is irresistibly led to think of blankets. A few black-looking ecclesiastics stalked about the place, like clerical ghosts, but apparently much respected and honoured.

A torrent called the Saltine descends from the mountain at this point, through a long ravine, that is not, however, very frightful in appearance, being far more distinguished by its size than by any thing particularly horrible. Through this broad and retiring vista, one can see upward, as far as the gate, or to the summit of the pass. The road itself has little to do, at first, with this ravine, though, in the end, it skirts its edge for a few miles, and finally doubles the upper end. So far from following it, immediately on quitting Brig, the route diverges from it nearly at right angles, winding its way on the broad breast of the pile, through open, shrubless pastures, of which it follows such portions as most favour the ascent. Nearly five miles of it were visible, before it became hid among the larches which grow higher against the hills. Judging by the eye, the distance from the town to the head of the ravine, which is in truth the greatest elevation of the pass, cannot materially exceed six miles, if, indeed, it be as much, nor did the angle appear to be as great as I had expected to find it. The distance one is obliged to travel, however, is about thirteen miles, the difference proceeding from the sinuosities of the road.

The valley of the Rhone narrows materially above Brig, and there is a fine view of a glacier of the Viescherhorn, one of the peaks of the Oberland, nearly opposite the town. The elevation of this spot above the sea is about 2400 feet. The distance, by the road, to the summit of the pass, is, as I have just stated, about thirteen miles; to the village of Simpeln, it is eighteen; to the frontier of Italy, twenty-three; to Crevola, or the level of the first Italian plain, thirty-one; and to Domo d'Ossola, the town where the day's work usually ends, four more; making the whole distance about thirty-five miles, of which, however, the last three or four are on a perfect flat. Having ascertained these facts, I returned to the inn, in order to catch an early nap, the indefatigable Caspar having commanded the trumpet to sound the *rappel* at three on the following morning.

Letter XXVIII.

My DEAR ———,

At the appointed hour we were all assembled in the *kitchen* of the inn, around a good fire, to enjoy the consolation of a cup of *café noir*, before commencing the day's work. This object happily achieved, we went out into the chill air of the morning, it being still so dark that it was not possible to see the length of the team. Caspar had lighted the carriage lamps, however, and, by their aid, I was enabled to discover that we had six horses, with an additional postilion. The *fourgon* was also promoted, on this occasion, to the dignity of a carriage and four. There was an air of work and preparation about all this, that got up the *touzy-mouzy* a little, and we had hopes of quitting Switzerland with a portion of that high excitement with which it had been entered. This was a grateful change, for the dull aspect of the Valais had actually thrown such a chill about my feelings, that I really began to fear I was falling into the apathy of one who had got to be a little *blasé*.

The ascent of the Simplon properly commences at the village already named, which we passed the previous evening, a mile or two before reaching Brieg, but which is not used as a stopping place by those who like good quarters. We had, therefore, to ascend, in the darkness, more than half a mile, by a cross road, before we felt the carriage turning into the more regular path. It does very well to talk about trotting up and down this celebrated route, by way of poetical embellishment, but our six cattle seemed very well disposed to take the matter much more leisurely. There were reaches of the road, it is true, where the thing was possible, and where, indeed, it was actually achieved by our own team, but much the greater part of the ascent was made on a walk.

I can say little more of the first two hours of our morning's work, than that it was a steady drag up a mountain of very even surface. I believe we passed in the obscurity, one of the most

XIII. The Gorge of the Tamina *Switzerland*, 185–87

xiv. Tell's Chapel and the Meadow of Grütli *Switzerland,* 155–57

xv. Baths of Pfeffers *Switzerland*, 184

xvi. The Simplon Pass *Switzerland*, 278–82

admired parts of the Swiss section of the road, but I much doubt if there be actually any thing so delightfully horrible, as is pretended, on that side of the mountain. When the day dawned, we found ourselves on the side of a ravine, called the Ganter, and not far from a point where the road led round its head, making a complete bend. Here W[illiam] and myself alighted and walked the rest of the distance to the summit, preceding the carriage the whole way, with great ease to ourselves: pretty good proof in itself that there was not much trotting. Indeed, the postilions soon after dismounted, walking by the side of their horses, most of the time. I do not think, however, that it would be necessary to lock the wheels much of the way, in descending, or that it would be at all dangerous to go down the whole declivity, on this side of the mountain, on a reasonable trot.

We passed a solitary tavern near the head of the ravine mentioned, where some English travellers had spent the night. Not far from this inn, we went through a bit of forest, after which the road came out *en corniche*, along the edge of a larger and deeper ravine, or that in which the Saltine flows, and up which I had obtained the view the previous evening. Many writers speak of the terrific appearance of these two ravines: of trees growing nearly in a line with their sides: of their vast depth, and of the nervousness with which one gazes downwards, into the gloomy abysses. All this struck me as being singularly exaggerated. From Brieg to the summit, I did not see a single point where there could have been any great difficulty in constructing a road, or a single spot where a man of ordinary nerves might not stand with great indifference, on the extreme edge of the path. The mountain was on vast scale; the road was certainly laid out with great science and method; the ravines, if not frightful, were yawning, and of great depth, and there can be no doubt that in many places, torrents, landslips, avalanches, and falling rocks may, occasionally, do much mischief. One of the latter had done material injury this very summer, but none of these dangers obtrude themselves on the eye of the traveller in ascending. Here and there, a small stone Refuge stands by the road-side, a place of shelter in the winter, and during storms: signs that the route is not without its difficulties in particular seasons.

Shortly before doubling the head of the last ravine, we got a good view into the great valley, Brieg looking quite near, but dreary as ever. At the point where the road bends, the ravine terminates, and the mountain above it rises more abruptly to a peak, crowned by a glacier. As the road here is necessarily cut into the earth, a roof of stone has been built over it, in order to cast the avalanches into the ravine. It is a damp and disagreeable gallery, and I should think too lightly constructed to offer a sufficient resistance to any very serious fall of snow. It is fair to presume, however, that it is suited to its purposes.

W[illiam] and myself reached the toll-house about nine, and fully twenty minutes before the carriage, notwithstanding Caspar had mounted and endeavoured to raise a trot, for the last mile or two. Our appearance alone and on foot caused some astonishment in the good woman who came out to greet us; nor did she seem to understand our errand, until looking down the road she saw the rest of the party toiling their way up. The delay gave us an opportunity to put some questions, which were readily and I thought intelligently answered. She told us, among other things, that the annual repairs of the road cost 30,000 francs, and that the receipts were, in common, less than 25,000. When I asked her what had become of all the milestones which the guide-books commemorate, she laughed heartily, and replied, that she "had read of them, too, but that she had been sixteen years on the mountain, without ever having had the good fortune to see one!" This is the way the world is quizzed by those arch rogues who live by the quill! This woman was as lively as the air she breathed; and several hearty jokes passed between her and the facetious Caspar, after his arrival, he proving to be an old acquaintance. They had an amicable difference, however, as to the amount of the toll that ought to be paid for the *fourgon*, which she classed among the carriages that are suspended on springs—while the *ci-devant* dragoon affirmed that he had ridden on it many a league without ever suspecting there was any thing like a spring in any part of the uneasy machine. "Ask this young woman," said Caspar, pointing to the Abigail who rode by his side, "whether she thinks it has any springs; if she says it has as much as there is in that rock, I will pay double your demand." This sally produced a laugh between them that might have been heard, on a still day, at Brieg, and in which the discomfited and jolted Lucie bore an unwilling part.

A short distance from the toll-house is a cross, which marks the precise summit. At this point one is about 6600 feet above the sea, and 4000 above Brieg. Not far from the cross, a *hospice* is constructing, for the purpose of giving travellers shelter. An old building of the same nature, but of very inferior pretensions, stands in a little valley hard by, deserted and dilapidated. The latter, it would seem, was a private charity; but the new edifice belongs to the brotherhood of Augustines of the Great St. Bernard.

There is little interest in the summit of the Simplon. It has breadth and vastness; but its aspect is that of a rocky mountain pasturage. A few glaciers are in sight, but none of any particular beauty on the immediate pile. The descent to the village of Simpeln is easy, and the distance is near five miles; the whole of which may be said, virtually, to lie on the summit of the passage, for, though Simpeln is six or seven hundred feet lower than the *hospice*, it is reached before the main descent commences. The village is inconsiderable, and the inn small and indifferent. *Au reste*, it is something to dwell in a town that lies 6000 feet above the level of tide.

At this place we saw two chamois, the first living animals of the species with which we had met. They were kept in a stable, and were sufficiently tame to be comfortable, but there was a hop-and-skip look about their eyes. These animals were not larger than a half-grown kid; though they appeared to be young, and may not have reached their full size.

To sum up the details of the northern side of the Simplon, I shall add that it fell materially short of the grand and terrific effects we anticipated from the descriptions we had not only heard, but read. There is no part of it which, as a road, presents either the appearance, or the reality, of the danger that you are accustomed to encounter so often in descending the mile that lies between the top of the Vision and your own little village; though there is much more of it, and every thing about it is on a vastly larger scale. If you will permit youself to imagine eight Visions piled one on the other, in a way to reduce the inclination fully one half, and then suppose the road to wind its way, by very gradual ascents, up its capacious breast, you would get a very tolerable idea of the Swiss portion of the Simplon.

What a different thing is that of Italy!—Throughout the Alps, as I have already told you, their northern faces are much less precipitous than their southern. You are not, however, to suppose from this fact that there is any thing beyond its poetry, in the florid accounts we have had of the effects produced, on invaders and travellers, by glimpses obtained of the plains of Italy, from the summits of any of these passes. The upper peaks of the Alps being visible from the low country of Lombardy, it follows that the low country of Lombardy must be visible (though at a great distance and quite indistinctly) from the upper peaks of the Alps; but no one beyond a chamois hunter or a solitary adventurer ever gets there to behold it. From the summit of the Simplon road, I question if the smallest fragment of Italy is to be seen, even in the peak of a distant rock. The mountains are too near and crowded to admit of glimpses beyond the limits of the particular valley, or gorge, in which the traveller may happen to be.

The books not only tell us that carriages trot up the Simplon, but some of them go so far as to add that they trot down it without locking the wheels. The prudent Caspar viewed the matter differently. While we were at breakfast, he took an occasion to let me know that the iron *sabot* would be good for nothing by the time we reached the frontier of Italy, if we depended on that alone, and that cheap wooden shoes were kept at the tavern for the express purpose of rendering the descent more economical. I bought one of the latter forthwith, and, by way of commentary on the popular account of the matter, will just add that when it was thrown away, it was worn as thin as the blade of a knife. Having made this very necessary provision, we left the village between twelve and one.

The first mile was a complete demonstration of the difference between the northern and the southern faces of the Alps. The mountain falls away rapidly; though the sharpness of the pitch is much diminished by following a very circuitous and winding path. It was certainly possible to trot some of the way down even this declivity, by the aid of the shoe; and it is even usual in America to descend sharper pitches, with loaded stages, without locking a wheel at all. But you will remember that impeding a carriage in this manner, or impeding any thing else, is a practice almost unknown in America—ill comporting with the hurry of the national character. Some one might get ahead of the laggard who should stop to put a shoe beneath a wheel!

We soon reached the first of the celebrated galleries, which are also features of the route that, I think, are usually exaggerated. The mere effect of passing through these artificial caverns, amid frowning precipices and foaming torrents, and along a road that, in reality, is as smooth and safe as a garden walk, is, beyond a doubt, both exciting and strange; but as mere public works these galleries are neither extraordinary nor unusual. The "Hole of Uri" is precisely the same thing, and much more ancient, though smaller. Were the rock entirely blown away, these passes would create much less wonder and conversation, while the labour and cost would evidently have been materially increased. But you can more easily appreciate the labour, if not the effect in a picturesque sense, by learning the dimensions. The longest of these galleries is a little more than six hundred feet, the height is about twenty, and the breadth twelve. The rock is a compact granite, with few veins. The single cutting on the Erie Canal, near Lockport, as a mere public work, materially surpasses all the cuttings and blastings on all the Alpine passes put together, although there are now two other roads, but little, if any, inferior to this of the Simplon.*

Notwithstanding all the mistakes which have arisen from indiscriminating descriptions, poetic feeling, or popular error, no passage of the Alps can possibly be other than grand, and, at certain seasons, dangerous. The magnificent nature among which the Simplon road is compelled to pass, coupled with its extent, form its principal peculiarities. There is, perhaps, no one insulated point on the whole route, which, taken by itself, merely as gallery, bridge, or road, is not surpassed, even in its own way, by some similar object, in some other part of Switzerland. Thus, no bridge is equal in boldness, thread-like lightness, and giddy altitude to that of the Reuss, near Ursern; nor do I know that there is any greater cutting than at that point; but

* That of the St. Gothard, which has since been completed, makes a fourth, and that by Nice a fifth.

there is *so much* of this labour, and skill, and hardihood, compressed into a single route, in descending the Simplon, that
while one is passing rapidly through such a scene, the mind,
without stopping to analyze the parts, is apt to carry away an
impression of an entire and undivided whole. You are kept for
hours among some of the grandest objects of the sublimest
scenery of Europe, if not of the world; and few pause to detect
the means that conspire to produce the impressions that all feel.

Soon after quitting the village, as has just been said, we commenced descending, by a road that made a wide sweep, and at
the end of a mile or two we entered the gallery. At this point the
descent became more gradual, and we trotted on, at a good
pace, for some distance farther. The gorge, through which the
road runs, deepened as we proceeded, until the cliffs impended
over it, in places, and in walls that were absolutely projecting, I
should think, fully a thousand feet. Here the scenery became
wildly, not to say awfully, grand, and one certainly feels a
strange sensation of wonder, at finding himself travelling
through such savage passes, along a road with a surface like a
floor.

I cannot pretend to give you a very accurate notion of distances, for the moments flew swiftly, and my attention was too
much attracted to the scenery, to take heed of their passage. I
should say, however, it was at a point less than two leagues from
the village, that we passed the portion of the road with which I
was most struck, considering it merely as a work of art. At this
spot, it became necessary to descend from one level of the
gorge to another that lay at some distance beneath. This object
the engineers had been obliged to achieve within a very short
space, and over a broken and steep surface of ragged rocks. It
was done, by short zig-zags, so admirably calculated, both as to
the inclination and the turns, as to enable old Caspar to wheel
his four grays, on a gentle trot, through the whole descent, with
as much accuracy as he, or any one else, could have wheeled a
squadron of dragoons. The beauty, precision, strength, ingenuity and judgment with which the road had been constructed among these difficulties, drew exclamations of delight
from us all.

On reaching the bottom of this descent, we crossed the
stream, a torrent that was raging in a rocky dell, the whole of

the way, at no great distance from us, by an admirably bold bridge, and passed beneath beetling cliffs that rendered the head dizzy to gaze at. The appearance of these cliffs instantly explained the nature of one of the chief dangers that beset the traveller, in crossing the Alps. Without adverting to the avalanches, in the spring and autumn, here was a long bit of the road where, at any moment, pieces of the rock, weighing from one pound to a dozen, might fall, from a height of several hundred feet, on the head of the passenger beneath. I saw a hundred fragments that had been half detached from their native beds by the frosts, suspended in perpendicular lines nearly a thousand feet above me; and little freshly made piles, that had been raked together by the workmen, lined the road side for some distance. Occasionally, a small chip was shaken down by the passage of our own carriages, and, in one instance, a piece fell quite near the *calèche;* though it was too small to do any injury, had it even hit it. Old Caspar looked up, and shook his head, as we went beneath these sublime crags, intimating that it was fortunate for us it was not spring, which is the season of danger. Apart from the snows, the constant freezing and thawing of that period of the year detach considerable masses from the rocks themselves.

Every one has a tolerably accurate notion of what it is to descend a long hill; but all other descents sink into insignificance compared to these of the Alps. We were constantly and steadily going down, literally, for hours; nor do I remember on the whole route, after quitting Simpeln, a single foot of ascent. Perfectly level ground, even, was very unfrequent, if, indeed, strictly speaking, it occurred anywhere.

As a matter of course, the glens grew deeper and deeper; and there were parts of the road that resembled yawning and frightful entrances into the very "bowels of the land." We passed a tall, quaint, deserted building of stone, seven stories in height, and a *hospice*, whose roof had been beaten in, most probably, by the snow. These were nearly all the signs of the abodes of men that relieved the savage wildness of the descent for miles, as, unlike the northern face of the mountain, there was neither pasturage nor any thing else to induce human beings to dwell amid these sterile crags.

We drew near a small chapel, in a rock, where Caspar

flourished his whip, calling out the talismanic word, *"Italie!"* I pulled off my cap, in reverence; nor do I believe one of the party passed this frontier without a throbbing of the pulses a little quicker than common. All this was produced purely by the imagination, for there was nothing visible to denote a change of country, beyond the little chapel already named. At length, we reached a hamlet of a few houses, called Isella, where there is a custom-house and a post station. A dozen postilions, in smart new liveries, were in the road, apparently watching the arrival of some important personage, whom we learned was the Grand-duchess Helena. The custom-house officers were quite civil, giving us no trouble, although one of them took occasion to hint that a *fourgon* ought to pay an unusually liberal fee.

We had a continuation of the same scenery for some time after quitting Isella, when suddenly we burst upon a little verdant opening that gave us a foretaste of the peculiarities of Italy. The valley widened, and, on one side, the mountain became less abrupt, in a way to admit of cultivation, and of the abodes of men. The habitable district was very limited, being no more than a sharp acclivity of some two or three thousand acres; but it was literally teeming with the objects of a rural civilization. The whole *côte* was a leafy cloud of lively foliage, above which peeped the roofs of cottages, wherever a cottage could stand. Tall, gaunt-looking church towers rose out of this grateful forest, in such numbers as to bespeak at once the affluence of Romish worship, and the density of the population. The glimpse was soon over; but it left a lively impression of the principal objects, as well as of the crowded character of ordinary Italian life.

The mountains approached each other again, and we went rolling down a gentle descent for miles, through gorges less wild than those above, but gorges that were always imposing and savage. Here the torrent was spanned by some beautiful bridges, that were intended to receive the foot passenger, or, at the most, a packhorse. They were of hewn stone, with pointed arches, and of extreme lightness and boldness. One or two were in ruins,—a fact that bespoke their antiquity, and contributed to their interest.

At length the mountains terminated, and an open space appeared, to denote the end. A transverse valley spread itself athwart the jaws of the gorge, and a massive bridge was thrown across the torrent at right angles to our course. Old Caspar cracked his whip, and soon whirled us into an entirely new region. The country was still Alpine, the valley into which we now entered being completely imbedded in sublime mountains; but the severity of the scenery unaccountably disappeared, and was replaced by softer hues and a gentler nature; even the naked rocks appearing less stern and repulsive than those we had left on the banks of the Rhone. The vegetation was naturally more exuberant, and it had been less nipped by frosts; the fruits were much more generous; and all the appliances of civilization were more abundant, and, if I may so express it, more genial. The change, beyond all question, was strikingly obvious; and could these things have been seen, from any of the great passes of the Alps, I make no doubt the followers of Hannibal would really have raised a shout in exultation. As it was, it is to be presumed, they deferred their rejoicings until they got down to the plains, whence they have been carried back to the mountain tops, by a poetical license.

As we turned out of the gorge of the Doveria, into the valley of the Toccia, the carriage passed a huge column of marble, that lay, half completed, by the side of the rock from which it had been quarried. This was a fit emblem of Italy; nor was its effect thrown away. The bridge across the torrent, too, was in a style and on a scale to impress us favourably, and I believe we all felt as if we had made an important step, in our approaches to a higher condition of civilization, in matters of luxury, at least, if not in matters of more general utility.

It was Sunday, and the road was lined with peasants, in their holyday attire. The females agreeably disappointed us, a large portion being unusually pretty. Fair complexions and blue eyes were the common peculiarities, though the first seemed *warmed* by the heat of a powerful sun. The men were, also, reasonably good-looking, being generally short, but sturdy. We saw little obvious misery; but, on the other hand, every appearance of gayety and contentment. As we drove into the town of Domo d'Ossola, the crowds in the streets were like bees before a hive; and Caspar was compelled, literally, to walk his horses, to prevent an accident.

What a change in the inn! The rooms were vast and airy; the

bed I occupied was near seven feet square, and the attendants were nimble and profoundly respectful; qualities, however, that, ere long, we could gladly have bargained for the probity which usually distinguishes the Swiss *garçon*, however much he may happen to be addicted to criticisms on a traveller's French.

Letter XXIX.

M<small>Y DEAR</small>————,

I had not yet lost the keen sense of pleasure produced by the consciousness of being in Italy, when we left Domo d'Ossola, with the rising of the sun, on the following morning. This pleasure, however, had its alloy, for there had been a robbery, and a man shot, about a fortnight before, and we were now approaching the scene of the outrage. The rumour of this robbery first reached me at Lausanne, on my way back from Geneva, at which time the Simplon was said to be the spot where the assassins had lain in wait for their prey. My charge being so numerous, and so perfectly helpless, I had not been without uneasiness on the subject, as we gradually drew nearer to the mountain, and I took various private occasions to question the servants of the inns on the subject. But nothing was to be gained from them; for it was all important to man, woman, and child, in the Valais, that the Simplon road should not lose its good name. Believing that the facts must be known at Brieg, I seized a favourable moment, when a little previous gossip had established amicable relations between the cook and myself, to interrogate that important functionary touching the circumstances. He admitted that something of the sort had occurred somewhere in Italy, in what kingdom he could not pretend to say; and, alluding to my using the term *assassins*, he stoutly denied that the murderers were *assassins* at all, but, to use his own words, "merely some *people** who wished to kill the *maître de poste*." I presume he inferred, as I was not a *maître de poste*, this explanation would set my heart at rest.

W[illiam] and myself had examined our fire-arms, in coming up the Simplon, and found them as unfit for service as a city watch; and, in descending the mountain, wonder and admiration kept us all so much occupied, that I believe no one thought

* *Des gens.*

a moment about an incident so vulgar as a robbery. At Domo d'Ossola, the wary Caspar, who had a natural regard for the safety of postilions, came at last at the truth, which simply amounted to the fact, that one of the corps had been shot off his horse, and the party he was driving rifled. This robbery had been committed about three weeks before, in a bit of low swampy land, at no great distance from Domo d'Ossola. There was so evident an absurdity in supposing that another outrage of this nature was more likely to occur at the precise spot in question than at any other, that I dismissed all uneasiness, and this the sooner, because the incident had stimulated the officers of justice, who would be likely, for a time at least, to hunt the offenders out of the district. Caspar viewed the matter differently, for, as we approached the suspected place, he drew himself up in the saddle, like a man who was expecting a shot. The villains had chosen their stand with judgment, the scene of the exploit being a lonely willow bottom, where there was no habitation near, and where it was not possible to see any distance, on either side. Old Caspar reconnoitred this position knowingly, as he trotted through it; nor did he fail to urge the cattle to do their best, so long as there was any hazard of an ambush, or the possibility of being overtaken by a bullet.

A little incident of this nature has, at least, the merit of keeping one's eyes open, after an early start, and, on me, it produced the effect of closing the organs of hearing to most of the tales about banditti, and the dangers of mountain passes, with which the ears of travellers in Italy are occasionally beset. We got through the terrible willow swamp unscathed; and I was just felicitating Caspar on his good fortune, when we came suddenly out upon the shores of Lago Maggiore; a scene that drove all ideas of robbers and of unpleasant *rencontres* from the mind.

Here, every thing was warm and Italian. Though the valley of Domo d'Ossola had, in some measure, prepared us for the transition, the change was great and unexpected. We had been transferred, as it were in a minute, from a rustic and retired population, into the midst of one that had the conventional air of the world. The region was still Alpine; but the mountains, while they formed a magnificent framework to the picture, became accessories; leaving the lake, with its sunny reaches; its shores lined with towns, villas, hamlets, churches, castles; its banks teeming with men; the islands; the steamboats ploughing their way through water pure as air; the inns thronged with loiterers; the vineyards, and the groves of olives, as the principal features. Although there was everywhere a bustle, no one seemed toiling. The warm, genial region really appeared as if it supported all these thousands by its own spontaneous efforts; and there was a careless indifference in the peasantry that denoted perfect security, and a firm reliance on Providence. Such were the first impressions produced by this sudden descent into the midst of a scene that is so truly Italian, although near the uttermost limits of that enchanting country!

The change of climate alone was such as, in general, it requires weeks of travelling to obtain. The weather had been good, since quitting Berne, a part of the first day excepted; but there was a chilliness that constantly proclaimed its uncertainty, and occasionally a flurry of snow, or of rain, had driven through the gorges, before or behind us, which, though it was our good fortune to escape them, kept us constantly alive to the fluctuations, and to the inhospitable character, of the climate. Here, however, one felt a sense of deep security, and there was no apprehension of being overtaken by a premature arrival of the seasons. In this respect the autumn was like our own, though still more bland and genial. In addition to having reached the southern side of the Alps, we had descended to a level that was but slightly elevated above the sea, and all this had been effected in a few hours.

The carriage stopped at Baveno, a village that is stretched along the shore of the lake, directly opposite the celebrated Borromean islands. Even the inn was classical in its form, and entirely different from its Swiss neighbours. The door was crowded by another group of smart postilions, in waiting for the Grand-duchess. These rogues, one and all, protested that they knew nothing of any robbery.

We breakfasted; and, leaving orders for Caspar to follow, took a boat for *Isola Bella*. This island has been too often described to require a detailed account of its singularities, for, judged by the laws of a severe taste, the vast expenditure that has been made on it, has resulted rather in oddities than in beauty. There is a large house, which the Italians call a palace; it is constructed in the usual mixed style of magnificence and meanness that marks most of the private architecture of the country, which is usually fine in its forms and proportions, but, the carvings in stone excepted, deficient in the details. There is also a garden laid out in a succession of terraces, in the form of a pyramid, that is adapted rather to surprise and amuse, than to win upon the taste or the affections. A great deal of money has been expended, and it is said that there is a very rare and precious collection of plants; but the whole thing struck me as singularly misplaced, amid the scenery of the mountains. The appearance of these islands, seen from the shore, cannot well be other than pretty; but, after the first feeling of novelty subsides, I should think any one would prefer to see a rustic church, a ruin, or a quaint old castle on this island, than to see the laboured invention of the *Borromées*. An island, in the immediate vicinity of *Isola Bella*, is completely covered by a hamlet of fishermen, and really, I think it a much more pleasant object than its neighbour. Some admire the contrast between the two; but it struck me as being too glaring and extravagant; like that of seeing a peasant in a full dressed circle, or a courtier, in his bag and sword, dancing on a village green.

Isola Madre stands a little aloof, and, with its swell of land, natural aspect, and solitary villa, is much better suited to the landscape it embellishes, than its competitor of the palace and terraces. Still, there is something so unusual and elaborate in the latter, that it serves very well to amuse the traveller for an hour or two, and may even give pleasure for a longer period to those who, feeling a deep reverence for money, look upon all its capricious creations with profound veneration.

We were shown through the house, and found some of the grottos grateful retreats even on the 13th of October. The King of Sardinia had just left the place, to which he had made a visit of two or three days.

The row was a pleasing exchange from the monotony of the carriage. We did not return to the inn, but, to prolong the pleasure, pulled down the lake a mile or two, where we landed; the road literally following the margin of the water for the rest of the day. A party of dark, sunny-looking urchins were lying in wait, to tempt us to part with a franc or two, in exchange for some grapes and other fruits, which, as usual, were transferred to our pockets and reticules, at prices exceeding some three or four times their real value.

I cannot give you the details of the rest of this day's drive at length, for one of the principal characteristics of an Italian landscape is the multiplicity of its objects. You will, however, form some idea of the region that we had reached, from a few of its leading features. The lake is irregular, with countless bays and promontories, and many windings. Its length is not much less than forty miles, and its width varies from four to six. The immediate shores are not so precipitous as those of the finer of the Swiss waters; but they are uniformly bold, and there are everywhere noble backgrounds of Alps. The strand admits of room for the highway, and, here and there, a village, or a small town, is crowded between the first terrace of the ascents and the water. In whatever direction the eye was turned, it rested on villas, buried among fruit trees; castles, or convents, on headlands, or heights; the buildings of towns clustered together, so as to resemble vast edifices; villages without number, while nearly the whole of the immediate shore wore the air of a hamlet. The grouping and separate appearance of the minor objects, moreover, were strikingly picturesque. Fishermen anchored on their grounds, or gliding athwart the glassy lake, with all their appliances disposed as one would introduce them into a picture; boats beached in beautiful disorder on the sands; with the rich colours of flaring female attire mixed up with, and throwing a warmth around, all. There was not so much a glow upon the landscape as a dreamy, warm mistiness, which softened the outlines, and threw back the chiselled peaks into distance.

About the middle of the afternoon, we alighted and ascended the hill by a convenient road, to a sort of table land, which, near its lower end, stretches along the western shore of the lake. This is the hereditary property of the family of Borromeo, the little town of Arona, the birth-place of St. Charles of that name, being beautifully situated beneath a promontory, a mile or two farther down the road. On this table land or terrace has been erected a statue of the saint, representing him in the robes of a cardinal. Like the *Isola Bella* of the same family, there is more to surprise than to please, in this huge conceit. I do not know the entire height of the statue and pedestal, but I should think that both together exceed one hundred feet. The statue alone is said to be seventy feet high. I mounted by a long ladder to the top of the pedestal, and ascertained that the statue was made of sheet copper, and then descended, having no ambition to say that I had stood in a nose, and gazed at a landscape through the eyes of San Carlo. It is possible, however, literally to perform the latter feat, a ladder being provided within the statue for the especial service of all who have such cockney propensities.

The view from the terrace, or table land, on which this statue stands, was commanding; and, in addition to the objects which your own imgination by this time ought to enable you to supply, it differed from most of the scenery of the Swiss lakes, in the overflowing affluence of its artificial parts.

The road continued to follow the shore of the lake, and the hills imperceptibly melted away into the plain, until they were gradually left behind us; the last of the Alps! Just at dusk, we drove up to the banks of the river that forms the outlet of Lago Maggiore, which was flowing through a perfectly level country. A town was on the opposite shore, and a boat soon appeared to receive us. The carriages were driven in, and we slowly crossed the stream, which was the Ticino, a tributary of the Po. The town is named Sesto Calende. We now quitted Piedmont, and entered the dominions of the Emperor of Austria, in his kingdom of Lombardy. Here we had some little trouble with the baggage, but not more, probably, than is rendered necessary by the management of the interests of a large and important state.

Letter XXX.

DEAR ———,

We were off before the dawn; but the light soon enabled us to perceive that we had taken leave of our grand nature, and that we were now in a country that was *beau*, in the sense of the Frenchman, without being *pittoresque*. This was the commencement of the plain of Lombardy, which stretches from the Alps to the Apennines, from the mountains of Genoa to the marshes of the Adriatic. In a north and south direction, this plain has an average length of about one hundred and fifty miles; nor is its breadth materially less. It gradually falls away towards the Adriatic, into which it pours all its waters; but the descent is so very imperceptible, and really is so small, that it is entirely lost to the eye of the traveller. We were now on its verge; but an hour sufficed to bury us as effectually among its vines and fruit trees, so far as the prospect was concerned, as if we had already reached its centre.

The cultivation was like that of a garden; and the fields were still veiled with vines and trees in a way to put views quite out of the question. The soil, a light sandy loam, is generous and warm; and vegetables, and even grain, are very commonly grown in the midst of all this foliage. The road was nearly a continued hamlet, and tall, gaunt, square church-towers rose out of the interminable but low forest, literally in scores, and as rigid, upright, lank, and precise, as an old-school New England parson. W[illiam] was tickled with this conceit,—some one remarking that the towers resembled so many dogmatical sentinels, stretching up their starched necks to overlook their flocks. Many of them were built of bricks, stuccoed. But nearly every dwelling we now met was covered with a coarse white plaster.

The population began rapidly to dwindle in size, and to have less of the bright, animated look which had so much pleased us in Piedmont. The men, in general, were both slight and short;

and we thought that while the poor looked very poor, they did not appear to endure much real suffering. We were not greatly annoyed by beggars; the peasants seeming to be occupied and earnest;—much more so, indeed, than we had been taught to expect.

After stopping at a village to breakfast, we pushed forward for Milan. The country is so very low that we did not get the smallest evidence of our near approach to a capital until we were within a mile or two of it, when the pinnacles of the cathedral thrust their white fret-work above the carpet of leaves. An open space like a glacis, a half-finished arch at the termination of the Simplon road, the walls, and the gate, announced the city.

Milan struck us as a neat and reasonably busy town, with a population of very decent outward appearance, but as less gay and conventional than we expected to find it. The houses were rather low, a fault that invariably detracts from the magnificence of a town, impressing it with a provincial look. Still the air of the place was highly respectable, and it seemed to contain many excellent private residences. These were the impressions made on entering.

The hotels were crowded, and it was with great difficulty that we got the rooms necessary to our accommodation, at a second rate tavern, where we consoled ourselves, with baths and rest, after a six days' march.

The next day we commenced the regular duties of travellers, much refreshed and with renewed courage. Our first object was the celebrated picture of the Last Supper, by Leonardo da Vinci. You doubtless know that it is painted *al fresco,** on the wall of the refectory of a convent. The colours are a good deal faded, and the picture does not appear to have been sufficiently cared for; but there were no signs about it of its having received the injuries mentioned by Eustace, who accuses the French of having fired bullets at the different figures. There was a spot or two in the wall, *beneath the picture*, that had been replastered, and the *laquais de place* affirmed that a few bullets had actually

* *Fresco* paintings are made by using *water-colours* on *green* mortar. As the first touch of the pencil must remain, it is a style of art that requires great readiness, with a perfect knowledge of drawing, to succeed. Of course, the design is sketched and matured before the plaster is laid.

been discharged at these spots. He was a decided Bonapartist, however, and probably thought that by assigning particular places to the bullets in question, he effectually got rid of the charge of abusing the work of Leonardo. I do not believe that the *picture* ever received the injuries named. Of the beauties of this work it is unnecessary to say any thing, for the design and general character are well known, and the nicer merits that usually distinguish an original happen, in this instance, to be much impaired by neglect and time. With a view to preserve a *fac simile*, a magnificent copy was making, in the same room, and the vividness of its colours served to render those of the great master even duller than they would otherwise have appeared.

From this picture we proceeded to the cathedral. My profound reverence for edifices of this kind had induced me to pay two or three stolen visits, the previous afternoon and evening; and one, also, by moonlight, had given me a foretaste of the effects of this unrivalled structure. I say unrivalled, for it stands absolutely alone in its own peculiar style.

The cathedral of Milan is yet unfinished. It was commenced in 1386, and it has consequently been nearly five hundred years beneath the hammer and chisel! The material is a white marble, and the style a mixed gothic. When we recollect the period in which the edifice was commenced, it is fair to presume that the original designs have not been rigidly respected, for the best and purest specimens of the gothic structures of Europe date from about the 14th century, although the most extraordinary must be referred to an earlier period.

This cathedral has strictly a Grecian front, engrafted on a gothic fabric. But the gothic itself is so unlike any thing else we had been accustomed to see, that we were less unpleasantly struck with this discrepancy than we could have supposed. The change of style has probably been an after-thought. The principal peculiarity of the edifice, however, is the great number of its pinnacles, which rise up, like inverted *stalactites*, from every part of its summit. These pinnacles give the building a mosque-like and imaginative air; though its Christian character is preserved by placing the statue of some orthodox saint on each of them. Incredible tales are told of the number of statues that are placed on and about the building, which some accounts pretend amounts to many thousands. The statues impair the fretted appearance of the style less than might be supposed, the proportions being too well maintained to permit them to become more than modest accessories. As a general effect, they rather add to, than detract from, the tracery and net-work look which so peculiarly belong to the order.

Most of the pinnacles have been run up since the reign of Napoleon commenced, and they have a fresh and unsullied look, compared to that of the older parts of the building; W[illiam], not unaptly, likening the whole to the appearance of the Alps, with their grey bases of granite, and their white summits of snow.

Of the size of this cathedral I shall give you an odd account. I have made a calculation of its cubic contents, allowing in the best manner I could for the irregularity of its form, and, estimating the number of churches in New York at one hundred, after computing their average dimensions, the result shows that the *Duomo* of Milan is materially larger than all the places of worship in our aspiring Manhattan put together! Its length is near 500 feet; its breadth varies from 190 to near 300; its interior height from about 80 feet (in the chapels) to 250 beneath the cupola; and the statue of the Virgin, which crowns the principal pinnacle, is near 400 feet from the ground. I have made this comparison, as the best means I know of, to arouse you from your American complacency on the subject of the use of the adjectives, "grand," "majestic," "elegant," and "splendid," in connexion with our architecture. The latter word, in particular, is coming to be used like a household term; while there is not, probably, a single work of art, from Georgia to Maine, to which it can, with propriety, be applied. I do not know a single edifice in the Union that can be considered more than third rate, by its size and ornaments; nor more than one or two that ought to be ranked even so high. We have succeeded better in forms, of which we have a few imitations that are as faultless as any you will meet with here. In hamlets, in villages, and even in country towns, we may possibly surpass Europe, as a whole; but when it comes to capitals, and the use of the adjectives I have just quoted, it may be well to remember that there is no city in the republic that has not decidedly the air and the habits of a provincial town; and this too, usually, without possessing the works of art that are quite commonly found in this hemisphere, even in places of that rank, or a single public building to which the term magnificent can, with any fitness, be adjudged.

We ascended the roof of the *Duomo*, which resembled a bit of table-land, on a small mountain. The view was limited, in all directions but one, by an horizon like that of the ocean,—the eye ranging over a vast extent of cultivated plain, covered, as usual, with fruit trees, out of which rose the gaunt towers of churches, stretching up their necks like so many watchful camelopards. But the hoary Alps were ranged along the northern margin of the landscape, looking warm and cheerful. Monte Rosa was the most conspicuous, affording us, for the first time, a distinct view of its sublime proportions. The glaciers were brilliant, but dreamy, no longer turning their faces coldly on us. Even the eternal snows appeared to have received a milder tint from the genial climate of Italy.

I bent my eyes, in vain, athwart the endless plain to the south, in the hope of catching some dim outline of the Apennines. If they are ever visible from Milan, the haze of the atmosphere prevented their being seen on this occasion. But, though the organs of sight were so limited, the spirit was free. I was transported across the seemingly boundless plain, into lower Italy, which is, in fact, *the* Italy we love, and began to enjoy, in anticipation, the pleasures of a residence in a country that, unlike its sterner neighbour, gradually wins upon the feelings, until it becomes the object of our dearest affections. Adieu, then, to Helvetia, with her caverns, her fields of eternal ice, her cascades, her green and broad mountain sides, her pastoral abodes, her winding and rocky paths, her aerial bridges, her infernal glens, her forests of dark larches, and her congress of hoary mountain peaks; and away for the glowing vales and purple rocks of *Parthenope!*

Explanatory Notes

5.18 *la belle Gabrielle*: Gabrielle d'Estrées was mistress of Henry IV of
France (1553–1610).

5.22 *gras*: "fat" or, in this case, mud.

7.9–10 the table of abdication, and the leg that was kicked: After the
capitulation of Paris on 31 March 1814, the French Senate
on 2 April declared that Napoleon had forfeited the throne of
France and Italy "for the welfare of France, and for the peace
of the world." The abdication took place at Fontainebleau. In
his Journal, Cooper remarked of the abdication table in the
Salle de Diane: "Mean little table, mark said to be made by the
kick of the Empereur" (*Letters and Journals*, I, 271).

8.7–8 the tragedy of Monaldeschi: Giovanni, Marquis Monaldeschi,
favorite of Queen Christina of Sweden, was assassinated in the
Galerie des Cerfs at Fontainebleau on 10 November 1657. The
Queen accused him of high treason, but the reasons for his
murder are obscure.

9.26 a sort of hunting lodge of Louis XV: Cooper and his family
spent the summer and autumn of 1827 at St. Ouen, just north
of Paris (see *Gleanings in Europe: France*, Chapter XVI). It was
therefore but a short drive for the novelist's friend, the Hon.
James Brown, then United States Envoy to France.

10.34–35 Osages . . . making a sensation: A group of Osage Indians
from the Arkansas River region were touring France at this
time as a sort of exhibit of Indian life. The Coopers saw them
in Paris and again in Dijon. The following notice appeared in
the *Journal Politique et Littéraire de la Côte-d'Or*, on Sunday,
20 July 1828: "Spectacle de dimanche: *Le Barbier de Séville*,
l'Epreuve villageoise. Les Osages assisteront à cette représenta-
tion, et il leur servi une collation entre les deux pièces. Ces
Indiens seront visibles à l'hôtel du *Parc*, dimanche et lundi
seulement, de dix à sept heures du soir. Prix: un franc."

12.10 *Mesdames de Silléry et de Genlis*: Madame de Silléry-Genlis boasts
in her *Memoirs* (1825) that, in her search for novelty, she and
her husband set out on a donkey one day, disguised as peas-

ants, to buy all the milk in the vicinity and have a bath *à la Romaine*. Cooper is incorrect in his impression that there were two ladies involved in the exploit.

12.33 Helvetic Confederation: Neuchâtel, long a Prussian possession, was admitted to the Swiss Confederation on 6 April 1815 as the twenty-first canton, though it remained under Prussian protection until 1857. See pp. 23–24.

15.11 *chevaux de renfort*: horses added to a carriage for a difficult passage.

17.2–4 Château de Joux . . . Toussaint: Like most biographers of Toussaint L'Ouverture, Cooper stresses Napoleon's calculated cruelty in destroying the black hero by incarcerating him in the grim, bitterly cold prison of Joux, actually Fort de Joux, a medieval stronghold. Toussaint died of exposure at Joux in April 1803 after less than a year of confinement.

17.35 Paris, as seen from Montmartre: See *Gleanings in Europe: France*, Chapter V.

19.14 "*touzy-mouzy*": According to his daughter Susan, Cooper was at this time "in a perpetual state of *toosy-moosy*—a word borrowed from Lord Byron, and which became a favorite expression of his own, conveying, in a modest form, the impression of an indescribable amount of poetical enjoyment." Susan Fenimore Cooper, "Introduction," *The Water-Witch* (New York, 1876), x.

20.22 Nott stoves: These "base-burning" stoves, ancestors of self-feeding stoves and furnaces, were patented in the 1820s and 1830s by the Rev. Eliphalet Nott, President of Union College, for burning anthracite coal. Their ornate classical exteriors, with pedimented flues and decorative ironwork, ingeniously concealed their utilitarian function. See reproductions in Josephine Peirce, *Fire on the Hearth: The Evolution and Romance of the Heating-Stove* (Springfield, Mass., 1951), pp. 126–30.

24.12 Ebel: J. G. Ebel, *Manuel du voyageur en Suisse*. Traduit de l'Allemand. Septième edition Française. Première et deuxième partes, contenent le manière du voyager, l'itinéraire, les plans et cartes. Paris: Langlois, 1827. (Boxed with *Carte Itinéraire de la Suisse*, par Henri Keller. Revue et corrigé d'après *Le Manuel du Voyageur dans ce Pays* par Ebel. Paris: Langlois, 1827.)

25.20 canton of Berne: The Cooper party crossed the border into Bern on 22 July (*Letters and Journals*, I, 273). Ebel notes of it that it was "le plus grand et le second en rang dans la Confédération Suisse" (p. 188), and Picot calls it "le plus grand, le plus peuplé et le plus puissant de toute la Suisse" (*Statistique de la Suisse* [Geneva, 1819], p. 171).

27.25 peculiar aristocracy: Bern was at this time the capital of the
Swiss confederacy and the most aristocratic of the cantons. Its
powerful patrician government, dating back to the fourteenth
century, had been swept away by the French in 1798 and partially restored in 1815 by the Congress of Vienna. After the
Revolution of 1830–1831 and until 1848, Bern shared the role
of capital with Zürich and Lucerne.

29.38 Erlachs . . . celebrated: The family of Erlach had been associated with Bern since the twelfth century. Utrich d'Erlach
brought military distinction to his city in 1298 and Rodolph
Louis d'Erlach commanded the army of the Swiss Confederation in 1802. In the centuries between, many Erlachs served
Bern, Switzerland and France.

32.31–33 A horse . . . with life: On 25 July 1654, a student named
Weinzaepfli was thrown over the balustrade by a frightened
horse. He landed in a kitchen garden, broke both arms and
legs, but recovered (Ebel, Pt. III, 192).

33.40 Monsieur Tonson: a ubiquitous, imaginary character in William
Moncrieff's farce of the same name. Morebleu, a refugee
French barber, is besieged and bewildered by strangers seeking
his ward Adolphine de Courcy and calling incessantly for a
nonexistent Monsieur Tonson, whose name (and existence)
derive from the French pronunciation of Thompson, the
name of the girl's father.

35.18 Nahl: The sculptor was Samuel Nahl (1748–1813), a native of
Bern.

37.13 conceit of Roubilliac: Among the more celebrated works of the
French sculptor Louis François Roubillac (1659–1762) was a
monument to Lady Elizabeth Nightingale erected in 1758. See
Arthur P. Stanley, *Historical Memorials of Westminster Abbey*
(Philadelphia, 1899), II, 89–90, for a description and reproduction. The name is variously spelled "Roubiliac," "Roubillac," and "Roubilliac."

37.24–25 Hofwyl. . . . Fellenberg: Philip Emanuel von Fellenberg
(1771–1844), patrician of Bern, made his extensive farm,
called Hofwyl, an experimental institute of agriculture and
education. He maintained two model farms, two small factories
for making farm instruments, an agricultural institute, a college of general studies, and a charity school. See Compte Capo
d'Istria's *Rapport à S. M. l'empereur Alexandre* (2nd ed. Geneva,
1817) and Fellenberg's own periodical *Feuilles agronomique de
Hofwyl* (Arau, 1808–1817).

37.39–40 Windham and his friend Pococke: William Windham

(1717–1761), a young British military man, explored the Mer de Glace in the valley of Chamonix in June 1741 in company with the celebrated British traveller Richard Pococke (1704–1765). An inscribed boulder commemorates the visit. Windham's *Letter from an English Gentleman to Mr. Arland, Giving an Account of a Journey to the Glacières or Ice Alps of Savoy* (1744) was one of the earliest printed descriptions of Chamonix and Mont Blanc.

40.38–39 Jung Frau, or the virgin: The 1830 edition of Ebel questioned the hitherto accepted assumption, repeated here by Cooper, that the Jungfrau was so named because it had never been scaled. According to Ebel (1830, p. 366), the brothers Meyer of Arau, approaching from the eastern side, had reached the summit in the summer of 1811. The western side was not scaled until 1865.

41.29 a recent French traveller in the United States: The identity of this traveller is not established. He could not have been Tocqueville, for whom Cooper had written a letter of introduction to American friends and with whose *La démocratie en Amérique* (1835) Cooper was in general agreement. For various possible identifications, see Frank Monaghan, *French Travellers in the United States* (New York, 1933).

43.2 We left la Lorraine: The date was 4 August 1828. An outline of this tour, with distances and estimated time, is given in Ebel, *Manuel* (Paris, 1827), a combination of itineraries #22 and #23. Cooper seems to have used Ebel's itineraries in planning his tours, but not to have followed any one itinerary strictly. His Journal notes for this first tour are full and detailed (*Letters and Journals*, I, 274–84).

45.1 Berne republicanism: The Swiss Confederation was established by the Congress of Vienna, but individual cantons were left to go their own ways internally; and most, including Bern, reverted to conservative patterns of the past. Under the general movement towards republican reform in Europe between 1830 and 1833, many cantons, including Zürich, Lucerne, and Bern, liberalized their constitutions in favor of more social and political involvement. As Cooper's notes on pages 27 and 45 are intended to suggest, observations made in 1828 were not necessarily valid in 1836.

50.38 By half past 6 A.M.: Cooper's Journal entry for 5 August 1828 begins: "At 7 o'clock we left Lauterbrunnen on horseback. We had our general guide, two conducteurs and four horses. The saddles for the ladies were supplied with supports for the back, and were both easy and safe" (*Letters and Journals*, I, 275–76).

51.34 *batz*: a small Swiss coin, then worth one seventh of a French franc.

51.39 Messrs. R[ay] and L[ow]: "There were very few Americans travelling in Switzerland in those years. Only two came to Berne during the summer we passed there, Mr. [Richard] Ray and Mr. [Nicholas] Low, of New York." Susan Fenimore Cooper, "Small Family Memories," *Correspondence of James Fenimore-Cooper*, ed. James Fenimore Cooper (New Haven, 1922), I, 71.

59.8 *Ranz des Vaches*: native songs of the shepherds and herdsmen of the Swiss mountains.

67.31–32 Captain C——, of the Navy and . . . Mr. O., an old and intimate friend: Cooper probably referred to Captain Ichabod Wolcott Chauncey and James De Peyster Ogden.

68.36 Meinherr W[alther]: Walther was the farmer, neighbor and agent from whom the Coopers rented La Lorraine. The two families evidently became fond of each other.

69.35–36 Mr. [John], and Lady [Charlotte Denison]: In his Journal entry for 24 August 1828, Cooper stated: "While at the fosse des ours [in Bern], met Mr. and Lady Charlotte Denison, who had just returned from the Oberland" (*Letters and Journals*, I, 292). Mr. Denison was John Evelyn Denison, later Viscount Ossington, whom Cooper had known in New York in 1824.

69.40 Captain [Cooper]: Captain Benjamin Cooper (d. 1850), a distant relative of the novelist.

72.3 Soleure and Treves: Soleure was a Roman *castrum* and its name "Solodurum" is found in Roman inscriptions. Here in 1038 the Burgundian nobles finally surrendered to the German king, Conrad II. Trevi, in Perugia, is situated on a steep hill, one and a half miles southeast of the presumed site of the Roman Trebiae.

73.24–25 We lived adjoining a convent at Paris: The Coopers' first residence in Paris, Faubourg St. Germain, Rue St. Maur, No. 12, was an apartment, *au seconde*, above a girls' boarding school conducted by Mesdames de la Tour and Kautz. See Robert E. Spiller, *Fenimore Cooper, Critic of His Times* (New York, 1931), pp. 108–12.

74.1–2 memory . . . Spain: In 1806 Cooper had visited England and Spain as a sailor before the mast on a merchant vessel. He was then seventeen.

76.14 Schœnbrunnen: Schönbrunn Palace, the splendid residence of the Hapsburgs on the outskirts of Vienna.

76.37 as Dogberry says, "'fore God, they are both in a tale": *Much Ado about Nothing*, IV.ii.30–31.

77.30 Zimmerman: Johann Georg von Zimmermann (1728–1795), Swiss philosopher and medical authority. Much sought after as a court physician, he practiced and wrote extensively, not merely on medical subjects.

80.14–15 much-talked-of cataract: According to Ebel (p. 534), the Falls of the Rhine were the "grandest in Europe, and form[ed] one of the most astonishing scenes that nature present[ed] in Switzerland."

81.29 Picot says: Picot (pp. 365–66) describes how the act of 1803 gave equal political rights to the bourgeoisie.

83.25–26 the spot where John Huss was burned: The place of Huss's execution held special interest because of the reputed intrigue by which King Sigismund enticed Huss to Constance by a "safe conduct" guaranteeing his return to Bohemia whatever the judgment against him. Later, he was removed from the Dominican convent, supposedly for reasons of safety, to the charge of the bishop of Constance at Gottlieben on the Rhine. Here he was burned at the stake on 6 July 1415 and his ashes and the earth on which they rested thrown into the Rhine.

84.5–6 Shakspeare's ignorance . . . coast of Bohemia: *The Winter's Tale*, III.iii.1ff.

85.1 orange tree referred to in a former letter: See *Gleanings in Europe: France*, Letter X.

94.25 St. Gall, a town and canton: Cooper seems to have derived some of his historical background for St. Gall from Louis Simond (1822), I, 76 and some from Picot (1819), p. 576 ff.

96.14 my theory: See Cooper's Chapter IV, "On Distinctive American Principles," *The American Democrat* (Cooperstown, 1838).

101.35 the cradle of Helvetic liberty: In the thirteenth century, the free men of Schwyz took a leading part in the movement for cooperative self-defense which is the cornerstone of Swiss political theory, and, in 1294, convened the first recorded meetings of the "Landsgemeinde" of that canton. In commemoration of the victory at Morgarten by the men of Schwyz over Leopold of Austria, the confederacy of the three forest cantons took the name of Swiss.

103.2–3 my . . . connexion, Mr. McAdam: Mrs. Cooper's older sister, Anne Charlotte De Lancey (1786–1852) had become the second wife of the road builder, John Loudon McAdam (1756–1836). See *Gleanings in Europe: England*, Letter XXII.

103.30 inscription . . . traveller: In his Journal for 31 August 1828,

Cooper wrote: "At Kuznacht . . . we were struck with an inscription on a neat tablet of white marble, which was let into the wall of the church within a few feet of the highway. On approaching it we found it was placed there to commemorate the death of F[rederick] W[arren] Goddard of Boston who was drowned in August 1820 by the upsetting of a boat" (*Letters and Journals*, I, 309). Wordsworth met Goddard (b. 1800) and traveled with him for two days just before his death. They had climbed the Righi together at sunrise and there separated "at an hour and on a spot well suited to the parting of those who were to meet no more." Wordsworth recalled the circumstances in "Elegiac Stanzas," addressed to Goddard, and in a long paragraph prefixed to the poem.

105.19 "unknowing and unknown":
"I wander in the ways of men,
    Alike unknowing and unknown:"
        Robert Burns, "Lament for James, Earl of Glencairn,"
        11. 35–36.

116.15–16 the Titlis, my Bernese discovery: See 38.8–20. Mt. Titlis, in the Canton of Unterwald, is 10,000 feet above sea level.

120.9 wounded lion: The "Lion of Lucerne," measuring twenty-eight feet in length, was constructed in 1821 from a model designed by Albert B. Thorvaldsen (1770–1844). Hewn from natural sandstone, the dying animal reclines in a grotto, pierced by a broken lance, sheltering the Bourbon lily with its paw.

120.15 the two celebrated animals of Canova: Sculptures of Antonio Canova (1757–1822) almost always represented the human figure. Cooper was thinking here of the two magnificent marble lions in the foreground of the tomb of Clement XIII (1792) in St. Peter's at Rome. For an engraving by Henry Moses, see *The Works of Antonio Canova, in Sculpture and Modelling*, text by Countess Albrizzi and Count Cicognara (London, 1849), unpaged.

123.3–5 *garde champêtre . . . gens d'armes*: The distinction is essentially the same as that between municipal police and state constabulary in the United States.

134.21 our own "Vision": Mt. Vision, on the eastern side of Lake Otsego, overlooking Cooperstown.

150.17 Winkelried has a statue: The monument of Arnold von Winkelried to which Cooper refers is represented opposite page 150 in an engraving from W. H. Bartlett's drawing. According to legend, Winkelried broke the phalanx of Duke Leopold III of Austria at the Battle of Sempach (1386) by gathering "with a wide embrace, into his single heart, a sheaf of fatal Austrian spears."

152.1 *toujours des vignes*: After discussing other products of the canton of Zürich, Ebel (p. 643) concludes: "Cependant la culture de la vigne est beaucoup plus considerable."

152.16 Tellen's Platte: the shelf of rocks near Küssnacht upon which William Tell is reputed to have sprung in escaping from Gessler's boat.

156.10 Walter Furst . . . two associates: Cooper was not as familiar with the story of the oath of the Grütli as he might have been, for three fountains supposedly erupted at the spot at which thirty-three men from the cantons of Uri, Schwyz and Unterwalden, led by Walter Furst, Werner Stauffacher, and Erni Arnold, vowed their fealty to each other and to the liberation of their soil on 7 November 1307.

158.36–37 the Benedictine convent of Einsiedeln: Dating from the time of Charlemagne, Notre-Dame-des-Ermites was rebuilt between 1704 and 1719 on the foundations of six or seven earlier abbeys, all destroyed by fire. Cooper described Einsiedeln in the following chapter of *Switzerland*, in his Journal entries for 11–12 September 1828 (*Letters and Journals*, I, 324–26), and in *The Heidenmauer* (1832), Chapter XXIV.

159.10–11 The ruins of Goldau . . . Righi: On 2 September 1806, a conglomerate strata of the Rossberg, approximately two miles long, 1,000 feet wide, and 100 feet thick, was dislodged and precipitated 3,000 feet into the valley below, burying the prosperous village of Goldau and three other villages. The Lake of Lowertz, filled with the debris to about a fourth of its capacity, flooded, causing further devastation. Some 500 people perished. The account in Ebel's *Manuel* to which Cooper refers is on pp. 170–72.

165.3 battle of Morgarten: On 15 November 1315, a small contingent of Swiss from the Forest Cantons defeated a brilliant company of invading knights led by Leopold of Austria, reaffirming Swiss expulsion of their Austrian governors eight years earlier and reinforcing Swiss independence.

174.25 *char à banc*: A *char à banc* was a large carriage with cross benches. The word *char* seems to have been used to designate almost any traveling vehicle.

176.11 battle of Naefels: On 9 April 1388, a handful of men from Glarus and Schwyz defeated Albert of Austria and freed the canton of Glarus once more from Hapsburg rule.

177.19 *Schrabzieger*: Cooper's etymology is fanciful. Schabziger, as the word is correctly spelled, is a green cheese whose name derives from "schab" ("abschaben," "to scrape") and "zeiger" ("curdled milk"). Schabziger is heavily flavored with melilot, a kind of clover also used for hay. Cooper's misspelling "Schrabzieger" in the copy-text suggests that he was associating this ingredient with "schrab."

181.37 dearborn: a light four-wheeled wagon, used in country districts in the United States.

182.6 ancient masters: bailiffs.

184.25 abbey of Pfeffers: Founded in 713, the Benedictine abbey of Pfeffers was virtually a principality between 1196 and 1798. It was suppressed in 1838 because of internal dissention.

189.10–12 Sir Joseph Banks . . . fleas and lobsters: "Sir Joseph Banks and the Boiled Fleas," a satiric poem by John Wolcot (Peter Pindar), portrays the President ("queen bee") of the Royal Society reduced to "dire dismay" by the ignominious failure of his latest experiment—the boiling of 1,500 fleas to see if they would turn crimson. Under duress, he confesses to the assembled Society:

"Since you *must* know, *must* know . . .
Fleas are not lobsters, d—mn their souls."
The Works of Peter Pindar . . . (Boston, Charles Williams, 1811), II, 102–05.

193.38–40 Luckily . . . province: Cooper is not entirely accurate here. Liechtenstein was part of the Rhine Confederation from 1806 to 1815 and of the German Confederation from 1815 until it became independent in 1886.

199.34 Rhetian language: According to Picot (p. 431), "Illantz est la seule ville des Grisons où on parle le roman."

202.8 Abbey of Disentis: The Benedictine abbey of Disentis dated from the seventh century, though it was burned by French soldiers in 1799 and had not regained its former authority.

213.16 new bridge: completed in 1830.

218.30 Sir Herbert Taylor: A minor political and military functionary, Taylor (1775–1839) was private secretary to the Duke of York and to George III.

226.3 Mr. Huskisson: As M.P., President of the Board of Trade, and Cabinet member, William Huskisson (1769–1830) was an influential advocate of free trade. Cooper was inclined to regard British promotion of free trade as a pretext for British exploitation of existing commercial advantages.

229.40 Owen system: The Scottish philanthropist Robert Owen

(1771–1858) aspired to elevate the entire community through reformation of society according to a Rousseauistic or even Godwinian model. The failure of his socialistic experiment at New Harmony, Indiana, in 1828, three years after its purchase from the Rappites, took with it much of Owen's fortune.

231.15–16 Monsieur de Watteville: Major General de Watteville's regiment of foreign troops reinforced Major General Drummond in British actions at Fort Erie during August 1814. Drummond blamed the British rout on the panic of de Watteville's corps.

231.17 Colonel Fischer: Lieutenant-Colonel Victor Fischer led a British column of 1,300 men, one of three columns, in the abortive British attack on Fort Erie on 15 August 1814. For an account of the action, see Reginald Horsman, *The War of 1812* (New York, 1969), pp. 179–82.

235.17 Swiss *Cressy*: At the Battle of Morat (1476), to which Cooper here compares the Battle of Crecy (1346), a small army of Swiss decisively defeated a much larger force led by Charles the Bold, Duke of Burgundy. Charles is said to have lost 15,000 men and all their ammunition and baggage. At Crecy, the English under Edward III inflicted a similarly decisive defeat under seemingly hopeless odds on the army of King Philip of Valois.

237.26–238.13 The winter . . . Payerne: The General who attracted Cooper's attention at a soirée of the Countess Sophie Schouvaloff was Baron Henri Jomini (1779–1869), who had left the service of the French in 1813 to become an aide to the Emperor Alexander. The "very celebrated Russian, of a most unpronounceable name," who answered Cooper's question, was the Admiral Tchechekoff. See Cooper's Journal for 3 September 1832, *Letters and Journals*, II, 326.

238.22–239.14 It is . . . . saddle: The Queen of Rudolph II had become a folk heroine in Payerne in the tenth century. Among other accomplishments she built a church and a Benedictine abbey. The French Swiss recalled her benefactions in the expression: "Ce n'est plus le temps où Berthe filiat."

239.12 "ten and six-pence sterling":
"The present representatives
Of Hotspur and his 'gentle Kate,'
Are some half-dozen serving-men . . .
And one, half groom, half seneschal,
Who bowed me through court, bower, and hall,
From donjon-keep to turret wall,

For ten-and-sixpence sterling."
Fitz-Greene Halleck, "Alnwick Castle," 11.118–28.

241.30 democratic *crachats*: i.e., spittle. In describing a judge she met in the West, Harriet Martineau said, "He had a quid in his cheek whenever I saw him, and squirted tobacco-juice into the fireplace or elsewhere at intervals of about twenty seconds." Henry S. Commager, *America in Perspective* (New York, 1948), p. 67. See also Jane L. Mesick, *The English Traveller in America (1785–1835)* (New York, 1922), p. 72.

243.6–23 meteor-like passages of Charles X . . . *Mars*: See *Gleanings in Europe: France*, Chapter V.

252.31–32 Geneva . . . a canton so short a time: Geneva was admitted to the Confederacy on 14 September 1814 as the twenty-second canton.

252.34–35 Louis Simond: Simond (1767–1831) was a brother-in-law of Charles Wilkes and a distant relative of Mrs. Cooper. He published travel journals on Great Britain, Switzerland, Italy, and Sicily.

253.27 General Moreau: The French General Jean Victor Moreau (1763–1813) spent most of his final years in political exile in Morrisville, Pennsylvania, and in New York City. He died in battle in the service of the Czar, fighting against Napoleon, two months after his return to Europe.

254.17 "Great-Hearts" or "Valiants": characters in Bunyan's *Pilgrim's Progress*, i.e., Mr. Great-heart and Mr. Valiant-for-truth.

254.28 Ferney . . . Voltaire: Voltaire purchased land for the village of Ferney in 1759, established manufactories, attracted industrious residents, built a château, and constructed a church. Cooper's disapproval of Voltaire is expressed more frankly in his manuscript Journal for 28 September 1828 (*Letters and Journals*, I, 342) than in *Switzerland*.

255.21–23 As Dogberry says . . . villains: *Much Ado about Nothing*, IV.ii.19–20.

256.34 Voltaire, his will: Cooper erred. Voltaire's house was not sequestered; and his library and many MSS were sold to Catherine II by Mme. Denis, his heir, soon after his death.

265.18 the region of Rousseau: An exile after the publication of *Emile* (1762), Rousseau spent two idyllic months in a small house or inn on the Isle of St. Peter in the Lake of Bienne before the Bernese government evicted him. His description of the island and the lake contributed measurably to their reputation.

271.30–32 "*Les Valaisans . . . leur bonheur*": Picot, pp. 538–39.

272.18 a very ancient and a very curious hermitage: the hermitage of Notre-Dame-du-Sex, said to have been founded in the sixteenth century.

274.4 *Teniersism*: Cooper presumably means the scene bore accidental resemblance to the landscapes of David Teniers, Elder or Younger. In Paris in 1831, he bought a picture reputed to be a portrait of the wife of one of the Teniers, probably the Younger.

292.11 these islands: Isola Bella and Isola Madre in Lake Maggiore were owned by the Borromeo family. Isola dei Pescatori, which lies between them and which Cooper does not refer to by name, belonged to the fishermen who inhabited it.

296.33 injuries mentioned by Eustace: See John Chetwode Eustace's *Classical Tour through Italy* (Third Edition, London, 1815), IV, 30, a popular reference and guide book for tourists.

299.33 *Parthenope*: Parthenope, the earliest name for Naples, was founded by Rhodian navigators in the ninth century B.C. on a site where, reputedly, a siren called Parthenope had lived. The name was revived briefly in the seventeenth century by insurrectionists of the "Parthenopean Republic."

Appendix A
Bentley's Analytical Table of Contents

LETTER I.   Page 5
Departure. Accident to Postilion. An old Frenchman.
Palace of Fontainebleau. Auxerre. Avallon. Beautiful
scenery. Dijon. The Osages.

LETTER II.   12
Genlis. Mountain Ranges. Auxonne. Frontier Fortresses.
Distant view of Mont Blanc. Ascent of the Jura. Salins.
Novel Scenery. Pontarlier. Mountain Barrier. Château de
Joux. Toussaint. Napoleon. Varying Scenery. Frontier of
Switzerland. Appearance of the Country. Picturesque
Valley. Mountain Pass. Val Travers. Swiss Cottages.
Solitary Pedestrian. Arrival at Neuchâtel.

LETTER III.   23
Town of Neuchâtel. Sublime view of the Alps. Particulars
respecting the Canton of Neuchâtel. Extensive Plain.
River Aar. Aarberg. Swiss Château. Canton of Berne.
Excellence of the Roads. Arrival at Berne.

LETTER IV.   27
Berne. Its History and Government. Swiss Nobility. True
Nobility. Erroneous Notions of a Republic.

LETTER V.   32
Country round Berne. Public Promenades. Buildings.
Population. Swiss Vehicle. Agriculture. Cattle Ranges.
Gleaners. Hindelbank. Hofwyl. French and Swiss People.
Discover a Glacier. Difficulty of conveying impressions of
Grand Scenery. Alps at Sunset. Oberland Alps. Works of
European Travellers on America.

LETTER VI.   43
Proceed to Thun. Grand-duchess Anna. Town and Lake
of Thun. Excursion to the latter. Castle of Spietz.
Respective Ignorance of Americans and Europeans. The
Jung Frau. Neuhaus. Unterséen. Valley of Lauterbrunnen.
Fall of the Staubbach. Town of Lauterbrunnen. Ascent
of the Oberland Alps.

LETTER VII.   56
Grindelwald. Its Glaciers. Mountain Music. The Eiger.
Departure for the valley of Meyringen. Ascent of the Great
Scheideck. Mountain Cascades. Valley of Meyringen.
Brientz. River Aar. Cascade of the Giesbach. Interlachen.
Neuhaus. Unterséen. Return to la Lorraine. Inhabitants of
the Oberland.

LETTER VIII.   65
View of the Alps. Peak of the Wengern. Burial-places of
Berne. Swiss-American Valley. Goîtres. Drunkenness.
Pasquinades on America. Anecdote. Germans in America.
Baths of Berne. Scenery of America.

LETTER IX.   71
Route to Soleure. Town and Canton of Soleure. Wayside
Crosses. Female Costume. Rites of the Romish Church.
Olten. Aarberg. Aarau. Baths of Schinznach. Mountain of
the Wülpelsberg. Town and Castle of Habsbourg. Brugg.
Kœnigsfeld. Baden. The Rhine. Kaiserstuhl.

LETTER X.   80
Schaffhausen. Banks of the Rhine. Amateur Beggars. The
Zellersee. Reichenau. Constance. Great Council Hall.
Huss's Cell. Thurgovie. Roschach. Canton of St. Gall.
Rheineck. Visit Austria. Swiss Architecture. The Rhine.
Reach Alstetten. A Dilemma. Youthful Beggars. Naked
Region. Gais. Teufen. Town of St. Gaul. Polity of
Appenzell. Herisau. Lichtensteig. Female Pilgrims.
Sublime Scenery. Reach Rapperschwyl.

LETTER XI.   100
Rapperschwyl. Lake of Zurich. Bridge. Schwytz. Sunday.
Scenery between Rapperschwyl and Zurich. Town and
Canton of Zurich. Switzerland and America.

LETTER XII.   106
The Albis. Zug. Take a Boat for Art. Democracy and
Aristocracy. Village of Art. Ruins of Goldau. Pious
Flirtation. A Scene thoroughly Swiss. "Our Lady of the
Snows." View from Righi Staffel. From the summit of the
Righi Kulm. Melancholy Event. German Swaggerers.
Sunrise.

LETTER XIII.   119
Descent. Pilgrims. Gessler and Tell. Take a boat for
Lucerne. Remarkable Objects of that Town. Lake of
Sempach. Arnold de Winkelried. Langenthal. A hearty
Innkeeper. Erroneous Notions of Liberty. Return to la
Lorraine.

LETTER XIV.   130
Cantonal Courtesy. Left Bank of the Aar. Approach to
Thun. Power of opposing Invasion. Proceed to Neuhaus.
An English Couple. Unterséen. An Aristocratic Guide.
Panoramic View from the Rügen. An English Girl. Valley
of Interlachen. Brienz. Waterfalls. Monetary System. View
from the Brünig. Lungern. Polity of Unterwalden.
Imperfection of the Confederated System. Church of St.
Nicholas de Flüe. Crosses. Sarnen. Mistaken for an
Englishman.

LETTER XV.   150
Stantz. Female Costume. Three Travellers. Road to
Stanzstad. Lake of Lucerne. Stanzstad. Proceed by Boat
towards Brunnen. Dangerous Positions for Dwellings.
Accident at Weggis. District of Gersau. Brunnen. The
Grütli. Walter Furst's Conspiracy. Dangers of the Lake of
Lucerne. Town of Schwytz. Seewen. Catastrophe at
Goldau. Rothenthurm. Alsacian Pilgrims. Pile of Buildings
resembling St. Peter's at Rome.

LETTER XVI.   167
Traditions respecting the Shrine of Einsiedeln. Superstition
attends the extreme Classes of Society. Arrival of Pilgrims.
The Church. Feelings of Devotion. Rarity of Female
Beauty. Unseemly Ceremonies. Opportunity of becoming
Martyr. Temporary Chapels. Extensive View. Delightful
Descent. Hire a Char. A dogmatic Waiter. Canton of
Glaris. Bishop of Coire. Town of Glaris. Schrabzieger
Cheese. Proceed to Wesen.

LETTER XVII.   180
Country between the Lakes of Wallenstadt and Zurich.
Wesen. Lake and Town of Wallenstadt. Sargans. Its
Castle. Route for Germany and Italy. Change in the Course
of the Rhine. Ruins of Châteaux. Deep Gorge. Baths of
Pfeffers.

LETTER XVIII.   188
Baths of Pfeffers. Manner of using them. Benefit received
therefrom. Leave the Baths. View near the Abbey.
Principality of Liechtenstein. Exquisite Spot. Canton of the
Grisons. Picturesque Sites. Hire a Phaeton. Coire. German
Companion. Richenau. Junction of the Upper and Lower
Rhine.

LETTER XIX.   197
Depart for Source of the Rhine. Unsophisticated Highway.
Uncertain Route. Effect of White Buildings. A Wood-
chopper. Reach the Main Road. Trins. Flims. Lax. Lose
our Way. Ilantz. Language of the Grisons. Barren Country.
Religion of the Grisons. Trons. Beautiful View. Disentis.
A Dilemma. Rough Accommodation. An "Interpreter."
Watch against Fire.

LETTER XX.   205
Abbey of Disentis. First Château of the Rhine. Rejoined by
Guide. Reduced width of the Rhine. Jüf. Deserted Valley.
Snow Storm. Change Functions with Guide. The Ober Alp.
Sources of the great Swiss Rivers. Novel View in
descending the Mountain. Hospital. Andermatt. Valley of
Ursern. Price for a Guide. The Reuss. Gloomy Cave. The
Devil's Bridge. Pass of the St. Gothard. New Road.
Extraordinary Scenery. Herds of Goats.

LETTER XXI.   215
Hospital. Realp. Ascent of the Furca. Quick Descent. View
of the Oberland Range. Stone Huts. Canton of Valais. The
Gallenstock. Glacier of the Rhone. Solemn Spectacle. Party
of English. Two grand Discoveries. Source of the Rhone.
Ascent of the Grimsel. "Lake of the Dead." The Hospice.
Sensation of Dreariness. Gradual Descent. Picturesque
Stone Bridges. Handeck. Falls of the Aar. Lines of
Packhorses. Reach Meyringen.

LETTER XXII.   223
A Discussion on West India Slavery. Hire a Char for
Brienz. Interlachen. Chamois Hunters reach the summit of
the Jung Frau. Unterséen. Galignani's Messenger. The
"Twelve Millions." New Tariff. Peculiarity in the English
Character. Its cause. Policy of England. Effect of
Vituperation. English, American, and French Press. Mr.
Huskisson and Free Trade. Fatigue of Sight-seeing. Depart
for Berne. Lake of Thun. Mercenary Soldiers. Swiss
Chivalry at Thun. Perfidy of Voiturier. Part with Guide.
La Lorraine.

LETTER XXIII.   234
Time for seeing Switzerland. Departure. Morat. The Swiss
Cressy. Erratum in Ebel. Ancient Aventicum. Roman
Remains. Avenche. Payerne. Anecdote. Bertha of
Bergundy. Start for Lausanne. Swiss-American Landscape.
Hire Voiturier at Lucens. Conversation with a lively
Vaudoise. European Blunders. Reach Lausanne.

LETTER XXIV.   243
Country near Lausanne. The Town. Unusual bustle.
Charles X. Grand-duchess Helena and her Daughter. Lake
of Geneva. Port of Lausanne. A mutual Recognition.
Democratic Attention to Royalty. Democracy and Marks of
Honour. Anecdote. Mr. ———'s Decorations. Excursion
on the Lake of Geneva. Arbitrary Regulation. Land at
Geneva.

LETTER XXV.   250
European Places of Interest. Geneva. Window-gazing.
The Port. A Pensioned Steamboat. View from the
Ramparts. Interview with M. Simond. Population and
Government. Ferney. Residence of Voltaire. Church
erected by him. Interesting Fact connected with his Will.
Anecdote of a French Functionary. Return to Lausanne.
Outrage by Voiturier. Proceed towards Berne. Voiturier
punished, after reaching la Lorraine. Ancient Aventicum.

LETTER XXVI.   260
Preparations for a journey Southward. Agreement with
Voiturier. Climate of Switzerland and America. Adieu to la
Lorraine. Payerne. Quails. English Travellers. Moudon.
An "Auberge inévitable." Ravishing View. Climate of
Vévey. Foraging Postilion. Fairy Scene. Feeling of calm
Satisfaction. An American Resident. Castle of Chillon.
Trial of speed with a Steamboat. Villeneuve.

LETTER XXVII.   269
Road from Villeneuve. Bex. Dent de Morcles——du Midi.
Important Pass. St. Maurice. The Crétins. Reflections.
Inhabitants of the Valais. Curious Hermitage. Feats of an
Ancestor. Accident by a "Sac d'eau." Valley of the Rhone.
Waterfall. Martigny. Town of Sion. Ravages of Nature.
Dreary Abodes. Commencement of the Simplon. Brieg. The
Saltine. Broad Vista. Distances to places between Brieg and
Domo d'Ossola.

LETTER XXVIII.   278
Departure from Brieg. Ascent of the Simplon. Lively
Tollhouse Woman. Summit of the Simplon. Descent to the
Village of Simpeln. Character of the Northern side of the
Simplon. Exaggerated Descriptions. Descent from
Simpeln. The celebrated Galleries. Peculiarities of the
Simplon Road. Grand Scenery. Admirable Construction of
Road. Dangerous Cliffs. Continued Descent. Frontiers of
Italy. Populous Acclivity. New Region. Huge Column of
Marble. Groups in Holiday Attire. Reach Domo d'Ossola.

LETTER XXIX.   289
Rumour of a Robbery on the Simplon. Inquiries about it
fruitless. Scene of the outrage. Shores of Lago Maggiore.
First impressions of the scene. Delightful change of
Climate. Baveno. The Borromean Islands. Isola Bella. Isola
Madre. Row down the Lake. Leading features of the
Region. Arona. Statue of St. Charles Borromeo. The last of
the Alps. The Ticino.

LETTER XXX.   295
The Plain of Lombardy. Rich Cultivation. The
Churchtowers. The Populace. Approach to Milan.
Impressions on entering the Town. The Last Supper, by
Leonardo da Vinci. The Cathedral of Milan. Style of the
building. Its numerous Pinnacles and Statues. Its great
dimensions. Inferiority of America in its cities. View from
the roof of the Duomo of Milan. Adieu to Helvetia.

Appendix B
Guide to Parallel Passages in the 1828 Journal and the Cooper Edition

Entry Date in 1828 Swiss Journal	Journal Text in *Letters and Journals*, vol. I	Expanded Text in Cooper Edition
Monday, 14 July– Thursday 22 July	pp. 270–273	pp. 5–33
Friday, 1 August	273	34–35
Saturday, 2 August	273	35–37
Sunday, 3 August	274	40–41
Monday, 4 August	274–275	43–50
Tuesday, 5 August	275–279	50–59
Wednesday, 6 August	279–280	58.20–29
		59–63
Thursday, 7 August	280–281	63–64
Friday, 8 August	281	64–65
Saturday, 9 August	281–282	65–66
Sunday, 10 August	282–283	——
Monday, 11 August	283	66
Tuesday, 12 August	283–284	34.13
		60.10–18
		34.18–28
		40.12–22
		39–41
		passim
Wednesday, 13 August	285	——
Thursday, 14 August	285	——
Friday, 15 August	285	41
Saturday, 16 August	285	78.30–32
		71.30–32
Sunday, 17 August	290–291	37–38
Monday and Tuesday, 18 and 19 August	291	66.23–34
		50.22–33
Wednesday, 20 August	291	66.35–38
Thursday, 21 August	291–292	37
		66.30–34
Friday, 22 August	292	66–67
Saturday, 23 August	292	67, 69.25–33

Sunday, 24 August	292	69
Monday, 25 August	293–294	71–74
Tuesday, 26 August	294–296	74–79
Wednesday, 27 August	296–297	80–83
Thursday, 28 August	297–302	82–90
Friday, 29 August	302–305	90–97
Saturday, 30 August	305–307	97–99
Sunday, 31 August	307–309	100–105
Monday, 1 September	309–310	106–116
Tuesday, 2 September	310	116–121
Wednesday, 3 September	311	121–122
Thursday, 4 September	311	122–127
Friday, 5 September	311	——
Saturday, 6 September	311–312	123
Sunday, 7 September	312	——
Monday, 8 September	312–314	130–136
Tuesday, 9 September	314–319	136–149
Wednesday, 10 September	319–321	150–161
Thursday, 11 September	321–326	161–171
Friday, 12 September	326–328	171–179
Saturday, 13 September	329–331	180–187
Sunday, 14 September	331–334	187–196
Monday, 15 September	334–335	197–203
Tuesday, 16 September	336–338	203–214
Wednesday, 17 September	339	215–221
Thursday, 18 September	339	221–224
Friday, 19 September	339	231–233
Saturday, 20 September	339–340	——
Sunday, 21 September	340	——
Monday and Tuesday, 22 and 23 September	340	234
Wednesday, 24 September	340–341	234–239
Thursday, 25 September	341	239–244
Friday, 26 September	341	244–249
Saturday, 27 September	342	251–254
Sunday, 28 September	342	254–257
Monday, 29 September	343	257.6–29
Tuesday, 30 September	343	257–258
Wednesday, 1 October	343	258–259
Wednesday, 8 October	348	260–262
Thursday, 9 October	348	263–268
Friday, 10 October	348–349	269–275
Saturday, 11 October	349–350	275–277
Sunday, 12 October	350	277–288
Monday, 13 October	350	289–294
Tuesday, 14 October	351	295–296
Wednesday, 15 October	351	296–299

TEXTUAL APPARATUS

Textual Commentary

No manuscript of *Gleanings in Europe: Switzerland* is known to survive, though Cooper's Journal entries between 14 July and 15 October 1828 may be considered a pre-copy-text form.[1] Three English-language editions appeared, all in 1836. The first, entitled *Sketches of Switzerland* (BAL 3871), was published in two volumes in Philadelphia by Carey, Lea and Blanchard on 20 May, in an impression of 2,500 copies stereotyped by L. Johnson.[2] The second, retitled *Excursions in Switzerland* (BAL 3872), was published in two volumes in London on 28 May by Richard Bentley,[3] in an impression of 1,500 copies printed by Samuel Bentley. The title page of this issue contained the phrase "Successor to Henry Colburn" under the publisher's name. A re-issue of undetermined size, designated "Second Ed[n]" in the Bentley Papers, appeared on 7 September, with a reset half-title page and a partially reset title page, omitting the reference to Colburn and carrying the words "NEW EDITION." A subsequent re-issue, undated and of undetermined size, carried the phrase "TWO VOLUMES IN ONE" on its reset title page, and a final re-issue, entitled *Travels and Excursions in Various Parts of the World: Switzerland.—Vol. I.*, appeared as Volumes I and II of an eleven-volume re-issue of Cooper's Travel Works sometime in 1838 or later.[4] The third English-language edition, a resetting of the Bentley retaining the Bentley title, was published in Paris on 25 July, in one volume under the separate imprints of Baudry's European Library and A. and W. Galignani.[5] The Baudry/Galignani edition, printed by J. Smith, exists in two issues, differentiated only by the half-title and title pages.[6] Its size is undetermined.

In the absence of the manuscript Cooper furnished to the Carey firm as printer's copy, the copy-text of the present edition is the Carey, Lea and Blanchard text, set in Philadelphia and proofread by the author in New York City between 22 December 1835 and early March 1836.[7] The Bentley edition, set from Carey, Lea and Blanchard sheets furnished to Bentley by the author as printer's copy,[8] incorporates over 1,100 variants, mostly in accidentals. The Baudry/Galignani edition—which perpetuates Bentley's variants, corrects a few errors in its source, and generates more errors of its own—is demonstrably a corrupt derivation from the British edition, insulated at two removes from possible authorial intervention.[9]

While the Baudry/Galignani edition has no conceivable claim to authority in the establishment of the present text, the status of the Bentley edition is less obvious and invites full scrutiny. Since Cooper could not—by reason of time and distance—have corrected Bentley's proofs,[10] the Bentley edition could be authorial only if Cooper originated some or all of its variants by entering scribal changes on the revised, stereotyped Carey, Lea and Blanchard sheets (now lost) as they passed through his hands between 12 and 20 March on their way to the British publisher. Disproof of this possibility rests on the cumulative weight of four distinct kinds of evidence: knowledge of Cooper's usual procedure at this point in his career in supplying Bentley with printer's copy, awareness of Cooper's special author-publisher relationships at this time, the number and nature of the textual variants, and certain characteristics of the Carey, Lea and Blanchard stereotype plates.

In sending printer's copy from one country to another between 1823 and 1850, Cooper customarily forwarded duplicate sets of his earliest corrected sheets by different conveyances. He supplied duplicates to guard against the possibility of loss or delay which might have had the effect of voiding the British copyright, and he sent corrected proof (that is, revises) to escape the gratuitous labor of entering corrections in multiple sets of proof.[11] He followed this general procedure faithfully with *Switzerland*, forwarding proof of Volume I on or about 20 March, of Volumes I and II on 20 April, and of Volume II (or I and II) on 23 April.[12] If Cooper had intended to make any significant number of revisions for the Bentley text, he would have entered them first in the Carey proofs so that they would appear in the American edition and so that they would not have to be entered twice or more times in the printer's copy intended for Bentley. The likelihood that he would have troubled himself or a member of his family to enter numerous changes unnecessarily in several sets of sheets seems exceedingly faint.

The assumption that most, if not all the variants originated in Bentley's printing office is, for a variety of reasons, far more credible, especially in view of Cooper's peculiar relationship with the British publisher at this time. As a practical publisher interested in sales, Bentley had tactfully resisted Cooper's impulse to write travel books. "[W]orks of that class," he wrote from London on 14 May 1835, "do not succeed here nearly as well as popular novels"; and he diminished his offer of pay accordingly.[13] Bentley had not forgotten that Cooper had been "under articles" since 1831 to write a "Lake-*marine* story," set on "Lake Ontario, with scenes on the Great Lakes, with Indians intermingled";[14] and, as work on the travels proceeded, he reminded the novelist that his

> admirers in Europe generally, would be highly gratified by another Story of the Sea from you. In suggesting this to your consideration I trust you will not think I presume further than the long and pleasant intercourse which you have permitted to subsist between us as author, and publisher might happily warrant[.][15]

Comprehending his disadvantage, which the recent failure of *The Monikins* (1835) had not improved, Cooper promised Bentley in a letter of 20 March 1836, "You can put this work [the travels] into any form that best suits yourself";[16] and, in a letter of 18 April transmitting printer's copy, he extended this liberty in regard to format to a loosely defined freedom in regard to text:

> I wish your proof reader to look close after the proofs, for this work has been printed in Philadelphia, and I have not had sufficient opportunity to correct it. I think the French ought to be in Italics, certainly all but the proper names, and even some of them. But this is an affair I leave to you.[17]

Cooper's permissive attitude suggests why Bentley felt free to make a relatively large number of changes—even substantive ones—in the text of *Switzerland*, and suggests further why Cooper was not concerned to revise sheets that he sent to Bentley.

Bentley's lively concern for the British reception of *Switzerland* is immediately apparent in striking improvements of format: in a meticulously analytical Table of Contents organized chapter by chapter with the appropriate sections repeated as topical summaries at the beginnings of chapters,[18] in the running heads prepared individually for each page, and in the handsome 12-point pica type and heavy leading. In his reprinting, Bentley not only followed Cooper's explicit injunction to put the French in italics, he accepted Cooper's implicit invitation—or so it seems—to "improve" the text in hundreds of other particulars, hoping no doubt to make the work more attractive to British readers.

Close examination of the 1,116 Bentley variants reveals none (with the possible exception of three longer substantive variants to be discussed separately) that could not have originated with the British publisher. Most of the variants—1,044—are in accidentals, principally in punctuation, spelling and capitalization, changes easily predictable in British reprints of American books. Bentley's text, for example,

frequently substituted British for American spellings. Classified and
tabulated, most of these accidental variants are identifiable as house
styling.[19] Similarly, sixty-nine or all but three of the substantive variants are most readily explained on the assumption that they originated in the taste, judgment and styling of the British printing office.
Corrections of errors in the Carey, Lea and Blanchard text account
for twenty-six; and corruptions introduced by the Bentley account for
nine.[20] Three of the substantive variants in the Preface (the substitution of "American" for "native" at 2.32, of "his country" for "the
country" at 3.4, and of "America" for "this country" at 3.39) are
transparently adaptations of an American text for a British audience.
Moreover, thirty additional substantive variants, none longer than
three words and none exhibiting Cooper's characteristic boldness in
revision, can be classified and tabulated in patterns of deletions, addi-
tions, substitutions, and transpositions.[21] Such "improvements" were
well within the competence of a skilled copyeditor; and, as Bentley
knew, Cooper would be grateful for this assistance if the alterations
were truly "improvements."

Another possible source of variants must be considered, however.
At least four variants—and probably more—could be explained by
late revision of the Carey stereotype plates. The three extended substantive variants, in which ambiguities in the Bentley are resolved in
the Carey text, insinuate Cooper's revising hand in the American
plates *after* the first installment of Bentley's printer's copy had been
sent. The peculiar circumstances of the transmission of copy to Bentley and certain characteristics of the Carey plates favor this assumption. In a letter of 12 March 1836, the Carey firm informed Cooper
that two sets of sheets of the first volume, which contained the variants in question, awaited him at Wiley and Long's bookstore in New
York and advised:

> Such alterations of the french words & other matters as you
> wish attended to will be done if you will mark them on one of
> the copies & return at an early day[.]
>
> You are no doubt aware that the plates are cast & of course
> the alterations should occupy the same space to avoid recasting
> whole pages—[22]

That Cooper did correct revises for Carey is shown by an entry of late
May 1836 in the Carey and Lea Cost Book charging $46.75 for altera-
tions at $.25 per alteration.[23] Most, though not all, of the 187 altera-
tions of the plates for *Switzerland* appear to have been italicizations
of the French. On 20 March, almost certainly before he could have
received Carey's second revises, Cooper wrote Bentley to report that

he was sending a set of sheets for the first volume and would forward a duplicate "in a few days." This duplicate, which would presumably have contained Cooper's final revisions, was not forwarded until 20 April, a month later, and then with sheets for Volume II. In order to publish on 28 May, Bentley would almost surely have had to have Volume I, set from the unsatisfactory printer's copy, in print before the second revises of Volume I arrived with the first sheets of Volume II. Even so, Bentley's lead time was insufficient to enable him to achieve the prior publication he always sought.

Carey's warning that the "alterations should occupy the same space to avoid recasting" invites inspection of the spacing of these three variants in the copy-text as a means of testing the hypothesis of Cooper's intervention. In the first (74.20–21), a passage concerning fortified places in Switzerland, sixty-nine spaces in the Carey match seventy-one in the Bentley, a correspondence almost too exact to be coincidental.[24] In the second (81.18–19), a reference to the sublimity of Niagara Falls, eleven spaces in the Carey match fourteen spaces in the Bentley.[25] An abnormally wide blank space at the end of the sentence in the Carey is sufficient to accomodate three superfluous spaces. In the third (121.15–16), a description of Swiss dwellings, forty-six spaces in the Carey match forty-two spaces in the Bentley.[26] Again the close correspondence in the number of spaces favors revision in the Carey plates, for revision in the Bentley edition would not have required calculation of the spacing. Since the 187 alterations in the plates, whose cost is recorded in the Carey and Lea Cost Book, almost surely exceeded the number employed to italicize the French, some of the other sixty-eight substantive variants may originate with late revision of the Carey plates. At 28.35, where the Carey reads "men" and the Bentley "negroes," an inequality of spacing between the words in the line in the copy-text strongly suggests the substitution of a word shorter by three or four letters. Other possible substitutions, some of which must have included punctuation, are too evenly matched to be detected from spacing alone.

All available evidence, then, external and internal, tends to confirm that the Carey, Lea and Blanchard is not only the copy-text, but the only authorial text of *Gleanings in Europe: Switzerland*. The only text potentially under his full control, it is the form of the text closest to the author's hand, and evidently the only form in which the author made revisions. The Bentley edition, for all its improvements of format, does not purport to be a faithful reproduction of the copy-text. It freely adapts Cooper's diction, spelling, and style to supposed preferences of British readers, imposes alien house styling on the copy-text, and either perpetuates or creates ambiguities in the three longest and most significant variant passages, ambiguities which the copy-text satisfactorily resolves. Since the Bentley variants are in no sense authoritative, they are not recorded in a Rejected Readings list.

The present edition corrects obvious errors in the copy-text, errors in both substantives and accidentals. Since spellings of many Swiss place names had not been standardized either in their French or German forms in the 1820s and 1830s, copy-text spellings of place names are retained if they are acceptable alternative spellings. When copy-text spellings are not acceptable alternatives, emendation is made first on the basis of Cooper's Journal spelling—if it is an acceptable variant—or, in the absence of Journal entries, on the basis of contemporaneously-published sources. Ebel, Keller's map, Picot, Simond and other contemporary travel books have been examined to confirm variant copy-text spellings, and, in a few instances, to correct errors in the copy-text.[27] No attempt has been made to regularize or modernize acceptable variant spellings.

Cooper's injunction to Bentley that the latter put "the French" into italics and Carey's promise to attend to "alterations of the french words" establish that Cooper wanted French words and phrases italicized in *Switzerland*. This instruction, together with the marked increase of italic forms in Volume II, shows that Cooper was belatedly formulating a consistent policy for italics which was sporadically applied to Volume I, and most fully represented in Volume II, after page fifty. Presumably because of Carey's warning about the cost, Cooper made few if any corrections in the stereotype plates already cast.[28] According to the policy Cooper evolved, French, German and Latin sentences and phrases are italicized. The present edition has, therefore, italicized foreign words and phrases in Volume I and the first fifty pages of Volume II. Conversations in French, forms of address like *Monsieur* and *son excellence*, and words like *château*, *sac d'eau*, *Kirschwasser* and *bitte, bitte* are emended in accordance with Cooper's practice in Volume II, 50 ff.[29] But because Cooper's letter to Bentley makes a qualified exception of proper names, the present edition has not emended them, retaining their roman and italic forms as they appear in the copy-text.[30]

The present edition supplements the copy-text in one way. Following the convention of the time, the copy-text of *Switzerland* refers to the names of persons by a letter followed by a three- or four-em dash. When possible, for the convenience of the reader, the present edition supplies these names within square brackets: for example, at 22.14 "W——" becomes "W[illiam]"; at 51.39 "R—— and L——" become "R[ay] and L[ow]."

The present edition of *Gleanings in Europe: Switzerland* is an unmodernized critical text, no portion of which has been silently emended. Variant but acceptable spellings of names of places and other words have been retained, but visual appurtenances of the copy-text, such as general typestyling and the styling of chapter openings, spacing of indentations, the styling of italic punctuation after italic words, and the use of periods after letter numbers have not been retained. Thus, the present edition reproduces the copy-text in its entirety except for ordinary visual appurtenances and duly recorded emendations, including corrections of obvious errors, the insertion of names in square brackets, and changes in italics in accordance with Cooper's expressed wish.

NOTES

1. See *The Letters and Journals of James Fenimore Cooper*, ed. James Franklin Beard (Cambridge, Mass., 1960), I, 270–350; MS: Yale Collection of American Literature, Beinecke Rare Book and Manuscript Library, Yale University, hereafter referred to as YCAL. These Journal entries were recorded in a bound notebook measuring 6½" x 8⅜", entitled on the cover "Holland and Switzerland/France and Italy." See also *Letters and Journals*, I, xxxiv–xxxv. That the Journal entries were not copy-text, but were substantially reconceived and rewritten is clear from the most casual comparison; but that Cooper followed essentially the same chronology, expanding and supplementing his Journal to produce the manuscript of *Switzerland* is equally clear.
2. Robert E. Spiller and Philip C. Blackburn, *A Descriptive Bibliography of the Writings of James Fenimore Cooper* (New York, 1934), p. 84; David Kaser, *The Cost Book of Carey & Lea, 1825–1838* (Philadelphia, 1963), p. 199.
3. The publication date of 28 May 1836 is furnished by Bentley's own publication list (BM Add Mss 46,637), a compilation of earlier records not available and presumed destroyed. This list is the best available authority. London *Literary Gazette* advertisements of 30 April and 7 May, designating a one-volume work, obviously preceded publication; and an advertisement of 28 May in the same journal referred to the work as *"just ready."* A review appeared in the *Literary Gazette* on 4 June.
4. Bentley Papers, BM Add Mss 46,637, 37v–38r. The entry for the "Second Ed^n" (or NEW EDITION) reports neither printer nor number of copies printed, and none of the other issues is referred to in the Bentley Papers. Hinman collation of copies of

the first two issues shows that the texts—except for the reset title pages and half-title pages—are identical except for minor imperfections of inking. Visual examination of sample pages of two volumes in the eleven-volume re-issue, not available for Hinman collation, also reveals identical texts. Examination of the gatherings of the issues establishes the identity of the first issue. The text for each of the issues begins on the B gathering, but only the title-page of the issue containing the phrase "Successor to Henry Colburn" is contained in an eight-leaf gathering which includes the Preface and the Table of Contents. All other issues contain separate two-leaf gatherings of the half-title and title pages. All of this evidence strongly suggests that the Bentley issues are comprised of new title-page gatherings bound with portions of the original 1,500 copies.

5. *Bibliographie de la France* (Paris, 1836), XXV, 3699, 3700.
6. The first gathering of the Baudry imprint consists of the half-title page, with the printer's imprint on the verso, conjugate with the title page. In Galignani copies examined, the two-leaf gathering is replaced by a tipped-in, single-leaf title page. Both issues are apparently from the same typesetting, but it has not been possible to determine if more than one impression occurred.
7. Carey and Lea to JFC, 21 December 1835; *Letters and Journals*, III, 207; MS: YCAL.
8. The sheets Cooper furnished to Bentley as printer's copy were presumably one of the sets Carey and Lea sent to Cooper for this purpose with a covering letter dated 12 March 1836 indicating that the plates were cast; MS: YCAL.
9. The following texts were collated in preparation of the present edition: copies of the Carey, Lea and Blanchard text owned by James F. Beard, the Emory University Library (DQ 23.C785), the Library of Congress (PQ 23.C6 office), the University of Delaware Library (Spec. DQ 23.C62.1836), the University of Texas at Austin (Aw C78sk 1836, copy 1; Aw C78sk 1836 [copy 2], the Williams College Library (L&T 3.C78s); copies of the Bentley text (first issue) in the Case Western Reserve University Library (813.24.E8), the National Library of Scotland (Lloyd 610–611), the University of Cincinnati Library (DQ 23.C6 1836); copy of the Bentley "NEW EDITION" owned by James F. Beard; copy of the Bentley "TWO VOLUMES IN ONE" in the National Library of Ireland (91494 C 8); copy of the eleven-volume re-issue in the Beinecke Library (Za C786 C840T); copies of the Baudry text owned by James F. Beard,

and in the University of Washington Library (914.94 C78c) and the University of Wisconsin Library (G38.C77); copy of the Galignani text owned by James F. Beard. Forty-nine additional copies of these texts have been examined in libraries in the United States, Great Britain and Ireland.

10. Typically an exchange of letters between Cooper and Bentley took a month or longer. Bentley accepted the note of payment for the first volume on 20 April 1836, a month after it was sent (Bentley *Letterbooks*, BM Add Mss 46,640).

11. Cooper began the practice of forwarding duplicate sets of printer's copy to British publishers in 1823 with *The Pioneers* and continued it until his final book *The Ways of the Hour* in 1850. If scribal corrections had been entered in one set and omitted in the other, he would presumably have had the forethought to warn his publisher in advance, as he did for *The Pioneers*. In fact, no evidence from any source suggests that he entered such corrections subsequent to *The Pioneers*, apparently because he was careful to forward duplicate sets of sheets in their final form. See *Letters and Journals*, I, 91; VI, 156, and passim.

12. *Letters and Journals*, III, 207, 209–210; JFC to Richard Bentley, 23 April 1836; MS: University of Texas.

13. Richard Bentley to JFC, 14 May 1835; MS: YCAL.

14. *Letters and Journals*, II, 53.

15. Bentley to JFC, 30 May 1836; MS: YCAL.

16. *Letters and Journals*, III, 207.

17. Ibid., 210.

18. This Table of Contents is reproduced for the reader's convenience in Appendix A, pp. 313–319. The spellings of persons and places in the Table of Contents have been changed, when necessary, to agree with spellings in the present edition.

19. These variants fall into twenty-four categories:

Internal Punctuation	420 instances
Hyphenation of compound words	
Two words to one hyphenated word (e.g., new fashioned→new-fashioned)	143 instances
Hyphenated word to two words (e.g., hill-side →hill side)	10 instances
Hyphenated word to one word (e.g., post-master→postmaster)	11 instances
One word to hyphenated word (e.g., halfway →half-way)	6 instances
Two words compressed to one word (e.g., any thing →anything)	44 instances

One word expanded to two words (e.g.,
halfway→half way)   1 instance
Italics
 Foreign words and phrases in roman italicized
 (e.g., Monsieur→*Monsieur*)   133 instances
 Italicized foreign words and phrases made into
 roman (e.g., *caste*→caste)   23 instances
Spelling variants
 Correct spellings changed to British
 preferences (e.g., gray→grey)   76 instances
 Corrections of incorrect spellings (e.g.,
 Tuetonic→Teutonic)   18 instances
 Correct spelling made incorrect (e.g.,
 camelopard→cameleopard)   1 instance
Capitalization
 Uncapitalized to capitalized (e.g., states
 →States)   31 instances
 Capitalized made lower case (e.g., Con-
 federation→confederation)   52 instances
Variant in terminal sentence punctuation
(e.g., taste. At→taste,—at)   4 instances
Accent marks
 Accent marks in foreign words added or
 corrected (e.g., á→à)   44 instances
 Accent marks in foreign words deleted (e.g.,
 Küsnacht→Kusnacht)   2 instances
Asterisk indicating footnote shifted or changed
 to dagger (e.g., *→†)   6 instances
Ligature removed (e.g., phæton→phaeton)   1 instance
Addition or deletion of apostrophes (e.g.,
 hours→hours')   3 instances
Quotation marks inserted (e.g., *poir-r-es*,
 →*poir-r-es*,')   3 instances
Quotation marks shifted (e.g., "the era→the
 "era)   1 instance
Arabic numbers written out (e.g., 6→six)   10 instances
Ordinal number changed to Arabic (e.g., first
 →1st)   1 instance
20. Actual and supposed substantive corrections of errors in the
    Carey edition: 20.17, scarce [in the Carey]→scarcely [in the
    Bentley]; 24.5, is→are; 27.8, valley→valleys; 43.3, Lorrainein
    →*Lorraine* in; 44.40, is→was; 43.15, SaxeCoburg→Saxe
    Coburg; 59.3, sung→sang; 80.24, most→more; 95.22, history

→histories; 110.32, one of the→the one; 111.24, baths→paths; 119.2, protected→protecting; 126.26, trusts→trust; 149.15, *Des*→*De*; 164.20, forbid→forbids; 191.30, spu→spur; 203.24, dose→doze; 207.8, the *deleted*; 224.28, suf/cient→sufficient; 257.39, hief→chief; 262.20 and 262.29, la→le; 271.31, *sout* →*sont*; 276.14, strong hold→stronghold; 278.1, XXIX→ XXVIII; and 289.1, XXX→XXIX. Substantive errors initiated by the Bentley edition: 93.28, Naked earth→Nakedearth; 98.5, châteaux→château; 128.38, or *deleted*; 153.23, site→sight; 194.34, a *deleted*; 224.29, Herbert→Hebert; 252.7, sneers→ snares; 262.29, *talents*→*talens*; and 289.27, inferred→interred.

21. Substantive styling changes of Carey readings: 1.19–20, is probably [in the Carey]→probably is [in the Bentley]; 2.14, was commenced→commenced by the writer; 2.22, interest→interests; 3.8, factions→faction; 3.9, that is *deleted*; 3.33, those→ these; 4.2, conclusions→conclusion; 6.28, probably→probable that; 13.36, that→which; 13.37, which→that; 16.6, a want of filth→*a want of filth*; 19.4, serpenting→serpentining; 32.6, the *deleted*; 47.28, lay a crowded→lay crowded a; 41.20, who→as; 49.21, a hotel→an hotel; 64.38, *Or Thoun. *deleted*; 67.23, conclusion→conclusion that; 77.40, *the*→the; 86.37, yet *deleted*; 88.20, wander→crawl; 91.10, revolution→*revolution*; 107.20, commonly→usually; 109.10, of the head *deleted*; 120.16, on the whole *deleted*; 156.35, sail→sail to be; 192.15, my→the; 217.7, through the pastures *deleted*; 290.8, that *deleted*; and 290.15, who was *deleted*.

22. Carey and Lea to JFC, 12 March 1836; MS: YCAL.

23. Kaser, p. 199.

24. The variant readings here and in footnotes 25 and 26 are set off by double bars.

CAREY EDITION	BENTLEY EDITION
Through an opening in the hills, we got a glimpse of Aarberg, a town of Berne, which was once a Roman station, ‖ and is now the only fortified place in Switzerland, unless Geneva can be called one. ‖	Through an opening in the hills, we got a glimpse of Aarberg, a town of Berne, which was once a Roman station, ‖ and is now one of the very few fortified places that are still left in Switzerland. ‖

25.

CAREY EDITION	BENTLEY EDITION
Niagara, however, like every thing truly sublime, grows upon the senses,	Niagara, however, like everything truly sublime, grows upon the senses, and, in

and, in the end, certainly stands without a rival. Its grandeur ||overshadows accessories.|| Lights and shadows embellish ordinary landscapes, but of what consequence is it to the awful sublimity of an eclipse, that there is a cloud or two, more or less, within the visible horizon?

the end, certainly stands without a rival. Its grandeur ||looks down all the accessories.|| Lights and shadows embellish ordinary landscapes, but of what consequence is it to the awful sublimity of an eclipse, that there is a cloud or two, more or less, within the visible horizon?

26. CAREY EDITION
Our road now lay by the open country, and, though always through a beautiful district, it offered little, ||except in the neatness and architecture of the dwellings,|| of a very interesting kind.

BENTLEY EDITION
Our road now lay by the open country, and, though always through a beautiful district, it offered little, ||except in its neatness, and in the novel architecture,|| of a very interesting kind.

27. Johann Gottfried Ebel, *Manuel du Voyageur en Suisse* (Paris, 1827 —a French reprint, one of many subsequent editions from the German original); Henri Keller, "Carte Itinéraire de la Suisse," included in Ebel; Jean Picot, *Statistique de la Suisse* (Geneva, 1819); Louis Simond, *Voyage en Suisse* (Paris, 1822). With the exception of Simond, a relative of Mrs. Cooper mentioned in *Switzerland* whose book Cooper had read, each work is specifically referred to as a source in *Switzerland*.

28. See Carey and Lea to JFC, 12 March 1836; MS: YCAL.

29. Anglicized foreign words are italicized only when the italic form is present in Volume II. For example, "*Café*," which is italicized in Volume II, is italicized at 91.10, while "connoisseur," which does not appear in Volume II, is not italicized in Volume I. Authority for the anglicization of foreign words is Webster's *Dictionary* (1828).

30. The only exception to this practice is when the proper name is contained within a foreign phrase. Thus, at 5.19 *la belle Gabrielle* is italicized, while the name Compiègne at 6.35 is not.

Textual Notes

The following notes explain emendations requiring more specific information than the Textual Commentary could provide.

12.33 Although "Neufchâtel" appears in several contemporary travel books—Louis Simond's entry begins "Neuchâtel, or properly Neufchâtel" (*Travels in Switzerland* [London, 1822], p. 15)— Cooper's Journal refers to "Neuchâtel," the correct spelling of the Swiss Canton, lake and town; "Neufchâtel" refers to a French town.

32.23 This rare alternate spelling of the German word *Plattform* is retained because it appears in *Letters and Journals*, I, 273; since it is a foreign word, it is also italicized in the present edition.

54.3 The present edition emends the incorrect form "Munch" to "Monch," Cooper's Journal spelling and an acceptable variant spelling of the town.

55.12 The present edition corrects the erroneous form "Grindewald" to "Grindelwald," in agreement with Cooper's most frequent Journal spelling and that of contemporaneous travel books.

77.30 Here "Bruck" and at 93.28 "Broek" are corrected to the acceptable variant spelling "Brugg" on the basis of Cooper's Journal entry, "Brug." The context of the passage reveals that Cooper is referring to this town rather than to the town of Brügg, in the Canton of Bern.

83.6 The copy-text form "Stockhorn," the name of a mountain, must be a misprinting of "Steckborn," the name of the village recorded at this point in Cooper's Journal.

93.28 See textual note at 77.30.

143.38 Though "saltation" is a valid word meaning "leaping, bounding, or jumping; a leap," the context here clearly calls for political "salutation."

151.16 The present edition corrects the erroneous form "Stanztad" to "Stanzstad," an acceptable variant spelling present in Cooper's Journal.

159.8 The present edition corrects the erroneous form "Scewen" to "Seewen," in agreement with Cooper's Journal and the generally accepted spelling.

164.32–33 The erroneous copy-text form "Rotenthurm," a town referred to in Cooper's Journal as "Rosenthurm," is corrected
here to the generally accepted spelling of "Rothenthurm."

220.31 The present edition emends "*Hôpital*" to "*hospice*" to avoid the
ambiguity of the copy-text, since Cooper is clearly not referring to the nearby town "*Hospital*" (or "*Hôpital*"), but to the
general term for a shelter or place of rest employed in this
context by Ebel, *Manuel du Voyageur en Suisse* (Paris, 1827).

234.17 The syntax here makes sense only if the missing "if" is supplied at the beginning of the dependent clause.

236.10 In this quotation from Ebel, p. 314, the present edition corrects the accent mark on this word to agree with its source.

281.2 The present edition prints in roman type the name of a woman
who was a member of the Cooper household staff.

Emendations

The following list records all changes in substantives and accidentals introduced into the copy-text. The reading of the present edition appears to the left of the square bracket; the authority for that reading, followed by a semicolon, the copy-text reading and the copy-text symbol appear to the right of the bracket. Within an entry, the curved dash ~ represents the same word that appears before the bracket and is used in recording punctuation variants; the caret ʌ represents a punctuation mark missing in the copy-text. An asterisk before an entry indicates that the entry is discussed in Textual Notes. A dagger † before an entry indicates that the entry is discussed in Explanatory Notes. The present edition, designated CE, is the authority for all emendations.

The following text is referred to:

A   *Sketches of Switzerland*. Philadelphia: Carey, Lea and Blanchard, 1836.

5.2	Dᴇᴀʀ ———,] CE; Dᴇᴀʀ ———ʌ A
5.4	*porte cochère*]CE; porte cochère A
5.4	*rue de Sèvres*]CE; rue de Sêvre A
5.16	*barrière du Trône*] CE; barrière du Trone A
†5.19	*la belle Gabrielle*] CE; la belle Gabrielle A
†5.23	*gras de Paris*] CE; gras de Paris A
5.26	*limonière*] CE; limonière A
5.34	*calèche*] CE; calèche A
6.5	*sacr-r-r-es*] CE; sacr-r-r-es A
6.10	*la nouvelle France*] CE; la nouvelle France A
6.13	*ancien régime*] CE; ancien régime A
6.15	*recherché*] CE; recherché A
6.21	*Monsieur*]CE; Monsieur A *Also italicized at* 149.6 (Monsieur's), 149.8 *and* 149.12.
6.25–26	*Aha! voyez-vous, mes enfans—les anciennes modes ont aussi leur mérite*]CE; Aha! voyez vousʌ mes enfans—les anciennes modes ont aussi leur mérite A
6.39	*château*] CE; château A *Also italicized at* 8.13, 12.9,

	12.17, 12.21, 12.22, 25.7, 35.32, 43.27, 47.1, 64.12, 66.25, 74.24, 75.22, 80.17, 87.15, 89.31, 97.22, 97.40, 98.7, 100.6, 118.25, 122.9, 122.12, *and* 131.6.
7.7	*salle de Diane*]CE; salle de Diane A
8.9	*salle de Diane*]CE; salle de Diane A
9.12	*la petite Suisse*]CE; la petite Suisse A
9.13	*fauxbourgs*]CE; fauxbourgs A
9.28	*son excellence*]CE; son excellence A *Also italicized at* 9.30 *and* 9.35.
9.30	*Monsieur l'ambassadeur*]CE; Monsieur l'ambassadeur A
9.31	*est un grand*]CE; est un grand A
9.38	*un grand*]CE; un grand A
10.5	*La belle France*]CE; La belle France A
10.5–6	*la France utile*]CE; la France utile A
11.17–18	*contre tems*]CE; contre tems A
12.2	MY DEAR ———,]CE; MY DEAR ———ʌ A
†12.11	*Mesdames de Silléry et de Genlis*]CE; Mesdames de Silléry et de Genlis A
*12.33	Neuchâtel]CE; Neufchâtel A *Also corrected at* 16.12, 21.5, 21.23, 22.4, 23.10, 23.24, 23.31, 24.3, 24.19, 24.37, 25.3, 25.38, 33.40, 44.4, 145.13, *and* 235.6.
13.22	[Mrs. Cooper]]CE; A——— A *Also identified at* 16.14, 81.8, 265.32, 266.30, 266.35, *and* 270.17.
13.33	*Mont Blanc, monsieur*]CE; Mont Blanc, monsieur A
14.14	Doubs]CE; Doub A
†15.11	*chevaux de renfort*]CE; chevaux de renfort A
16.28	*mêlée*]CE; mêlée A
†17.4	Toussaint]CE; Touissant A
18.8	*gens d'armes*]CE; gens d'armes A *Also italicized at* 34.38, 88.24, *and* 123.4–5
18.17	*entrée*]CE; entrée A
19.23–24	Neuchâtelois]CE; Neufchâtelois A
19.36	pass]CE; ~, A
20.35	*n'est-ce*]CE; *n'est ce* A
20.39	*celui-ci*]CE; *celui ci* A
20.40	*crois*]CE; *croix* A
20.40	*à*]CE; *a* A
21.2	*d'être cultivé*]CE; *d'etre cultiver* A
21.14	*coup d'œils*]CE; coup d'œils A
22.14	W[illiam]]]CE; W——— A *Also identified at* 50.39, 55.25, 62.14, 63.16, 82.29, 82.33, 83.4, 91.18, 97.16,

105.23, 109.2–3, 109.30, 110.36, 111.3, 112.2,
116.29, 116.33, 121.12, 262.11, 262.31, 279.6,
280.11, 289.29, 295.26, *and* 298.9–10.

24.6	Neuchâtelois]CE; Neufchâtelois A
24.22	*calèche*]CE; caléche A
24.22–23	*à la mode de l'Allemagne*]CE; à la mode de l'Allemagne A
24.33	Basle]CE; Bâsle A
24.36	us only]CE; ~, ~, A
26.13	*Bürgerschaft*]CE; Bürgerschaft A *Also italicized at* 28.38, 29.5, 30.38, *and* 34.6.
28.28	*seigneurie*]CE; seigneurie A
*32.23	*Platteform*]CE; Platteform A
33.22	*calèche*]CE; caléche A
33.28	*char-à-banc*]CE; char-à-banc A
33.29	*char-à-banc*]CE; char-à-banc A
37.37	Teutonic]CE; Tuetonic A
†37.39	Windham]CE; Wyndham A
38.5	P[aul]]CE; P——— A
43.3	Lorraine in]CE; Lorrainein A
43.15	Saxe Coburg]CE; SaxeCoburg A
43.20	*rencontres*]CE; rencontres A
44.32	*la belle batelière*]CE; la belle batelière A
45.12	*la belle batelière*]CE; la belle batelière A
51.34	*batz* and *half-batz*]CE; batz and half-batz A
51.37	*batz*]CE; batz A
†51.39	R[ay] and L[ow]]CE; R——— and L——— A
*54.3	Monch]CE; Munch A
*55.12	Grindelwald]CE; Grindewald A *Also corrected at* 56.3, 56.23, 57.3, 58.10, 58.29, 58.39, 59.2, 59.11, 59.30, 62.6, 62.14, 62.19, 64.9, 136.10, 216.35, 217.28, 219.16, *and* 224.11.
57.15	snow.]CE; ~ˬ A
61.3	*lämmergeyer*]CE; lämmergeyer A
61.28	*jets d'eau*]CE; jets d'eau A
63.13	*chaises*]CE; *chaìses* A
65.31	*à la Suisse*]CE; à la Sùisse A *Also italicized at* 74.17–18 *and* 114.33.
66.5–6	*immortelle*]CE; immortelle A
66.39	*goîtres*]CE; goîtres A
67.6	hangable]CE; hangible A
67.9	*goîtreism*]CE; goîtreism A

67.12	*goître*]CE; goître A
†68.13	W[alther]]CE; W——— A *Also identified at* 68.36, *and* 261.19.
68.16–17	*que messieurs les Anglais n'aiment pas trop les Américains*]CE; que messieurs les Anglais n'aiment pas trop les Américains A
69.30	*à la française*]CE; à la Française A
†69.34–35	Mr. [John], and Lady [Charlotte Denison]]CE; Mr. ———, and Lady ——— ——— A
†69.40	Captain [Cooper]]CE; Captain —— A
71.3	Lorraine]CE; *Lorraine* A
72.10	Before]CE; before A
72.26	*châteaux*]CE; châteaux A *Also italicized at* 72.26, 75.15, 83.9, 91.37, 98.5, *and* 130.22.
72.33	*ne plus ultra*]CE; ne plus ultra A
73.37–38	*Sœurs de Charité*]CE; Sœurs de Charité A
74.16–17	*à l'Américain*]CE; à l'Américaine A
76.6	Knights']CE; Knight's A
77.18	Slav]CE; Slave A
*77.30	Brugg]CE; Bruck A
78.18	capitol]CE; capital A
79.31	*Kaiser*]CE; Kaiser A
79.32	*Stuhl*]CE; Stuhl A
81.30	*aristo-démocratique*]CE; *aristo-democratique* A
*83.6	Steckborn]CE; Stockhorn A
86.26	*Schlösser*]CE; schlœsser A
89.20	*bon vivant*]CE; bon vivant A
90.10	Basle]CE; Bâsle A
91.10	*Café*]CE; Café A
92.38	*bitte, bitte*]CE; bitte, bitte A
*93.28	Brugg]CE; Broek A
95.15	celibates]CE; celibites A
96.8	*Rhodes*]CE; Rhodes A
96.16	*Rhode*]CE; Rhode A
100.13	*place d'armes*]CE; place d'armes A
107.6	*batteaux*]CE; batteaux A
109.12	*viâ la rue Vivienne*]CE; viâ la rue Vivienne A
111.27	*fêtes*]CE; fêtes A
117.13	*ne plus ultra*]CE; ne plus ultra A
119.13	Grütli]CE; Griitli A
122.19	*beau idéal*]CE; beau idéal A
123.3	*garde champêtre*]CE; garde champêtre A

124.3	*gensdarmerie*]CE; gensdarmerie A
127.2	scarcely]CE; sarcely A
127.3	occurrence]CE; occurence A
130.1	LETTER XIV]CE; LETTER X A
132.6	*n'est-ce*]CE; *n'est ce* A
133.37	*Monsir*]CE; Monsir A
134.32	*fête*]CE; fête A
135.19	*rencontres*]CE; rencontres A
137.10	*sacs d'eau*]CE; sacs d'eau A
139.38	*Louis d'or*]CE; Louis d'or A
140.1	*Louis*]CE; Louis A
140.2	*Louis d'or*]CE; Louis d'or A
140.28	for.]CE; ~ʌ A
143.8	*imperium in imperio*]CE; imperium in imperio A
*143.38	salutation]CE; saltation A
146.20	Catholic]CE; catholic A
147.39	*Landsgemeinde*]CE; Landsgemeinde A
149.15	*De*]CE; *Des* A
*151.16	Stanzstad]CE; Stanztad A *Also corrected at* 151.21, 151.27, 151.38, *and* 152.17.
154.34	*Landsgemeinde*]CE; Landsgemeinde A
154.35	*Landamman*]CE; landamman A
156.28	*batteau*]CE; batteau A
158.15	Gessler]CE; Gesler A
*159.8	Seewen]CE; Scewen A *Also emended at* 160.12 *and* 160.18.
*164.32–33	Rothenthurm]CE; Rotenthurm A
165.2	Egeri]CE; Engeri A
171.8	*Boulevard*]CE; *Boulevards* A
172.35	*Kirschwasser*]CE; Kirschwasser A
174.13	Lachen]CE; Lacken A
174.40	*poir-r-es*,']CE; ~,ʌ A
†176.28–29	*Schrabzieger*]CE; Schrabzieger A
177.19	*Schrabzieger*]CE; Schrabzieger A
177.39	*Trifolium melilot. cærul.*]CE; Trifolium melilot. cærul. A
182.8	*bâtiment*]CE; batiment A
182.18	Schaffhausen]CE; Schaff hausen A
183.5	*voilà*]CE; *voila* A
188.3	*Io Pæan*]CE; IO PÆAN A
190.29	*Kirschwasser*]CE; *Kirchs wasser* A
191.30	spur]CE; spu A

192.34	*Almanach*]CE; *almanach* A
194.5	*châteaux*]CE; *chateaux* A
196.4	*Schlöss*]CE; *schloss* A
196.5	*Schlöss*]CE; *schloss* A
203.31	*shibboleth*]CE; *shiboleth* A
212.39	Urnerlock.]CE; ~ʌ A
213.6	Lucerne]CE; Luzerne A
213.11	Tessin]CE; Tessino A
*220.31	*hospice*]CE; *Hôpital* A *Also emended at* 220.37 *and* 221.27.
224.28	sufficient]CE; sufcient A
226.37	*dénouement*]CE; *dénoument* A
230.24	*à*]CE; *á* A
231.25	*coteries*]CE; *côteries* A
*234.17	if you]CE; you A
234.21	*Téméraire,*)]CE; ~,ʌ A
*236.10	*diamètre*]CE; *diamêtre* A
237.29	Russians]CE; Russsians A
†237.38	General [Jomini]]CE; General ——— A *Also identified at* 238.5, 238.14, *and* 238.27.
239.9	pommel]CE; pummel A
240.27	fabricate.]CE; ~ ? A
240.28	*cela*]CE; *celà* A *Also corrected at* 240.38 *and* 241.18.
240.29	pins.]CE; ~ ? A
240.30	*Où*]CE; *Ou* A
240.39	too,]CE; ~ʌ A
241.3	*plaisante*]CE; *plaîsante* A
242.30	*dénouement*]CE; *dénoument* A
243.14–15	*rencontres*]CE; rencontres A
243.20	*cuirassiers*]CE; *curaissiers* A
243.23	*Champ*]CE; *Champs* A
246.12	motion,]CE; ~ʌ A
254.32	C[ooperstow]n]CE; C———n A
257.39	chief]CE; hief A
261.15	C[ooperstow]n]CE; C———n A
262.20	*le*]CE; *la* A
262.29	*le*]CE; *la* A
267.18	*Arrêtez*]CE; *Arrétez* A
268.4	*bateaux-à-vapeur*]CE; *bateaux-à-vapeurs* A
268.4	"Napoleon]CE; ʌ~ A
268.4	steamboats,"]CE; ~,ʌ A
268.10	*remise*]CE; *rémise* A
270.16	*côtelettes*]CE; *cotelettes* A

271.31	*sont*] CE; *sout* A
276.14	stronghold] CE; strong hold A
278.1	LETTER XXVIII] CE; LETTER XXIX A
278.18	*blasé*] CE; *blazé* A
*281.2	Lucie] CE; *Lucie* A
289.1	LETTER XXIX] CE; LETTER XXX A
292.15	*Borromées*] CE; *Borromii* A

Word-Division

List A records compounds or possible compounds hyphenated at the end of the line in the copy-text and resolved as hyphenated or one word as listed below. If the words occur elsewhere in the copy-text or if Cooper's manuscripts of this period fairly consistently followed one practice respecting the particular compound or possible compound, the resolution was made on that basis. Otherwise first editions of works of this period were used as guides. List B is a guide to transcription of compounds hyphenated at the end of the line in the Cooper Edition: compounds recorded here should be transcribed as given; words divided at the end of the line and not listed should be transcribed as one word.

LIST A

6.29	pipe-stem	105.15	passer-by
8.5	wax-work	107.2	self-assumed
9.18	eyebrows	108.29	door-yards
20.20	tea-cup	110.21	broad-backed
23.25	common-place accounts	114.29	neighbour-waters
25.14	nobleman	119.33	head-land
29.38	countrymen	122.4	landlady
36.15	tomb-stone	147.10	head-irons
43.14	Grand-duchess	148.12	state-house
49.9	dust-like	165.8	half-deserted
61.15	*touzy-mouzy*	171.36	bareheaded
69.31	-the-way	175.22	twenty-five
73.40	make-weights	177.33	rough-cast
78.1	Grand-duke	187.14	lower-region
81.24	Boat-houses	201.30	well-drilled
84.11	forty-five	203.14	drum-like
87.3	custom-house	206.22	*ser-vi-*
88.6	whisky-drinking	213.21	bridge-builder
88.25	double-headed	240.20	every-day
97.1	forty-two	241.21	ill-intentioned

244.2	Grand-duchess	274.8	north-east
249.24	felucca-like	278.12	*touzy-mouzy*
251.20	window-frame	286.11	Grand-duchess
257.16	by-the-	297.36	mosque-like

LIST B

5.7	common-place		
6.40	well-known	124.30	co-ordinate
9.2	vine-growing	139.36	five-franc
10.15	vineyards	143.18	half-canton
19.16	semi-barbarous	174.19	quaint-looking
22.10	hill-side	177.5	cider-mill
35.7	-the-way	185.13	dirty-looking
36.15	tomb-stone	194.29	rough-cast
36.40	sand-stone	203.4	well-behaved
37.31	seventy-four	229.20	self-evident
45.17	south-east	232.33	battle-ground
50.12	mountain-abutment	241.30	silver-forkisms
58.39	drum-head	244.3	two-and-
73.5	re-entered	249.20	oyster-men
88.5	tobacco-chewing	262.25	London-built
89.35	mosque-like	265.34	*touzy-mouzy*
101.20	vine-leaves	278.12	*touzy-mouzy*
107.2	self-assumed	293.16	head-lands
108.8	firebrands	297.36	mosque-like
108.15	cool-headed		

INDEX

Index

This index includes persons, places, things, and topics of concern mentioned or alluded to in Cooper's text, including his own footnotes. Subjects glossed in the Explanatory Notes of this edition are indicated by an asterisk (*) placed before the appropriate page number. The abbreviation m. is employed for items of brief or unspecified mention.

Aar, river: valley, 24, 122, 234; description, 28, 32–33, 74–75; course, 40, 63–64, 182, 220–22; plain, 71, 77; sources, 209; falls, 222; m., 25, 27–28, 43, 45, 52, 66, 130, 138
Aarau, 75
Aarberg, 25, 74, 122
Achsenberg, 156
Acropolis, 274
Adriatic Sea, 295
Æolian harp, 103, 193
Africa, 149, 271
l'aigle d'or, 83, 86
Albis, pass, 106
Alexander I (Russ.), 238
Almanach de Gotha, 192
Alpbach, 138
Alpnach, 151
Alps: definition, 34, 51; upper peaks, 43, 50, 53, 56–58, 102, 116–17, 282; minor peaks, 45, 52; size, 47–48, 55, 136; general description, 39–41, 44–45, 47–48, 53–55, 65–66, 97, 99, 261–62, 282–83, 299; southern peaks, 116, 190–91, 291; pastures, 136, 152, 176, 181, 194, 216; northern peaks, 190–91; Vorarlberg, 191; life in, 210; m., 12, 23–25, 32, 55, 86, 112, 115, 117, 122, 130, 148, 155, 164, 173, 181–82, 195, 206, 209, 213, 217–18, 234, 239–40, 245, 264, 269, 273, 282–83, 285, 287, 290, 293–95, 298–99

Alsaciens, 165, 170
Altstetten, 90–91
Am Stoss, 90–93, 173
America, see United States
Andermatt, 210–11, 215
Anjou, Philip, Duke of, Philip V (Sp.), 8
Anna, see Johanna, Grand Duchess
Apennines, mountains, 295, 299
Apollo, 37
Appenzell, canton, 87, 93, 95, 145, 201; districts, 96
Argovie (Aarau), canton, 28, 30, 75, 123, 145
Arkansas, 130
Arona, 293
Art, village, 107–09, 115, 118
Athens, 274
Atlantic Ocean, 11, 252
Augustines of Great St. Bernard, 281
Austrasia, 46
Austria, House of, 29, 76; princes of, 77; army, 178, 201; emperor, 193, 294; empire, 76, 193; m., 29, 84, 88, 91, 121, 131, 139, 150, 231
Auxerre, 8
Auxonne, 13
avalanches, 53–54, 57, 108–09, 136, 142, 153, 159–60, 210, 279, 285
Avallon, 9–10
Avenche (Aventicum), 235–37, 258–59

Baden, 77–78, 80, 84
Baden, Grand Duke of, 78–79, 84

Baden-Baden, 78
Baden-Baden, Grand Duke of, 78
Banks, Sir Joseph, *189
Basle, 24, 74, 90, 120, 145
Bavaria, 84
Baveno, 291
beau, le, 21, 152, 244, 295, see also the following entry
beautiful, the, or beauty, 10, 18, 20, 27, 32, 38, 44, 48, 59, 70, 98, 112, 114–15, 120, 130, 133, 142, 151–52, 170, 197–98, 212–13, 217, 244, 274
Belgium, 2, 13, 95
Bellinzone, 213
Benedictine monks, 158, 185, 187, 201, 205
Bern, canton: history, *25, 27–31, 104; government, *27–31, *45; quarries, 66; bears (emblem), 73, 139; m., 37, 64, 75, 91, 123, 140, 145, 174, 176, 220, 231
Bern, city: description, 26–28, 32–35; Platteform, 32; altitude, 35; cemeteries, 65–66; bears, 69; m., 37–38, 40, 46, 57, 63, 65, 67, 75, 94, 130, 216, 230–34, 252, 257–61, 291
Bertha, Queen, (Burg.), *238–39
Berthier, Marshal Pierre Alexander, 24
Besançon, 15
Bex, 269
Bible, 85, 234
Bienne, lake, 25
Black Aar Peak (Finster Aar Horn), 221
Black Forest, 77, 170
Blonay, 266
Blümlis Alp, 131
Bodensee, see Constance
Bohemia, *84
Bordeaux, Duke of, 8
Borromean Islands, 291–92
Borromeo, family, 293
Boston, 103, 143
Boullion, Godfrey of, 85
Bourbon, family, 7; House of, 7–8
Bourbon, Anthony, Duke of, 7
Brandenburgh, House of, 23
Brazil, 70
Brieg, see Brig

Brientz, lake, 62–63
Brientz, village, 63
Brienz, lake, 133–36, 222, 244
Brienz, village, 137, 147, 223
Brig (Brigg, Brieg), 276–81, 289
Britons, 149
Broadway (N.Y.), 109, 177
Brown, James, *9
Brooklyn, 253
Brugg, 77, 93
Brünig (Brunig, Brüning), pass, 138, 140–42, 148
Brunnen, 153, 155–58
Brunswick troops, 68
Bunyan, John, 112, 194, *254
Bürgerschaft, 26, 29, 258
Burgundy, country, 10, 13, 27, 46, 235, 238; people of, 234–36
Burgundy, Duke of (Charles the Bold, Count of Charolais), 235
Burgundy, kings of, 72, 238
Butter Hill, 2
Byron, Lord, 19

Cæsar, Julius, 13
Calais, 13, 15
Calvin, John, 249
Canada, country, 18
Canada, falls, 114
Canova, Antonio, *120
Capitol (U.S.), 78
Carrouge, 263
Caspar (JFC's guide), 265–70, 276–78, 280, 282, 284–87, 290–91
Catholic, see Roman Catholic
Catskill, see Kaatskill
chamois, 50, 116, 281
Champ de Mars, 243
Charenton, 5
Charlemagne, 167
Charles VI (Habsbourg), 76
Charles IX (Fr.), 7
Charles X (Fr.), 8, 11, 73, *243, 256
Châtelard, 266
château, definition, 12
Château de Joux, *17
Chillon, 267
China, 260
cholera, 226
Christ, Jesus, 36, 172
Circassian market, 152
Clarens, 266

Claude Lorrain, 264
Clermont, Louis de, 7
Clermont, Robert, Count of, 7
Clovis I, 238
Cohoos, falls, 80–81, 237
Cohoos, river, 237
Coire, 194–95, 202, 206
Coire, Bishop of, 175
Condé, Princes of, 7
Compiègne, 6
Congress (U.S.), 126–28
Constance, town, 83–84; Great
    Council, 84–85; cathedral, 85; m.,
    87, 90, 94
Constance (Bodensee), lake, 82–84,
    86–87, 94, 173, 182–83, 275
Constantine, Grand Duke (Russ.), 43
Constitution (Br.), 125
Constitution (U.S.), 128
Conti, Princes of, 7
Cooper, Captain Benjamin, *69–70
Cooper, Paul (JFC's son), 38
Cooper, Susan Augusta (Mrs. JFC),
    13, 16, 81, 265–66, 270
Cooper, William Yeardley (JFC's
    nephew), 22, 50, 55, 62–63,
    82–83, 91, 97, 105, 109–12, 116,
    121, 262, 279–80, 289, 295, 298
Cooperstown, 254, 261
Copenhagen, 267
Corneille, Pierre, 264
Corinthian architecture, 236
Corydon, 60
Council of Blood, 143
Cressy, battle, *235
Crétins, 270–71
Crevola, 277
Cricq, M. de St., 256
Croix Blanche, inn, 131

Denison, Lady Charlotte, *69
Denison, John, *69
Dent de Midi, 191, 269
Dent de Morcles, 191, 269
Dents, mountains, 269
Devil's Bridge, 155, 212
Diet (Switz.), 96, 175, 192, 275
Dijon, 10–12, 196
Disentis, 201–02, 204–06
Disentis, Abbey of, *202, 205
Dogberry, *76, *255
Dole, 14–15

Dominican convents, 85, 122
Domleschg, 199
Domo d'Ossola, 277, 287, 289–90
Doubs, river, 14–15
Doveria, gorge, 287

Ebel, Johan Gottfried, travel book,
    *24, 40, 76, 100–01, 106, 142, 162,
    164, 184, 217, 220, 236, 239
Egeri, lake, 165
Egypt, 88
Eiger, mountains, 54, 59–60, 134
Einsiedeln, convent, *158, 167–72,
    175, 188–89
Einsiedeln, Mary of, 167, 169
Elizabeth I (Br.), 125
Elizabethan architecture, see
    French-Elizabethan architecture
Enghein, Louis Antoine, Duke of, 7
England, travellers, 17, 41, 131–35,
    218–19, 223; vegetation, 18, 108;
    King of, 23, 124–25, 127, 247; at-
    titudes towards Americans, 46, 68,
    226–27, 232; government, 123,
    124–29, 226; newspapers, 226–29;
    trade, 226–29; m., 2, 18, 41, 43,
    47, 50, 67, 90, 106, 135, 140, 146,
    148–49, 176, 195, 215, 218–19,
    223–28, 237, 240–41, 243, 244,
    248, 250, 253, 257–58, 262, 265,
    279
English language, 19, 67–68, 79, 91,
    148–49, 224
Entlibuch, valley, 121
Erie, fort, 231
Erie, lake, 87
Erie Canal, 283
Erlach, family, *29–30, 35; tomb, 35–
    36
Estrées, Gabrielle d', *5
Eugene, Prince (Aust.), 78
Europe, attitudes towards Ameri-
    cans, 3–4, 9–11, 41–42, 46, 68,
    149, 241; scenery, 21, 32, 70, 284;
    governments, 29, 46, 69, 77, 104;
    m., 4–8, 10–12, 14, 28, 35, 42–43,
    46, 69, 72, 76–77, 84–86, 90, 96,
    102–05, 111, 123, 131, 135, 137,
    140, 149, 158, 170, 176, 192, 218,
    221, 224, 240, 242, 251, 262, 284,
    297–98
Eustice, John Chetwode, *296

Faucon, le, inn, 26
Federalist Party (U.S.), 247
Fellenberg, Philip Emanuel, *37
Fernay, *254–55
Finster Aar Horn, 221
Fischer, Colonel Victor, *231
Fiznau, 154
Flemish painting, 274
Flims, 199
Flora, 60
Florence, 260
Flüe, St. Nicholas de, 147–48
Fluelen, 151, 155–56, 158, 213
Fontainebleau, palace, 6–8
Fontainebleau, town, 6
Forest Cantons, 142, 145, 164
Fort Erie, 231
Four Cantons, Lake of, 114, 159
France, travellers and soldiers, 5–6,
    19–21, 132–34, 148, 296–97;
    towns, 6, 16, 179, 181, 254; gov-
    ernment, 7–8, 11, 25; inns, 8–9,
    14–15; attitudes towards Ameri-
    cans, 9, 11, 20–21, 41, 148, 249;
    character, 9, 24, 134; agriculture,
    10, 14; châteaux, 12; armies, 19,
    133–34, 201; revolution (1789),
    28, 72, 104, 106, 108, 134, 227;
    Empire, 227; newspapers, 228; m.,
    2, 9–13, 30, 37, 66–67, 72–74, 77,
    94, 106, 123, 131–32, 139–40,
    146, 148, 152, 165, 167, 176, 179,
    211, 231, 250–51, 254–57
Franche Comté, 13, 73
Francis of Lorraine, 76
Francis I (Fr.), 6
Francis II (Fr.), 7
Franz, Francis I (Aus.), 79
Fraubrunnen, 71
Free Trade, 225–30
French-Elizabethan architecture, 7
French language, 11–12, 20, 24, 91,
    149, 151, 174–75, 190, 203, 233,
    245, 288
French Revolution (1789), see France
frescoes, 296
Fribourg, 239
Furca, pass, 211, 215–18, 220
Furst, Walter, 119, *156

Gabrielle, see d'Estrées
Gais (Gaiss), 93, 97, 199

Galignani's Messenger, 224
Gallenstock, 217
Ganter, ravine, 279
Geneva, canton, 24, 105, 145, 249,
    *252, 254, 256
Geneva (Léman), lake, 72, 173, 182,
    242, 244, 246, 248, 252, 263–65,
    273
Geneva, port, 249, 251–52
Geneva, town, 74, 242, 248–53,
    256–57, 260–61, 289
Genlis, see Mme. de Silléry-Genlis
Genlis, town, 12
Genoa, 264, 295
George, lake, 102
Georgia, 298
German language, 59, 63, 79, 89,
    91–92, 133, 200
Germany, travellers and soldiers, 37,
    68–69, 116–17, 133–34, 155–58,
    170, 192, 195–96, 202, 221; states,
    46, 192; beggars, 82–83; m., 2, 13,
    35, 41, 68–69, 72, 78–79, 83–84,
    120, 140, 144, 146, 170, 172–73,
    177, 182–83, 192, 194, 227
Gersau, 154
Gessler, bailiff, 118–19, 158
Giesbach, falls, 63
Gil Blas, Adventures of, 258
glaciers, 14, 38–41, 47, 50, 54–57,
    59–62, 187, 206, 209–10, 217,
    219–20, 225, 273, 280–81, 299
Glaris, canton, 175–79, 253
Glaris, town, 176–78
Glarus, canton, 99
Glarus, town, 99
Glys, 276
Goddard, Frederick Warren, *103
Godfrey of Boullion, 85
Goethe, Johann Wolfgang von, 264
goîtres, 66–67, 270
Goldau, town, 108–09, 115, 163;
    landslide, 108–10, *159, 163, 273;
    m., 158, 161
Gondemar of Burgundy, 238
Gorcum coach, 5
Gothic architecture, 297
Great Britain, see England
Great Hearts, *254
Great St. Bernard, 190, 269, 274, 281
Great Scheideck Mountain, 51, 55,
    60–61

Greek architecture, 297
Grimsel, lake, 220
Grimsel, mountain, 218–22, 241
Grindelwald, town, 57–59, 62, 64
Grindelwald, valley, 55–59, 62, 64,
  136, 216–17, 219, 224
Grisons, canton, 95, 145, 155, 192–
  93, 200–01, 209, 275
Grütli, 155–56, 158; leaders, 119
Habsbourg, House of, 27, 76, 146–
  47, 160; village, 76; castle, 76–
  77
Haldenstein, 193
Halleck, Fitz-Greene, 239
Ham (Bib.), 225
Hamburgh, 196, 226
Handeck, 222
Hannibal, 191, 287
Hanover, King of, 247
Hapsbourg, see Habsbourg
Hebes, 120
Hebrew language, 91
Helena, Grand Duchess (Russ.), 161,
  244–46, 286, 291
Helvetia, 24–25, 136, 158, 299; free-
  dom, 30, 101, see also Switzerland
Helvetic Confederation, *12, 23–25,
  27, 29, 99
Henry III (Fr.), 7
Henry IV (Fr.), 5, 7–8
Herefordshire, 132
Herisau, 96–97, 176
Héristal, Pepin de, 94
Hessian troops, 68–69
Hindelbank, 35–36, 125–26
Hofwyl, *37
Hohentwiel, 82
Hohenzollern, House of, 167
Hole of Uri (Urnerlock), 212, 215,
  283
Holland, 2, 5, 198, 226–27, 251
Holstein, 221
Horn, 86
Hospital, 210–11, 215
Hudson, river, 62, 70, 114
Huns, 77, 236
Huskisson,William, *226, 228
Huss, John, *83–85

Ilantz, 199–201
Indian corn, 14
Indian tribes, 199–200

Interlachen, 48–49, 52, 57, 63, 133,
  136, 223
Irish people, 150
Isabella II (Sp.), 8
Isella, 286
Isle of St. Peter, 25
Isola Bella, *291–93
Isola Madre, *292
Istanbul, see Stamboul
d'Istria, Count Capo, 237
Italian language, 91, 199–200, 204,
  250
Italy, government, 46, 192; old landscape paintings, 113, 141; architecture, 200, 281, 291–92, 295; climate, 264, 291, 299; frontier, 277,
  282, 286; agriculture, 286, 291,
  295; inns, 287–89, 291–93, 296;
  beggars, 292, 296; fishermen, 292–
  93; m., 2, 74, 77, 155, 167, 169–70,
  182, 191, 195–96, 208, 212–13,
  215–16, 238, 250, 259–60, 275,
  277, 282, 286–87, 290–91, 293,
  295, 299

Jericho, 234, 236
Jerusalem, 234
Jesuits, 256, 276
Johanna, Grand Duchess (Russ.), 43
John Bull, 132
Johnson, Dr. Samuel, 188
Jomini, General Antoine Henri,
  *237–38
Joseph II (Aust.), 77
Journalism, standards, 226–29
Jüf, 207
Jungfrau, mountain, *40, 47, 50,
  52–54, 63–65, 116, 132, 134, 136,
  190, 216, 224
Jura, mountains, 11–17, 21–22, 24,
  32, 48, 71–72, 74, 122, 130, 263

Kaatskill (Catskill), mountains, 113–
  14, 131, 181, 206
Kaatskill, falls, 114
Kaiserstuhl (Emperor's Seat), 79, 90
Keller, map of, 216, 263
Kennebunk, 46, 130
kirschwasser, 172, 190, 233
Kœnigsfeld, 77
Küznacht (Küsnacht), 103, 113, 118–
  19, 151–52

Lachen, 174
Lady of the Hermits, 167, 171–72
La Fayette, Marquis de, 227
La Fayette Place, 78
Lake of the Dead, 220
Landenberg, 148
Landsgemeinde, 147, 154
Langenthal, 122–23
Langhans, family of, 35; tomb, 36–37
Langhans, Madame Anna Magdalena, 66, 126
larch, 15, 17–18, 20, 49–50, 75, 99, 111, 134, 197–98, 210, 276, 299
Last Supper, The, 296
Latin language, 94, 109, 199, 205
Lausanne, 239–42, 244–45, 257–58, 263, 289
Lauterbrunnen, town, 52, 56, 134
Lauterbrunnen, valley, 48–56, 62–63
Lax, 199
Legion of Honour, 247
Léman, lake, see Geneva
Léman, ship, 245–46, 248
Leonardo, see Vinci
Leopold, Prince of Saxe-Coburg, 43
Leopold (Aust.), 100
Lichtensteig, 97–98
Liechtenstein, *192–93, 197, 199
Limmat River, 24, 77–79, 103–04
Linth River, 176, 179–80
Lion of Lucerne, *120
Little St. Bernard, 269
Little Scheideck Mountain, 51, 55, 61, 64
Lockport (N.Y.), 283
Lombardy, 282, 294–95
London, 5, 225, 262
London newspapers (*Times, Courier, Standard*), 226
Loretto, 167
Lorraine, la (JFC's country house), 38, *43, 63–64, 67–68, 71, 121, 127, 130, 140, 216, 233–34, 258, 261
Louis IX, St. Louis (Fr.), 7–8
Louis XIII (Fr.), 8
Louis XIV (Fr.), 8, 13
Louis XV (Fr.), *9
Louis Phillipe I (Fr.), 8
Louisiana, 11
Louvre, 12

Low, Nicholas, *51
Lower Walden, 143
Lowerz, lake, 110, 115, 158–59, 161, 164
Lowerz, town, 161, 164
Lucca, Duke of, 8
Lucchese, princes of, 8
Lucens, 240
Lucerne, canton, 122–23, 152, 175
Lucerne, lake, 112, 115, 151, 156, 158–60, 173, 176, 181, 213, 244
Lucerne, town, 107, 113, 118–21, 148, 151–53, 234
Lucie, cook, 280–81
Lungern, lake, 141
Lungern, town, 141–43, 147

McAdam, John Loudon, *103, 243
Magdalen, Mary, 111, 120, 174
Maggiore, lake, 213, 290, 294
Maine, 31, 298
Manhattan, 33, 67, 94, 162, 178, 298
Maria, Grand Duchess (Russ.), 244
Maria Theresa (Aust.), 76
Marne, river, 5
Marseilles, 13
Martigny, 274
Massachusetts, 31, 46
Mayensfeld, 191
Mediterranean, sea, 12, 70, 84, 176, 220, 264
Melchthal, Arnold de, 119, 147
Mèilleurie, 265–66
Melun, 6
Methodist religion, 257
Mettenberg, mountains, 60
Meyringen, town, 51, 61, 63, 222
Meyringen, valley, 59, 62, 138, 140
Michael, Grand Duke (Russ.), 161
Milan, 2, 196, 296–99
Milton, John, 163, 264
Mitres (Mythen), 158
Mohawk River, 8, 80, 88
Monaco, 192
Monaldeschi, Giovanni, *8
Monch, mountain, 54
Mont Bénon, 244
Mont Blanc, 2, 13–14, 17–18, 22, 116, 190–91, 240, 248, 252, 269
Mont Cenis, 191
Monte Rosa, 116, 190, 269, 299
Montmartre, *17

Montreux, 266
Mont Velan, 274
Morat, town, 234–36, 261
Morat, lake, 234–35, 259
Moreau, General Jean Victor, *253
Morgarten, battle, *165
Moudon, 263
Mount Pilatus, 141, 148

Naefels, battle, *176, 178–79
Nahl, Samuel, *35, 37
Naples, 8, 231, 267
Napoleon Bonaparte, *7, 13, *17, 24,
   168, 192, 238, 268, 270, 272, 298;
   wars, 265; followers, 297
Navarre, 7
Neuchâtel, canton, *12, 21–24, 33,
   145; industry, 19; people, 19, 24;
   history, 23–24
Neuchâtel, lake, 22–23, 25, 44, 235
Neuchâtel, town, 16, 21–25
Neuhaus, 47, 63, 132
New Englanders, 122, 295
New Forest (Br.), 77
New Goldau, 161
New York, city, 78, 162, 249, 252–
   53, 260; churches, 298, see also
   Manhattan
New York, state, 18, 25, 31, 87, 106,
   113, 266
Niagara, falls, 18, 80–81, 114, 237
Nice, 131, 283
Niesen, mountain, 40
Norman horses, 5
North America, 103
North Sea, 220
Notre Dame de Neiges, 109, 111, 118
Nott stoves, *20

Ober Alp, 206, 210–11, 215, 220
Oberland, region, 32, 34, 40–41, 44,
   48, 59, 62, 64, 90, 107, 140, 176
Oberland, mountains, 22, 38, 40,
   116, 148, 216, 248, 252, 269, 277
Olten, 74
Ontario, lake, 87
oriental baths, 189
Orleans, 8
Orleans, House of, 8
Osage Indians, *10–11
Otsego Hall, 254
Otsego, county, 66
Otsego, lake, 105, 134

Otsego, town, 66
Ouchy, 245
Our Lady of the Snows, 109, 111,
   118
L'Ouverture, Toussaint, F. D., *17
Owen, Robert, system, *229
Ox, inn, 167, 171

Paon, inn, 99, 101–02
Paradise Lost, 163
Paris, 2, 5, 8–9, 11–12, *17, 73, 95,
   104, 171, 224, 237, 243, 247, 250,
   255–56
Parliament (Br.), 124–28, 226
Parma, Duchy of, 8
Parthenope, *299
Payerne, 237–41, 258, 262
Pepin, King, 72
Pfeffers, baths, *184–89, 194
Phidias, 20, 78
Philadelphia, 232
piazza, meaning, 250
Picot, Jean, *81, 104, 199, 238, 271
picturesque (pittoresque), 10, 18–21,
   27, 32, 43, 45, 48–50, 53–56,
   60–61, 64, 73–74, 89, 115, 135,
   142, 152, 170, 174, 182, 193–94,
   201–02, 214–15, 221–22, 244,
   274–75, 283, 293, 295
Piedmont, 294–95
Pierre, gardener, 9
Pilatus, Mount, 141, 148
Pilgrim's Progress, 112, 194, *254
Pine Orchard, 113–14
Pippin III (Frank.), 72
Pitt, William, 125
Pius VII, 7
Pococke, Richard, *37
Poland, 131
Pontarlier, 16
Pontine, marshes, 180
Portales, Count (Neuchâtel), 33
Po River, 294
Portugal, 146
Pottowattomies, King of, 25
Protestant religion, 72, 76, 96–97,
   105, 145, 169–71, 201, 220
President (U.S.), 126–28
Prussia, kings, 23, 247
Prussia, states, 24, 73, 167
Prussian people, 116
Puritanism, 185

Quarterly Review, 243

Racine, Jean, 37, 264
Ragatz, 183, 185, 187, 189
Ranz des Vaches, *59, 64, 89
Rapperschwyl, 99–103, 173–74, 176, 186
Ray, Richard, *51
Realp, 215
Reichenau, 83
Reichenbach (Rich Fall), 63
Reuss, river, 24, 77, 120, 209, 211–12, 283
Rhetian people, 200
Rhetian language, *199–200, 204
Rheineck, 87
Rhine, river, 24, 72, 77–79, *80–85, 88–90, 177, 182–83, 185, 190–93, 195–201, 205–09, 227, 275
Rhine, valley, 91, 209
Rhinthal, valley, 87–90, 93, 183
Rhodes, districts, 96
Rhone, river, 15, 190–91, 217–20, 250, 269–70, 275, 287
Rhone, valley, 209, 211, 218, 245, 263, 273–74, 277
Richenau, 195–96
Righi, river, 109
Righi Kulm, 113–18, 122, 141, 152–55, *159–61, 163, 219
Righi Staffel, 112–14, 118
Ritter Saal, 76
Roland, castle of, 13
Roman Catholic religion, 71–74, 76, 96–97, 105–06, 109, 142, 144–47, 165, 167–72, 175, 201, 275, 286
Roman ruins, 72, 74, 77–78, 235–37
Rome, 72, 144–45, 165, 231, 235, 237, 239, 259, 271; people, 77–78, 239, 274–75
Roschach, 87
Rosenlaui, glacier, 61
Rosenlaui, mountain, 62–63
Rossberg, *159–64
Rothenthurm, 164
Rotterdam, 88
Rotzberg, 151
Roubilliac, Louis François, *37
Round Top Mountain, 181
Rousseau, Jean Jacques, 25, 249, *265

Rügen, 134
Russia, 77, 131, 134, 201, 237–38, 244

St. Charles (San Carlo), 293–94
St. Cloud, 243
St. Domingo, 17
St. Gall, canton, 86–87, *94–95, 97, 102, 145, 175, 179, 193
St. Gall, town, *94–95
St. Gingoulph, 265–66
St. Gothard, 155, 190, 208–13, 215–16, 269, 283
St. Lawrence River, 227
St. Louis, see Louis IX
St. Martin, Boulevard, 171
St. Maurice, 270, 272, 274
St. Peter, Isle of, 25
Saint Peter's (Rome), 165
Salins, 14–15, 18
Saltine, river, 276, 279
San Marino, 154, 192
Saone, river, 13
Sardinia, King of, 292
Sargans, 182–83
Sargans, Count of, 182
Sarnen, 113, 141, 147, 150
Savoy, 14, 56, 131, 245, 263, 265, 270
Saxe-Coburg, Duke of, 43
Saxony, princes of, 112
Schabziger cheese, *176–77
Schaffhausen, canton, 80, 145, 253
Schaffhausen, town, 81–82, 86, 90, 182
Scheideck, see Great and Little Scheidecks
Schiller, J. C. F. von, 264
Schinznach, baths, 75, 77
Schonbrunn Palace (Schœnbrunnen), *76
Schouvaloff, Countess Sophie, *237
Schrabzieger cheese, see Schabziger
Schwytz (Schweitz), canton, 30, 99, *101–03, 108, 146, 150, 153–54, 159, 164, 175–76, 253
Schwytz, town, 115, 155, 158
Scottish people, 94, 149–50
Seewen, 159–60
Seine, river, 9, 251
Sempach, battle, 121
Sempach, lake, 121

Senate (U.S.), 127
Sesto Calende, 294
Sèvres, rue de, 5
Shakers, 93
Shakespeare, William, 37, *84, 264
Sigismund, emperor (Rom.), 85
Silléry-Genlis, Mme. de, *12
Simond, Louis, *252
Sion, 274
Simpeln, 277, 281, 285
Simple Council, 143
Simplon, pass, 213, 269–70, 272,
    276, 278–79, 281–84, 289, 296
Slavic people, 77
Sœurs de Charité, 73
Soleure, 50, *71–73, 123
Spain, 8, 33, *74, 78, 134, 146, 231
Spietz, Castle, 45–47
Splügen, pass, 182, 195–97, 213, 269
Stäel, Madame de, 134
Staffel, 114, 118
Stamboul (Istanbul), 152
Stantz, 141, 150
Stanzstad, 151–52
Staubbach, falls, 48–49, 51–52, 55,
    61
Stauffach, Werner, 119
Steckborn, 83
Stein, 82
Steinach, 86
Stockhorn, mountain, 130
Stuarts, reign of (Br.), 125
Suabia, 79
sublime, the, 2, 5, 20, 37–41, 44, 61,
    65, 81, 91, 99, 103, 114–16, 133,
    142, 147, 153, 155, 169, 176, 192,
    217, 233, 243–45, 261, 264, 284,
    287, 299
Swedes, 64
Swiss-German language, 147
Switzerland:
    abbeys, 77, 94–95, 99, 167, 190–
        92, 202, 205;
    agriculture, 19, 34–35, 43, 49, 66,
        73, 82–83, 90, 96–97, 108, 110,
        122, 148, 154–55, 161, 176,
        181–83, 191, 201, 207, 214,
        264–65;
    architecture, 15, 20, 43, 49, 71, 74,
        76, 78, 89, 177–78, 196, 205,
        236, 250, 264;

banks, lack of, 139–40;
baths, 69, 75, 78, 111, 133, 184,
    189–90;
beggars, 51–52, 82–83, 92, 97,
    106–07;
boats, 44, 47, 86–87, 103, 107, 132,
    135, 137, 151–52, 155–58,
    180–81, 223, 245–46, 248–49,
    252, 264, 267;
châteaux, 25, 35, 43, 47, 64, 66, 72,
    74–75, 80, 83, 87, 89, 97–98,
    100, 118, 122, 130–31, 183,
    193–94, 197, 201, 205, 239–40,
    254, 266;
churches, 35–36, 71, 73–74, 78,
    89, 92, 95, 99, 102–03, 109, 113,
    126, 137, 140, 142, 147, 150,
    161, 164, 200, 206–07;
convents, 71, 73, 82, 97, 106, 122,
    158, 174, 238;
costumes, 73, 78, 86, 89, 101, 109,
    150, 170, 183, 190, 194, 200, 246;
crosses, 72–74, 114, 147, 201, 216,
    254, 281;
defence, 13, 19, 28, 71, 74, 148,
    234, 269;
disasters, 45, 58, 103, 108, 116–17,
    137, 156, 159, 161–64, 273;
food, 15, 86, 91, 104–05, 111, 122,
    133, 142, 172, 174, 176–77, 270;
government, 24, 80–81, 96, 98,
    104–06, 118, 131, 133, 143–47,
    154, 175, 192, 231, 253, see also
    Bern;
history, 23–25, 27–30, 78, 84–85,
    94–95, 104–06, 119, 121, 152,
    154, 165, 201, 231, 234–39,
    253–54, 271–73, see also Bern;
houses, 18–20, 32, 43, 73, 89–90,
    93, 102, 114, 154, 158, 165,
    176–78, 194, 198, 200, 250–51,
    267;
industry, 14, 19, 80, 86–88, 94–98,
    104, 122, 154, 176–77, 256;
inns, 21, 26, 48–50, 56, 58–59, 61,
    67, 79–80, 82–83, 88–92,
    96–97, 99, 103, 111, 113, 117–
    18, 122, 131, 133, 147–48, 161,
    167, 171, 174–75, 178, 194–97,
    200, 202–03, 205–06, 210,
    214–15, 220–23, 238, 242–43,

250, 257, 262–63, 267, 276–79, 281, 285, 291;
lakes, 44, 102, 115, 173–74, 180, 182, 235, 293–94;
languages, 200; see also English, French, German, Italian and Rhetian;
legends and superstitions, 32, 58, 77, 119, 146–47, 166–69, 185;
monetary system, 139–40, 211;
mountain climbing, 50, see also Alps;
occupations, 19, 34–35, 44, 66, 88, 90, 97, 110, 123–24, 174, 214, 231–33, 256, 258;
ports, 47, 87, 101, 103–04, 120, 152, 155, 245, 251;
prisons, 71, 85, 104;
religion, 24, 74, 94–95, 109, 144–47, 165–66, 170–72, 175–76, 201, 220, 275, see also Protestant and Roman Catholic religion;
roads, general characteristics of, 16, 24, 60, 103, 197, 202, 283;
ruins, 19, 24–25, 72, 74–79, 82, 87, 95, 97, 102, 108, 110, 113, 118, 134–35, 151, 159–60, 163–64, 182–83, 191, 193, 201, 215, 236, 239–40, 285

Tamina, river, 184–87, 190
Taylor, Sir Herbert, *218, 224
tea, 15, 64, 111, 122, 260
Tchechekoff, Admiral, *237
Tell, William, 41, 108, 118–19, 121, 152, 155
Tellen's Platte (Tellen's Place), *152, 156–58
Téméraire, Charles le, 234
Teniersism, *274
Tessin, 213
Teufen, 93–94
Teutonic race, 37
Thorwaldsen, Albert B., *120
Thoun, see Thun
Thun, lake, 40, 43–45, 63–64, 130, 133, 230, 244
Thun, town, 43–44, 47, 62, 64, 130–32, 171, 231–32
Thurgovie, canton, 82, 86, 145
Ticino, river, 294

Titlis, mountain, 38, *116, 120
Titus, emperor (Rom.), 236
Toccia, 287
Toggenburg (Tockembourg, Tockemburg, Tockenberg), district, 97–98, 145, 173
Tonson, Monsieur, *33
Toussaint L'Ouverture, F. D., *17
"touzy-mouzy," *19, 158, 196, 265, 278
Trenton, falls, 114
Trèves (Trier), *72
Trins, 198
Trône, barrière du, 5
Trons, 201, 208
Tuileries, 12, 120
Tuscans, 200
Tyrol, 56, 86, 90, 131, 172

Ufnau, 102, 173
United States: patriotism, 2–3, 114; European attitudes towards Americans, 9, 11, 42, 44, 67–69, 97, 232, 237, 240–41, 247–48; American attitudes towards Europe, 11, 27–28, 41, 43, 46, 69, 105, 123, 250; American behaviour, 44, 250, 271, 298; inns, 44, 122, 175; baths, 69; scenery, 70, 240; architecture, 71, 76, 78, 148, 298; government, 123, 126–29, 247, 253; industry, 88, 240; m., 2–3, 11, 14–15, 25, 30–31, 38, 72, 74, 84, 87–88, 90, 97, 100–01, 104, 107, 118, 123, 130, 139, 146, 149, 170, 185, 187, 195, 197–201, 203, 218, 221, 223, 225, 227–28, 231, 237, 245, 247–48, 250–53, 262, 282–83, 298
Unterséen, 48, 52, 64, 133, 136, 223–24
Unterwalden, canton, 38, 121, 139–40, 143–44, 175, 201, 253; Upper Unterwalden (Obwalden), 143, 147; Lower Unterwalden (Nidwalden), 143, 150
Uri, canton, 38, 155, 175, 209, 213, 254
Uri, lake, 156
Uri, Hole of (Urnerlock), 212, 215, 283
Ursern, 209, 211, 283

Uznach, 99, 174

Valais, canton, 24, 67, 191, 217, 220, 269–71, 275, 278, 289
Valiants, *254
Val Travers, 16, 19–20, 24, 62, 66, 152
Vatican, 165
Vaud, canton, 24, 28, 30, 145, 240–41, 246, 263
Venus, 120
Verrières, les, 20
Versailles, 85
Vespasian, emperor (Rom.), 236
Vévey, 246, 264–65, 274
Viescherhorn, 277
Village of Fools, 45
Villeneuve, 266–68
Vinci, Leonardo da, 296–97
Vision, mountain, *134, 281
Vivienne, la rue, 109
Voltaire, François Marie, 244, *254–56
Voltaire, Quai, 255
Vorarlberg, mountains, 88, 91, 93, 131, 191

Wallenstadt, lake, 179–82, 191, 244, 263
Walther, Ludwig Gottlieb, *68, 261
Wagram, Prince of, 24
Washington (D.C.), 6
Washington, George, 8, 225
waterfalls, 48, 61, 63, 80, 113, 137–38, 181, 222, 274
Watteville, General de, *231

Watwyl, 97–98
Weggis, 153, 159
Weinzaepfli, *32
Wengern Alp, 53–55, 64–65, 134, 136
Wesen, 179–81, 188
West Indies, 70, 223
Westminster Abbey, 37
Wetterhorn, mountain, 59–61
White Mountains, 40
Wildeck, château, 75
Windham, William, *37
Winkel, 151
Winkelried, Arnold de, 121, 139, *150
Wülpelsberg, mountain, 75
Wünster, Rudolph, 45, 62
Wurtemburg, 82, 84, 86, 244

Yankees, 69, 88
yeomanry, 34, 120
Yonne River, 8

Zæringue, (Zæringen), 27
Zell, town, 83
Zellersee, 83
Zimmerman, Dr. Johann George von, *77
Zolliken, 103
Zug, canton, 106, 175, 253
Zug, lake, 106–07, 114–15, 118, 162
Zug, town, 106–07, 121, 253
Zurich, canton, 80, 82, 102–06, 145, 152, 182
Zurich, lake, 98, 100, 102–03, 106, 115, 173, 179–80, 244
Zurich, town, 103–06, 182